Beyond Little Hearts For His Glory

An Early Learning Program for Ages 6-8

Written by Carrie Austin, M.Ed.

Editor:	Cover Designer:
Julie Grosz	Merlin DeBoer

Heart of Dakota Publishing
www.heartofdakota.com

Special Thanks to:

- Our Lord and Savior, Jesus Christ, for giving us the vision to train up our children in the Lord. May He be glorified through this work.

- My parents, Ken and Marlene Mellema, for their faithful example of living for Christ and their steadfast commitment to family that has lasted a lifetime. I can only hope to follow carefully in their footsteps and learn from their example.

- Julie Grosz for her countless hours of editing, endless convention trips, steadfast support and enthusiasm, and willingness to pilot this program with her own children. I am blessed to have Julie in my life.

- Dave and Cindy Madden for forging a new path by homeschooling their seven precious children. Thank you for showing all of us a better way to live our lives for Christ. We will never be the same.

- Mike Austin for his unwavering support and love, consistent hard work without complaint, patient encouragement, and constant prayers. Without him, there would be no *Beyond Little Hearts For His Glory*.

- Cole and Shaw Austin, my sons, and Rachel Madden, my niece, for posing for the cover of this book. They are truly an inspiration to me and are wonderful blessings from our Father in heaven.

Copyright 2006, updated 2010 by Carrie Austin
Heart of Dakota Publishing, Inc.
1004 Westview Drive
Dell Rapids, SD 57022

Website: www.heartofdakota.com
Phone (605) 428-4068

All rights reserved. No part of this book may be stored in a retrieval system, reproduced or transmitted in any form or by any means - graphic, electronic, mechanical, photocopying, recording, or otherwise - without prior written permission from the author.

Printed in the U.S.A.
ISBN 0-9747695-7-6

Table of Contents

	Section
Introduction	Introduction
Pioneers from Spain Settle St. Augustine ..... Language Arts and Math	Unit 1
Pioneers from England Settle Jamestown ..... Language Arts and Math	Unit 2
Trouble with King James in England .... Language Arts and Math	Unit 3
Pilgrims Leave England for Holland .... Language Arts and Math	Unit 4
English Pilgrims Settle in Holland .... Language Arts and Math	Unit 5
Life in Holland .... Language Arts and Math	Unit 6
The Pilgrims Move from Amsterdam to Leiden .. Language Arts and Math	Unit 7
English Pilgrims Travel to America .... Language Arts and Math	Unit 8
Landing in America .... Language Arts and Math	Unit 9
Pilgrims Settle in Plymouth .... Language Arts and Math	Unit 10
Pilgrims Build Houses at Plymouth .... Language Arts and Math	Unit 11
Samoset and Squanto Help the Pilgrims .... Language Arts and Math	Unit 12

The First Thanksgiving at Plymouth . . . . Unit 13
Language Arts and Math

More Problems for the Pilgrims at Plymouth . . . . Unit 14
Language Arts and Math

Dutch Pioneers Settle New Amsterdam . . . . Unit 15
Language Arts and Math

King Philip Declares War on the Pilgrims . . . . . . Unit 16
Language Arts and Math

Two Pilgrim Children Become Captives. . . . . Unit 17
Language Arts and Math

Trouble in the New Land . . . . Unit 18
Language Arts and Math

Life for the Puritans in Colonial Times. . . . . Unit 19
Language Arts and Math

Colonial Schools . . . . Unit 20
Language Arts and Math

Pioneers from France Settle Detroit . . . . Unit 21
Language Arts and Math

Life in Colonial Philadelphia and Boston . . . . . . Unit 22
Language Arts and Math

Trouble Before the Revolutionary War . . . . Unit 23
Language Arts and Math

The Time of the American Revolution . . . . Unit 24
Language Arts and Math

Young Soldiers in the Continental Army . . . . Unit 25
Language Arts and Math

The Beginning of the United States of America . . Unit 26
Language Arts and Math

The First American President . . . . Unit 27
Language Arts and Math

Pioneers Go West on the Wilderness Road . . . . . Unit 28
Language Arts and Math

Pioneers Travel West on the Ohio River. . . . . Unit 29
Language Arts and Math

Pioneers Go West by Covered Wagon . . . . Unit 30
Language Arts and Math

Pioneers on the Santa Fe Trail . . . . Unit 31
Language Arts and Math

The Oregon Trail and the California Trail . . . . . . Unit 32
Language Arts and Math

Pioneers from Norway Settle on the Plains . . . . . Unit 33
Language Arts and Math

The Transcontinental Railroad . . . . Unit 34
Language Arts and Math

Appendix . . . . Appendix
    Overview of Reading Choices
    Scheduled Books for Emerging Readers
    Bibliography: Suggested Storytime Titles
    Spelling Lists for Units 1-34
    Math Alternate Schedule: *Primary Mathematics 2A & 2B*
    Poetry and Rhymes for Units 1-34
    Other Books by this Author

Introduction

Complete Plans
Beyond Little Hearts for His Glory features 34 units with complete daily plans. These plans are designed to provide an enjoyable, balanced approach to learning. Little preparation is required, and all of the skill areas are covered. Each day of plans is divided into the following 2 parts: "Learning the Basics" and "Learning Through History".

Learning the Basics
The "Learning the Basics" part of the program focuses on language arts and math. It includes activities for spelling, copywork, basic grammar, mechanics, and usage, math exploration, and choices for reading and storytime.

Learning Through History
The "Learning Through History" part of the program gives a chronological overview of early American history from 1565-1860. The daily history stories emphasize God's plan throughout history. A weekly Bible passage wraps up each unit by focusing on an example of Godly character that corresponds with the history stories. The following areas are linked with the daily stories: Bible memory work, Bible study, devotional topics, science discovery, art projects, geography, timeline and history activities, poetry, gross motor skills, and music.

Easy to Use
Each unit contains 5 days of instruction. Easy daily plans are divided into 9 boxes, which can be spaced throughout the day as time allows.

Quick Activities
Beyond Little Hearts for His Glory was written with the busy homeschool teacher in mind. It provides a way to do great activities without all of the usual planning and preparation. Quick and easy activities require little or no preparation and use materials you're likely to have on hand.

Fun Ideas
Engaging daily lessons take approximately 120-150 minutes to complete. They are filled with ideas that get kids moving, exploring, and learning in a meaningful way.

Flexible
Lesson plans are written to allow you to customize the program to suit your child's needs. A choice of resources is provided. Resources noted in the plans with a 'star' are considered necessary. Resources noted in the plans with a 'checkmark' provide a text or music connection to the activity.

Resources

All of the 'star' and 'checkmark' resources noted in *Beyond Little Hearts for His Glory* are available from Heart of Dakota Publishing. Order resources online at www.heartofdakota.com, by mail using the printable online order form, or by telephone at (605) 428-4068. Resource titles are listed below.

'Star' Resources (considered necessary)

★ *American Pioneers and Patriots* by Caroline D. Emerson (Christian Liberty Press, 2002)

★ *Stories of the Pilgrims* by Margaret B. Pumphrey, Revised by Michael J. McHugh and Elizabeth Arwine (Christian Liberty Press, 2007)

★ *Boys and Girls of Colonial Days* by Carolyn Sherwin Bailey (Christian Liberty Press, 2002) Note: There are two versions of this book with a 2002 copyright. The newer version uses a larger font. If you are using the older version of this book, use the old version page numbers in the plans.

'Star' Resource Choices (considered necessary choices)

★ If your child is a beginning reader, choose one of the following phonics options:
   1. *The Reading Lesson* by Michael Levin and Charan Langton (Mountcastle Company, 2000)
   2. *Reading Made Easy* by Valerie Bendt (Bendt Family Ministries, 2001)
   3. Your own phonics program

★ If your child is an emerging reader, choose one of the following emerging reader options:
   1. Scheduled Book Set for Emerging Readers (see Appendix for list)
   2. Your own program

★ If your child is an independent reader, choose one of the following options:
   1. *Drawn into the Heart of Reading: Level 2/3* by Carrie Austin (Heart of Dakota Publishing, 2000)
   2. Your own program

'Checkmark' Resources (provide text and music connections)

✔ *Morning Bells* by Frances Ridley Havergal (SMF Press, 2001)

✔ *God's Wonderful Works* by Eric D. Bristley and Edward J. Shewan (Christian Liberty Press, 1999)

✔ *Primary Mathematics 1A & 1B, U.S. Edition* by Singapore Ministry of Education (Times Media, 2003) **or** *Primary Mathematics 2A & 2B, U.S. Edition* by Singapore Ministry of Education (Times Media, 2003)

✔ *Hide 'Em In Your Heart Vol. II* by Steve Green (Sparrow, 2003)

"Learning Through History" Components

Reading About History
The "Learning Through History" part of each unit has a theme centered around stories from early American history. The themes are organized in chronological order from the years 1565-1865. God's plan is emphasized throughout the themes. History stories are read aloud to the students each day using the following resources: *American Pioneers and Patriots, Stories of the Pilgrims,* and *Boys and Girls of Colonial Days* by Christian Liberty Press. A weekly Bible passage wraps up each unit by focusing on an example of Godly character that corresponds with the history stories. These stories provide the focus for this part of the plans. The areas listed on this page are all linked to the daily stories.

Poetry and Rhymes
A different classic poem is introduced in each unit. Each poem was chosen for its enduring quality and its ability to withstand the test of time. Many famous poets are represented. The poems also reinforce the history theme.

Bible Memory Work
A new memory verse is introduced in each unit. Each memory verse has a practical meaning for young students, and also reinforces God's plan throughout history. A variety of daily memory activities incorporate gross motor skills to help students enjoy memorizing these important verses.

Bible Study
Daily Bible study questions are meant to instill Biblical values by training children to read and reflect on God's word. The questions work best with the King James or NIV version of the Bible. Each unit includes the following Bible study activities in coordination with the history stories:
  *Day 1: introduction and interpretation of the memory verse
  *Day 2: personal application of the memory verse
  *Day 3: observation of Godly character through devotional reading
  *Day 4: practical application of the devotional character trait
  *Day 5: exploration of a Bible passage focusing on Godly living

Devotional Activity
One day in each unit lists a text connection from *Morning Bells* by Frances Ridley Havergal. Each devotion is linked to the history theme, and also emphasizes basic Biblical lessons in an understandable way. A related narrative, corresponding Scripture verse, and a quote from a poem or hymn are part of each devotion.

Corresponding Music
Musical selections from *Hide 'Em in Your Heart Volume II* by Steve Green correspond with the Bible memory verses in the program. The original songs recite the Bible verses using a variety of musical styles.

"Learning Through History" Components
(continued)

Art Activity
One day in each unit includes an art activity that reinforces the historical theme. These activities help students practice some of the basic skills needed to express themselves and create freely.

Science Exploration
Two days in each unit include short, discovery activities that are linked to the history readings. Hands-on exploration in the areas of life science, physical science, and earth science help children make connections to the world around them. *God's Wonderful Works* by Christian Liberty Press is referenced as a science text connection for the lessons.

Geography
One day in each unit includes exploration of a geography concept that stems from the history story. Concepts range from learning about the continents and oceans, to tracing the routes of explorers, to reading maps, and following directions. The included activities help students gain basic geography skills while learning about the world around them. A world map or globe and a map of the United States is needed for several of the geography activities.

Timeline and History Activities
One day in each unit includes a history activity that reinforces the history story. To understand the flow of history, students will keep a basic timeline of the major events studied throughout the year. The students will also participate in short, engaging activities that make the history stories come alive.

"Learning The Basics" Components

Language Arts
For the language arts portion of each unit, four days are devoted to spelling and one day is devoted to basic grammar, mechanics, and usage skills. Daily copywork provides written language practice.

Spelling
Four days in each unit include spelling activities to guide students to spell words necessary for writing and daily use. A choice of two different word lists is provided in the Appendix for each unit. Word lists contain words from the Dolch word list, Fry's word list, and other grade level lists of high frequency words.

Each unit emphasizes one spelling word pattern. Eight words on each list are pattern words. The other two spelling words on each list are target words that do not follow the spelling pattern. Spelling strategies are taught using a multi-sensory approach that emphasizes picturing the word mentally.

A brief scope and sequence of the spelling patterns is listed by unit below (Number '1' corresponds to Unit 1, number '2' corresponds to Unit 2, etc.):
- 1 - short 'a'
- 2 - short 'e'
- 3 - short 'i'
- 4 - short 'o'
- 5 - short 'u'
- 6 - short vowel words ending in double consonants 'ff', 'zz', 'll', 'ss', 'gg'
- 7 - review
- 8 - long vowel words ending in a single 'o', 'y', or 'e'
- 9 - long 'a' formed by silent final 'e'
- 10 - long 'i' formed by silent final 'e'
- 11 - long 'o' formed by silent final 'e'
- 12 - words with 'u' formed by silent final 'e'
- 13 - review
- 14 - 'or' as in 'horn'
- 15 - 'er' as in 'her'
- 16 - 'ir' as in 'girl'
- 17 - 'ar' as in 'farm'
- 18 - review
- 19 - long 'a' spelled 'ay' as in 'day'
- 20 - long 'a' spelled 'ai' as in 'sail'
- 21 - long 'e' spelled 'ee' as in 'keep'
- 22 - long 'e' spelled 'ea' as in 'eat'
- 23 - final 'y' that says long 'e' as in 'baby'
- 24 - review
- 25 - long 'o' spelled 'ow' as in 'grow'
- 26 - 'ow' as in 'cow'
- 27 - 'oo' as in 'moon'

"Learning The Basics" Components
(continued)

    28 - 'oo' as in 'book'
    29 - 'aw' as in 'saw'
    30 - 'oi' or 'oy' as in 'boil' or 'boy'
    31 - review
    32 - color words
    33 - number words
    34 - days of the week and seasons
    Extra: contractions

Note: See the Appendix for actual word lists for each of the spelling patterns listed above. If you have a spelling program that you prefer, feel free to substitute your own program for this part of the plans.

Grammar, Mechanics, and Usage
    One day in each unit focuses on basic grammar, mechanics, and usage skills. Lessons are mainly oral using guided conversation between you and your child. The lessons are purposefully short and designed to focus on one rule or concept per lesson. In this manner, students are exposed to a variety of language skills in a low-key way. The concepts in the lessons are only introduced and are not meant to be mastered at this level.

    A brief scope and sequence of the grammar, mechanics, and usage concepts is listed by unit below (Number '1' corresponds to Unit 1, number '2' corresponds to Unit 2, etc.):
    1 - sentences and fragments
    2 - run-on sentences
    3 - sentences: subjects and predicates
    4 - sentences: statements
    5 - sentences: questions
    6 - sentences: questions and statements
    7 - sentences: commands
    8 - sentences: commands
    9 - sentences: exclamations
    10 - sentences: exclamations and statements
    11 - sentences: statements, questions, commands, exclamations
    12 - nouns
    13 - proper nouns: first names
    14 - proper nouns: full names
    15 - initials of full names
    16 - capitalizing 'I'
    17 - proper nouns: names of days of the week
    18 - proper nouns: names of days of the week
    19 - proper nouns: names of the months
    20 - proper nouns: names of the months

"Learning The Basics" Components
(continued)

   21 - writing dates
   22 - common and proper nouns: places
   23 - proper nouns: addresses of places
   24 - common nouns: things
   25 - plural nouns: adding '-s' and '-es'
   26 - commas in a series
   27 - action verbs
   28 - verbs: using 'is' and 'are'
   29 - verbs: using 'was' and 'were'
   30 - verbs: using 'has' and 'have'
   31 - contractions
   32 - alphabetical order
   33 - alphabetical order
   34 - friendly letters

Copywork

Daily written language practice is provided through copywork. By copying from a correctly written model, students gain practice in handwriting, spelling, grammar, capitalization, punctuation, and vocabulary. Copywork also prepares students to eventually write their own compositions.

Copywork sessions should be limited to 5-10 minutes. Work should be required to be done neatly and correctly. It is more important for students to produce careful, quality work, rather than a large quantity that is carelessly done. Copywork assignments can be done in a notebook or on loose-leaf paper to be collected in a binder.

Four days each week, students are directed to copy a portion of the poem being studied in the unit. A different classic poem is introduced each unit. Each poem was chosen for its enduring qualities and its ability to withstand the test of time. Many famous poets are represented.

Some students will be able to copy directly from the typed poems in the Appendix. Other students will need you to write a line or two from the poem on paper for them to copy directly below it.

One day each week, students will copy a sentence or a list of words related to the grammar, usage, or mechanics concept covered in that unit.

Reading

A reading instruction reminder is listed in the plans daily. If your child is a beginning reader, choose one of the phonics programs suggested in the Appendix, or use your own. If your child is an emerging reader, choose to follow the *Emerging Reader's Schedule* in the Appendix, or use your own program. If your child is an independent reader, choose *Drawn into the Heart of Reading: Level 2/3,* or use your own reading program.

"Learning The Basics" Components
(continued)

Since I believe reading instruction is a very personal decision for each family, I specifically designed *Beyond Little Hearts for His Glory* to work with any reading program that you choose.

Storytime

Daily storytime sessions are based on literature that is read aloud from the following nine genres: Biography, Adventure, Historical Fiction, Fantasy, Mystery, Nonfiction, Humor, Realistic Fiction, and Folk Tale. Each type of literature is read aloud for 20 days, except for Folk Tale which is read aloud for 10 days.

The instructions and activities are written to be used with any literature. This flexibility allows you to use your own discretion in selecting literature to read aloud to your students. The structure also allows you to select the pace at which you'll complete your read aloud selection.

A suggested list of read-aloud titles is provided in the Appendix. This list of titles is <u>not necessary</u> to complete the program. It is an optional list to help you choose literature for each genre to read-aloud. Each book on the list was very carefully chosen as an excellent read-aloud for this listening level. Heart of Dakota Publishing sells three different packages of the listed read-aloud selections on the website www.heartofdakota.com, or call (605) 428-4068 for more information.

Each unit includes the following reading activities in coordination with the read-aloud assignments:
* Day 1: introduce and study different types of literature
* Day 2: model narration to foster comprehension
* Day 3: identify and analyze a different story element for each genre
* Day 4: relate personally to one Godly character trait, compare Biblical and book characters, and select one area to improve
* Day 5: practice narration by retelling the story in a variety of ways

Math Exploration

Daily math lessons are included in the "Learning the Basics" part of the plans. These activities use concrete objects and hands-on experiences to introduce mathematical concepts through guided exploration. The workbooks *Primary Mathematics 1A & 1B* by Times New Media provide a text connection for each math lesson.

A brief scope and sequence of the math concepts is listed by unit below (Number '1' corresponds to Unit 1, number '2' corresponds to Unit 2, etc.):
1 - numbers '1' - '10': comparing sets, missing numbers, number pairs
2 - pairs of numbers with sums up to '10'
3 - addition: missing addends, addition stories, number sentences
4 - addition: commutative property, number combinations, sentences

"Learning The Basics" Components
(continued)

5 - addition sums to '10', introduction of subtraction: stories, sentences
6 - subtraction: sentences, fact families, counting backward
7 - addition & subtraction sentences, word problems, ordinal numbers
8 - ordinal numbers, review of concepts
9 - grouping and counting up to '20', comparing and ordering numbers
10 - adding and subtracting by grouping tens and ones
11 - adding and subtracting up to '20': counting up or back, fact families
12 - review, plane and solid figures: recognizing, naming, comparing
13 - plane and solid shapes: comparing sizes, completing patterns
14 - comparing: length, height, weight; nonstandard measurement
15 - weights: measuring and comparing; review, comparing groups
16 - sets: comparing, matching one-to-one, adding, subtracting
17 - graphs, numbers to '40': matching, counting, number words
18 - grouping: tens and ones, missing addends, counting patterns
19 - tens and ones: writing numbers, adding, subtracting
20 - tens and ones: counting to add or subtract; addition facts
21 - subtraction: facts, with zeros, patterns; addition: 3 addends
22 - review, introduction to multiplication as repeated addition
23 - multiplication: symbols, stories, number sentences; review
24 - review, introduction of division as sharing equally
25 - dividing items into equal groups, fractions: halves, quarters
26 - shapes: halves, quarters; telling time: hour, half hour
27 - writing times: hour, half hour; review, numbers to '100'
28 - numbers to '100': tens and ones, number words, adding, patterns
29 - numbers to '100': sequencing, hundreds chart, tens and ones
30 - adding numbers up to '100', double-digit addition with regrouping
31 - counting back to subtract up to '100', double-digit subtraction
32 - double-digit subtraction with regrouping, review, counting money
33 - money: counting, writing amounts, comparing sets, making change
34 - review of previous concepts

Note: If you have already covered the concepts listed above, follow the alternate math schedule in the Appendix using *Primary Mathematics 2A & 2B: U.S. Edition*.

If you have a different math program that you are already comfortable using, feel free to substitute it for the "Math Exploration" part of the plans. However, you may find that you enjoy using the actvities suggested in the "Math Exploration" box anyway.

Beyond Little Hearts For His Glory Lessons

Learning Through History

Focus: Pioneers from Spain Settle St. Augustine

Unit 1 - Day 1

Reading About History

Read about history in the following resource:

★ *American Pioneers and Patriots* p. 2 and 12

Key Idea: When pioneers from Spain came to settle in Florida, they crossed the ocean in sailing ships. Travel was very different in those days.

Poetry and Rhymes

Read aloud the poem *"The Storm"* (see Appendix) to the students. Do not share the title. Ask students to suggest some titles for the poem. Share the real title. Read the poem again with the students.

"Lightening & the Flood"

Key Idea: Read and appreciate a variety of classic poetry.

Geography

Outline a huge circle on the floor with masking tape. Say, *This circle is Earth. Earth has 7 continents. A continent is a large body of land surrounded by water.* On separate pieces of paper write these continent names: Asia, Africa, Antarctica, North America, South America, Australia, and Europe. Help students tape each continent name on Earth in the correct place. Give students actions to follow using the continent names (i.e. *Hop on one foot from Africa to Asia*). Other actions might be to walk backward, tiptoe, crawl, twirl, stomp, or gallop. Last, have students use p. viii in *American Pioneers and Patriots* as a guide while they scoot on a pillow to show Columbus' route and Magellan's route.

Key Idea: Explorers discovered that the Earth had 7 continents.

Bible Study

Psalm 4:8 is the memory verse for this unit. Read the verse out loud. Ask, *What does it mean to feel peaceful? How can you feel peaceful even when there may be many things that make you worried? Who keeps you safe? How can Psalm 4:8 comfort you?* Say the verse together 3 times. Add hand motions to help students remember the words.

Key Idea: Even though the pioneers had a long, hard trip ahead of them, they knew the Lord was watching over them.

Corresponding Music

✓ *Hide 'Em in Your Heart Vol. 2*
CD - Track 20; Cassette - Side B
Song: *"I Will Lie Down and Sleep"*

Learning the Basics

Focus: Language Arts and Math

Unit 1 - Day 1

Language Arts

Choose **either** spelling list **1 or** 2 (see Appendix for lists). Write each spelling word on a separate index card. Guide students to study each card one at a time, flip it over, write the word from memory on paper, flip the card back over to check the spelling, and erase and correct any mistakes. <u>Copywork</u>: Have students copy part of the poem *"The Storm"*.

<u>Key Idea</u>: Practice spelling words with the short 'a' sound as in 'hat'.

Reading Choices

Choose **one** of the reading options listed below (see Appendix for details).

★ *A phonics program*

★ *Scheduled Books for Emerging Readers*

★ *Drawn into the Heart of Reading Level 2/3*

<u>Key Idea</u>: Use a step-by-step program for reading instruction.

Storytime

Choose at least one biography to read aloud for the next 20 days of plans (see Appendix for suggested titles). To introduce the genre, *Biography*, hand each student a sack. Give students a limited amount of time to find 5 items to put in their sack that tell something about themselves. Have students share their items and explain their reasons for choosing each item. Say, *A biography is a true story of a person's life written by another person. Just like we learned about you as you shared about yourself, we can learn about others by reading about their lives.* Read a portion of the biography you chose.

<u>Key Idea</u>: Introduce the genre: *Biography*.

Math Exploration

Make cards with the number words 'one' - 'ten' written on them. Tell students to count silently or in a whisper as you clap your hands up to ten times. Stop clapping and ask students to say the number of times that you clapped. Then, have students hold up the matching number word card.

✔ <u>Text Connection</u>: *Primary Mathematics Workbook 1A* p. 7-8

<u>Key Idea</u>: Practice counting the numbers '1' - '10' and matching each number to the corresponding number word.

Learning Through History

Focus: Pioneers from Spain Settle St. Augustine

Unit 1 - Day 2

Reading About History

Read about history in the following resource:

★ *American Pioneers and Patriots* p. 3-5

Key Idea: Pedro, Catalina, and their parents left Spain on a ship bound for America. Pedro was excited, but Catalina was worried. The ship was crowded and hot.

Poetry and Rhymes

Read aloud the poem *"The Storm"* (see Appendix) with the students. Discuss the poem's meaning. If you choose, photocopy the poem, cut it apart, and have the students place it in the correct order.

Key Idea: Read and appreciate a variety of classic poetry.

Science Exploration

Say, *The earth has five oceans: the Atlantic, the Pacific, the Arctic, the Antarctic, and the Indian Ocean. The oceans have currents which make paths in the water as they move. Let's try moving a boat using a current.* Fill a sink or tub partway with water. Cut a small, flat boat shape out of an index card. The boat should have a pointed front but still lay flat. Place the boat on top of the water. Say, *Fill a dropper, baster, or squirty toy with water. Hold it beneath the surface of the water behind the boat. Squeeze the water out. The boat should move forward. Try to move the boat around the sink or tub using the current.*

✔ Text Connection: *God's Wonderful Works* p. 45

Key Idea: Pedro and Catalina crossed the Atlantic Ocean in a boat.

Bible Study

Say Psalm 4:8 while the students join in on the parts they know. Use the hand motions you added on Day 1. Say, *Name some things that worry you. What should you do when you are worried? After you pray about your worries, how should you feel?* Next, have students do 5 jumping jacks. After 5 jumping jacks, have the students recite the entire Bible verse. Prompt the students as needed. Repeat the activity several times.

Key Idea: The pioneers knew that only the Lord could keep them safe.

Corresponding Music

✔ *Hide 'Em in Your Heart Vol. 2* CD - Track 20; Cassette - Side B Song: *"I Will Lie Down and Sleep"*

Learning the Basics

Focus: Language Arts and Math

Unit 1 - Day 2

Language Arts

Use the spelling list from Day 1. Say the first spelling word. Use it in a sentence. Repeat the word. Ask students to write the word on a markerboard or a piece of paper from memory. Give students the matching word card from Day 1 to compare with their spelling. Guide students to correct any mistakes. Repeat the activity with all 10 words.
<u>Copywork</u>: Have students copy part of the poem *"The Storm"*.

<u>Key Idea</u>: Practice spelling words with the short 'a' sound as in 'hat'.

Reading Choices

Choose **one** of the reading options listed below (see Appendix for details).

★ A phonics program

★ *Scheduled Books for Emerging Readers*

★ *Drawn into the Heart of Reading Level 2/3*

<u>Key Idea</u>: Use a step-by-step program for reading instruction.

Storytime

Read aloud the next portion of the biography that you selected. Without looking back at the story, model retelling or narrating the part of the biography that you read today to the students. Remember to tell the most important points and to add details from the story to the retelling without overwhelming the students. After the retelling, ask, *What question would you like to ask the person in this book?* On paper, write the question that the students dictated to you. Have the students copy the question on paper underneath your writing.

<u>Key Idea</u>: Model retelling a story from a single reading.

Math Exploration

Set out 1-10 objects in a row (i.e. blocks, cans of food, spoons, paperclips, or crayons). Ask students to make a matching set of objects underneath the row that you made. Count each set with the students to compare and make sure the sets are equal. Then, have students write the corresponding number for each set on paper or on markerboard.

✔ <u>Text Connection</u>: *Primary Mathematics Workbook 1A* p. 9-10

<u>Key Idea</u>: Practice counting and writing the numbers '1' - '10'.

Learning Through History

Focus: Pioneers from Spain Settle St. Augustine

Unit 1 - Day 3

Reading About History

Read about history in the following resource:

★ *American Pioneers and Patriots* p. 6-8

Key Idea: After the ship passed the Canary Islands, there was a big storm at sea. The mainmast broke. The pioneers prayed that the Lord would calm the sea.

Poetry and Rhymes

Read aloud the poem *"The Storm"* (see Appendix) with the students. Read the poem aloud a second time, pausing after each line or two for students to add their own actions to the poem. The actions should make sense with the poem.

Key Idea: Read and appreciate a variety of classic poetry.

Science Exploration

Say, *Some sea creatures like the whale and the dolphin have blubber to protect them from cold water temperatures. Blubber is fat.* Fill a sink with very cold water. Have students coat one of their hands with a thick layer of vegetable shortening. Tell students to place both hands in the cold water. After one minute, have students take both hands out. Ask, *Is one hand colder than the other? Why might the hand with the shortening be warmer than the hand without shortening? Shortening is similar to blubber. How do you think blubber helps a whale or a dolphin?*

✔ Text Connection: *God's Wonderful Works* p. 73-74 and 77

Key Idea: During their stormy sea voyage, the pioneers heard stories about crocodiles and sea creatures.

Bible Study

Say Psalm 4:8 with the students. Use the hand motions you added on Day 1. Next, have students hop on their left foot until you say, *Freeze*. After they 'freeze', have the students recite the entire Bible verse. Prompt students as needed. Have students switch to the right foot, and repeat the activity.

✔ Text Connection: *Morning Bells* p. 64-66

Key Idea: The pioneers trusted God to watch over them.

Corresponding Music

✔ *Hide 'Em in Your Heart Vol. 2* CD - Track 20; Cassette - Side B Song: *"I Will Lie Down and Sleep"*

Learning the Basics

Focus: Language Arts and Math

Unit 1 - Day 3

Language Arts

Using the spelling list from Day 1, choose 3 or more words that the students need to practice. Guide students to use each of the words that you chose in a sentence. On a markerboard or a piece of paper, write down the sentences as the students dictate them to you. Underline the spelling word in each sentence. Have the students copy the sentences on a piece of paper. Help students check their sentences and correct any mistakes.

Copywork: Have students copy part of the poem *"The Storm"*.

Key Idea: Practice spelling words with the short 'a' sound as in 'hat'.

Reading Choices

Choose **one** of the reading options listed below (see Appendix for details).

★ A phonics program
★ *Scheduled Books for Emerging Readers*
★ *Drawn into the Heart of Reading Level 2/3*

Key Idea: Use a step-by-step program for reading instruction.

Storytime

Read aloud the next portion of the biography that you selected.

Say, *Characters are the people or animals in a story. Who is the most important character in the biography?* Take turns with the students naming things about the main character. Then, take turns thinking of questions to ask about the main character.

Key Idea: Introduce the story element: *character*.

Math Exploration

Say, *Hold up any number of fingers from '1' to '10'. I will also hold up any number of fingers from '1' to '10'. Let's compare our two sets of fingers to see who has more. Say the numbers to compare them. For example, '8' is more than '5'. Let's repeat the activity, but this time we'll compare our two sets of fingers to see who has less. For example, '3' is less than '6'.* Repeat the activity alternating answers to compare more or less. If the two sets have the same number, make sure to point out that the sets are equal.

✔ Text Connection: *Primary Mathematics Workbook 1A* p. 11-12

Key Idea: Compare two sets to see which has more or less.

Learning Through History

Focus: Pioneers from Spain Settle St. Augustine

Unit 1 - Day 4

Reading About History

Read about history in the following resource:

★ *American Pioneers and Patriots* p. 9-11

Key Idea: Pedro used his knife to keep the door shut during the storm. After the storm, the ship stopped in Puerto Rico for repairs. Then, it sailed for America. Pedro's father rewarded Pedro with his own knife.

Poetry and Rhymes

Read aloud the poem *"The Storm"* (see Appendix) with the students. Have students draw pictures that reflect the poem's meaning on either a photocopy of the poem or on their copywork. File the finished poem in a special place.

Key Idea: Read and appreciate a variety of classic poetry.

History Activity

Divide a sheet of white paper into 5 equal columns and 9 equal rows. Label the columns from left to right across the top of the paper as follows: 1400, 1500, 1600, 1700, 1800. Say, *This will be our timeline. We will save it and add important events as we study them. Each of these columns stands for 100 years. Who do you know that has lived to be almost 100? Today we read about St. Augustine being settled in 1565. Let's find the column that says 1500. Draw a small fort in that column. Write 'St. Augustine, 1565' under it. Earlier, we read about Columbus. He sailed in 1492. Let's find the 1400 column. Draw a small ship in that column. Write 'Columbus, 1492' under it.*

Key Idea: The Spanish people settled at St. Augustine in Florida.

Bible Study

Say Psalm 4:8 with the students. Use the hand motions you added on Day 1. Ask, *What are some of the things that you need? Who helps take care of your needs? How can you show that you trust God to take care of you?* Next, have the students do 5 sit-ups. After 5 sit-ups, have the students recite the entire Bible verse.

Key Idea: When the pioneers were afraid, they prayed for the Lord to keep them safe. They trusted Him.

Corresponding Music

✓ *Hide 'Em in Your Heart Vol. 2* CD - Track 20; Cassette - Side B Song: *"I Will Lie Down and Sleep"*

Learning the Basics

Focus: Language Arts and Math

Unit 1 - Day 4

Language Arts

Use the spelling list from Day 1. Say each word and use it in a sentence. Have students write each word and check it with the matching word card from Day 1. Guide students to correct any mistakes. For each missed word, have students jump in place and spell the word out loud, jumping each time they say a letter.
<u>Copywork</u>: Have students copy part of the poem *"The Storm"*.

<u>Key Idea</u>: Practice spelling words with the short 'a' sound as in 'hat'.

Reading Choices

Choose **one** of the reading options listed below (see Appendix for details).

★ A phonics program

★ *Scheduled Books for Emerging Readers*

★ *Drawn into the Heart of Reading Level 2/3*

<u>Key Idea</u>: Use a step-by-step program for reading instruction.

Storytime

Say, *Responsibility means being accountable to God and to others as you carry out your duties in a faithful way.* Read aloud the key verse 1 Peter 4:10 to illustrate *responsibility*. List some duties that you are responsible for carrying out. Now, have students list duties that they are responsible for carrying out. Read aloud the next portion of the biography that you selected. Then, ask, *How do the characters show responsiblity? What could the characters do to be more responsible?*

<u>Key Idea</u>: Introduce the Godly character trait: *responsibility*.

Math Exploration

Make cards with the numbers '1' - '10'. Place the cards in a row facedown in order from '1' - '10'. Flip over the second card. Ask students to name the next three numbers in the row ('3', '4', '5'). Students may check their answer by flipping over the next three cards in the row. Return the cards to their facedown position. Flip over the ninth card. Ask students to count backward to name the three numbers before the ninth card ('8', '7', '6'). Have students check their answer. Repeat the activity, turning over different cards.

✔ <u>Text Connection</u>: *Primary Mathematics Workbook 1A* p. 13-14

<u>Key Idea</u>: Count up or back to find the missing numbers in a sequence.

Learning Through History

Focus: Pioneers from Spain Settle St. Augustine

Unit 1 - Day 5

Reading About History

Read the following passage from your own Bible:

Psalm 18:1-6

Key Idea: When the pioneers were afraid, they called out to God, just like King David did in this Psalm. They knew that God heard their cries, and they trusted God to protect them.

Poetry and Rhymes

Read aloud the poem *"The Storm"* (see Appendix) with the students. Without looking at the words, have the students recite as much of the poem as they can from memory. Prompt students as needed.

Key Idea: Read and appreciate a variety of classic poetry.

Artistic Expression

Cut a large shield out of tagboard or construction paper. Cover the shield with aluminum foil. Tape the foil to the shield in the back. Cut out a strip of paper and tape or staple it to the back of a shield as a handle. Allow students to choose to either paint or etch on their shield. If students choose to paint, use tempera paint applied with cotton swabs. If students choose to etch, use a sharp pencil or the point of a stretched out paperclip for etching. Guide students to illustrate symbols on the shield that go along with Psalm 18:1-6. Possible symbols might include a horn, a rock, a music note, a heart, rays of light, or a fort.

Key Idea: The Lord is your shield. When you are scared, you need to trust God to protect you.

Bible Study

Ask, *In Psalm 18:1-3, what does King David say about God? In Psalm 18:4-6, what is King David describing? What can you learn from King David about trusting God? How can you trust God even when times are hard?* Ask students to share their memory verse, Psalm 4:8, with someone special. Suggestions for sharing the verse include saying it to another family member, saying it to someone by telephone, reciting it to a stuffed animal, or writing it to mail.

Key Idea: The pioneers trusted God to be their help and strength.

Corresponding Music

✓ *Hide 'Em in Your Heart Vol. 2* CD - Track 20; Cassette - Side B
Song: *"I Will Lie Down and Sleep"*

Learning the Basics

Focus: Language Arts and Math

Unit 1 - Day 5

Language Arts

Say, *A sentence is a group of words that tells a complete thought. Sentences have two parts. One part tells who or what the sentence is about. The other part tells what that person or thing is doing. If a sentence is missing one of the parts, it is called a fragment. I will read you a group of words. Tell me whether the words make a sentence* (S) *or a fragment.* (F) *The dog ran away.* (S) *The man in the car.* (F) *Helen is shopping.* (S) *That cat is striped.* (S) *Running fast.* (F) *Playing outside.* (F) *I love pizza.* (S) *My eyes are blue.* (S)
<u>Copywork</u>: Have students dictate one sentence about themselves to copy.

<u>Key Idea</u>: Introduce the difference between sentences and fragments.

Reading Choices

Choose **one** of the reading options listed below (see Appendix for details).

★ A phonics program

★ *Scheduled Books for Emerging Readers*

★ *Drawn into the Heart of Reading Level 2/3*

<u>Key Idea</u>: Use a step-by-step program for reading instruction.

Storytime

Read aloud a short portion of the biography that you selected. Give students a chance to orally retell the portion of today's story that you read aloud. Use the following prompts as needed: *What happened in the beginning of the part that we read today? What happened during the middle of the part that we read today? What happened at the end?*

<u>Key Idea</u>: Give students practice retelling a portion of a biography.

Math Exploration

Draw a group of green circles on the left side of a piece of paper to be a cabbage patch. Draw a group of orange triangles on the right side of the paper to be a carrot patch. Give students 6 marshmallows or cotton balls to be bunnies. Have students act out addition stories on their papers (i.e. 4 bunnies were in the cabbage patch. 2 bunnies were in the carrot patch. 4 bunnies and 2 bunnies make 6 bunnies.) After several practices, allow students to act out their own bunny stories.

✓ <u>Text Connection</u>: *Primary Mathematics Workbook 1A* p. 15

<u>Key Idea</u>: Name different pairs of numbers that make '6'.

Learning Through History

Focus: Pioneers from England Settle Jamestown

Unit 2 - Day 1

Reading About History

Read about history in the following resource:

★ *American Pioneers and Patriots* p. 16 and 25

Key Idea: Many men settled in Jamestown to find gold. They didn't want to work. Captain Smith said they must work to eat. Since there were no stores, most things had to be made.

Poetry and Rhymes

Read aloud the poem *"Father, We Thank Thee"* (see Appendix) to the students. Do not share the title. Ask students to suggest some titles for the poem. Share the real title. Read the poem again with the students.

"Flowers of God"

Key Idea: Read and appreciate a variety of classic poetry.

Science Exploration

Say, *The pioneers were not sure what animals they might see in the new land. Name some animals that are found in different parts of the world than where you live. Choose one or more animals from another climate to read about in the science text pages listed below or in an encyclopedia. After reading, choose one way to show what you learned. Ideas for sharing information may include drawing a picture, building a model with playdough or clay, narrating a play using toys or stuffed animals, or building a 3-D model with paper or building bricks.*

✓ Text Connection: *God's Wonderful Works* p. 89-91, 97-99, 101, or 108

Key Idea: The new land was strange. It was very different from England.

Bible Study

Galations 6:9 is the memory verse for this unit. Read the verse out loud. Ask, *What does it mean to be weary? Should you become weary or give up when you are doing good things? Why not? If you do not give up, what does the verse say will happen?* Say the verse together 3 times. Add hand motions to help students remember the words.

Key Idea: The men in Jamestown needed to learn to work hard and trust God for the blessings.

Corresponding Music

✓ *Hide 'Em in Your Heart Vol. 2* CD - Track 7; Cassette - Side A Song: *"If We Don't Lose Heart"*

Learning the Basics

Focus: Language Arts and Math

Unit 2 - Day 1

Language Arts

Choose **either** spelling list 1 **or** 2 (see Appendix for lists). Write each spelling word on a separate index card. Guide students to study each card one at a time, flip it over, write the word from memory on paper, flip the card back over to check the spelling, and erase and correct any mistakes.

Copywork: Have students copy part of the poem *"Father, We Thank Thee"*.

Key Idea: Practice spelling words with the short 'e' sound as in 'bed'.

Reading Choices

Choose **one** of the reading options listed below (see Appendix for details).

★ A phonics program

★ *Scheduled Books for Emerging Readers*

★ *Drawn into the Heart of Reading Level 2/3*

Key Idea: Use a step-by-step program for reading instruction.

Storytime

Say, *Tell me what was happening in the biography the last time that we read together.* Read aloud the next chapter title. Discuss what it could mean. Briefly look at the pictures in the next chapter and discuss them to preview what you will read today. Read aloud the next portion of the biography that you selected. Pace your reading to complete the biography during the next 15 days of plans.

Key Idea: Preread to build anticipation for the next part of the biography.

Math Exploration

Quickly sketch the outline of two trees on a piece of paper. Give each student 8 raisins or fruit bits to use as fruit on the trees. Have the students act out addition stories on their papers (i.e. One tree has 5 pieces of fruit. The other tree has 3 pieces of fruit. How many pieces of fruit are on both trees?) As you tell each story, write the addition sentence on paper or markerboard (i.e. 5 + 3 = 8). Introduce the "+" and "=" signs. Repeat the activity using different numbers of fruit that equal '8'. Have students write the corresponding addition sentence for each problem.

Key Idea: Combine two sets together using addition up to '8'. Write the corresponding addition sentences.

Learning Through History

Focus: Pioneers from England Settle Jamestown

Unit 2 - Day 2

Reading About History

Read about history in the following resource:

★ *American Pioneers and Patriots* p. 17-19

Key Idea: Sally's mother trusted her to watch her little brother, Richard. Sally could knit, mend, and babysit. She was a good helper to her mother.

Poetry and Rhymes

Read aloud the poem *"Father, We Thank Thee"* (see Appendix) with the students. Discuss the poem's meaning. If you choose, photocopy the poem, cut it apart, and have the students place it in the correct order.

Key Idea: Read and appreciate a variety of classic poetry.

Science Exploration

Say, *Squirrels are part of the rodent family. They are noted for their agility and for their ability to glide in the air. Tree squirrels fall by stretching out their legs and flattening their bodies and tail. This slows the speed of their fall. Let's try an experiment to show how squirrels "fall". Crumple a sheet of paper into a ball. Let it drop. Now try the experiment with a flat sheet of paper. Describe how the crumpled paper dropped. Describe how the flat paper dropped. Which paper fell faster? Why might flattening their bodies help tree squirrels "glide" through the air?*

✔ Text Connection: *God's Wonderful Works* p. 112-113

Key Idea: Sally's brother, Ralph, had caught a wild, baby squirrel. He was keeping it in a box as a pet. Richard wanted to play with the squirrel.

Bible Study

Say Galations 6:9 while the students join in on the parts they know. Use the hand motions you added on Day 1. Say, *Name some good things that you do without expecting someone to thank you. Will things always go well when you are trying to do something good? Why not? How can this Bible verse comfort you?* Next, have students do 3 push-ups. After 3 push-ups, have the students recite the entire Bible verse. Repeat the activity several times.

Key Idea: Sally worked hard to do what her mother asked her to do.

Corresponding Music

✔ *Hide 'Em in Your Heart Vol. 2* CD - Track 7; Cassette - Side A
Song: *"If We Don't Lose Heart"*

Learning the Basics

Focus: Language Arts and Math

Unit 2 - Day 2

Language Arts

Use the spelling list from Day 1. Say the first spelling word. Use it in a sentence. Repeat the word. Ask students to write the word on a markerboard or a piece of paper from memory. Give students the matching word card from Day 1 to compare with their spelling. Guide students to correct any mistakes. Repeat the activity with all 10 words.
Copywork: Have students copy part of the poem *"Father, We Thank Thee"*.

Key Idea: Practice spelling words with the short 'e' sound as in 'bed'.

Reading Choices

Choose **one** of the reading options listed below (see Appendix for details).

★ A phonics program
★ *Scheduled Books for Emerging Readers*
★ *Drawn into the Heart of Reading Level 2/3*

Key Idea: Use a step-by-step program for reading instruction.

Storytime

Read aloud the next portion of the biography that you selected. Without looking back at the story, begin retelling or narrating the part of the biography that you read today. After a short time, tap the student and say, *Your turn.* The student should pick up the narration where you left off. After a short time, the student should tap you and say, *Your turn.* Continue taking turns narrating in this manner until today's reading has been retold. Then, say, *Name one thing that you learned about the main character today.* Write it on paper for students to copy.

Key Idea: Take turns retelling a story from a single reading.

Math Exploration

Complete the assigned lesson in the workbook listed below.

✔ Text Connection: *Primary Mathematics Workbook 1A* p. 16-17

Note: Use counters as needed to find the different combinations that make '7' and '8'.

Key Idea: Add two numbers together to find the different combinations that make '7' and '8'.

Learning Through History

Focus: Pioneers from England Settle Jamestown

Unit 2 - Day 3

Reading About History

Read about history in the following resource:

★ *American Pioneers and Patriots* p. 20-21

Key Idea: While Sally was helping her mother, Richard woke up and ran away. Sally prayed for God to help her find Richard. She found him in the woods. When she got back, the house was on fire.

Poetry and Rhymes

Read aloud the poem *"Father, We Thank Thee"* (see Appendix) with the students. Read the poem aloud a second time, pausing after each line or two for students to add their own actions to the poem. The actions should make sense with the poem.

Key Idea: Read classic poetry.

Geography

Give each student a white piece of paper and markers or crayons. Say, *You will be making a map of the places from today's story. Listen carefully as I read.* Read the first six paragraphs of *American Pioneers and Patriots* p. 21 aloud. Say, *At the bottom of your paper, draw a brown, rectangular wall. In the middle of your paper draw green rows of corn. At the top of your paper, draw a forest of trees. Next, make a gate in the wall leading to the cornfield. Now, as I reread the same portion of the story that I read before, add footprints to your map to show where Richard went. Draw red strawberries at the place where Sally found Richard.*

Key Idea: Richard was missing. God helped Sally find him.

Bible Study

Say Galations 6:9 with the students. Use the hand motions you added on Day 1. Next, have students skip around the room until you say, *Freeze.* After they 'freeze', have the students recite the entire Bible verse. Have students repeat the activity.

✔ Text Connection: *Morning Bells* p. 85-87

Key Idea: Sally did the best she could with the duties that were given to her. You need to do the best you can with the duties you are given.

Corresponding Music

✔ *Hide 'Em in Your Heart Vol. 2* CD - Track 7; Cassette - Side A Song: *"If We Don't Lose Heart"*

Learning the Basics

Focus: Language Arts and Math

Unit 2 - Day 3

Language Arts

Using the spelling list from Day 1, choose 3 or more words that the students need to practice. Guide students to use each of the words that you chose in a sentence. On a markerboard or a piece of paper, write down the sentences as the students dictate them to you. Underline the spelling word in each sentence. Have the students copy the sentences on a piece of paper. Help students check their sentences and correct any mistakes.

<u>Copywork</u>: Have students copy part of the poem *"Father, We Thank Thee"*.

<u>Key Idea</u>: Practice spelling words with the short 'e' sound as in 'bed'.

Reading Choices

Choose **one** of the reading options listed below (see Appendix for details).

★ A phonics program

★ *Scheduled Books for Emerging Readers*

★ *Drawn into the Heart of Reading Level 2/3*

<u>Key Idea</u>: Use a step-by-step program for reading instruction.

Storytime

Read aloud the next portion of the biography that you selected. Say, *Describe how the main character looks* (i.e. hair, eyes, build, age, clothing, special features). Ask students to draw a picture of the main character's face and body. Allow students to color their pictures if they have time. Save the students' pictures for Unit 3 - Day 3.

<u>Key Idea</u>: Focus on the story element: *character*.

Math Exploration

Set out 2 cups. You will need 9 counters (i.e. dry cereal pieces, marshmallows, buttons, or coins). Divide the 9 counters into the 2 cups. Have the students count the number of items in each cup. Guide students to write an addition sentence on paper that represents the combined total of the cups. Repeat the activity to find all the different combinations that equal '9' (1 + 8 = 9, 2 + 7 = 9, 3 + 6 = 9, 4 + 5 = 9, 9 + 0 = 9, 8 + 1 = 9, 7 + 2 = 9, 6 + 3 = 9, 5 + 4 = 9, and 0 + 9 = 9).

✔ <u>Text Connection</u>: *Primary Mathematics Workbook 1A* p. 18

<u>Key Idea</u>: Combine two sets to find all the pairs of numbers that equal '9'.

Learning Through History

Focus: Pioneers from England Settle Jamestown

Unit 2 - Day 4

Reading About History

Read about history in the following resource:

★ *American Pioneers and Patriots* p. 22-24

Key Idea: The people of Jamestown worked together to put out the fire. Instead of blaming one another, the family praised God for saving their house and their family. Their friends shared food with them.

Poetry and Rhymes

Read aloud the poem *"Father, We Thank Thee"* (see Appendix) with the students. Have students draw pictures that reflect the poem's meaning on either a photocopy of the poem or on their copywork. File the finished poem in a special place.

Key Idea: Read and appreciate a variety of classic poetry.

History Activity

On a markerboard or a piece of paper, draw a timeline of a year starting with January and ending with December. Say, *This is a timeline of one year. There are 12 months in one year. Each year you have a birthday. Circle the month of your birthday on this timeline. Get out the timeline you started in Unit 1. On the timeline you started in Unit 1, each column stands for 100 years. That means that each column stands for 100 of your birthdays. To have 100 birthdays, you would need to go through the months on our one year timeline 100 times. Today we read about Jamestown being settled in 1607. Let's find the column that says 1600. Draw a small fort in that column. Write 'Jamestown, 1607'.*

Key Idea: Some English people settled at Jamestown in Virginia.

Bible Study

Say Galations 6:9 with the students. Use the hand motions you added on Day 1. Ask, *What are some jobs that you do at home? How well do you do those jobs when no one else is watching? Who is always watching you? How can saying Galations 6:9 help you be a harder worker?* Next, have students run in place. When you say, *Freeze,* have the students stop and recite the entire Bible verse. Repeat the activity.

Key Idea: The pioneers wanted to do what was right in God's eyes.

Corresponding Music

✓ *Hide 'Em in Your Heart Vol. 2*
CD - Track 7; Cassette - Side A
Song: *"If We Don't Lose Heart"*

Learning the Basics

Focus: Language Arts and Math

Unit 2 - Day 4

Language Arts

Use the spelling list from Day 1. Say each word and use it in a sentence. Have students write each word and check it with the matching word card from Day 1. Guide students to correct any mistakes. For each missed word, have students write the word on paper and trace around it 3 times using 3 different colors.
Copywork: Have students copy part of the poem *"Father, We Thank Thee"*.

Key Idea: Practice spelling words with the short 'e' sound as in 'bed'.

Reading Choices

Choose **one** of the reading options listed below (see Appendix for details).
★ A phonics program
★ *Scheduled Books for Emerging Readers*
★ *Drawn into the Heart of Reading Level 2/3*

Key Idea: Use a step-by-step program for reading instruction.

Storytime

Say, *Responsibility means being accountable to God and to others as you carry out your duties in a faithful way.* Review the key verse for *responsibility*, 1 Peter 4:10. Read aloud 2 Thessalonians 3:6-13. Ask, *How did Paul's actions show responsibility?* Read aloud the next portion of the biography that you selected. Then, ask, *How does the main character in the biography show responsibility? What would the Biblical character, Paul, do differently from the character in your book?*

Key Idea: Focus on the Godly character trait: *responsibility*.

Math Exploration

Divide a piece of paper in half by drawing a line down the center of the paper. Give students 10 counters. Tell students to divide the counters on the two sides of the paper (i.e. Place 6 counters on one side of the paper and 4 counters on the other side). Help students write the corresponding number sentence to match the counters (i.e. 6 + 4 = 10). Guide students to repeat the activity to find all the different ways to make '10'.

✔ Text Connection: *Primary Mathematics Workbook 1A* p. 19

Key Idea: Combine two sets to find the different ways to make '10'.

Learning Through History

Focus: Pioneers from England Settle Jamestown

Unit 2 - Day 5

Reading About History

Read the following passage from your own Bible:

★ Ruth 1:3-5; 2:1-12; 4:13-17

Key Idea: The pioneers could have given up and gone home. Just like Ruth, they faithfully stayed. God blessed Ruth for her faithfulness. Even though the pioneers had many hard times, God was watching over them.

Poetry and Rhymes

Have students get out the poems that they saved from the previous units. Ask students to select one or more poems to review. Read aloud the selected poems with the students.

Key Idea: Read classic poetry.

Artistic Expression

Give each student a piece of brown or black construction paper. Say, *Fold over a 1" strip of the paper and press down on the crease. Flip the paper over and repeat the folding process. Continue accordian-folding the paper. Set the folded paper on the table to be a bumpy field.* Give students yellow or gold paper to cut out bundles of grain. Each bundle should be several inches high. Say, *Glue the bundles to the folds of the brown or black paper, so the bundles look like they are standing up in the field. Cut small pieces of yellow paper to glue in the bottom of the folds in the field to be stray pieces of grain.*

Key Idea: Ruth faithfully worked to gather grain from Boaz's field for food. God used Boaz to take care of Ruth and Naomi.

Bible Study

Ask, *In the Bible passage we read from Ruth, what good things did Ruth do? Did she become weary in doing good?* Discuss what Ruth teaches us about reaping blessings if we continue to do good when times are hard. Ask, *How can you help others?* Ask students to share their memory verse, Galations 6:9, with someone special. Suggestions for sharing the verse include saying it to another family member, saying it to someone by telephone, reciting it to a stuffed animal, or writing it to mail.

Key Idea: Ruth worked hard and trusted God for help. You can too.

Corresponding Music

✔ *Hide 'Em in Your Heart Vol. 2*
CD - Track 7; Cassette - Side A
Song: *"If We Don't Lose Heart"*

Learning the Basics

Focus: Language Arts and Math

Unit 2 - Day 5

Language Arts

Say, *A sentence is a group of words that tells a complete thought. A run-on sentence has more than one complete thought. Help me divide the following run-on sentence into 2 sentences: I am hungry I am eating a sandwich.* Say, *Periods are like stop signs. Run-on sentences are missing periods. So, the sentences just run on and on. Listen as I read the following run-on sentence: A train must stop to get fuel It cannot keep going and going without stopping My family is waiting for the train to pick us up I hope the train will stop for us soon.* Say, *Let's read it again and listen for the right places to stop and add periods.* <u>Copywork</u>: Have students copy one of the sentences.

<u>Key Idea</u>: Correct run-on sentences.

Reading Choices

Choose **one** of the reading options listed below (see Appendix for details).

★ A phonics program
★ *Scheduled Books for Emerging Readers*
★ *Drawn into the Heart of Reading Level 2/3*

<u>Key Idea</u>: Use a step-by-step program for reading instruction.

Storytime

Read aloud a short portion of the biography that you selected. Give students a chance to orally **retell** today's reading while mimicking the character's actions. Prompt students after each action by asking, *What happened next?* If needed, guide the retelling by reading the important sentences from today's reading for students to act out.

<u>Key Idea</u>: Give students practice retelling a portion of a biography.

Math Exploration

Complete the assigned lesson in the workbook listed below.

✔ <u>Text Connection</u>: *Primary Mathematics Workbook 1A* p. 20-22

Note: Use counters as needed to find the missing part of a set that will equal the given total.

<u>Key Idea</u>: Count up to find the missing part of a set that will equal the total '6', '7', '8', or '9'.

Learning Through History

Focus: Trouble with King James in England

Unit 3 - Day 1

Reading About History

Read about history in the following resource:

 Stories of the Pilgrims p. 1-5

Key Idea: The Brewster family ran an inn in Scrooby, England. The king's messenger came to let William Brewster know that Queen Anne was coming to stay at the inn on her way to her new home.

Artistic Expression

Give each student a piece of grey paper. Help students use a black crayon or marker to outline large stones on the paper to make a stone wall. Guide students to color or paint green vines trailing up the wall between the stones. Then, direct students to wad up a paper towel or napkin, dab it in red paint, and blot the paint along the vines to be roses.

Key Idea: The Brewster's house had once been a palace. Now, it was an inn for travelers. The house had a beautiful garden with ponds filled with fish. The outside walls of the house were covered by a climbing rosebush.

Poetry and Rhymes

Read aloud the poem *"Uphill"* (see Appendix) to the students. Do not share the title. <u>Ask students to suggest some titles</u> for the poem. Share the real title. Read the poem again with the students.

"Travels"

Key Idea: Read and appreciate a variety of classic poetry.

Bible Study

1 John 4:15-16a is the memory verse for this unit. Read the verse out loud. Ask, *If you believe in Jesus, how does God dwell or live within you? How can we live the way God wants us to live? Can we be good enough to earn God's love? Why does God love us even though we sin?* Say the verse together 3 times. Add hand motions to help students remember the words.

Key Idea: The Brewster family tried to live for God. They wanted others to see God's love in them.

Corresponding Music

✓ *Hide 'Em in Your Heart Vol. 2* CD - Track 5; Cassette - Side A Song: *"God Is Love"*

Learning the Basics

Focus: Language Arts and Math

Unit 3 - Day 1

Language Arts

Choose **either** spelling list 1 **or** 2 (see Appendix for lists). Write each spelling word on a separate index card. Guide students to study each card one at a time, flip it over, write the word from memory on paper, flip the card back over to check the spelling, and erase and correct any mistakes.

<u>Copywork</u>: Have students copy part of the poem *"Uphill"*.

<u>Key Idea</u>: Practice spelling words with the short 'i' sound as in 'sit'.

Reading Choices

Choose **one** of the reading options listed below (see Appendix for details).

★ A phonics program

★ *Scheduled Books for Emerging Readers*

★ *Drawn into the Heart of Reading Level 2/3*

<u>Key Idea</u>: Use a step-by-step program for reading instruction.

Storytime

Say, *What things have gone wrong for the characters in your biography? What problems do the characters in your biography have right now? What would you do to help the characters, if you could?*

Read aloud the next portion of the biography that you selected. Pace your reading to complete the biography during the next 10 days of plans.

<u>Key Idea</u>: Set a purpose for reading the next part of the biography.

Math Exploration

Hold up both hands and show 7 fingers. Ask, *How many more fingers are needed to make '10'?* Write the matching number sentence on paper or markerboard for students to complete (7 + ___ = 10). Repeat the activity showing different numbers of fingers and writing the matching number sentences. After several examples, give students a chance to hold up their fingers and ask you to answer.

✓ <u>Text Connection</u>: *Primary Mathematics Workbook 1A* p. 23-24

<u>Key Idea</u>: Find the missing addend in number sentences with a sum of '10'.

Learning Through History

Focus: Trouble with King James in England

Unit 3 - Day 2

Reading About History

Read about history in the following resource:

★ *Stories of the Pilgrims* p. 6-12

Key Idea: Patience talked with the queen in the garden. She told Queen Anne about the church meetings they had at the inn. The queen kindly warned Patience not to tell any other strangers her secret.

Poetry and Rhymes

Read aloud the poem *"Uphill"* (see Appendix) with the students. Discuss the poem's meaning. If you choose, photocopy the poem, cut it apart, and have the students place it in the correct order.

Key Idea: Read and appreciate a variety of classic poetry.

Science Exploration

Set out 2 small plates to be flowers. Spread the plates out. Sprinkle crushed yellow potato chips, crackers, or dry cereal in the center of **one** plate to be pollen. Have students pretend to be bees by landing on the pollinated flower with their fingers. Ask, *What happens as the bee crawls on the flower?* Then, have the bees fly and land on the new flower. Have the bees shake the pollen onto the new flower. Ask, *What happens when the bee lands on a new flower?* Say, *Flowers need bees to pollinate them and help them make seeds. Bees need the yellow pollen on the flowers for food and the sweet nectar to make honey.*

✔ Text Connection: *God's Wonderful Works* p. 52

Key Idea: Queen Anne admired the blooming flowers in the garden.

Bible Study

Say 1 John 4:15-16a while the students join in on the parts they know. Use the hand motions you added on Day 1. Ask, *What are some ways that you can show love to others? When you show love to others, who will people see in you?* Next, have students do 5 toe touches. After 5 toe touches, have the students recite the entire Bible verse. Prompt the students as needed. Repeat the activity.

Key Idea: The Brewster children were excited to be helpful and show God's love to the guests at the inn.

Corresponding Music

✔ *Hide 'Em in Your Heart Vol. 2* CD - Track 5; Cassette - Side A
Song: *"God Is Love"*

Learning the Basics

Focus: Language Arts and Math

Unit 3 - Day 2

Language Arts

Use the spelling list from Day 1. Say the first spelling word. Use it in a sentence. Repeat the word. Ask students to write the word on a markerboard or a piece of paper from memory. Give students the matching word card from Day 1 to compare with their spelling. Guide students to correct any mistakes. Repeat the activity with all 10 words. <u>Copywork</u>: Have students copy part of the poem *"Uphill"*.

<u>Key Idea</u>: Practice spelling words with the short 'i' sound as in 'sit'.

Reading Choices

Choose **one** of the reading options listed below (see Appendix for details).

★ A phonics program
★ *Scheduled Books for Emerging Readers*
★ *Drawn into the Heart of Reading Level 2/3*

<u>Key Idea</u>: Use a step-by-step program for reading instruction.

Storytime

Read aloud the next portion of the biography that you selected. Without looking back at the story, write a retelling of the part of the biography that you read today leaving blanks in place of key words (i.e. _____ was a young boy who lived in _____. He enjoyed drawing, painting, and playing with _____. His father was a _____.). Key words can be names, places, descriptive words, times of day, seasons, etc. Work with the students to reread the written narration and fill in the missing words.

<u>Key Idea</u>: Model retelling a story from a single reading.

Math Exploration

Complete the assigned lesson in the workbook listed below.

✔ <u>Text Connection</u>: *Primary Mathematics Workbook 1A* p. 25-26

<u>Key Idea</u>: Tell addition stories to show how many items there are altogether.

Learning Through History

Focus: Trouble with King James in England

Unit 3 - Day 3

Reading About History

Read about history in the following resource:

★ *Stories of the Pilgrims* p. 13-17

Key Idea: King James ordered the people of Scrooby to go to his church. He did not want them to worship on their own. He sent soldiers to watch them and to find out where they were meeting.

Poetry and Rhymes

Read aloud the poem *"Uphill"* (see Appendix) with the students. Read the poem aloud a second time, pausing after each line or two for students to add their own actions to the poem. The actions should make sense with the poem.

Key Idea: Read classic poetry.

Science Exploration

Find a dark room. Tape a piece of white paper and a piece of black or dark paper next to each other on a wall. Turn off the lights in the room and stand several feet back from the papers. Have students shine the flashlight on the white paper and then on the black paper. Ask, *Which paper seems brighter? What do you notice about the black paper? What do you notice about the white paper? Why would the white paper look brighter? Light colors, like white, reflect light. Dark colors, like black, absorb light.*

✔ Text Connection: *God's Wonderful Works* p. 16

Key Idea: The dark night absorbed the people hiding in the chapel, making it hard for the King's soldiers to see them.

Bible Study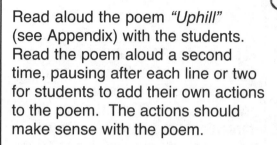

Say 1 John 4:15-16a with the students. Use the hand motions you added on Day 1. Next, have students lay on their backs and peddle their feet in the air like they are riding a bicycle. When you say, *Freeze,* the students should stop and recite the entire Bible verse. Repeat the activity.

✔ Text Connection: *Morning Bells* p. 100-102

Key Idea: The people of Scrooby loved the Lord more than anything else. They met to worship God and show Him how much they loved Him.

Corresponding Music

✔ *Hide 'Em in Your Heart Vol. 2*
CD - Track 5; Cassette - Side A
Song: *"God Is Love"*

Learning the Basics

Focus: Language Arts and Math

Unit 3 - Day 3

Language Arts

Using the spelling list from Day 1, choose 3 or more words that the students need to practice. Guide students to use each of the words that you chose in a sentence. On a markerboard or a piece of paper, write down the sentences as the students dictate them to you. Underline the spelling word in each sentence. Have the students copy the sentences on a piece of paper. Help students check their sentences and correct any mistakes.
<u>Copywork</u>: Have students copy part of the poem *"Uphill"*.

<u>Key Idea</u>: Practice spelling words with the short 'i' sound as in 'sit'.

Reading Choices

Choose **one** of the reading options listed below (see Appendix for details).

★ A phonics program
★ *Scheduled Books for Emerging Readers*
★ *Drawn into the Heart of Reading Level 2/3*

<u>Key Idea</u>: Use a step-by-step program for reading instruction.

Storytime

Read aloud the next portion of the biography that you selected.

Get out the pictures from Unit 2 - Day 3 that the students drew of the main character. Help students think of several items or things that are important to the main character in the story. Have students write or draw each of these things around their drawing of the main character on the paper.

<u>Key Idea</u>: Focus on the story element: *character*.

Math Exploration

Cut a large circle out of brown paper to make a pizza crust. Give students 10 red hots, bits of licorice, or red circles to be pepperoni. Have students act out addition stories with the pizza (i.e. There are 6 pieces of pepperoni on the pizza. Add 3 more. There are 9 pieces of pepperoni altogether.) After several examples, have students act out their own addition stories using the pizza.

✓ <u>Text Connection</u>: *Primary Mathematics Workbook 1A* p. 27

<u>Key Idea</u>: Tell addition stories to show how many items there are altogether.

Learning Through History

Focus: Trouble with King James in England

Unit 3 - Day 4

Reading About History

Read about history in the following resource:

⭐ *Stories of the Pilgrims* p. 18-20

Key Idea: King James caught the people worshiping in a barn and put the men in jail. The people wanted to be free to worship God according to the Bible. So, they secretly planned to leave England and move to Holland in the autumn.

Poetry and Rhymes

Read aloud the poem *"Uphill"* (see Appendix) with the students. Have students draw pictures that reflect the poem's meaning on either a photocopy of the poem or on their copywork. File the finished poem.

Key Idea: Read classic poetry.

Geography

Ask, *How do we know that the world is round instead of flat?* Show students Magellan's route on p. viii of *American Pioneers and Patriots*. Say, *If the world was flat like a table, what would have happened to Magellan as he sailed?* Instead, Magellan's crew sailed around the world and came back to the place where they started. Another way we know that the world is round has to do with the horizon. The horizon is where the land and sky meet. If you stand outside and look around you, it will appear that you are standing in the center of a huge circle. No matter where you are in the world, you will find this to be true. This helps us understand that the surface of the world is round.

Key Idea: The Pilgrims planned to sail to Holland.

Bible Study

Say 1 John 4:15-16a with the students. Use the hand motions you added from Day 1. Say, *What are some ways that you can show God that you love Him? How does Satan keep you from showing your love for God? Who did God send to Earth as an example of His love? How can you be more like Jesus?* Next, have students gallop by leading with their left foot until you say, *Freeze*. After they 'freeze', have the students recite the entire Bible verse. Have students switch to the right foot and do it again.

Key Idea: The Pilgrims wanted to be able to serve and worship God freely.

Corresponding Music

✓ *Hide 'Em in Your Heart Vol. 2*
CD - Track 5; Cassette - Side A
Song: *"God Is Love"*

Learning the Basics

Focus: Language Arts and Math

Unit 3 - Day 4

Language Arts

Use the spelling list from Day 1. Say each word and use it in a sentence. Have students write each word and check it with the matching word card from Day 1. Guide students to correct any mistakes. Direct students to write each missed word with fingerpaint or sidewalk chalk. <u>Copywork</u>: Have students copy part of *"Uphill"*.

<u>Key Idea</u>: Practice short 'i' words.

Reading Choices

Choose **one** of the reading options listed below (see Appendix for details).

★ A phonics program

★ *Scheduled Books for Emerging Readers*

★ *Drawn into the Heart of Reading Level 2/3*

<u>Key Idea</u>: Use a step-by-step program for reading instruction.

Storytime

Say, *Responsibility means being accountable to God and to others as you carry out your duties in a faithful way.* Review the key verse 1 Peter 4:10. Say, *Name some ways that we are accountable to God* (i.e. read His word, follow His commands, answer to Him for our behavior). Discuss, *How are you using the gifts that God has given you to serve others?* (i.e. keeping your room clean, watching younger siblings, sharing, doing tasks cheerfully and carefully). Read aloud the next portion of the biography that you selected. Ask, *How do the book characters show responsibility by serving others? Do the characters show the opposite trait, irresponsibility?*

<u>Key Idea</u>: Focus on the Godly character trait: *responsibility*.

Math Exploration

On paper, outline a blue pond, a green tree, and a brown fence to make a backyard scene. Give each student 10 bits of tinfoil to be fireflies. Have students act out addition stories with the backyard scene (i.e. 4 fireflies are by the pond. 3 fireflies are by the fence. How many fireflies are there altogether?). Have students write a number sentence to match the addition story (i.e. 4 + 3 = 7). Repeat the activity using different numbers of fireflies.

✔ <u>Text Connection</u>: *Primary Mathematics Workbook 1A* p. 28

<u>Key Idea</u>: Write addition number sentences to match addition stories.

Learning Through History

Focus: Trouble with King James in England

Unit 3 - Day 5

Reading About History

Read the following passage from your own Bible:

★ Romans 12:9-21

Key Idea: The pilgrims wanted to do what was right in God's eyes. They were more worried about God than King James. We need to serve the Lord first, even if it is not always easy.

Poetry and Rhymes

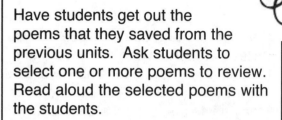

Have students get out the poems that they saved from the previous units. Ask students to select one or more poems to review. Read aloud the selected poems with the students.

Key Idea: Read classic poetry.

History Activity

Say, *King James believed that no one could disagree with the king. He believed he was above all people and above the church. Let's play a game to see if you agree with King James. Stand in the center of the room. The front wall is King James' court. The back wall is prison. Roll one dice and follow the directions I give for that roll. '1' = Go to King James' church. Take one step forward. '2' = Put God before the King. Take two steps back. '3' = Do not question the King. Take one step forward. '4' = Worship your own way. Take two steps back. '5' = Disagree with the King. Take 2 steps back. '6' = Worship King James' way. Take 1 step forward.* Ask, *Did you end up in King James' court or in prison? Why?*

Key Idea: King James persecuted anyone who did not believe as he did.

Bible Study

Say, *In Romans 12:9-10, how does God say we should show love to others? Name some ways you can put others before yourself. What does Romans 12:17-21 tell you to do if someone hurts you? Who will judge those who hurt you?* Ask students to share their memory verse, 1 John 4:15-16a, with someone special. Suggestions for sharing the verse include saying it to another family member, saying it to someone by telephone, reciting it to a stuffed animal, or writing it to mail.

Key Idea: The Pilgrims followed Christ's example and put others first.

Corresponding Music

✔ *Hide 'Em in Your Heart Vol. 2*
CD - Track 5; Cassette - Side A
Song: *"God Is Love"*

Learning the Basics

Focus: Language Arts and Math

Unit 3 - Day 5

Language Arts

Say, *Sentences have two parts. One part tells who or what the sentence is about. This is called the subject. The other part tells what that person or thing is doing. This is called the predicate.* Get out 10 index cards. Ask students to think of 5 different subjects to complete the following sentence: _____ *is outside.* Help students write the 5 subjects on 5 different cards. Capitalize the first letter of each subject. Ask students to think of 5 different predicates to complete the following sentence: *The cat _____.* Help students write the 5 predicates on 5 different cards. **Do not** capitalize the first letter. Put a period at the end of each predicate. Have students pair subject cards with predicate cards to make 5 sentences.

Key Idea: Introduce subjects and predicates.

Reading Choices

Choose **one** of the reading options listed below (see Appendix for details).

★ A phonics program
★ *Scheduled Books for Emerging Readers*
★ *Drawn into the Heart of Reading Level 2/3*

Key Idea: Use a step-by-step program for reading instruction.

Storytime

Read aloud a short portion of the biography that you selected. Guide students to retell today's reading by saying, *Tell me what you remember from today's story.* Prompt students as needed to include the important events (i.e. *What about _____? How about _____?*).

Key Idea: Give students practice retelling a portion of a biography.

Math Exploration

Complete the assigned lesson in the workbook listed below.

✔ Text Connection: *Primary Mathematics Workbook 1A* p. 29-30

Key Idea: Use the pictures to tell addition stories. Complete the matching number sentences.

Learning Through History

Focus: Pilgrims Leave England for Holland

Unit 4 - Day 1

Reading About History

Read about history in the following resource:

★ *Stories of the Pilgrims* p. 21-25

Key Idea: When the Pilgrims tried to leave Holland, the captain of the ship betrayed them. The Pilgrims ended up in prison. Elder Brewster planned to leave for Holland again in the spring.

Poetry and Rhymes

Read aloud the poem "*Daybreak*" (see Appendix) to the students. Do not share the title. Ask students to suggest some titles for the poem. Share the real title. Read the poem again with the students.

Key Idea: Read and appreciate a variety of classic poetry.

Science Exploration

Say, *Light goes through some things. Other things block light.* Get out items to test (i.e. tissue, aluminum foil, waxed paper, cling wrap, notebook paper, colored construction paper, paper bag, plastic bag, lightweight fabric, or an arm chair cover). To test each item, have students hold the items up to a sunny window one at a time. If it isn't a sunny day, use a flashlight as the light source instead. Prior to testing each item, ask students to predict whether the light will shine through the item or whether the light will be blocked.

✔ Text Connection: *God's Wonderful Works* p. 10

Key Idea: The Pilgrims waited in darkness on the beach. In the beginning, the whole world was filled with darkness. Then, God made the lights in the sky.

Bible Study

Matthew 6:19-21 is the memory verse for this unit. Read the verse out loud and discuss its meaning with the students. Ask, *What does Jesus mean in Matthew 6:19? Where does Jesus say we should store up our treasure? What treasure is Jesus talking about? How can we store up treasure in heaven?* Say the verse together 3 times. Add hand motions to help students remember the words.

Key Idea: The Pilgrims treasured God and His word above all else.

Corresponding Music

✔ *Hide 'Em in Your Heart Vol. 2*
CD - Track 18; Cassette - Side B
Song: "*Where Your Treasure Is*"

Learning the Basics

Focus: Language Arts and Math

Unit 4 - Day 1

Language Arts

Choose **either** spelling list 1 **or** 2 (see Appendix for lists). Write each spelling word on a separate index card. Guide students to study each card one at a time, flip it over, write the word from memory on paper, flip the card back over to check the spelling, and erase and correct any mistakes.

<u>Copywork</u>: Have students copy part of the poem *"Daybreak"*.

<u>Key Idea</u>: Practice spelling words with the short 'o' sound as in 'hop'.

Reading Choices

Choose **one** of the reading options listed below (see Appendix for details).

★ A phonics program

★ *Scheduled Books for Emerging Readers*

★ *Drawn into the Heart of Reading Level 2/3*

<u>Key Idea</u>: Use a step-by-step program for reading instruction.

Storytime

Ask students to help you make a list of the characters in the biography. Next, have students place a star beside the names of the mainly good characters and a checkmark beside the names of the mainly bad characters. Discuss the reasons for the students' decisions. Read aloud the next portion of the biography that you selected. Pace your reading to complete the biography during the next 5 days of plans.

<u>Key Idea</u>: Set a purpose for reading the next part of the biography.

Math Exploration

On paper, draw a rectangle on the left side to be a crayon box and a circle on the right side to be a table. Give students 10 crayons. Have students act out addition stories with their crayons (i.e. Put 6 crayons in the box and 2 on the table. How many crayons are there altogether?). Guide students to write both possible addition sentences that go with the story (i.e. 6 + 2 = 8 and 2 + 6 = 8). Point out to students that the order of the addends doesn't matter. The answer is still the same. Repeat the activity with different numbers of crayons.

<u>Key Idea</u>: Demonstrate the commutative property of addition to show that order doesn't matter.

Learning Through History

Focus: Pilgrims Leave England for Holland

Unit 4 - Day 2

Reading About History

Read about history in the following resource:

★ *Stories of the Pilgrims* p. 26-30

Key Idea: As the Pilgrims tried to leave England again, the ship's captain sailed away with only the men. The women and children were taken to prison. King James finally decided to let them leave England.

Poetry and Rhymes

Read aloud the poem *"Daybreak"* (see Appendix) with the students. Discuss the poem's meaning. If you choose, photocopy the poem, cut it apart, and have the students place it in the correct order.

Key Idea: Read classic poetry.

Science Exploration

Get out a coin, a paper towel or a napkin, and an eyedropper or a baster. Lay the coin flat on the paper towel. Guide students to use the dropper or baster to gently squeeze drops of water onto the face of the coin, one drop at a time. Ask students to predict the number of drops that will fit on the coin before the tension breaks and the water runs over. After the experiment, explain that ships on the ocean are held up by the surface tension of the water. If a ship gets too heavy, it will sink.

✔ Text Connection: *God's Wonderful Works* p. 9

Key Idea: The Dutch captain's ship got a hole in it and almost sank during several terrible storms at sea. Everyone on the ship prayed to reach Holland safely.

Bible Study

Say Matthew 6:19-21 while the students join in on the parts they know. Use the hand motions you added on Day 1. Say, *Name some special things that you own. Will you be able to take those things to heaven? Why not? What is really important to God?* Next, have students do windmills by touching their right hand to their right foot, and then their left hand to their left foot. After 5 windmills, have the students recite the Bible verse. Repeat the activity.

Key Idea: The treasures of the earth are not as important as God's will.

Corresponding Music

✔ *Hide 'Em in Your Heart Vol. 2*
CD - Track 18; Cassette - Side B
Song: *"Where Your Treasure Is"*

Learning the Basics

Focus: Language Arts and Math

Unit 4 - Day 2

Language Arts

Use the spelling list from Day 1. Say the first spelling word. Use it in a sentence. Repeat the word. Ask students to write the word on a markerboard or a piece of paper from memory. Give students the matching word card from Day 1 to compare with their spelling. Guide students to correct any mistakes. Repeat the activity with all 10 words.

<u>Copywork</u>: Have students copy part of the poem *"Daybreak"*.

<u>Key Idea</u>: Practice spelling words with the short 'o' sound as in 'hop'.

Reading Choices

Choose **one** of the reading options listed below (see Appendix for details).

★ A phonics program
★ *Scheduled Books for Emerging Readers*
★ *Drawn into the Heart of Reading Level 2/3*

<u>Key Idea</u>: Use a step-by-step program for reading instruction.

Storytime

Read aloud the next portion of the biography that you selected. Ask students to retell or narrate what you read today. Remind students to tell the most important parts and to include details from the story in the retelling. As students work together to retell the story, write, type, or tape record the students' narration. When the students are finished, read the narration out loud. Highlight, circle, or underline one main idea from the narration for the students to copy.

<u>Key Idea</u>: Keep a sample of the students' narrations for the genre: *Biography*.

Math Exploration

Complete the assigned lesson in the workbook listed below.

✓ <u>Text Connection</u>: *Primary Mathematics Workbook 1A* p. 31-33

<u>Key Idea</u>: Find the different number combinations that equal '5', '6', '7', '8', '9', and '10'.

Learning Through History

Focus: Pilgrims Leave England for Holland

Unit 4 - Day 3

Reading About History

Read about history in the following resource:

★ *Stories of the Pilgrims* p. 31 - top of p. 34

Key Idea: The rest of the Pilgrims finally arrived in Amsterdam, Holland. Everyone was glad to see their friends and family members again. The Pilgrims shared what they had with one another.

Poetry and Rhymes

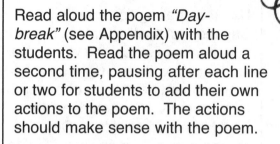

Read aloud the poem *"Daybreak"* (see Appendix) with the students. Read the poem aloud a second time, pausing after each line or two for students to add their own actions to the poem. The actions should make sense with the poem.

Key Idea: Read classic poetry.

Geography

Say, *If you stand outside and look at the horizon at something very far away, you may only see the top of the object. That is because part of it is hidden by the sloping curve of the earth. The curving face on a compass stands for the horizon. The needle on a compass will always point to the north. If you don't have a compass, you can stand with your right hand pointing to where the sun rises (which is east), and your left hand pointing to where the sun sets (which is west). Then, north will be in front of you, and south will be behind you. In this way, you can always tell your directions.* Use small slips of paper to label the walls in several rooms to show the directions.

Key Idea: The city of Amsterdam looked like it was floating in the water.

Bible Study

Say Matthew 6:19-21 with the students. Use the hand motions you added on Day 1. Next, have students squat down, hop up, and squat back down again. After the last squat, have the students recite the entire Bible verse. Prompt students as needed. Repeat the activity.

✓ Text Connection: *Morning Bells* p. 49-51

Key Idea: Others could see that the Pilgrims were different because Christ lived in their hearts. Does Christ live in your heart?

Corresponding Music

✓ *Hide 'Em in Your Heart Vol. 2* CD - Track 18; Cassette - Side B Song: *"Where Your Treasure Is"*

Learning the Basics

Focus: Language Arts and Math

Unit 4 - Day 3

Language Arts

Using the spelling list from Day 1, choose 3 or more words that the students need to practice. Guide students to use each of the words that you chose in a sentence. On a markerboard or a piece of paper, write down the sentences as the students dictate them to you. Underline the spelling word in each sentence. Have the students copy the sentences on a piece of paper. Help students check their sentences and correct any mistakes.

Copywork: Have students copy part of the poem *"Daybreak"*.

Key Idea: Practice spelling words with the short 'o' sound as in 'hop'.

Reading Choices

Choose **one** of the reading options listed below (see Appendix for details).

★ A phonics program

★ *Scheduled Books for Emerging Readers*

★ *Drawn into the Heart of Reading Level 2/3*

Key Idea: Use a step-by-step program for reading instruction.

Storytime

Read aloud the next portion of the biography that you selected.

Say, *Which character in the biography would you choose as a friend? Why? Using what you know about the character you chose, what is one gift that the character might enjoy receiving? Explain.*

Key Idea: Focus on the story element: *character*.

Math Exploration

Give each student a piece of paper. Have them follow directions to draw a meadow scene. Say, *On the bottom of the page draw 4 ladybugs. Draw 1 more ladybug crawling along. How many are there altogether? Write a matching addition sentence under the ladybug picture (4 + 1 = 5).* Say, *On the top of the page, draw 7 clouds. Draw 3 more clouds floating by. How many clouds are there altogether? Write a matching addition sentence under the clouds (7 + 3 = 10).* Continue adding to the picture by telling addition stories with birds, ants, flowers, and trees.

✓ Text Connection: *Primary Mathematics Workbook 1A* p. 34-35

Key Idea: Write addition sentences.

Learning Through History

Focus: Pilgrims Leave England for Holland

Unit 4 - Day 4

Reading About History

Read about history in the following resource:

★ *Stories of the Pilgrims* p. 34-37

Key Idea: In Holland, the Pilgrims saw many new things. They saw storks, windmills, and streets made of water. They learned that Holland is a low country protected from the sea by dikes. They also learned to watch for leaks in the dike.

Poetry and Rhymes

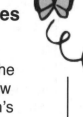

Read aloud the poem *"Daybreak"* (see Appendix) with the students. Have students draw pictures that reflect the poem's meaning on either a photocopy of the poem or on their copywork. File the finished poem in a special place.

Key Idea: Read classic poetry.

History Activity

Ask, *What is a dike?* Have students use the description from today's story to help them build a clay or play-dough dike across a sink or bowl. When the dike is finished, add water to one side of the dike. Make sure the water can't flow over or around the dike. Place an object to be a house on the dry side of the dike. Tell students that you will make a small leak in the dike. When students see the leak, they should shout, *Ring, Ring* to sound the alarm. Then, they should quickly patch the leak. Last, have students add to their timeline. Say, *We read about the Pilgrims in Holland in 1608. Let's find the column that says 1600. Draw a small windmill in that column. Write 'Pilgrims in Holland, 1608' under it.*

Key Idea: The Pilgrims finally arrived in Amsterdam, Holland.

Bible Study

Say Matthew 6:19-21 with the students. Use the hand motions you added on Day 1. Say, *When you become a Christian, Christ gives you a new heart. What does that mean? If Christ lives in your heart, how will you act? How can you show others that Christ lives in your heart?* Next, have students hop backward 5 times. After 5 hops, have the students recite the entire Bible verse. Repeat the activity several times.

Key Idea: A Christian's heart wants to please Christ. It is made new. The Pilgrims were Christians.

Corresponding Music

✔ *Hide 'Em in Your Heart Vol. 2*
CD - Track 18; Cassette - Side B
Song: *"Where Your Treasure Is"*

Learning the Basics

Focus: Language Arts and Math

Unit 4 - Day 4

Language Arts

Use the spelling list from Day 1. Say each word and use it in a sentence. Have students write each word and check it with the matching word card from Day 1. Guide students to correct any mistakes. For each missed word, have students trace it in dry cornmeal, oatmeal, or sand on a plate.

<u>Copywork</u>: Have students copy part of the poem *"Daybreak"*.

<u>Key Idea</u>: Practice spelling words with the short 'o' sound as in 'hop'.

Reading Choices

Choose **one** of the reading options listed below (see Appendix for details).

★ A phonics program
★ *Scheduled Books for Emerging Readers*
★ *Drawn into the Heart of Reading Level 2/3*

<u>Key Idea</u>: Use a step-by-step program for reading instruction.

Storytime

Say, *Responsibility means being accountable to God and to others as you carry out your duties in a faithful way.* Review the key verse 1 Peter 4:10. Read aloud the next portion of the biography that you selected. Ask, *Was the main character usually responsible or irresponsible? Explain. Are you usually responsible or irresponsible? Draw a picture showing one way that you could be more responsible. Post your picture in a place where you will see it often.*

<u>Key Idea</u>: Focus on the Godly character trait: *responsibility*.

Math Exploration

Complete the assigned lesson in the workbook listed below.

✔ <u>Text Connection</u>: *Primary Mathematics Workbook 1A* p. 36-37

<u>Key Idea</u>: Follow the directions to complete the pictures. Write the corresponding addition sentences.

Learning Through History

Focus: Pilgrims Leave England for Holland

Unit 4 - Day 5

Reading About History

Read the following passage from your own Bible:

★ Luke 12:13-21

Key Idea: The parable of the rich man warns us to think of others before ourselves. The Pilgrims used what they were given to further God's kingdom, not their own.

Poetry and Rhymes

Have students get out the poems that they saved from the previous units. Ask students to select one or more poems to review. Read aloud the selected poems with the students.

Key Idea: Read classic poetry.

Artistic Expression

Give each student a red piece of paper. Have students lay the paper in front of themselves with the long side on the top. Guide students to fold the right side of the paper to the center. Then, help students fold the left side of the paper to meet the other side of the paper in the center. Students should end up with two flaps that look like barn doors. Have students use a white crayon or colored pencil to color an 'X' on each door. Next, have students copy Matthew 6:21 on a piece of white paper to glue inside the barn door flaps.

Key Idea: The rich man built bigger barns to store up his earthly treasure. But, he wasn't prepared when his time on earth was over. Be careful what you treasure and how you spend your time. You never know when Christ may return.

Bible Study

Ask, *In Luke 12:13-21 what does the parable of the rich man teach us? What was wrong with how the rich man acted? If you are always asking for things, what does your heart love? How can you show God that He is more important to you than earthly things?* Ask students to share their memory verse, Matthew 6:19-21, with someone special. Suggestions for sharing the verse include saying it to another family member, saying it to someone by telephone, reciting it to a stuffed animal, or writing it to mail.

Key Idea: The Pilgrims faithfully served God and obeyed Him.

Corresponding Music

✓ *Hide 'Em in Your Heart Vol. 2*
CD - Track 18; Cassette - Side B
Song: *"Where Your Treasure Is"*

Learning the Basics

Focus: Language Arts and Math

Unit 4 - Day 5

Language Arts

Write the following sentence on a markerboard or a piece of paper: *The rain makes the grass grow.* Say, *What does this sentence tell you? Which part is the subject? Which part is the predicate? What do you notice at the beginning of the sentence? What do you see at the end of the sentence?* Say, *Sentences begin with capital letters. Telling sentences end with periods. Telling sentences are called statements. Let's practice writing some statements. Get an object to describe* (i.e. rock, leaf, twig, flower). Have students write several statements describing their chosen object. If students are not able to write, have them dictate the statements for you to write.

<u>Key Idea</u>: Introduce telling sentences as statements.

Reading Choices

Choose **one** of the reading options listed below (see Appendix for details).

★ *A phonics program*

★ *Scheduled Books for Emerging Readers*

★ *Drawn into the Heart of Reading Level 2/3*

<u>Key Idea</u>: Use a step-by-step program for reading instruction.

Storytime

Read aloud the final portion of the biography that you selected. You will need to select an adventure book to read aloud next. Have students choose a few props that will help them retell today's reading. Allow them to act out the story while they are retelling it to you.

<u>Key Idea</u>: Give students practice retelling a portion of a biography.

Math Exploration

Tape a long strip of masking tape on the floor and number it from '1' - '10'. Write "2 + 6 = ___" on a piece of paper or a markerboard. Say, *One way to make adding easier is to start with the higher number and count up. If we start with the '2' we must count up 6 more to get the answer. But, if we start with the '6' we only need to count up 2 more to get the answer.* Act out the problem on the number line by moving a stuffed toy. Repeat the activity using different numbers. Remind the students to always start with the larger number.

✔ <u>Text Connection</u>: *Primary Mathematics Workbook 1A* p. 38-39

<u>Key Idea</u>: Count on from the higher number to add.

Learning Through History

Focus: English Pilgrims Settle in Holland

Unit 5 - Day 1

Reading About History

Read about history in the following resource:

★ *Boys and Girls of Colonial Days* p. 1-6 (old version, p. 1-5)

Key Idea: Love Bradford was a Pilgrim girl that came to Amersterdam on a ship. Her father was in prison in England. A Dutch family let Love live with them.

Poetry and Rhymes

Read aloud the poem *"Song for a Little House"* (see Appendix) to the students. Do not share the title. Ask students to suggest some titles for the poem. Share the real title. Read the poem with the students.

"God gave me what I needed"

Key Idea: Read and appreciate a variety of classic poetry.

Science Exploration

Explain, *Light moves in waves through space.* To see how light waves move, fill a bowl almost full with water. Place your mouth level with the top of the bowl and blow gently across the surface of the water. Ask students to observe the water's surface. Ask, *What do you notice about the surface of the water? Can you see it rippling as I blow on it? This is kind of like the way that light moves in waves through space.*

✔ Text Connection: *God's Wonderful Works* p. 14

Key Idea: As the bright light from the sun broke through the clouds, Love got to see the city of Amsterdam for the first time. As time went on, Love waited patiently for the sun to shine on her tulip and for her father to come and find her.

Bible Study

Psalm 139:13-14 is the memory verse for this unit. Read the verse out loud and discuss its meaning with the students. Ask, *Who formed you in your mother's womb? How does Psalm 139:14 say that you are made? What does that mean? Do you think that God has a plan for your life? Why?* Say the verse together 3 times. Add hand motions to help students remember the words.

Key Idea: God created each of one of us. He has a plan for you, just as He had a plan for the Pilgrims.

Corresponding Music

✔ *Hide 'Em in Your Heart Vol. 2* CD - Track 12; Cassette - Side B Song: *"You Knit Me Together"*

Learning the Basics

Focus: Language Arts and Math

Unit 5 - Day 1

Language Arts

Choose **either** spelling list 1 **or** 2 (see Appendix for lists). Write each spelling word on a separate index card. Guide students to study each card one at a time, flip it over, write the word from memory on paper, flip the card back over to check the spelling, and erase and correct any mistakes.

Copywork: Have students copy part of the poem *"Song for a Little House"*.

Key Idea: Practice spelling words with the short 'u' sound as in 'cut'.

Reading Choices

Choose **one** of the reading options listed below (see Appendix for details).

★ A phonics program
★ *Scheduled Books for Emerging Readers*
★ *Drawn into the Heart of Reading Level 2/3*

Key Idea: Use a step-by-step program for reading instruction.

Storytime

Choose at least one adventure book to read aloud for the next 20 days of plans (see Appendix for suggested titles). To introduce the genre, *Adventure*, plan a short treasure hunt. Either write numbered clues for the student to follow, or draw a quick treasure map on a cut up paper bag. Have your chosen adventure book and a snack be the treasure at the end of the hunt. Explain that adventure books are suspenseful stories filled with action and excitement. Read a portion of the adventure book you chose.

Key Idea: Introduce the genre: *Adventure*.

Math Exploration

Complete the assigned lesson in the workbook listed below.

✔ Text Connection: *Primary Mathematics Workbook 1A* p. 40

Key Idea: Practice addition with sums up to '10'.

Learning Through History

Focus: English Pilgrims Settle in Holland

Unit 5 - Day 2

Reading About History

Read about history in the following resource:

★ *Boys and Girls of Colonial Days* p. 7-10 (old version, p. 6-9)

Key Idea: Love patiently waited for her father to come. When she brought the tulip she had grown down to the dike, she met her father. Her patience was rewarded.

Poetry and Rhymes

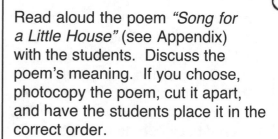

Read aloud the poem *"Song for a Little House"* (see Appendix) with the students. Discuss the poem's meaning. If you choose, photocopy the poem, cut it apart, and have the students place it in the correct order.

Key Idea: Read and appreciate a variety of classic poetry.

Artistic Expression

On brown paper, draw the outline of a flowerpot. Have students cut out the flower pot and glue it on blue paper. On pink paper, draw the outline of a tulip for students to cut out. Help them tape the pink tulip to the end of a pencil or a straw. Guide students to wrap the pencil or straw with crepe paper or ribbon and tape the end of it to the pencil or straw. Cut a slit near the top of the flowerpot. Direct students to place their pink tulip behind the paper and up through the slit in the pot. Show students how to raise the tulip slowly, so it looks like it is growing.

Key Idea: In the spring, Love's bulb grew into a beautiful pink tulip. Most of the tulips in Holland were red or yellow. Love's tulip was special. Love decided to sell her precious tulip to repay Jan and his mother.

Bible Study

Say Psalm 139:13-14 while the students join in on the parts they know. Use the hand motions you added on Day 1. Ask, *In what ways does God take care of you? How does Psalm 139:13-14 help you know how much God loves you?* Next, have students do 5 jumping jacks. After 5 jumping jacks, have the students recite the entire Bible verse. Prompt the students as needed. Repeat the activity.

Key Idea: God cared for Love Bradford and watched over her. He cares for you too.

Corresponding Music

✓ *Hide 'Em in Your Heart Vol. 2* CD - Track 12; Cassette - Side B Song: *"You Knit Me Together"*

Learning the Basics

Focus: Language Arts and Math

Unit 5 - Day 2

Language Arts

Use the spelling list from Day 1. Say the first spelling word. Use it in a sentence. Repeat the word. Ask students to write the word on a markerboard or a piece of paper from memory. Give students the matching word card from Day 1 to compare with their spelling. Guide students to correct any mistakes. Repeat the activity with all 10 words.

Copywork: Have students copy part of the poem *"Song for a Little House"*.

Key Idea: Practice spelling words with the short 'u' sound as in 'cut'.

Reading Choices

Choose **one** of the reading options listed below (see Appendix for details).

★ A phonics program

★ *Scheduled Books for Emerging Readers*

★ *Drawn into the Heart of Reading Level 2/3*

Key Idea: Use a step-by-step program for reading instruction.

Storytime

Read aloud the next portion of the adventure book that you selected. Without looking back at the story, model retelling or narrating the part of the adventure that you read today to the students. Remember to tell the most important parts and to add details from the story to the retelling without overwhelming the students. After the retelling, ask, *What big problem is there in the story?* On paper, write a summary of the students' answers to the question in one sentence. Have the students copy the answer on paper underneath your writing.

Key Idea: Model retelling a story from a single reading.

Math Exploration

Set out a cereal bowl. Place 10 pieces of dry cereal in the bowl. Take out some pieces of dry cereal. Ask students to figure out how many are left in the bowl (i.e. There are 10 pieces of cereal in my bowl. If I take out 3 pieces, how many cereal pieces are left in my bowl?). Students may count the remaining pieces in the bowl to find the answer. Repeat the activity using different numbers of cereal pieces. Point out that this is subtraction, which means "taking away".

✔ Text Connection: *Primary Mathematics Workbook 1A* p. 41-42

Key Idea: Introduce subtraction through stories that require taking away items.

Learning Through History

Focus: English Pilgrims Settle in Holland

Unit 5 - Day 3

Reading About History

Read about history in the following resource:

★ *Stories of the Pilgrims* p. 38-41

Key Idea: The Pilgrims found that Amsterdam looked different than England. The streets were canals and the houses were made of pink, red, and yellow bricks. Many houses leaned to one side.

Poetry and Rhymes

Read aloud the poem *"Song for a Little House"* (see Appendix) with the students. Read the poem aloud a second time, pausing after each line or two for students to add their own actions to the poem. The actions should make sense with the poem.

Key Idea: Read and appreciate a variety of classic poetry.

History Activity

Say, *The houses in Holland were very different from the houses in England. How are the houses in Holland different from the house that you live in?* Next, spend some time describing the house or houses that you lived in when you were a child. Make sure to describe any sights, sounds, or smells that you vividly remember from your home. Ask the students, *How was the house that I lived in as a child different from the house that you have today?*

Key Idea: The homes in Holland were made of colored bricks. They were built very close together on stilts. The kitchens were tiled. Beds were tucked into the walls in the kitchen and hidden behind curtains upstairs.

Bible Study

Say Psalm 139:13-14 with the students. Use the hand motions you added on Day 1. Next, have students hop on their left foot until you say, *Freeze*. After they 'freeze', have the students recite the entire Bible verse. Have students switch to hopping on their right foot and repeat the activity.

✔ Text Connection: *Morning Bells* p. 10-12

Key Idea: The Pilgrims followed Jesus' example of being kind and good.

Corresponding Music

✔ *Hide 'Em in Your Heart Vol. 2* CD - Track 12; Cassette - Side B Song: *"You Knit Me Together"*

Learning the Basics

Focus: Language Arts and Math

Unit 5 - Day 3

Language Arts

Using the spelling list from Day 1, choose 3 or more words that the students need to practice. Guide students to use each of the words that you chose in a sentence. On a markerboard or a piece of paper, write down the sentences as the students dictate them to you. Underline the spelling word in each sentence. Have the students copy the sentences on a piece of paper. Help students check their sentences and correct any mistakes.

Copywork: Have students copy part of the poem *"Song for a Little House"*.

Key Idea: Practice spelling words with the short 'u' sound as in 'cut'.

Reading Choices

Choose **one** of the reading options listed below (see Appendix for details).

★ A phonics program

★ *Scheduled Books for Emerging Readers*

★ *Drawn into the Heart of Reading Level 2/3*

Key Idea: Use a step-by-step program for reading instruction.

Math Exploration

Set out a brown piece of paper to be a desert. Give students 2 different items to represent two kinds of snakes (i.e. regular macaroni and macaroni with stripes drawn on it, or red yarn and blue yarn). Have students act out subtraction stories with the snakes (i.e. There are 10 snakes altogether. 4 snakes are striped. How many are not striped?). Write the corresponding number sentence on markerboard or paper (10 - 4 = 6). Repeat the activity with a different story.

✓ Text Connection: *Primary Mathematics Workbook 1A* p. 43-44

Key Idea: Tell subtraction stories to find the missing number.

Storytime

Read aloud the next portion of the adventure book that you selected. Say, *Problems are things that are going wrong in the story which the characters must face as the pressures continue to build. What is the biggest problem in the story? Does it remind you of anything that has ever happened to you? Explain. How do you think that the characters could fix the problem?*

Key Idea: Introduce the story element: *problem* or *conflict*.

Learning Through History

Focus: English Pilgrims Settle in Holland

Unit 5 - Day 4

Reading About History

Read about history in the following resource:

★ *Stories of the Pilgrims* p. 42-45

Key Idea: The Pilgrim children learned many new things. They had to wait for the water barge to bring them fresh water. They met some Dutch children that lived in a canal boat. They learned to speak some Dutch.

Poetry and Rhymes

Read aloud the poem *"Song for a Little House"* (see Appendix) with the students. Have students draw pictures that reflect the poem's meaning on either a photocopy of the poem or on their copywork. File the finished poem in a special place.

Key Idea: Read classic poetry.

Geography

Get out a globe, or a world map, or have students to look at p. 34 of *God's Wonderful Works*. Say, *About three-fourths of the Earth's surface is covered with water. Look at all of the blue area on the map or globe. That is all water. Much of the water on earth is in the oceans. Try to name the 5 oceans on Earth* (i.e. Atlantic Ocean, Pacific Ocean, Indian Ocean, Arctic Ocean, and Antarctic Ocean). For help, have students refer to the world map, or globe, or to p. 45 of *God's Wonderful Works*. Say, *Most cities were built near the ocean or near water. Why do you think that's true?* (i.e. for travel and transportation, for trading goods, for food).

Key Idea: In Amsterdam, even the streets were made of water.

Bible Study

Say Psalm 139:13-14 with the students. Use the hand motions you added on Day 1. Say, *What do you know about Jesus as a child? Why do you think that God planned for Jesus to grow up here on earth? What are some things that you can learn from Jesus' example?* Next, have students do 5 sit-ups. After every 5 sit-ups, have the students recite the entire Bible verse.

Key Idea: The Pilgrim children learned about Jesus from their parents. God wants you to learn about Jesus from your parents too.

Corresponding Music

✓ *Hide 'Em in Your Heart Vol. 2*
CD - Track 12; Cassette - Side B
Song: *"You Knit Me Together"*

Learning the Basics

Focus: Language Arts and Math

Unit 5 - Day 4

Language Arts

Use the spelling list from Day 1. Say each word and use it in a sentence. Have students write each word and check it with the matching word card from Day 1. Guide students to correct any mistakes. Use a dark marker to write each missed word very largely on paper. Help students trace each missed word with glue. Allow the glue to dry in order to feel the words.
<u>Copywork</u>: Have students copy part of the poem *"Song for a Little House"*.

<u>Key Idea</u>: Practice spelling words with the short 'u' sound as in 'cut'.

Reading Choices

Choose **one** of the reading options listed below (see Appendix for details).

★ A phonics program
★ *Scheduled Books for Emerging Readers*
★ *Drawn into the Heart of Reading Level 2/3*

<u>Key Idea</u>: Use a step-by-step program for reading instruction.

Storytime

Say, *Fear of the Lord is revering the Lord and His commands and believing the Lord can turn harm into good for those who trust in Him.* Read aloud the key verse Deuteronomy 13:4 to illustrate *fear of the Lord*. Share examples of people that you show reverence to in your own life. Have students list people that they must revere. Read aloud the next portion of the adventure book that you selected. Then, ask, *What could the characters do differently to show more fear of the Lord?*

<u>Key Idea</u>: Introduce the Godly character trait: *fear of the Lord.*

Math Exploration

Complete the assigned lesson in the workbook listed below.

✔ <u>Text Connection</u>: *Primary Mathematics Workbook 1A* p. 45-46

<u>Key Idea</u>: Tell a subtraction story to match each picture. Write the corresponding number sentence.

Learning Through History

Focus: English Pilgrims Settle in Holland

Unit 5 - Day 5

Reading About History

Read the following passage from your own Bible:

★ Luke 2:39-52

Key Idea: As Jesus grew, God was pleased with Him. Jesus was filled with wisdom and grace. He was obedient to His parents. The Pilgrim children tried to be obedient to their parents and to God.

Poetry and Rhymes

Have students get out the poems that they saved from the previous units. Ask students to select one or more poems to review. Read aloud the selected poems with the students.

Key Idea: Read classic poetry.

Science Exploration

Say, *When babies are forming in their mother's wombs, you can already hear their little hearts beating.* Have students open and close one hand for 30 seconds to simulate a heart beating. Ask, *Did your hand get tired after awhile? Your heart beats many times each day without ever getting tired. God made our bodies in a wonderful way.* Hold an empty paper towel or toilet paper tube over your heart. Allow sutdents to put their ear on the other end of the tube like a stethoscope and listen to your heartbeat.

✔ Text Connection: *God's Wonderful Works* p. 129

Key Idea: Jesus' body had a beating heart just like your body. His body grew and changed just like yours.

Bible Study

Ask, *Even Jesus was once a baby in His mother's womb. In Luke 2:51-52, how did Jesus please God and His parents as He grew? What can you do to please God and your parents? Can you ever be as good as Jesus? What can you do to try to be more like Him?* Ask students to share their memory verse, Psalm 139:13-14, with someone special. Suggestions for sharing the verse include saying it to another family member, saying it to someone by telephone, reciting it to a stuffed animal, or writing it to mail.

Key Idea: Jesus was a child once too. He was holy and without sin.

Corresponding Music

✔ *Hide 'Em in Your Heart Vol. 2* CD - Track 12; Cassette - Side B Song: *"You Knit Me Together"*

Learning the Basics

Focus: Language Arts and Math

Unit 5 - Day 5

Language Arts

Write the following question on a markerboard or a piece of paper: *What is your favorite food?* Ask, *What is this sentence about? Does it tell you anything? What does it do instead of telling you something? What do you notice at the beginning of the sentence? What do you see at the end of the sentence?* Say, *Asking sentences end with question marks and are called questions.* Say, *I will ask you a question. You will answer with a statement. What is your favorite holiday?* (i.e. My favorite holiday is Christmas.) *Who are your family members? When is your birthday? Where is your favorite place to go? How are you feeling?* Next, have the students ask the questions. <u>Copywork</u>: Write one question for students to copy.

<u>Key Idea</u>: Introduce 'asking sentences' as questions.

Storytime

Read aloud a short portion of the adventure book that you selected. Ask students to retell today's reading. If students are stuck or give a short narration allow them to look at any pictures in the reading for ideas.

<u>Key Idea</u>: Give students practice retelling a portion of an adventure.

Reading Choices

Choose **one** of the reading options listed below (see Appendix for details).

★ A phonics program
★ *Scheduled Books for Emerging Readers*
★ *Drawn into the Heart of Reading Level 2/3*

<u>Key Idea</u>: Use a step-by-step program for reading instruction.

Math Exploration

Give students 10 counters (i.e. cans, spoons, forks, or blocks). Place the counters in one row. Tell students to place a pencil between the second and third counters to separate the counters into two groups. On paper or markerboard, write two subtraction sentences that would describe the groups (i.e. 10 - 2 = 8 or 10 - 8 = 2). Vary the activity by separating the ten counters into other groups or by using more than 10 counters.

✓ <u>Text Connection</u>: *Primary Mathematics Workbook 1A* p. 47

<u>Key Idea</u>: Write two subtraction number sentences to go with each picture.

Learning Through History

Focus: Life in Holland

Unit 6 - Day 1

Reading About History

Read about history in the following resource:

★ *Stories of the Pilgrims* p. 46-47

Key Idea: In Holland, there was a weekly scrubbing day. Everyone came out to wash their houses and windows. The Pilgrims had never seen anything like that!

Poetry and Rhymes

Read aloud the poem *"The Months"* (see Appendix) to the students. Do not share the title. Ask students to suggest some titles for the poem. Share the real title. Read the poem again with the students.

"Seasons"

Key Idea: Read and appreciate a variety of classic poetry.

History Activity

Say, *In Holland there was a weekly scrubbing day. With the help of someone older than you, choose something in your house that needs scrubbing - like your countertop, refrigerator, stove, dishwasher, table, or kitchen chairs. Use a bucket of soap and water to scrub the items you chose. Clean up when you are done.* Last, have students get out their timeline. Say, *While the Pilgrims were in Holland, King James was still King of England. Even though King James had some ideas that were wrong, God used him to allow the Bible to be translated into English. You can still read the King James version of the Bible today. Let's find the column that says 1600. Draw a small Bible in that column. Write 'King James' Bible, 1611' under it.*

Key Idea: The Pilgrims were getting used to living in Holland.

Bible Study

Review the memory verse, Psalm 4:8, from Unit 1. Read the verse out loud. Ask, *What does it mean to sleep in peace? Name some things that scare you. Which part of Psalm 4:8 tells you that the Lord watches over you? Does this mean nothing bad will ever happen to you? What does it mean?* Say the verse together 3 times. Review the hand motions that go with the verse from Unit 1, if you remember them.

Key Idea: Even though the Pilgrims were in a new country, they trusted God to watch over them.

Corresponding Music

✔ *Hide 'Em in Your Heart Vol. 2*
CD - Track 20; Cassette - Side B
Song: *"I Will Lie Down and Sleep"*

Learning the Basics

Focus: Language Arts and Math

Unit 6 - Day 1

Language Arts

Choose **either** spelling list 1 **or** 2 (see Appendix for lists). Write each spelling word on a separate index card. Guide students to study each card one at a time, flip it over, write the word from memory on paper, flip the card back over to check the spelling, and erase and correct any mistakes.

Copywork: Have students copy part of the poem *"The Months"*.

Key Idea: Practice spelling words with short vowels ending in double consonants.

Reading Choices

Choose **one** of the reading options listed below (see Appendix for details).

★ A phonics program
★ *Scheduled Books for Emerging Readers*
★ *Drawn into the Heart of Reading Level 2/3*

Key Idea: Use a step-by-step program for reading instruction.

Storytime

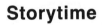

Say, *When you listen to an adventure story, the author makes sure to have suspenseful or exciting parts in the story that leave you wondering what will happen next. When I read an exciting part today, you should jump up and down.*

Read aloud the next portion of the adventure book that you selected. Pace your reading to complete the adventure during the next 15 days of plans.

Key Idea: Preread to build anticipation for the next part of the adventure.

Math Exploration

Complete the assigned lesson in the workbook listed below.

✔ Text Connection: *Primary Mathematics Workbook 1A* p. 48-49

Note: Students should explain each subtraction story in the workbook to you to make sure that they understand the concept of subtraction.

Key Idea: Use the pictures to fill in the missing numbers in the subtraction sentences.

Learning Through History

Focus: Life in Holland

Unit 6 - Day 2

Reading About History

Read about history in the following resource:

★ *Stories of the Pilgrims* p. 48-52

Key Idea: The Pilgrim boys delivered milk with their Dutch neighbor, Karl. Karl told them Dutch people believe storks bring luck. The Pilgrims didn't believe in luck. They believed in God's providence.

Poetry and Rhymes

Read aloud the poem *"The Months"* (see Appendix) with the students. Discuss the poem's meaning. If you choose, photocopy the poem, cut it apart, and have the students place it in the correct order.

Key Idea: Read and appreciate a variety of classic poetry.

Science Exploration

Say, *A stork is a water bird that walks in shallow water to look for food. Storks do not have webbed feet like many other water birds.* Fill a sink or tub partway with water. Wrap a slotted spatula with plastic wrap or aluminum foil. Say, *Paddle with the spatula in the water to show how webbed feet work. Now, take off the plastic wrap or foil and try paddling again. What did you learn about webbed feet? Why don't storks need webbed feet? Storks eat fish and frogs. What do fish and frogs eat?* On a markerboard or paper, list and discuss the following food chains:
1) stork --> frog --> insects
2) stork --> fish --> algae

✓ Text Connection: *God's Wonderful Works* p. 83, 116-117

Key Idea: The Dutch people believed it was bad luck to harm a stork.

Bible Study

Review the memory verse Galations 6:9, from Unit 2, by saying it while the students join in on the parts they know. Say, *In Galations 6:9, when does it say that we will reap blessings? Does luck have anything to do with the blessings that we receive? Where do all blessings come from?* Next, have students do 3 push-ups. After 3 push-ups, have the students recite the entire Bible verse. Repeat the activity several times.

Key Idea: All blessings come from God our Father in heaven.

Corresponding Music

✓ *Hide 'Em in Your Heart Vol. 2* CD - Track 7; Cassette - Side A Song: *"If We Don't Lose Heart"*

Learning the Basics

Focus: Language Arts and Math

Unit 6 - Day 2

Language Arts

Use the spelling list from Day 1. Say the first spelling word. Use it in a sentence. Repeat the word. Ask students to write the word on a markerboard or a piece of paper from memory. Give students the matching word card from Day 1 to compare with their spelling. Guide students to correct any mistakes. Repeat the activity with all 10 words.

<u>Copywork</u>: Have students copy part of the poem *"The Months"*.

<u>Key Idea</u>: Practice spelling words.

Reading Choices

Choose **one** of the reading options listed below (see Appendix for details).

★ A phonics program

★ *Scheduled Books for Emerging Readers*

★ *Drawn into the Heart of Reading Level 2/3*

<u>Key Idea</u>: Use a step-by-step program for reading instruction.

Storytime

Read aloud the next portion of the adventure book that you selected. Without looking back at the story, begin retelling or narrating the part of the adventure that you read today. After a short time, tap a student and say, *Your turn.* The student should pick up the narration where you left off. After a short time, the student should tap you and say, *Your turn.* Continue taking turns narrating in this manner until today's reading has been retold. Then, say, *Name one thing that you learned about the main character today.* Write it on paper for the students to copy.

<u>Key Idea</u>: Take turns retelling a story from a single reading.

Math Exploration

Draw one hill on a piece of paper. Give students 10 chocolate chips or raisins to be ants. Tell subtraction stories for the students to act out on their papers with their ants (i.e. There are 10 ants on the hill. 3 crawl away. There will be 7 ants left on the hill.) Write the corresponding number sentence on paper or markerboard for students to complete (i.e. 10 - 3 = ___). After several examples, have students use the ants to tell their own subtraction stories.

✔ <u>Text Connection</u>: *Primary Mathematics Workbook 1A* p. 50-51

<u>Key Idea</u>: Complete the subtraction number sentences.

Learning Through History

Focus: Life in Holland

Unit 6 - Day 3

Reading About History

Read about history in the following resource:

★ *Stories of the Pilgrims* p. 53-56

Key Idea: It grew very cold in Holland. The ground was covered with snow and the first day of skating on the frozen canal was a holiday.

Poetry and Rhymes

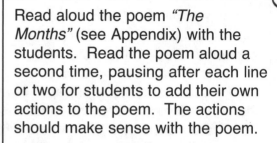

Read aloud the poem *"The Months"* (see Appendix) with the students. Read the poem aloud a second time, pausing after each line or two for students to add their own actions to the poem. The actions should make sense with the poem.

Key Idea: Read classic poetry.

Science Exploration

Say, *As the weather grew colder in Holland, the storks migrated to warmer places. We do not migrate. Instead, we need to dress warmly in cold weather. Let's see which kind of clothing is best at protecting us from the outside air.* Set out 2 plates. Place one ice cube on each plate. Make sure the ice cubes are close to the same size. Wrap one ice cube in a light cotton dishcloth. Wrap the other ice cube in a wool scarf, or place it inside a mitten. Set the timer for 15 minutes. After 15 minutes, guess which ice cube will have melted the least. Check your prediction. *What type of clothing should you wear in cold weather? Why?*

✔ Text Connection: *God's Wonderful Works* p. 31, 33, and 85

Key Idea: As winter came, the storks knew it was time to fly south. Soon, white snow fell, and the canal froze.

Bible Study

Ask, *What does it mean if something is whiter than snow? Does snow always stay white? Why not? Are you able to keep your 'heart' whiter than snow by never sinning? Why not? Who can wash your sins away?* Next, review the memory verse, 1 John 4:15-16a, from Unit 3 by saying it while the students join in on the parts they know. Have students run in place. When you say, *Freeze,* have the students stop and recite the entire verse. Repeat the activity.

Key Idea: God knows your heart is sinful. He sent Jesus to cleanse you.

Corresponding Music

✔ *Hide 'Em in Your Heart Vol. 2* CD - Track 5; Cassette - Side A Song: *"God Is Love"*

Learning the Basics

Focus: Language Arts and Math

Unit 6 - Day 3

Language Arts

Using the spelling list from Day 1, choose 3 or more words that the students need to practice. Guide students to use each of the words that you chose in a sentence. On a markerboard or a piece of paper, write down the sentences as the students dictate them to you. Underline the spelling word in each sentence. Have the students copy the sentences on a piece of paper. Help students check their sentences and correct any mistakes.
Copywork: Have students copy part of the poem *"The Months"*.

Key Idea: Practice spelling words with short vowels ending in **double consonants**.

Reading Choices

Choose **one** of the reading options listed below (see Appendix for details).

★ A phonics program
★ *Scheduled Books for Emerging Readers*
★ *Drawn into the Heart of Reading Level 2/3*

Key Idea: Use a step-by-step program for reading instruction.

Storytime

Read aloud the next portion of the adventure book that you selected. On paper, draw a simple stairstep diagram with 10 or more steps. Say, *Think back to the beginning of the adventure story. Help me write one problem on each step going up the staircase in the order that the problems happened in the story. We'll save the staircase to add more problems as we read.*

Key Idea: Focus on the story element: *problem* or *conflict*.

Math Exploration

Set out 10 of the same type of coins. Say, *Shake the 10 coins and drop them gently on the table. Count the number of coins that are heads and the number of coins that are tails. On a markerboard or a piece of paper, write four different number sentences that match your toss. For example, 4 heads + 6 tails = 10 coins, 6 tails + 4 heads = 10 coins, 10 coins - 4 heads = 6 tails, and 10 coins - 6 tails = 4 heads.*
If students toss an equal number of heads and tails there will only be two number sentences.

✔ Text Connection: *Primary Mathematics Workbook 1A* p. 52-53

Key Idea: Introduce fact families.

Learning Through History

Focus: Life in Holland

Unit 6 - Day 4

Reading About History

Read about history in the following resource:

★ *Stories of the Pilgrims* p. 57-59

Key Idea: The Pilgrims moved from Amsterdam to Leiden. They saw windmills, tulips, and strips of white linen bleaching in the sun. The Pilgrims were poor, but they hoped Leiden would be a good place to live.

Poetry and Rhymes

Read aloud the poem *"The Months"* (see Appendix) with the students. Have students draw pictures that reflect the poem's meaning on either a photocopy of the poem or on their copywork. File the finished poem in a special place.

Key Idea: Read and appreciate a variety of classic poetry.

Geography

Say, *A canal is a man-made street of water. Let's experiment with how water runs through the canals. Lay a cookie sheet flat in a sink or tub. Use an eyedropper or baster to drip quite a bit of water onto the flat cookie sheet. Then, lift the cookie sheet a little and tip it slightly. Watch the water run down the sheet in ribbons that look just like canals. Lift the cookie sheet higher and watch the water run even faster. This shows how the water from the canals runs down to end up in a river or the sea.*

Key Idea: The Pilgrims sailed in canal boats on the canals to move from Amsterdam to Leiden. They did not have many things to take with them when they moved.

Bible Study

Review the memory verse, Matthew 6:19-21, from Unit 4 by saying it while the students join in on the parts they know. Next, have students skip around the room until you say, *Freeze*. After they 'freeze', have the students recite the entire Bible verse. Have students repeat the activity.

✔ Text Connection: *Morning Bells* p. 34-36

Key Idea: The Dutch people worked hard to keep their homes, clothes, and cities clean. Only Jesus can keep our hearts clean.

Corresponding Music

✔ *Hide 'Em in Your Heart Vol. 2* CD - Track 18; Cassette - Side B Song: *"Where Your Treasure Is"*

Learning the Basics

Focus: Language Arts and Math

Unit 6 - Day 4

Language Arts

Use the spelling list from Day 1. Say each word and use it in a sentence. Have students write each word and check it with the matching word card from Day 1. Guide students to correct any mistakes. For each missed word, have students hop on one foot and spell the word out loud, hopping each time they say a letter.
<u>Copywork</u>: Have students copy part of the poem *"The Months"*.

<u>Key Idea</u>: Practice spelling words with short vowels ending in double consonants.

Reading Choices

Choose **one** of the reading options listed below (see Appendix for details).

★ A phonics program
★ *Scheduled Books for Emerging Readers*
★ *Drawn into the Heart of Reading Level 2/3*

<u>Key Idea</u>: Use a step-by-step program for reading instruction.

Storytime

Say, *Fear of the Lord is revering the Lord and His commands and believing the Lord can turn harm into good for those who trust in Him.* Review the key verse Deuteronomy 13:4. Read aloud Genesis 28:10-22. Ask, *How did Jacob's actions show fear of the Lord?* Read aloud the next portion of the adventure book that you selected. Then, ask, *How does the main character in the adventure show reverence or fear of the Lord? What would the Biblical character, Jacob, do differently from the character in your book?*

<u>Key Idea</u>: Focus on the Godly character trait: *fear of the Lord*.

Math Exploration

Complete the assigned lesson in the workbook listed below.

✔ <u>Text Connection</u>: *Primary Mathematics Workbook 1A* p. 54-55

Note: Use counters as needed to help with the problems.

<u>Key Idea</u>: Write number sentences using the '+' or '-' symbols so that the sentences make sense.

Learning Through History

Focus: Life in Holland

Unit 6 - Day 5

Reading About History

Read the following passage from your own Bible:

★ Psalm 51:1-7

Key Idea: This Psalm reminds us that we were all sinful from the time we were born. Jesus cleanses our sin when we ask for forgiveness.

Poetry and Rhymes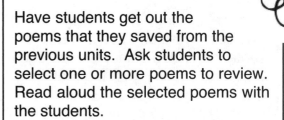

Have students get out the poems that they saved from the previous units. Ask students to select one or more poems to review. Read aloud the selected poems with the students.

Key Idea: Read classic poetry.

Artistic Expression

Fold a red 9" x 12" sheet of paper in half. Starting at the fold, draw half of a heart on one side of the paper. Have students keep the paper folded and cut on the line that you drew. Open the paper to see a whole heart. Cut two 2" vertical slits in the heart several inches apart. Then, measure and cut a strip of white paper that is 2" x 12". Say, *Draw the outline of a red heart on the first part of the strip and a black colored heart several inches further down the strip. Slide the strip of white paper up through the slit in the back of the heart, across the front of the heart, and down through the other slit. Pull the strip to see the black heart filled with sin and the white heart that's been washed clean.*

✔ Text Connection: *God's Wonderful Works* p. 128

Key Idea: The Pilgrims wanted to raise their children to glorify God and worship Him with all of their heart.

Bible Study

Ask, *In Psalm 51:1-7, what is David asking God to do? Is it important to ask Jesus to forgive you when you sin? Why? Who do your sins hurt? Since Jesus will forgive your sins, is it alright to keep on doing the same sins over and over?* Ask students to share their memory verse, Psalm 139:13-14, with someone special. Suggestions for sharing the verse include saying it to another family member, saying it to someone by telephone, reciting it to a stuffed animal, or writing it to mail.

Key Idea: Even though we were born as sinners, Jesus can forgive us and wash our sins away.

Corresponding Music

✔ *Hide 'Em in Your Heart Vol. 2* CD - Track 12; Cassette - Side B Song: *"You Knit Me Together"*

Learning the Basics

Focus: Language Arts and Math

Unit 6 - Day 5

Language Arts

Get out 7 index cards. On each card, write one of the following question words: which, what, when, where, why, how, who. Place an object in a paper bag. Say, *I have placed an object in this bag. Draw a card. To find out what the object is, ask a question about the object that begins with the word on the card (i.e. What color is it?). I will answer you with a statement (i.e. It is red and blue).* You may want to set a time limit for the questions so the students do not become frustrated. If there is time, have students hide an object in the bag and have you ask questions. <u>Copywork</u>: Write one question for students to copy.

<u>Key Idea</u>: Practice asking and answering questions.

Reading Choices

Choose **one** of the reading options listed below (see Appendix for details).

★ A phonics program
★ *Scheduled Books for Emerging Readers*
★ *Drawn into the Heart of Reading Level 2/3*

<u>Key Idea</u>: Use a step-by-step program for reading instruction.

Storytime

Read aloud a short portion of the adventure book that you selected. Give students a chance to orally retell today's reading by pretending to be one of the characters in the story telling you what is happening in the story. Prompt students as needed by asking, *What did ____ say to ____ when ...? Then, what happened? After that what did ____ say?*

<u>Key Idea</u>: Give students practice retelling a portion of an adventure.

Math Exploration

Tape a long strip of masking tape on the floor and number it '1'- '10'. Write "7 - 2 = ___" on a markerboard or a piece of paper. To solve the subtraction problem, have students stand on the number '7' on the number line and take two steps or hops back. Instruct students to count backward to subtract as they step back ('6', '5'). Last, have students write the number where they ended up on the line to complete the subtraction sentence. Repeat the activity using various subtraction sentences.

✓ <u>Text Connection</u>: *Primary Mathematics Workbook 1A* p. 56-57

<u>Key Idea</u>: Count backward to subtract.

Learning Through History

Focus: The Pilgrims Move from Amsterdam to Leiden

Unit 7 - Day 1

Reading About History

Read about history in the following resource:

★ *Stories of the Pilgrims* p. 60-62

Key Idea: The Pilgrims and the Dutch people dressed and worshiped very differently. However, they were kind to one another and lived peacefully together.

Poetry and Rhymes

Read aloud the poem *"Mother's Jewels"* (see Appendix) to the students. Do not share the title. Ask students to suggest some titles for the poem. Share the real title. Read the poem again with the students.

Key Idea: Read and appreciate a variety of classic poetry.

Science Exploration

Either write the following steps for making cloth on separate index cards or list them on a markerboard or paper in random order: shear the wool from the sheep --> wash the wool --> comb the wool --> spin the wool into thread --> dye the thread --> weave the thread into cloth --> pack the cloth in boxes --> load the boxes on the ship --> deliver the boxes of cloth to a store. Say, *Many Pilgrims worked in the mills in Holland to make cloth. Let's look at the steps for making cloth and put them in order.*

✔ Text Connection: *God's Wonderful Works* p. 11

Key Idea: It takes energy to do work. Many Pilgrims worked in the mills to make wool into cloth. What are some things that you do that take energy?

Bible Study

Psalm 119:9-11 is the memory verse for this unit. Read the verse out loud. Ask, *If something is pure or clean, what does that mean? How does Psalm 119:9-10 say you can keep your way pure or clean? What does it mean to hide God's word in your heart? In Psalm 119:11, what reason does it give you to hide God's word in your heart?* Say the verse together 3 times. Add hand motions to help students remember the words.

Key Idea: The Pilgrims wanted to live according to God's word.

Corresponding Music

✔ *Hide 'Em in Your Heart Vol. 2* CD - Track 21; Cassette - Side B Song: *"I Have Hidden Your Word"*

Learning the Basics

Focus: Language Arts and Math

Unit 7 - Day 1

Language Arts

Get out the spelling words on index cards that you saved from Unit 1 and Unit 2. Guide students to study each card one at a time, flip it over, write the word from memory on paper, flip the card back over to check the spelling, and erase and correct any mistakes.

Copywork: Have students copy part of the poem *"Mother's Jewels"*.

Key Idea: Review spelling words from Unit 1 and Unit 2.

Reading Choices

Choose **one** of the reading options listed below (see Appendix for details).

★ A phonics program
★ *Scheduled Books for Emerging Readers*
★ *Drawn into the Heart of Reading Level 2/3*

Key Idea: Use a step-by-step program for reading instruction.

Storytime

Say, *As we are reading today, we will be searching for one object or item that seems to be very important to the story. Listen and watch for an item that is mentioned often.*

Read aloud the next portion of the adventure book that you selected. Pace your reading to complete the adventure during the next 10 days of plans. Ask, *As we were reading today, what object or item seemed to be very important to the story? Explain why it's important. On paper, draw the item that we discussed.*

Key Idea: Set a purpose for reading the next part of the adventure.

Math Exploration

Complete the assigned lesson in the workbook listed below.

✔ Text Connection: *Primary Mathematics Workbook 1A* p. 58

Key Idea: Complete the subtraction sentences.

Learning Through History

Focus: The Pilgrims Move from Amsterdam to Leiden

Unit 7 - Day 2

Reading About History

Read about history in the following resource:

★ *Stories of the Pilgrims* p. 63-67

Key Idea: The Pilgrims wanted their children to speak English and remember the English ways. They wanted to have farms and land of their own. So, they decided to sail to America.

Poetry and Rhymes

Read aloud the poem *"Mother's Jewels"* (see Appendix) with the students. Discuss the poem's meaning. If you choose, photocopy the poem, cut it apart, and have the students place it in the correct order.

Key Idea: Read and appreciate a variety of classic poetry.

History Activity

Say, *The Pilgrim children began to speak Dutch better than English. Let's practice some Dutch words.* Practice saying the following English words in Dutch: yes (ja), no (nr), hello (hello), good-bye (vaarwel), tulip (tulp), love (liefde), God (God). Practice saying the following English sentence in Dutch: I love my church. (I liefde mijn kerk.) Try other Dutch sentences by replacing church with the Dutch words for sister (zuster), brother (broer), family (familie), and school (school). Now try this English sentence in Dutch: I love to play. (I liefde aan spel.) Try other Dutch sentences by replacing the word 'play' with the Dutch words for 'work' (het werk), 'eat' (eet), 'fish' (vissen).

Key Idea: The Pilgrim children were growing up like Dutch children.

Bible Study

Say Psalm 119:9-11 while the students join in on the parts they know. Use the hand motions you added on Day 1. Ask, *What are some ways that you can hide God's word in your heart? If God's word is in your heart, how will that help you?* Next, have students do 5 toe touches. After 5 toe touches, have the students recite the entire Bible verse. Prompt the students as needed. Repeat the activity several times.

Key Idea: God wants you to remember His ways and follow His word.

Corresponding Music

✓ *Hide 'Em in Your Heart Vol. 2* CD - Track 21; Cassette - Side B Song: *"I Have Hidden Your Word"*

Learning the Basics

Focus: Language Arts and Math

Unit 7 - Day 2

Language Arts

Get out the spelling cards that you saved from Unit 3. Say the first spelling word. Use it in a sentence. Repeat the word. Ask students to write the word on a markerboard or a piece of paper from memory. Give students the matching word card to compare with their spelling. Guide students to correct any mistakes. Repeat the activity with all 10 words.
Copywork: Have students copy part of the poem *"Mother's Jewels"*.

Key Idea: Review spelling words from Unit 3.

Reading Choices

Choose **one** of the reading options listed below (see Appendix for details).

★ A phonics program
★ *Scheduled Books for Emerging Readers*
★ *Drawn into the Heart of Reading Level 2/3*

Key Idea: Use a step-by-step program for reading instruction.

Storytime

Read aloud the next portion of the adventure book that you selected. Without looking back at the story, write a retelling of the part of the adventure that you read today leaving blanks in place of key words (i.e. _____ was a young woman who traveled to _____ with _____. She lost her _____ on the trip and felt so _____. But, she found it again when they reached _____). Key words can be names, places, descriptive words, time of day, seasons, etc. Work with the students to reread the written narration and fill in the missing words.

Key Idea: Model retelling a story from a single reading.

Math Exploration

Give students 10 items to use as counters (i.e. buttons, blocks, raisins, or spoons). Say, *We are going to play a game. The goal is to find as many ways to use up to 10 counters to get an answer of '5' as possible. You may add two numbers or subtract two numbers to equal '5'. For example, 3 + 2 = 5 and 6 - 1 = 5. List the number sentences on paper or a markerboard as you find them. We'll see how many you can find in five minutes.*

✔ Text Connection: *Primary Mathematics Workbook 1A* p. 59

Key Idea: Find addition and subtraction sentences that equal a given number.

Learning Through History

Focus: The Pilgrims Move from Amsterdam to Leiden

Unit 7 - Day 3

Reading About History

Read about history in the following resource:

★ *Stories of the Pilgrims* p. 68-69

Key Idea: Miles Standish went to the Pilgrim's church. He was a brave soldier and had a sword named, *Gideon.* He planned to go with the Pilgrims to America.

Poetry and Rhymes

Read aloud the poem *"Mother's Jewels"* (see Appendix) with the students. Read the poem aloud a second time, pausing after each line or two for students to add their own actions to the poem. The actions should make sense with the poem.

Key Idea: Read classic poetry.

Geography

Get out a globe or a world map. Say, *Find England on the globe or map. Hint: It is near the top of the globe or map. Now, find the Netherlands (or Holland). It is east of England. England and Holland are both found on which continent?* (Europe). *Now find Virginia in the United States. What ocean will the Pilgrims have to cross to get from Holland to the United States?* (Atlantic Ocean). *What channel will the Pilgrims go through to reach the ocean?* (The English Channel). *What might a channel be?* (a water route). *On what continent is the United States found?* (North America).

Key Idea: The Pilgrims planned to sail from Holland to Virginia in America in the spring.

Bible Study

Say Psalm 119:9-11 with the students. Use the hand motions you added on Day 1. Next, have students lay on their backs and peddle their feet in the air like they are riding a bicycle. When you say, *Freeze,* the students should stop and recite the entire Bible verse. Repeat the activity.

✔Text Connection: *Morning Bells* p. 43-45

Key Idea: The Pilgrims decided that going to America was the right thing to do. They sought God's will and trusted Him to provide for their needs.

Corresponding Music

✔*Hide 'Em in Your Heart Vol. 2* CD - Track 21; Cassette - Side B Song: *"I Have Hidden Your Word"*

Learning the Basics

Focus: Language Arts and Math

Unit 7 - Day 3

Language Arts

Get out the spelling word cards from Unit 4. Choose 3 or more words that the students need to practice. Guide students to use each of the words that you chose in a sentence. On a markerboard or a piece of paper, write down the sentences as the students dictate them to you. Underline the spelling word in each sentence. Have the students copy the sentences on a piece of paper. Help students check their sentences and correct any mistakes.

Copywork: Have students copy part of the poem *"Mother's Jewels"*.

Key Idea: Review spelling words.

Reading Choices

Choose **one** of the reading options listed below (see Appendix for details).

★ A phonics program
★ *Scheduled Books for Emerging Readers*
★ *Drawn into the Heart of Reading Level 2/3*

Key Idea: Use a step-by-step program for reading instruction.

Storytime

Read aloud the next portion of the adventure book that you selected. Take out the staircase diagram that you saved from Unit 6 - Day 3. Read aloud the problem on each step. If that problem has been solved, have students color that step. Then, add any new problems in the story to the upper steps of the staircase. Say, *We'll save the staircase to add more problems as we read.*

Key Idea: Focus on the story element: *problem* or *conflict*.

Math Exploration

On paper, draw three circles stacked up to be a snowman. Give students 10 counters to be buttons (i.e. raisins, chocolate chips, 'O' shaped cereal, or buttons). Give word problems for students to act out with their buttons (i.e. The snowman had 3 buttons. The children put on 3 more. How many buttons are there now?). Have the students write a matching number sentence (i.e. 3 + 3 = 6). Here is another example: The snowman had 7 buttons and 4 fell off. How many are left? Write "7 - 4 = 3".

✔ Text Connection: *Primary Mathematics Workbook 1A* p. 60-62

Key Idea: Decide when to add and when to subtract in word problems.

Learning Through History

Focus: The Pilgrims Move from Amsterdam to Leiden

Unit 7 - Day 4

Reading About History

Read about history in the following resource:

★ *Stories of the Pilgrims* p. 70-73

Key Idea: The Pilgrims worked hard to prepare for the trip to America. They spun and stitched and packed. They had to leave behind many pretty things. Their Dutch friends helped them get ready for the journey.

Poetry and Rhymes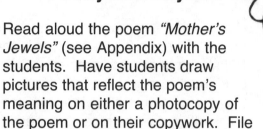

Read aloud the poem *"Mother's Jewels"* (see Appendix) with the students. Have students draw pictures that reflect the poem's meaning on either a photocopy of the poem or on their copywork. File the finished poem in a special place.

Key Idea: Read classic poetry.

Science Exploration

Say, *In the spring the Pilgrims were ready to sail to America. They traveled in canal boats to meet the ship in Delfshaven. Using ramps as levers made loading the canal boats easier. Let's see how.* Use a soup can as a barrel. Try to push the barrel up several steps of stairs. Now, place a flat lid or cookie sheet at an angle down several steps of stairs. Roll the barrel up the ramp. *Was it easier to move the barrel with a ramp? Why? How would the ramp have helped the men as they loaded the boats with supplies for their trip to America?*

Key Idea: The Pilgrims worked hard to load the boats with supplies for their move to America.

Bible Study

Say Psalm 119:9-11 with the students. Use the hand motions from Day 1. Ask, *What things are you tempted to keep for yourself? Where do all good things come from? Can God give you more than you have, if you share with others? How do you sin against God by being greedy with your Earthly treasures?* Have students gallop by leading with their left foot until you say, *Freeze*. After they 'freeze', have students recite the verse. Have students repeat the activity with their right foot.

Key Idea: The Pilgrims knew God could provide more than they had.

Corresponding Music

✔ *Hide 'Em in Your Heart Vol. 2*
CD - Track 21; Cassette - Side B
Song: *"I Have Hidden Your Word"*

Learning the Basics

Focus: Language Arts and Math

Unit 7 - Day 4

Language Arts

Get out the spelling word cards from Unit 5 and Unit 6. Say each word and use it in a sentence. Have students write each word and check it with the matching word card. Guide students to correct any mistakes. For each missed word, have students trace the word with their finger on a patch of carpet.
<u>Copywork</u>: Have students copy part of the poem *"Mother's Jewels"*.

<u>Key Idea</u>: Review spelling words.

Reading Choices

Choose **one** of the reading options listed below (see Appendix for details).

★ A phonics program
★ *Scheduled Books for Emerging Readers*
★ *Drawn into the Heart of Reading Level 2/3*

<u>Key Idea</u>: Use a step-by-step program for reading instruction.

Storytime

Say, *Fear of the Lord is revering the Lord and His commands and believing the Lord can turn harm into good for those who trust in Him.* Review the key verse Deuteronomy 13:4. Say, *Name some ways that we show reverence to God* (i.e. be quiet during prayer, listen in church, sing praises during worship, follow the Bible reading, pray for God's will). Share how the Lord has turned harm into good for you. Read aloud the next portion of the adventure that you selected. Ask, *How have the book characters experienced harm being turned into good? Do the characters show fear of the Lord?*

<u>Key Idea</u>: Focus on the Godly character trait: *fear of the Lord*.

Math Exploration

Complete the assigned lesson in the workbook listed below.

✔ <u>Text Connection</u>: *Primary Mathematics Workbook 1A* p. 63-65

<u>Key Idea</u>: Use the pictures to help solve the word problems. Decide whether to add or subtract.

Learning Through History

Focus: The Pilgrims Move from Amsterdam to Leiden

Unit 7 - Day 5

Reading About History

Read the following passage from your own Bible:

 Psalm 119:33-40

Key Idea: It was very important to the Pilgrims to raise their children to serve God. They did not want their children to become selfish or to long for worldly things.

Poetry and Rhymes

Have students get out the poems that they saved from the previous units. Ask students to select one or more poems to review. Read aloud the selected poems with the students.

Key Idea: Read classic poetry.

Artistic Expression

On white paper, use a dark marker to draw the outline of each student's hair, face, and shirt. Tape half of a white index card on the shirt to be a pocket. Leave the pocket open at the top. Direct students to look in the mirror and draw and color in their eyes, nose, mouth, and hair. Guide students to color the shirt on the paper to look like the shirt that they are wearing. When the students are done with their picture, have them copy Psalm 139:14 on a slip of paper. You may choose to write the verse for the students instead. Last, help students fold the slip of paper and put it in the pocket that is taped to the shirt.

Key Idea: The Lord made each of us in a very special way. We need to praise Him for making us just the way we are. He made us to glorify Him.

Bible Study

Say, *In Psalm 119:33-40, what does the writer of the Psalm ask God to do? What does the Psalm tell you to do to keep God's commands? Are you able to follow God's commands perfectly? Why do you need God's help to follow His commands?* Ask students to share their memory verse, Psalm 119:9-11, with someone special. Suggestions for sharing the verse include saying it to another family member, saying it to someone by telephone, reciting it to a stuffed animal, or writing it to mail.

Key Idea: The Pilgrims wanted their children to follow God's commands.

Corresponding Music

✓ *Hide 'Em in Your Heart Vol. 2*
CD - Track 21; Cassette - Side B
Song: *"I Have Hidden Your Word"*

Learning the Basics

Focus: Language Arts and Math

Unit 7 - Day 5

Language Arts

Write the following command on a markerboard or a piece of paper: *Sit down.* Ask, *What does this sentence do? What do you notice at the beginning of the sentence? What do you see at the end of the sentence?* Say, *Commands are sentences that order or request that you do something.* Say, *You will need to get one of your stuffed toys. I will give you commands to follow with your toy.* Say, *Place the toy beside you. Make your toy do a flip. Set your toy behind you. Pass your toy from your right hand to your left hand. Slide your toy in front of you. Walk your toy backward. Have your toy hop over your leg. Wave your toy's right hand.* Next, have the students give you commands to follow with the stuffed toy. <u>Copywork</u>: Write one command for the students to copy.

<u>Key Idea</u>: Introduce commands.

Reading Choices

Choose **one** of the reading options listed below (see Appendix for details).

★ A phonics program
★ *Scheduled Books for Emerging Readers*
★ *Drawn into the Heart of Reading Level 2/3*

<u>Key Idea</u>: Use a step-by-step program for reading instruction.

Storytime

Read aloud a short portion of the adventure book that you selected. Guide students to retell the important events in the chapter by saying, *Tell me the exciting parts from today's reading.*

<u>Key Idea</u>: Give students practice retelling a portion of an adventure.

Math Exploration

Place 10 stuffed toys in a line. Give the following directions for students to do with the stuffed toys: *The second toy in line jumps up. The fourth toy spins around. The sixth toy lays down. The eighth toy claps. The third toy stands on its head. The tenth toy gives a kiss. The fifth toy falls over. The seventh toy does a somersault.* Repeat the game allowing students to give you directions to follow with the toys.

✔ <u>Text Connection</u>: *Primary Mathematics Workbook 1A* p. 66-67

<u>Key Idea</u>: Practice using ordinal numbers.

Learning Through History

Focus: English Pilgrims Travel to America

Unit 8 - Day 1

Reading About History

Read about history in the following resource:

★ *Stories of the Pilgrims* p. 74-76

Key Idea: It was very hard for the Pilgrims to leave their Dutch friends. Holland seemed like home to the Pilgrim children who had grown up there. The Pilgrims trusted God to watch over them.

Poetry and Rhymes

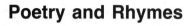

Read aloud the poem *"Where Lies the Land?"* (see Appendix) to the students. Do not share the title. Ask students to suggest some titles for the poem. Share the real title. Read the poem again with the students.

Key Idea: Read and appreciate a variety of classic poetry.

Artistic Expression

Say, *You will be making your own picture of the Mayflower. On brown paper, draw the outline of the boat. Cut it out. Glue the brown boat near the bottom of a piece of blue paper.*

Draw masts on the boat and color them brown. Cut out several white sails and glue them on your masts.

Use markers or colored pencils to add any missing details to your boat.

Last, use a Q-tip or small paintbrush and toothpaste to paint foamy waves around the Mayflower. Save your boat to use on Day 2.

Key Idea: When the Pilgrims reached Delfshaven, they boarded the *Speedwell*. After the ship was loaded, the Pilgrims sailed to England to meet the *Mayflower*.

Bible Study

1 Thessalonians 5:11 is the memory verse for this unit. Read the verse out loud. Ask, *What does it mean to encourage or comfort someone? Who does the verse say you should comfort or encourage? Why should Christians build each other up or edify one another? What is the opposite of building someone up?* Say the verse together 3 times. Add hand motions to help students remember the words.

Key Idea: The Pilgrims comforted and encouraged each other as they left for America.

Corresponding Music

✓ *Hide 'Em in Your Heart Vol. 2*
CD - Track 2; Cassette - Side A
Song: "Encourage One Another"

Learning the Basics

Focus: Language Arts and Math

Unit 8 - Day 1

Language Arts

Choose **either** spelling list 1 **or** 2 (see Appendix for lists). Write each spelling word on a separate index card. Guide students to study each card one at a time, flip it over, write the word on paper, flip the card back over to check the spelling, and erase and correct any mistakes. <u>Copywork</u>: Have students copy part of the poem *"Where Lies the Land?"*.

<u>Key Idea</u>: Practice spelling words with long 'o', 'y', or 'e' at the end.

Reading Choices

Choose **one** of the reading options listed below (see Appendix for details).

★ A phonics program

★ *Scheduled Books for Emerging Readers*

★ *Drawn into the Heart of Reading Level 2/3*

<u>Key Idea</u>: Use a step-by-step program for reading instruction.

Storytime

Say, *Remember that an adventure story is a suspenseful story filled with action and excitement. What clues do you notice in the pictures in the book (or on the cover) that show this is an adventure story? What kinds of places are shown in the pictures? Would you like to live in any of the places described in the story? Explain.*

Read aloud the next portion of the adventure book that you selected. Pace your reading to complete the adventure during the next 5 days of plans.

<u>Key Idea</u>: Set a purpose for reading the next part of the adventure.

Math Exploration

Place 10 cups in a row upside down. Direct students to turn their backs to the row of cups. Hide an object under one of the cups. Have students turn around and ask questions to figure out where the object is hidden (i.e. Is it hidden before the third cup? Is it between the fourth and the seventh cup? Is it hidden after the eighth cup?). When students think they know where the object is hidden, have them look under that cup to check if they are right. Repeat the activity by hiding the object under a different cup.

✔ <u>Text Connection</u>: *Primary Mathematics Workbook 1A* p. 68

<u>Key Idea</u>: Practice using ordinal numbers.

Learning Through History

Focus: English Pilgrims Travel to America

Unit 8 - Day 2

Reading About History

Read about history in the following resource:

★ *Stories of the Pilgrims* p. 77-79

Key Idea: Soon after the Pilgrims left England, the *Speedwell* began to leak. Both the *Mayflower* and the *Speedwell* sailed back to England. Only the *Mayflower* would be able to sail to America.

Poetry and Rhymes

Read aloud the poem *"Where Lies the Land?"* (see Appendix) with the students. Discuss the poem's meaning. If you choose, photocopy the poem, cut it apart, and have the students put it in order.

Key Idea: Read classic poetry.

History Activity

Say, *Get out your timeline. The Mayflower sailed for America in September, 1620. There were 102 passengers on board. It took 66 days for the ship to sail 2,750 miles across the Atlantic Ocean. Find the column on your timeline that says 1600. Draw a small boat in that column. Write Mayflower, 1620 under it.* Next, have students get out their boat pictures from Day 1. Cut a 2" horizontal slit in the boat. Tape a ziplock bag to the back of the picture, so the mouth of the bag opens around the slit. Say, *The Mayflower was about 113 feet long. It could hold 180 casks or barrels.* Give students dry 'O'-shaped cereal to use as casks. Have students count and load 180 casks onto their *Mayflower*, using the slit in the boat.

Key Idea: The boat was crowded.

Bible Study

Say 1 Thessalonians 5:11 while the students join in on the parts they know. Use the hand motions you added on Day 1. Say, *Name some ways that you can encourage or comfort someone else. Do you ever feel discouraged or sad? How can others encourage you?* Next, have students do windmills by touching their right hand to their right foot, and then their left hand to their left foot. After 5 windmills, have the students recite the Bible verse. Repeat the activity several times.

Key Idea: The Pilgrims encouraged one another during hard times.

Corresponding Music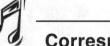

✔ *Hide 'Em in Your Heart Vol. 2*
CD - Track 2; Cassette - Side A
Song: *"Encourage One Another"*

Learning the Basics

Focus: Language Arts and Math

Unit 8 - Day 2

Language Arts

Use the spelling list from Day 1. Say the first spelling word. Use it in a sentence. Repeat the word. Ask students to write the word on a markerboard or a piece of paper from memory. Give students the matching word card from Day 1 to compare with their spelling. Guide students to correct any mistakes. Repeat the activity with all 10 words.

Copywork: Have students copy part of the poem *"Where Lies the Land?"*.

Key Idea: Practice spelling words with long 'o', 'y', or 'e' at the end.

Reading Choices

Choose **one** of the reading options listed below (see Appendix for details).

★ A phonics program

★ *Scheduled Books for Emerging Readers*

★ *Drawn into the Heart of Reading Level 2/3*

Key Idea: Use a step-by-step program for reading instruction.

Storytime

Read aloud the next portion of the adventure book that you selected. Ask students to retell or narrate what you read today. Remind students to tell the most important parts and to include details from the story in the retelling. As students work together to retell the story, write, type, or tape record the students' narration. When the students are finished, read the narration out loud. Highlight, circle, or underline one main idea from the narration for the students to copy.

Key Idea: Keep a sample of the students' narrations for the genre: *Adventure*.

Math Exploration

Place several snacks of different types in one bowl (i.e. 3 raisins, 4 crackers, 3 marshmallows, 2 dried fruit bits). Hold the bowl up and have students take one snack at a time and lay them in a row on the table. As each snack is placed in the row, students should announce its position (i.e. A raisin was first. The cracker was second. I got a marshmallow third.). After each student has ten or more snacks, give directions for students to eat the snacks (i.e. Eat the third snack. Eat the snack in seventh place.)

✔ Text Connection: *Primary Mathematics Workbook 1A* p. 69-70

Key Idea: Practice using ordinal numbers.

Learning Through History

Focus: English Pilgrims Travel to America

Unit 8 - Day 3

Reading About History

Read about history in the following resource:

★ *Stories of the Pilgrims* p. 80-82

Key Idea: As the *Mayflower* sailed to America, there were some days without any wind. But, there were also many storms. John Howland fell overboard during a storm and almost drowned.

Poetry and Rhymes

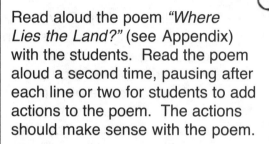

Read aloud the poem *"Where Lies the Land?"* (see Appendix) with the students. Read the poem aloud a second time, pausing after each line or two for students to add actions to the poem. The actions should make sense with the poem.

Key Idea: Read classic poetry.

Science Exploration

Say, *Fill a ziplock bag partway full of water. Add several drops of blue food coloring. Add 5 or 6 drops of oil. Seal the bag and shake it. What do you notice about the oil and the water? Oil is lighter than water, so it floats. Now, sprinkle some salt in the water. Seal the bag and shake it. Let the water settle. What happens to the oil now? The salt made the oil heavier, so the drops of oil began to sink. The Mayflower ran into some storms as sea. During one storm a man was swept overboard. Just like the oil, he floated for awhile and then he began to sink.*

✔ Text Connection: *God's Wonderful Works* p. 24-25

Key Idea: John Howland fell into the water during a storm at sea. As he began to sink, he grabbed a rope and pulled himself toward the ship.

Bible Study

Say 1 Thessalonians 5:11 with the students. Use the hand motions you added on Day 1. Next, have students squat down, hop up, and squat back down again. After the last squat, have the students recite the entire Bible verse. Prompt students as needed. Repeat the activity.

✔ Text Connection: *Morning Bells* p. 91-93

Key Idea: The Pilgrims needed patience and endurance. John Howland became impatient with the storms. He went up on deck and almost lost his life.

Corresponding Music

✔ *Hide 'Em in Your Heart Vol. 2* CD - Track 2; Cassette - Side A Song: *"Encourage One Another"*

Learning the Basics

Focus: Language Arts and Math

Unit 8 - Day 3

Language Arts

Choose 3 or more words from the spelling list from Day 1. Guide students to use each of the chosen words in a sentence. Write down the sentences as the students dictate them. Underline the spelling words. Have students copy the sentences on paper. Help students check them. <u>Copywork</u>: Have students copy part of the poem *"Where Lies the Land?"*.

<u>Key Idea</u>: Practice spelling words with long 'o', 'y', or 'e' at the end.

Reading Choices

Choose **one** of the reading options listed below (see Appendix for details).

★ A phonics program
★ *Scheduled Books for Emerging Readers*
★ *Drawn into the Heart of Reading Level 2/3*

<u>Key Idea</u>: Use a step-by-step program for reading instruction.

Storytime

Read aloud the next portion of the adventure book that you selected. Take out the staircase diagram that you saved from Unit 7 - Day 3. Read aloud any problems on the diagram that are not already on a colored step. If the problem has been solved by now, have students color that step. Ask, *What was the biggest problem in the story? Why do you think that was the biggest problem? Look at the staircase diagram. Did the biggest problem happen at the beginning, the middle, or the end of the story?* Point out that the problems in a story usually build and get bigger as the story goes on, until they are finally solved.

<u>Key Idea</u>: Focus on the story element: *problem* or *conflict*.

Math Exploration

These are the concepts that are covered in this review: counting '1' - '10', writing numbers '1' - '10', writing number words 'one' - 'ten', ordinal numbers, adding and subtracting to '10', and counting up and back to complete a number sequence. Review any concepts that students had difficulty understanding. Also, complete the assigned review in the workbook listed below.

✓ <u>Text Connection</u>: *Primary Mathematics Workbook 1A* p. 71-74

<u>Key Idea</u>: Review difficult concepts.

Learning Through History

Focus: English Pilgrims Travel to America

Unit 8 - Day 4

Reading About History

Read about history in the following resource:

★ *Stories of the Pilgrims* p. 83-87

Key Idea: During the trip, it began to get cold. Many Pilgrims became sick. Priscilla and Mary told stories and played games with the children to pass the time. Two new babies were born on the voyage.

Poetry and Rhymes

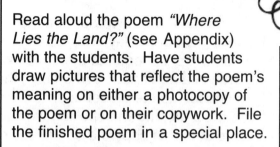

Read aloud the poem *"Where Lies the Land?"* (see Appendix) with the students. Have students draw pictures that reflect the poem's meaning on either a photocopy of the poem or on their copywork. File the finished poem in a special place.

Key Idea: Read classic poetry.

Science Exploration

Say, *Spin a pen on the floor. Now, spin yourself around several times. Which took longer to spin around, you or the pen? Why did it take you longer to spin around? You are much larger than the pen, so it takes you longer to spin around. The Earth is much larger than you, so it takes the Earth a whole day just to spin around one time. Each day lasts 24 hours. Now, count how many spins it takes you to cross a room. It takes the Earth 365 spins to go around the sun once. Each spin lasts a whole day. So, it takes the Earth a whole year to go around the Sun.*

✔ Text Connection: *God's Wonderful Works* p. 12 and 59-60

Key Idea: On the ship, some days were sunny and beautiful. Then, the days began to get colder. It was hard to be on the ship so many days.

Bible Study

Say 1 Thessalonians 5:11 with the students. Use the hand motions you added on Day 1. Say, *What does it mean to be impatient? When are some times that it is hard to wait or be patient? How can you remember to be less selfish and more patient? Who helps encourage you to be more patient?* Next, have students hop backward 5 times. After 5 hops, have the students recite the entire Bible verse. Repeat the activity.

Key Idea: The Pilgrims were getting tired of being on the ship. They worked together to help each other.

Corresponding Music

✔ *Hide 'Em in Your Heart Vol. 2*
CD - Track 2; Cassette - Side A
Song: *"Encourage One Another"*

Learning the Basics

Focus: Language Arts and Math

Unit 8 - Day 4

Language Arts

Use the spelling list from Day 1. Say each word and use it in a sentence. Have students write each word and check it with the matching word card from Day 1. Guide students to correct any mistakes. For each missed word, have students spell the word out loud clapping once each time they say a letter. <u>Copywork</u>: Have students copy part of the poem "Where Lies the Land?".

<u>Key Idea</u>: Practice spelling words with long 'o', 'y', or 'e' at the end.

Reading Choices

Choose **one** of the reading options listed below (see Appendix for details).

★ A phonics program
★ *Scheduled Books for Emerging Readers*
★ *Drawn into the Heart of Reading Level 2/3*

<u>Key Idea</u>: Use a step-by-step program for reading instruction.

Storytime

Say, *Fear of the Lord is revering the Lord and His commands and believing the Lord can turn harm into good for those who trust in Him.* Review the key verse Deuteronomy 13:4. Read aloud the next portion of the adventure book that you selected. Ask, *Did the book characters usually show reverence or fear of the Lord? Explain. Do you usually show reverence or fear of the Lord? Draw a picture showing one way that you could show more reverence or fear of the Lord. Post your picture in a place where you will see it often.*

<u>Key Idea</u>: Focus on the Godly character trait: *fear of the Lord*.

Math Exploration

These are the concepts that are covered in this review: addition and subtraction sentences, fact families, deciding when to add and when to subtract, interpreting word problems, and writing number sentences. Review any concepts that students had difficulty understanding. Also, complete the assigned review in the workbook listed below.

✔ <u>Text Connection</u>: *Primary Mathematics Workbook 1A* p. 75-78

<u>Key Idea</u>: Review difficult concepts.

Learning Through History

Focus: English Pilgrims Travel to America

Unit 8 - Day 5

Reading About History

Read the following passage from your own Bible:

★ Hebrews 11:1-16

Key Idea: Each of the people in this passage were faithful. They could not see what God had promised them, but they faithfully believed God's promises. The Pilgrims faithfully trusted God too.

Poetry and Rhymes

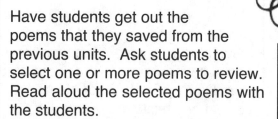

Have students get out the poems that they saved from the previous units. Ask students to select one or more poems to review. Read aloud the selected poems with the students.

Key Idea: Read classic poetry.

Geography

Get out a globe or a world map. Read Hebrews 11:8-10 and 16. Say, *A country is a nation and its territory or land. What is the name of the country where you live? Find it on the map or globe. Look on the map or globe and name the countries that border or surround the country where you live. Countries are usually divided up into states, provinces, or regions. What state, province, or region do you live in? Find it on the globe or map. Each state, province, or region usually has several big cities. A city is an important town. What city is located nearest to where you live? Find the city you named on the map or globe.*

Key Idea: Just like Abraham, the Pilgrims left one country to travel to another. They were faithful to God's plan for their lives.

Bible Study

Ask, *How does Hebrews 11:1 describe faith? In Hebrews 11:1-11, what can you learn about faith from Abel, Enoch, Noah, and Abraham? Will you always get everything you want if you are a Christian? What does Hebrews 11:13-16 teach you about faith?* Ask students to share their memory verse, 1 Thessalonians 5:11, with someone special. Suggestions for sharing the verse include saying it to another family member, saying it to someone by telephone, reciting it to a stuffed animal, or writing it to mail.

Key Idea: The Pilgrims faithfully trusted God's plan for their lives.

Corresponding Music

✔ *Hide 'Em in Your Heart Vol. 2* CD - Track 2; Cassette - Side A Song: *"Encourage One Another"*

Learning the Basics

Focus: Language Arts and Math

Unit 8 - Day 5

Language Arts

Say, *Commands are sentences that order or request you to do something. We are going to play a game of "Teacher Says". I will give you a command. If I begin the command with "Teacher Says", then you must follow the command. If I do not begin the command with "Teacher Says", you should not follow the command.* Some possible commands include: touch your toes, hop on one foot, clap your hands, stomp your left foot, spin once, reach up, do a jumping jack, run in place, rub your tummy, pull your ear, touch your knees, and pat your head. Next, have the students be the teacher and give commands for you to follow. <u>Copywork</u>: Write one command for students to copy.

<u>Key Idea</u>: Practice using commands.

Reading Choices

Choose **one** of the reading options listed below (see Appendix for details).

★ A phonics program
★ *Scheduled Books for Emerging Readers*
★ *Drawn into the Heart of Reading Level 2/3*

<u>Key Idea</u>: Use a step-by-step program for reading instruction.

Storytime

Read aloud the final portion of the adventure book that you selected. You will need to select a historical fiction book to read aloud next. Have students draw a scene from today's reading. When the drawings are complete, ask students to tell you about their pictures as a way of retelling what happened in the story.

<u>Key Idea</u>: Give students practice retelling a portion of an adventure.

Math Exploration

These are the concepts that are covered in this review: matching numbers with corresponding number words, ordinal numbers, finding one more or one less, addition and subtraction to '10', and using addition and subtraction in word problems. Review any concepts that students had difficulty understanding. Also, complete the assigned review in the workbook listed below.

✔ <u>Text Connection</u>: *Primary Mathematics Workbook 1A* p. 79-82

<u>Key Idea</u>: Review difficult concepts.

Learning Through History

Focus: Landing in America

Unit 9 - Day 1

Reading About History

Read about history in the following resource:

★ *Stories of the Pilgrims* p. 88-91

Key Idea: After 9 weeks on the *Mayflower,* the Pilgrims finally saw land. It wasn't the sunny land they had hoped to find. It was not a good place to settle.

Poetry and Rhymes

Read aloud the poem *"Maker of Heaven and Earth"* (see Appendix) to the students. Do not share the title. Ask students to suggest some titles for the poem. Share the real title. Read the poem again with the students.

"God"

Key Idea: Read and appreciate a variety of classic poetry.

Science Exploration

Tape a masking tape line around the middle of a ball or a globe. Say, *This imaginary line is called the Equator. It divides the Earth into 2 equal parts called the Northern Hemisphere and the Southern Hemisphere.* Hold the ball's or globe's 'Equator' next to a lamp with no shade. Say, *The sun's rays shine straight out to the Equator, making that part of Earth much hotter. It doesn't change seasons there, because it is so hot.* Use yarn to measure the distance from the light source to the Equator. Cut the yarn. Repeat the activity with the North and South Poles. Compare the lengths of the 3 pieces of yarn. Ask, *Why is it so cold at the North and South Poles?*

✓ Text Connection: *God's Wonderful Works* p. 34-35

Key Idea: The Pilgrims had hoped to land in a warmer climate.

Bible Study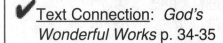

Colossians 3:23 is the memory verse for this unit. Read the verse out loud. Ask, *What does it mean to work at something heartily or with all your heart? Which things are you supposed to do heartily? Why are you supposed to work heartily in all you do? Who are you working to please?* Say the verse together 3 times. Add hand motions to help students remember the words.

Key Idea: The Pilgrims had a long, difficult voyage, but they worked heartily to find food and fuel. They planned to rest on the Sabbath day.

Corresponding Music

None this lesson

Learning the Basics

Focus: Language Arts and Math

Unit 9 - Day 1

Language Arts

Choose **either** spelling list 1 **or** 2 (see Appendix for lists). Write each spelling word on a separate index card. Guide students to study each card one at a time, flip it over, write the word on paper, flip the card back over to check the spelling, and erase and correct any mistakes.

<u>Copywork</u>: Have students copy part of *"Maker of Heaven and Earth"*.

<u>Key Idea</u>: Practice spelling words.

Reading Choices

Choose **one** of the reading options listed below (see Appendix for details).

★ A phonics program
★ *Scheduled Books for Emerging Readers*
★ *Drawn into the Heart of Reading Level 2/3*

<u>Key Idea</u>: Use a step-by-step program for reading instruction.

Storytime

Choose at least one historical fiction book to read aloud for the next 20 days of plans (see Appendix for suggested titles). To introduce the genre, *Historical Fiction*, have students act out the Pilgrims landing in America and looking for a place to live. Compare the students' portrayal to *Stories of the Pilgrims* p. 100-104. Ask, *Was the way you acted out the Pilgrims' landing more fictional or true? Historical fiction is a realistic telling of a real place and time from the past. It mixes truth with made-up details.* Read a portion of the historical fiction book you chose. Check the book summary to see which parts of the story may be true and which parts are fiction.

<u>Key Idea</u>: Introduce the genre: *Historical Fiction*.

Math Exploration

Complete the assigned lesson in the workbook listed below.

✓ <u>Text Connection</u>: *Primary Mathematics Workbook 1A* p. 83-85

<u>Key Idea</u>: Count up to '20' items by grouping them in tens and ones. Practice writing the numbers up to '20'.

Learning Through History

Focus: Landing in America

Unit 9 - Day 2

Reading About History

Read about history in the following resource:

★ *Stories of the Pilgrims* p. 92-95

Key Idea: On Monday, the Pilgrims went ashore. They worked hard to wash their clothes. The children gathered nuts and ran on the beach. By nightfall, their work was done.

Poetry and Rhymes

Read aloud the poem *"Maker of Heaven and Earth"* (see Appendix) with the students. Discuss the poem's meaning. If you choose, photocopy the poem, cut it apart, and have the students place it in the correct order.

Key Idea: Read classic poetry.

Artistic Expression

Say, *The sea star lives in saltwater on the ocean floor. It has 5 arms. Sometimes sea stars wash up on beaches near the ocean. Draw a sea star on brown, tan, or yellow paper. For help with the drawing, refer to p. 79 of* God's Wonderful Works. *Cut the sea star out. Make a mixture of half glue and half water. Paint the glue mixture on the sea star with a paintbrush. Crush dry cereal (i.e. corn flakes, shredded wheat, or square cereal pieces). Sprinkle the crushed cereal onto the sea star. Let it dry overnight.*

✓ Text Connection: *God's Wonderful Works* p. 79-80

Key Idea: The Pilgrims were on a beach by the ocean. They may have seen ocean animals like the sea star. God made each animal in His creation very special.

Bible Study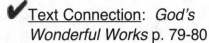

Say Colossians 3:23 while the students join in on the parts they know. Use the hand motions you added on Day 1. Say, *Name some jobs that you like to do. How well do you do those jobs? Name some jobs that you don't like to do. How well do you do those jobs? What does Col. 3:23 teach you about work?* Next, have students do 5 jumping jacks. After 5 jumping jacks, have the students recite the entire Bible verse. Prompt the students as needed. Repeat the activity.

Key Idea: The Pilgrims worked hard. Their work was not fun or easy to do.

Corresponding Music

None this lesson

Learning the Basics

Focus: Language Arts and Math

Unit 9 - Day 2

Language Arts

Use the spelling list from Day 1. Say the first spelling word. Use it in a sentence. Repeat the word. Ask students to write the word on a markerboard or a piece of paper from memory. Give students the matching word card from Day 1 to compare with their spelling. Guide students to correct any mistakes. Repeat the activity with all 10 words.
<u>Copywork</u>: Have students copy part of *"Maker of Heaven and Earth"*.

<u>Key Idea</u>: Practice spelling words with long 'a', ending in silent 'e'.

Reading Choices

Choose **one** of the reading options listed below (see Appendix for details).

★ A phonics program
★ *Scheduled Books for Emerging Readers*
★ *Drawn into the Heart of Reading Level 2/3*

<u>Key Idea</u>: Use a step-by-step program for reading instruction.

Storytime

Read aloud the next portion of the historical fiction book that you selected. Without looking back at the story, model retelling or narrating the part of the historical fiction book that you read today to the students. Remember to tell the most important points and to add details from the story to the retelling without overwhelming the students. After the retelling, ask, *What is the most important place in the story?* On paper, write a one-sentence answer that reflects the students' responses. Have students copy the sentence on paper.

<u>Key Idea</u>: Model retelling a story from a single reading.

Math Exploration

Give students 15 items (i.e. dry macaroni, beans, or blocks). Tell students to count the items they have been given. Say, *Now, I will show you a faster way to count your items. Make a group of 10 items. Place the group of 10 items in a ziplock bag. Point to the bag and say, '10'. Continue counting on from '10' to see how many items you have in all (i.e. '11', '12', '13', '14', '15').* Repeat the activity with various numbers of items up to '20'.

✔ <u>Text Connection</u>: *Primary Mathematics Workbook 1A* p. 86-87

<u>Key Idea</u>: Count up to '20' items by grouping them into 'tens' and 'ones'. Practice writing numbers up to '20'.

Learning Through History

Focus: Landing in America

Unit 9 - Day 3

Reading About History

Read about history in the following resource:

Stories of the Pilgrims p. 96-98

Key Idea: The Pilgrims continued to look for a place to live. The next day, the men saw some Indians. The Indians did not want the gifts that the Pilgrims offered them.

Poetry and Rhymes

Read aloud the poem *"Maker of Heaven and Earth"* (see Appendix) with the students. Read the poem aloud a second time, pausing after each line or two for students to add their own actions to the poem. The actions should make sense with the poem.

Key Idea: Read and appreciate a variety of classic poetry.

Science Exploration

Tape a masking tape line across one end of a table to be land. Mark a spot on the tape with a red 'X'. Give students a marble or a small wadded up ball of tinfoil to be a ship sailing on the ocean. The table is the ocean. Have students stand at the opposite end of the table from the tape and blow the ship across the ocean to land on the red 'X'. Ask, *Did you land on the red 'X'? Why, or why not?* Repeat the activity, but this time while the students are blowing the ship, you blow from the side, changing the direction of the ship. Ask, *Did you land on the red 'X'? Why, or why not?*

✔ Text Connection: *God's Wonderful Works* p. 38

Key Idea: The storm winds forced the Pilgrims to the north where it was colder. The Pilgrims landed in Massachusetts instead of in Virginia.

Bible Study

Say Colossians 3:23 with the students. Use the hand motions you added on Day 1. Next, have students hop on their left foot until you say, *Freeze*. After they 'freeze', have the students recite the entire Bible verse. Prompt students as needed. Have students switch to their right foot, and repeat the activity.

✔ Text Connection: *Morning Bells* p. 88-90

Key Idea: The Pilgrims worked hard to choose the right place to settle. It was an important decision.

Corresponding Music

None this lesson

Learning the Basics

Focus: Language Arts and Math

Unit 9 - Day 3

Language Arts

Using the spelling list from Day 1, choose 3 or more words that the students need to practice. Guide students to use each of the words that you chose in a sentence. On a markerboard or a piece of paper, write down the sentences as the students dictate them to you. Underline the spelling word in each sentence. Have the students copy the sentences on a piece of paper. Help students check their sentences and correct any mistakes.

Copywork: Have students copy part of the poem *"Maker of Heaven and Earth"*.

Key Idea: Practice spelling words with long 'a', ending in silent 'e'.

Reading Choices

Choose **one** of the reading options listed below (see Appendix for details).

★ A phonics program
★ *Scheduled Books for Emerging Readers*
★ *Drawn into the Heart of Reading Level 2/3*

Key Idea: Use a step-by-step program for reading instruction.

Storytime

Read aloud the next portion of the historical fiction book that you selected. Say, *The setting of a story is the place where the story happens. What places seem to be important in this story? Have you ever been to any places like the ones in the book? Explain. Does the story seem to be happening now or during some other time in the past? How can you tell?*

Key Idea: Introduce the story element: *setting*.

Math Exploration

Complete the assigned lesson in the workbook listed below.

✔ Text Connection: *Primary Mathematics Workbook 1A* p. 88-90

Key Idea: Complete addition number sentences by finding the missing sum.

Learning Through History

Focus: Landing in America

Unit 9 - Day 4

Reading About History

Read about history in the following resource:

Stories of the Pilgrims p. 99-101

Key Idea: The Pilgrim men found a deserted Indian village. They saw many wigwams. The men found Indian corn and took some back to the *Mayflower*. The Pilgrims were almost out of food.

Poetry and Rhymes

Read aloud the poem *"Maker of Heaven and Earth"* (see Appendix) with the students. Have students draw pictures that reflect the poem's meaning on either a photocopy of the poem or on their copywork. File the finished poem in a special place.

Key Idea: Read and appreciate a variety of classic poetry.

Geography

On a piece of paper draw 4 rows of 4 footprints in a grid formation. At the end of the top row, draw a basket of corn. In the bottom corner, make a compass rose labeled north, south, east, west. Say, *You are a Pilgrim. You will be following the Indian footprints to get to the corn. I will tell you which direction to go. To start, color the footprint on the bottom right hand corner. Now, go one footprint north, and color it in. Next, travel two footprints west, and color them in. Then, follow two footprints north, and color them in. Now, go two footprints east, and color them in. You should have reached the corn!* Make another grid and play again, having the students give directions instead.

Key Idea: The Pilgrims saw many Indian footprints. God helped the Pilgrims find an Indian village.

Bible Study

Say Colossians 3:23 with the students. Use the hand motions you added on Day 1. Ask, *Who should you work to please? What does it mean to dawdle or be idle? Is it a sin to be lazy? How do you know? How can Colossians 3:23 help you be a hard worker?* Next, have the students do 5 sit-ups. After 5 sit-ups, have the students recite the entire Bible verse.

Key Idea: The Pilgrims knew it would take hard work to settle in the new land.

Corresponding Music

None this lesson

Learning the Basics

Focus: Language Arts and Math

Unit 9 - Day 4

Language Arts

Use the spelling list from Day 1. Say each word and use it in a sentence. Have students write each word and check it with the matching word card from Day 1. Guide students to correct any mistakes. Add several inches of soapy water to a sink. For each missed word, have students "write" the word with their index finger in the soapy water.
<u>Copywork</u>: Have students copy part of the poem *"Maker of Heaven and Earth"*.

<u>Key Idea</u>: Practice spelling words with long 'a', ending in silent 'e'.

Reading Choices

Choose **one** of the reading options listed below (see Appendix for details).

★ A phonics program
★ *Scheduled Books for Emerging Readers*
★ *Drawn into the Heart of Reading Level 2/3*

<u>Key Idea</u>: Use a step-by-step program for reading instruction.

Storytime

Say, *Faith is having a strong belief that stands firm in the face of trouble.* Read aloud the key verse 2 Corinthians 4:18 to illustrate *faith*. List some ways that you are faithful. Then, have students list some ways that they are faithful.

Read aloud the next portion of the historical fiction book that you selected. Then, ask, *How do the characters show faithfulness? What could the characters do differently to show more faith?*

<u>Key Idea</u>: Introduce the Godly character trait: *faith*.

Math Exploration

Call out a number between '1' - '20' (i.e. '14'). Have students count on by ones from that number until you say, *Stop* (i.e. '15', '16', '17', '18', '19', etc.). Repeat the activity by calling out different numbers as a starting point. Then, vary the activity by calling out a number from '1' - '20' and having students count backward by ones instead (i.e. '14', '13', '12', '11', '10', etc.).

✔ <u>Text Connection</u>: *Primary Mathematics Workbook 1A* p. 91-92

<u>Key Idea</u>: Find the missing numbers in a numerical sequence.

Learning Through History

Focus: Landing in America

Unit 9 - Day 5

Reading About History

Read the following passage from your own Bible:

★ Nehemiah 4:6-23

<u>Key Idea</u>: God called Nehemiah to rebuild the wall in Jerusalem. Just like Nehemiah, the Pilgrims needed to build a protected town. The Pilgrims were willing to work hard at the job they felt God had called them to do, just like Nehemiah did.

History Activity

Use blocks or snap-together bricks to build a rectangular foundation for a wall. Say, *Your job is to build a wall on my foundation. Your wall must be 3 bricks high all the way around. When I say, "Go", you will want to build as fast as you can. My job is to attack the wall and slow down your building. Before I attack, I have to pound the floor 10 times, then I can knock down a small part of your wall. When you see an attack, stop building, make a trumpet sound, and go rebuild the part of the wall that I knocked down. Then, you can go back to building the rest of the wall, until I attack again.* Continue playing until the wall has been built 3 blocks high. Ask, *Did it take a long time to build the wall this way?*

<u>Key Idea</u>: It is hard to build a wall when you are worried about an attack.

Poetry and Rhymes

Have students get out the poems that they saved from the previous units. Ask students to select one or more poems to review. Read aloud the selected poems with the students.

<u>Key Idea</u>: Read classic poetry.

Bible Study

Ask, *In Nehemiah 4:6, how did the people feel about their work? In Nehemiah 4:7-9, what did the people do when there was trouble? What can you learn from Nehemiah 4:14-18 about God's protection when you do what He asks? In Nehemiah 4:19-23, what can you learn about working for God?* Ask students to share their memory verse, Colossians 3:23, with someone special. Suggestions for sharing the verse include saying it to another family member, saying it to someone by telephone, reciting it to a stuffed animal, or writing it to mail.

<u>Key Idea</u>: The Pilgrims worked hard and trusted God.

Corresponding Music

None this lesson

Learning the Basics

Focus: Language Arts and Math

Unit 9 - Day 5

Language Arts

Say, *Name two of your favorite things.* On a markerboard or a piece of paper, write 2 exclamatory sentences about the students' favorite things (i.e. We are having pepperoni pizza tonight! I can't wait to go swimming!). Ask, *What does each sentence do? What feeling is being shown in each sentence? What do you notice at the beginning of each sentence? What do you see at the end of each sentence?* Say, *Sentences that show strong feeling and end in an exclamation point are called exclamations.* <u>Copywork</u>: Ask the students to dictate an exclamation about another favorite thing. Write it for the students to copy.

<u>Key Idea</u>: Introduce exclamations.

Reading Choices

Choose **one** of the reading options listed below (see Appendix for details).

★ A phonics program

★ *Scheduled Books for Emerging Readers*

★ *Drawn into the Heart of Reading Level 2/3*

<u>Key Idea</u>: Use a step-by-step program for reading instruction.

Storytime

Read aloud a short portion of the historical fiction book that you selected. Give students a chance to orally retell the portion of today's story that you read aloud. Prompt students after the retelling to fill in missing details by using leading questions that begin with these words: *Who? What? When? Where? Why? How?*

<u>Key Idea</u>: Give students practice retelling a portion of a historical fiction book.

Math Exploration

On paper, write the numbers '1' - '20' in a row. Make three cards that say 'greater' and three that say 'smaller'. Shuffle the cards. Place them facedown. Give students 20 markers (i.e. coins, beans, blocks). Say, *Point to two numbers on the paper. Turn over the top card. Place a marker on the number that matches the card. For example, if you point to '19' and '11' and turn over a card that says 'smaller', place a marker on '11' because it is smaller than '19'.* Play until all 20 numbers are covered.

✓ <u>Text Connection</u>: *Primary Mathematics Workbook 1A* p. 93-94

<u>Key Idea</u>: Compare numbers using the concepts greater and smaller.

Learning Through History

Focus: Pilgrims Settle in Plymouth

Unit 10 - Day 1

Reading About History

Read about history in the following resource:

★ *Stories of the Pilgrims* p. 102 - 105

Key Idea: Francis Billington was a little boy who often got into mischief. One afternoon he got into the ship's powder room. He fired off a loaded musket that could have blown the ship to pieces. God was watching over the Pilgrims to keep them safe.

Poetry and Rhymes

Read aloud the poem *"What Are Heavy?"* (see Appendix) to the students. Do not share the title. Ask students to suggest some titles for the poem. Share the real title. Read the poem again with the students. "God"

Key Idea: Read and appreciate a variety of classic poetry.

Artistic Expression

Cut a large oval out of a 9" x 12" piece of red paper. Draw a large 'X' in the center of the oval. Then, draw one vertical line that goes through the center of the 'X'. Help students make cuts in the middle of the oval by following the lines you drew. Show students how to roll each resulting triangle piece back from the center by curling the paper around a pencil. Say, *Glue the oval to a black or blue sheet of paper. Write, "BOOM", on the red oval to stand for the explosion on the boat. Inside the oval, glue a white cotton ball to be Francis' scared, white face. Use a marker to dot 2 eyes and an 'O'-shaped mouth on the cotton ball.*

Key Idea: Francis was scared when the gun powder went off. God was watching over him.

Bible Study

Psalm 118:1 is the memory verse for this unit. Read the verse out loud. Ask, *Who does this verse say you should thank? Why should you thank the Lord? What does it mean to endure? How long does this verse say that the Lord's mercy and love will endure? Do you deserve this? Why?* Say the verse together 3 times. Add hand motions to help students remember the words.

Key Idea: The Pilgrims thanked the Lord for saving the *Mayflower*.

Corresponding Music

✔ *Hide 'Em in Your Heart Vol. 2* CD - Track 14; Cassette - Side B Song: *"Give Thanks to the Lord"*

Learning the Basics

Focus: Language Arts and Math

Unit 10 - Day 1

Language Arts

Choose **either** spelling list 1 **or** 2 (see Appendix for lists). Write each spelling word on a separate index card. Guide students to study each card one at a time, flip it over, write the word on paper, flip the card back over to check the spelling, and erase and correct any mistakes.

Copywork: Have students copy part of the poem *"What Are Heavy?"*.

Key Idea: Practice spelling words.

Reading Choices

Choose **one** of the reading options listed below (see Appendix for details).

★ A phonics program

★ *Scheduled Books for Emerging Readers*

★ *Drawn into the Heart of Reading Level 2/3*

Key Idea: Use a step-by-step program for reading instruction.

Storytime

Say, *List the important characters in the story. Did these people really live? When and where does the story take place?* If possible, show the location on a globe or a map. *What makes this book historical fiction, rather than fiction?* Point out that historical fiction often includes stories that have been retold for generations. In the retelling, the clothing, words, or characters are no longer completely accurate. Historical fiction also may include characters that have been entirely made-up. Read aloud the next portion of the historical fiction book that you selected. Pace your reading to complete the book during the next 15 days of plans.

Key Idea: Build anticipation for the next part of the historical fiction book.

Math Exploration

Divide a piece of paper in half. Give students 20 counters (i.e. buttons, raisins, or dry cereal). Write "9 + 6 = ____" on a markerboard or a paper. Have students place '9' counters on one half of the paper and '6' counters on the other half to model the addition sentence. For faster adding, show students how to move the counters to create a set of 10 on one half of the paper (i.e. move one counter from the '6' over to the '9' to make '10'). Then, count on from '10' to get the total. Repeat the activity using different addition sentences.

✔ Text Connection: *Primary Mathematics Workbook 1A* p. 95-96

Key Idea: Add two numbers by grouping the tens first.

Learning Through History

Focus: Pilgrims Settle in Plymouth

Unit 10 - Day 2

Reading About History

Read about history in the following resource:

★ *Stories of the Pilgrims* p. 106-109

Key Idea: It was getting cold, and still the Pilgrims searched for a place to settle. One morning, Indians attacked the search party. The Pilgrims' muskets drove the Indians away.

Poetry and Rhymes

Read aloud the poem *"What Are Heavy?"* (see Appendix) with the students. Discuss the poem's meaning. If you choose, photocopy the poem, cut it apart, and have the students place it in the correct order.

Key Idea: Read classic poetry.

Geography

Say, *A bay is a small area of water partly surrounded by land. A bay that gives shelter to ships is called a harbor. On a map or a globe, find Boston, Massachusetts. Look at the arm of land that comes out into the ocean near Boston. What bay do you notice inside that arm of land? The city of Plymouth is located south of Boston. It is in the Cape Cod Bay area. Point to the spot on the globe or map where you would find Plymouth. Plymouth is located on another small bay called Plymouth Bay.* Help students sketch the outline of Cape Cod Bay and Plymouth Bay using the map or globe as a reference. Guide students to add the cities of Boston and Plymouth to their sketch.

Key Idea: The Pilgrims were still looking for the right place to settle.

Bible Study

Say Psalm 118:1 while the students join in on the parts they know. Use the hand motions you added on Day 1. Say, *Name some things that you can thank God for giving you. If you are a Christian, will God always make sure that good things happen to you? Why not? What does Psalm 118:1 promise you?* Next, have students do 3 push-ups. After 3 push-ups, have the students recite the entire Bible verse. Repeat the activity several times.

Key Idea: The Pilgrims thanked God for keeping them safe.

Corresponding Music

✓ *Hide 'Em in Your Heart Vol. 2*
CD - Track 14; Cassette - Side B
Song: *"Give Thanks to the Lord"*

Learning the Basics

Focus: Language Arts and Math

Unit 10 - Day 2

Language Arts

Use the spelling list from Day 1. Say the first spelling word. Use it in a sentence. Repeat the word. Ask students to write the word on a markerboard or a piece of paper from memory. Give students the matching word card from Day 1 to compare with their spelling. Guide students to correct any mistakes. Repeat the activity with all 10 words. <u>Copywork</u>: Have students copy part of the poem *"What Are Heavy?"*.

<u>Key Idea</u>: Practice spelling words with long 'i', ending in silent 'e'.

Reading Choices

Choose **one** of the reading options listed below (see Appendix for details).

★ A phonics program
★ *Scheduled Books for Emerging Readers*
★ *Drawn into the Heart of Reading Level 2/3*

<u>Key Idea</u>: Use a step-by-step program for reading instruction.

Storytime

Read aloud the next portion of the historical fiction book that you selected. Without looking back at the book, begin retelling or narrating the part of the story that you read today. After a short time, tap the student and say, *Your turn.* The student should pick up the narration where you left off. After a short time, the student should tap you and say, *Your turn.* Continue taking turns narrating in this manner until today's reading has been retold. Then, say, *Name one thing that you learned about the main character today.* Write it on paper for students to copy.

<u>Key Idea</u>: Take turns retelling a story from a single reading.

Math Exploration

Complete the assigned lesson in the workbook listed below.

✓ <u>Text Connection</u>: *Primary Mathematics Workbook 1A* p. 97-98

<u>Key Idea</u>: Add two numbers by making a group of tens first and then counting on to find the total.

Learning Through History

Focus: Pilgrims Settle in Plymouth

Unit 10 - Day 3

Reading About History

Read about history in the following resource:

★ *Stories of the Pilgrims* p. 110-112

Key Idea: As the *Mayflower* sailed along the shore a winter storm came up. The Pilgrims were blessed to land on an island. They sailed on and finally found a place to settle.

Poetry and Rhymes

Read aloud the poem *"What Are Heavy?"* (see Appendix) with the students. Read the poem aloud a second time, pausing after each line or two for students to add actions to the poem. The actions should make sense with the poem.

Key Idea: Read classic poetry.

Science Exploration

Have students use clay or playdough to build a model in the sink of the land under the ocean. Refer to *God's Wonderful Works* p. 47 as needed. Say, *First, make the tallest part of the land with a flat top at sea level. Next, make the land angle down to a shelf that is further out and below sea level. Last, make a steep slide that slants down to the sink bottom which is the ocean floor. Add water to the sink until your model is covered. Fashion a boat out of aluminum foil and sail it into your bay. Did your boat get stuck? Why would it be important to check and see how deep the bay is?*

✔ Text Connection: *God's Wonderful Works* p. 47-48

Key Idea: The Pilgrims measured the depth of the water in the bay to be sure that large ships could dock with supplies.

Bible Study

Say Psalm 118:1 with the students. Use the hand motions you added on Day 1. Next, have students skip around the room until you say, *Freeze*. After they 'freeze', have the students recite the entire Bible verse. Have students repeat the activity.

✔ Text Connection: *Morning Bells* p. 67-69

Key Idea: The Pilgrims knew that the Lord was with them always. They trusted the Lord to keep them safe and help them find a new home.

Corresponding Music

✔ *Hide 'Em in Your Heart Vol. 2* CD - Track 14; Cassette - Side B Song: *"Give Thanks to the Lord"*

Learning the Basics

Focus: Language Arts and Math

Unit 10 - Day 3

Language Arts

Using the spelling list from Day 1, choose 3 or more words that the students need to practice. Guide students to use each of the words that you chose in a sentence. On a markerboard or a piece of paper, write down the sentences as the students dictate them to you. Underline the spelling word in each sentence. Have the students copy the sentences on a piece of paper. Help students check their sentences and correct any mistakes.

Copywork: Have students copy part of the poem *"What Are Heavy?"*.

Key Idea: Practice spelling words with the long 'i', ending in silent 'e'.

Reading Choices

Choose **one** of the reading options listed below (see Appendix for details).

★ A phonics program

★ *Scheduled Books for Emerging Readers*

★ *Drawn into the Heart of Reading Level 2/3*

Key Idea: Use a step-by-step program for reading instruction.

Storytime

Read aloud the next portion of the historical fiction book that you selected. Ask, *How is the place (or setting) in the story different from where you live?* Fold a piece of paper in half. On one half, have students draw a picture of where they live. On the other half, have students draw a picture of the setting of the story.

Key Idea: Focus on the story element: *setting*.

Math Exploration

Divide a piece of paper in half. Label the left side 'tens' and the right side 'ones'. Give students 15 counters (i.e. crayons, paperclips, or markers). Guide students to make a set of 10 counters on the 'tens' side of the paper and place the leftover counters on the 'ones' side. Tell students to add '3' more counters to the 'ones'. Help students add the counters to see how many there are in all. Note: Count the '10' first and then count on. Repeat the activity with different numbers of counters.

✔ Text Connection: *Primary Mathematics Workbook 1A* p. 99-101

Key Idea: Group numbers into 'tens' and 'ones' before adding.

Learning Through History

Focus: Pilgrims Settle in Plymouth

Unit 10 - Day 4

Reading About History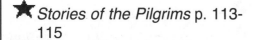

Read about history in the following resource:

★ *Stories of the Pilgrims* p. 113-115

Key Idea: The Pilgrims came ashore to see the place where their town would be built. Mary Chilton stepped out on Plymouth Rock. The rock is still there in Plymouth Bay today.

Poetry and Rhymes

Read aloud the poem *"What Are Heavy?"* (see Appendix) with the students. Have students draw pictures that reflect the poem's meaning on either a photocopy of the poem or on their copywork. File the finished poem in a special place.

Key Idea: Read classic poetry.

Science Exploration

Say, *God designed water to move in a cycle to continually provide Earth with the water it needs. To see how the water cycle works, add a 1/2 cup of water to a ziplock bag. Add several drops of blue food coloring to the water. Squeeze the air out of the bag and seal it tightly. Tape the bag to the inside of a window in a sunny location. Watch throughout the day for a cloud to appear in the bag over the water. Later, watch for the cloud to drip water down inside the bag as if it was raining.*

✔ Text Connection: *God's Wonderful Works* p. 32 and 46

Key Idea: The Pilgrims made sure that there was fresh water near their new home. Humans cannot survive long without fresh water to drink.

Bible Study

Say Psalm 118:1 with the students. Use the hand motions you added on Day 1. Ask, *What are some things that you fear? Is Jesus always with you? Do you always feel like Jesus is with you? If you don't feel Jesus, does that mean that He is not there? How do you know that Jesus is always with you?* Next, have students run in place. When you say, *Freeze,* have the students stop and recite the entire Bible verse. Repeat the activity several times.

Key Idea: The Pilgrims knew God was with them all of the time.

Corresponding Music

✔ *Hide 'Em in Your Heart Vol. 2* CD - Track 14; Cassette - Side B Song: *"Give Thanks to the Lord"*

Learning the Basics

Focus: Language Arts and Math

Unit 10 - Day 4

Language Arts

Use the spelling list from Day 1. Say each word and use it in a sentence. Have students write each word and check it with the matching word card from Day 1. Guide students to correct any mistakes. For each missed word, have students jump in place and spell the word out loud, jumping each time they say a letter.

Copywork: Have students copy part of the poem *"What Are Heavy?"*.

Key Idea: Practice spelling words with long 'i', ending in silent 'e'.

Reading Choices

Choose **one** of the reading options listed below (see Appendix for details).

★ A phonics program
★ *Scheduled Books for Emerging Readers*
★ *Drawn into the Heart of Reading Level 2/3*

Key Idea: Use a step-by-step program for reading instruction.

Storytime

Say, *Faith is having a strong belief that stands firm in the face of trouble.* Read aloud the key verse 2 Corinthians 4:18. Read aloud Joshua 14:6-14. Ask, *How did Caleb's actions show faith?* Read aloud the next portion of the historical fiction book that you selected. Then, ask, *How does the main character in the historical fiction book show faith? What would the Biblical character, Caleb, do differently from the character in your book?*

Key Idea: Focus on the Godly character trait: *faith*.

Math Exploration

Divide a piece of paper in half. Label the left side 'tens' and the right side 'ones'. Give students 16 snack pieces (i.e. marshmallows, fruit bits, dry cereal pieces). Guide students to make a set of 10 snacks on the 'tens' side of the paper and place the leftover snacks on the 'ones' side. Tell students to subtract '4' snacks from the 'ones' side by eating them. Help them count the remaining snacks to see how many are left. Note: Count the '10', first, and then count on. Repeat the activity with different numbers of snacks.

✔ Text Connection: *Primary Mathematics Workbook 1A* p. 102-104

Key Idea: Group numbers into 'tens' and 'ones' before subtracting.

Learning Through History

Focus: Pilgrims Settle in Plymouth

Unit 10 - Day 5

Reading About History

Read the following passage from your own Bible:

★ Psalm 40:1-5

Key Idea: Just like David in this Psalm, the Pilgrims waited patiently for the Lord to show them what to do. God gave them a place to settle. Like David, they praised God and put their trust in Him.

Poetry and Rhymes

Have students get out the poems that they saved from the previous units. Ask students to select one or more poems to review. Read aloud the selected poems with the students.

Key Idea: Read classic poetry.

History Activity

Reread Psalm 40:1-3 out loud. Say, *Let's play a game to help you practice waiting patiently like David. The goal of the game is for you to get from one end of the house or yard to the other end. To start, you must kneel and wait until I say, "Go". Then, hustle forward until I say, "Stop". When you stop, you must kneel and sing one verse of the song "God is So Good". Then, you must wait patiently until I say, "Go", again.* Play until the students reach the opposite end of the house or yard. Wait 1-5 minutes each time before you say, *Go*. Ask, *Was it hard to wait? Why? Is it hard to wait patiently for the Lord sometimes? Why? What can we learn about waiting from David?*

Key Idea: Sometimes it is hard to wait upon the Lord. But, He knows best.

Bible Study

Ask, *In Psalm 40:1, how did David wait for the Lord? Is it hard to be patient? In Psalm 40:2-3 what does God do for David? What are some things that you've waited for? What blessings did God give you when you were patient? Why might the Lord make you wait for some things?* Ask students to share their memory verse, Psalm 118:1, with someone special. Suggestions for sharing the verse include saying it to another family member, saying it to someone by telephone, reciting it to a stuffed animal, or writing it to mail.

Key Idea: David waited patiently on the Lord, and you can too.

Corresponding Music

✓ *Hide 'Em in Your Heart Vol. 2*
CD - Track 14; Cassette - Side B
Song: *"Give Thanks to the Lord"*

Learning the Basics

Focus: Language Arts and Math

Unit 10 - Day 5

Language Arts

Give each student an index card. Guide students to make a period on one side of their card and an exclamation point on the other side of their card. Say, *I will read a sentence. If it is an exclamation, jump up, wave the exclamation point side of the card, and shout, "Yahoo!". If the sentence is a statement, show the period side of the card, stretch and yawn, and say, "Ho-hum".* Read the following sentences: It's my birthday today! It is time for lunch. I love ice cream! It's a beautiful day! Today is Monday. I have a watch. I'm scared! I'm worried about the storm! It is bedtime. My pencil is red. I lost my favorite book! My dog is fluffy.
<u>Copywork</u>: Write a sentence for students to copy and add a '!' or a '.'

<u>Key Idea</u>: Practice '!' and '.'

Reading Choices

Choose **one** of the reading options listed below (see Appendix for details).

★ A phonics program
★ *Scheduled Books for Emerging Readers*
★ *Drawn into the Heart of Reading Level 2/3*

<u>Key Idea</u>: Use a step-by-step program for reading instruction.

Storytime

Read aloud a short portion of the historical fiction book that you selected. Give students a chance to orally retell the portion of today's story that you read aloud. Prompt students as needed using the following leading words: *First..., Next..., Then..., Last...*

<u>Key Idea</u>: Give students practice retelling a portion of a historical fiction book.

Math Exploration

Complete the assigned lesson in the workbook listed below.

✔ <u>Text Connection</u>: *Primary Mathematics Workbook 1A* p. 105-107

<u>Key Idea</u>: Group a number into 'tens' and 'ones' prior to subtracting.

Learning Through History

Focus: Pilgrims Build Houses at Plymouth

Unit 11 - Day 1

Reading About History

Read about history in the following resource:

★ *American Pioneers and Patriots* p. 30 and 38

Key Idea: After the Pilgrims decided to settle at Plymouth, they began building houses. They did not know how to build log cabins, so they built board houses.

Poetry and Rhymes

Read aloud the poem *"Don't Give Up"* (see Appendix) to the students. Do not share the title. Ask students to suggest some titles for the poem. Share the real title. Read the poem again with the students.

Key Idea: Read and appreciate a variety of classic poetry.

Geography

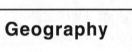

Say, *Look on the map on p. 27 of American Pioneers and Patriots. Which explorer sailed closest to the area where the Pilgrims settled in Massachusetts? What country did John Cabot sail from in 1497? Trace the path of Drake's voyage in 1578 with your finger. Sir Francis Drake was an English explorer that sailed around the world, just like the Spanish explorer Magellan did in 1521. Compare Drake's route on p. 27 with Magellan's route on p. viii. What differences do you notice in the routes that they took? Drake sailed up the coast of North America, while Magellan curved more west across the Pacific Ocean.*

Key Idea: The Pilgrims were not the first people to arrive at Plymouth Bay. Indians and explorers had been there many years before.

Bible Study

Psalm 143:10 is the memory verse for this unit. Read the verse out loud. Ask, *In Psalm 143:10, what does 'will' mean? Whose will are you supposed to follow? Why should you pray for God's will to be done, instead of your own? Who does this verse say will lead you? If you are willing to follow, where will the Spirit lead you?* Say the verse together 3 times. Add hand motions to help students remember the words.

Key Idea: The Pilgrims wanted to follow God's will for their lives. They prayed for Him to guide them.

Corresponding Music

None this lesson

Learning the Basics

Focus: Language Arts and Math

Unit 11 - Day 1

Language Arts

Choose **either** spelling list **1 or** 2 (see Appendix for lists). Write each spelling word on a separate index card. Guide students to study each card one at a time, flip it over, write the word from memory on paper, flip the card back over to check the spelling, and erase and correct any mistakes.

<u>Copywork</u>: Have students copy part of the poem *"Don't Give Up"*.

<u>Key Idea</u>: Practice spelling words with long 'o', ending in silent 'e'.

Reading Choices

Choose **one** of the reading options listed below (see Appendix for details).

★ A phonics program

★ *Scheduled Books for Emerging Readers*

★ *Drawn into the Heart of Reading Level 2/3*

<u>Key Idea</u>: Use a step-by-step program for reading instruction.

Storytime

Say, *Choose one character from the story. What things does this character do that you think are right? What things does this character do that you think are wrong? Who do you know that reminds you of this character?*

Read aloud the next portion of the historical fiction book that you selected. Pace your reading to complete the book during the next 10 days of plans.

<u>Key Idea</u>: Set a purpose for reading the next part of the historical fiction book.

Math Exploration

Tape a long strip of masking tape on the floor and number it from '1' - '20' to be a number line. Give the students a toy car. Write "6 + 11 = ____" on a markerboard or piece of paper. To add, instruct students to place their car on the '11' and drive it down the number line '6' more spots to find the total. Point out that it is easier to start with the larger number when adding, so you don't have to count on as far. Repeat the activity with different addition sentences that have sums less than '20'.

✔ <u>Text Connection</u>: *Primary Mathematics Workbook 1A* p. 108

<u>Key Idea</u>: Add by counting on from the larger number.

Learning Through History

Focus: Pilgrims Build Houses at Plymouth

Unit 11 - Day 2

Reading About History

Read about history in the following resource:

★ *American Pioneers and Patriots* p. 31-32

Key Idea: Thomas wanted to help his father and the other men as they cut down the trees. But, he kept getting in the way. The men were in a hurry to get the houses built.

Poetry and Rhymes

Read aloud the poem *"Don't Give Up"* (see Appendix) with the students. Discuss the poem's meaning. If you choose, photocopy the poem, cut it apart, and have the students place it in the correct order.

Key Idea: Read and appreciate a variety of classic poetry.

Science Exploration

Say, *The Pilgrims used axes as wedges to split the wood of the trees apart. Let's look at other wedges. A doorstop is used to wedge or hold a door open.* Slide a triangular-shaped block under a door to demonstrate. Say, *The blades of a scissors are wedges. They cut by wedging the paper apart.* Cut a piece of paper to demonstrate. Say, *The slide on a zipper has 2 wedges in it. When you zip up a zipper, the wedges force the teeth in the zipper together. When you unzip a zipper, the wedges force the teeth apart.* Use a zipper to demonstrate. Ask, *How would you describe a wedge?*

✔ Text Connection: *God's Wonderful Works* p. 100 and 111

Key Idea: As his father was cutting trees, Thomas was startled by a porcupine. He thought it was Indians.

Bible Study

Say Psalm 143:10 while the students join in on the parts they know. Use the hand motions you added on Day 1. Ask, *Name some times that you have done what you wanted instead of what God wanted. What happened? Is it always easy to do God's will? How can you do what God wants you to do?* Next, have students do 5 toe touches. After 5 toe touches, have the students recite the entire Bible verse. Prompt the students as needed. Repeat the activity.

Key Idea: Thomas wanted to help. But, he did what his father asked.

Corresponding Music

None this lesson

Learning the Basics

Focus: Language Arts and Math

Unit 11 - Day 2

Language Arts

Use the spelling list from Day 1. Say the first spelling word. Use it in a sentence. Repeat the word. Ask students to write the word on a paper or a markerboard from memory. Give students the matching word card from Day 1 to compare with their spelling. Guide students to correct any mistakes. Repeat the activity with all 10 words. <u>Copywork</u>: Have students copy part of the poem *"Don't Give Up".*

<u>Key Idea</u>: Practice spelling words.

Reading Choices

Choose **one** of the reading options listed below (see Appendix for details).

★ A phonics program
★ *Scheduled Books for Emerging Readers*
★ *Drawn into the Heart of Reading Level 2/3*

<u>Key Idea</u>: Use a step-by-step program for reading instruction.

Storytime

Read aloud the next portion of the historical fiction book that you selected. Without looking back at the story, write a retelling of the part of the story that you read today leaving blanks in place of key words (i.e. _____, _____, and _____ lived in a cabin in the _____. They had a dog named _____. The family worked hard on their _____. One day in _____, a storm came howling across the pairie. It was very _____.). Key words can be names, places, descriptive words, times of day, seasons, etc. Work with the students to reread the written narration and fill in the missing words.

<u>Key Idea</u>: Model retelling a story from a single reading.

Math Exploration

Place several handfuls of an item in a bowl (i.e. dry macaroni, small cubes, or plastic counters). Tell students to take one handful of items out of the bowl and lay them on the table. Guide students to count the items and write the total on a markerboard or a piece of paper. Say, *Write the number that would be one more than the total. Write the number that is one less than the total.* Repeat the activity, but this time ask students to write numbers that are two more or two less than the total.

✔ <u>Text Connection</u>: *Primary Mathematics Workbook 1A* p. 109

<u>Key Idea</u>: Practice counting on or subtracting by one or two.

Learning Through History

Focus: Pilgrims Build Houses at Plymouth

Unit 11 - Day 3

Reading About History

Read about history in the following resource:

★ *American Pioneers and Patriots* p. 33-34

Key Idea: Thomas wanted to help the men. No matter what he did, he always seemed to be getting in the way. It didn't seem like he could do anything right.

Poetry and Rhymes

Read aloud the poem *"Don't Give Up"* (see Appendix) with the students. Read the poem aloud a second time, pausing after each line or two for students to add actions to the poem. The actions should make sense with the poem.

Key Idea: Read classic poetry.

Artistic Expression

Help students make oiled paper window coverings. Cut out a square of paper from a paper bag. Lay the paper on a sheet of waxed paper to keep the work surface clean. Guide students to blot cooking oil on the paper bag using cotton balls or paper towels. Have students hold the oiled paper up to a sunny window to see how the light shines through. Lay the oiled paper on the waxed paper to dry. You may also have students use notched Lincoln Logs to build a house. They may cut and tape oiled paper in place of the windows of the house that they build.

✔ Text Connection: *God's Wonderful Works* p. 133

Key Idea: Thomas was having a hard day. He accidentally cut his skin with his knife. Then, he shot an arrow through a new, oiled paper window.

Bible Study

Say Psalm 143:10 with the students. Use the hand motions you added on Day 1. Next, have students lay on their backs and peddle their feet in the air like they are riding a bicycle. When you say, *Freeze,* the students should stop and recite the entire Bible verse. Repeat the activity.

✔ Text Connection: *Morning Bells* p. 70-72

Key Idea: Thomas kept getting into trouble. He wanted to do the right thing, but he needed to ask God for help. Then, he would be able to please God.

Corresponding Music

None this lesson

Learning the Basics

Focus: Language Arts and Math

Unit 11 - Day 3

Language Arts

Using the spelling list from Day 1, choose 3 or more words that the students need to practice. Guide students to use each of the words that you chose in a sentence. On a markerboard or a piece of paper, write down the sentences as the students dictate them to you. Underline the spelling word in each sentence. Have the students copy the sentences on a piece of paper. Help students check their sentences and correct any mistakes.
<u>Copywork</u>: Have students copy part of the poem *"Don't Give Up"*.

<u>Key Idea</u>: Practice spelling words with long 'o', ending in silent 'e'.

Reading Choices

Choose **one** of the reading options listed below (see Appendix for details).

★ A phonics program
★ *Scheduled Books for Emerging Readers*
★ *Drawn into the Heart of Reading Level 2/3*

<u>Key Idea</u>: Use a step-by-step program for reading instruction.

Storytime

Read aloud the next portion of the historical fiction book that you selected. In the center of a piece of paper, draw a circle. Draw 6 or more arrows coming out from the circle like spokes on a wheel. Ask the students, *Where does this story take place?* Write the answer in the center of circle. Say, *List some words that describe the place.* At the end of each arrow, write a descriptive word that the students shared.

<u>Key Idea</u>: Focus on the story element: *setting*.

Math Exploration

Complete the assigned lesson in the workbook listed below.

✔ <u>Text Connection</u>: *Primary Mathematics Workbook 1A* p. 110-111

Note: Use counters as needed to help students add and subtract.

<u>Key Idea</u>: Add and subtract numbers up to '20'.

Learning Through History

Focus: Pilgrims Build Houses at Plymouth

Unit 11 - Day 4

Reading About History

Read about history in the following resource:

★ *American Pioneers and Patriots* p. 35-37

Key Idea: The Pilgrims finally had a place to live. The winter that came next was long and hard. Later, some Indians came to help the Pilgrims.

Poetry and Rhymes

Read aloud the poem *"Don't Give Up"* (see Appendix) with the students. Have students draw pictures that reflect the poem's meaning on either a photocopy of the poem or on their copywork. File the finished poem in a special place.

Key Idea: Read classic poetry.

History Activity

Say, *The Pilgrims were ready to raise the frame of their house. Let's experiment with a frame of your own. Connect 4 straws, tinker toys, or craft sticks together with tape to make a square frame.* Ask, *Can you move the sides of your frame without breaking it? Does your frame seem very strong? How could you add one more straw, tinker toy, or craft stick to make your frame stronger?* Note: Guide students to tape the fifth piece across the middle of the frame diagonally, from one corner to another. Say, *Now get out your timeline. Let's find the column that says 1600. Draw a small log house in that column. Write 'Plymouth, Massachusetts, December 21, 1620'.*

Key Idea: Thomas quickly climbed up to help fit the beams together. He saved the frame of the house from falling.

Bible Study

Say Psalm 143:10 with the students. Use the hand motions from Day 1. Ask, *What are some things that you have had to wait to do until you are older? Do you have to wait until you are older to do God's will? Name some little things that you can do to please God now. How will you feel when you do God's will?* Next, have students gallop by leading with their left foot until you say, *Freeze*. After they 'freeze', have the students recite the Bible verse. Have students switch to the right foot and repeat the activity.

Key Idea: It is more important to please God than to please others.

Corresponding Music

None this lesson

Learning the Basics

Focus: Language Arts and Math

Unit 11 - Day 4

Language Arts

Use the spelling list from Day 1. Say each word and use it in a sentence. Have students write each word and check it with the matching word card from Day 1. Guide students to correct any mistakes. For each missed word, have students write the word on paper and trace around it 3 times with 3 different colors.
<u>Copywork</u>: Have students copy part of the poem *"Don't Give Up"*.

<u>Key Idea</u>: Practice spelling words.

Reading Choices

Choose **one** of the reading options listed below (see Appendix for details).

★ A phonics program
★ *Scheduled Books for Emerging Readers*
★ *Drawn into the Heart of Reading Level 2/3*

<u>Key Idea</u>: Use a step-by-step program for reading instruction.

Storytime

Say, *Faith is having a strong belief that stands firm in the face of trouble.* Read aloud 2 Corinthians 4:18. Say, *Name ways that you can stand firm in the face of trouble* (i.e. refuse to do things that are wrong, trust God in hard times, believe God can turn harm into good, pray). Discuss, *How do we fix our eyes on what is unseen?* (i.e. trust God for the future, believe in God even though we can't see Him, look forward to heaven someday). Read aloud the next portion of the historical fiction book that you selected. Ask, *How do the book characters fix their eyes on what is unseen? Do the characters show the opposite trait, unbelief?*

<u>Key Idea</u>: Focus on the trait: *faith*.

Math Exploration

Complete the assigned lesson in the workbook listed below.

✔ <u>Text Connection</u>: *Primary Mathematics Workbook 1A* p. 112-113

Note: Use counters as needed to help students add and subtract.

<u>Key Idea</u>: Add and subtract numbers up to '20'.

Learning Through History

Focus: Pilgrims Build Houses at Plymouth

Unit 11 - Day 5

Reading About History

Read the following passage from your own Bible:

★ John 4:27-38

Key Idea: In this passage, Jesus talks about doing God's will. Jesus speaks of the harvest of Christians who will reap eternal life. The Pilgrims planted crops and trusted God for the harvest on earth. They looked forward to life in heaven.

Poetry and Rhymes

Have students get out the poems that they saved from the previous units. Ask students to select one or more poems to review. Read aloud the selected poems with the students.

Key Idea: Read classic poetry.

Science Exploration

Say, *In today's Bible passage, Jesus talks about sowing, reaping, and harvesting. Let's see what those words mean.* Give students a basket of dry beans, popcorn seeds, or cereal pieces to sow by scattering them across the floor. Next, give students a butter knife to be a sickle. Have students "cut under" each seed with their sickle to reap the crop. Last, have students harvest the crop by gathering it and placing it in a basket. Guide students to kneel and thank God for the harvest once it has all been gathered.

✓ Text Connection: *God's Wonderful Works* p. 53

Key Idea: We practiced harvesting today, so that we can have a better understanding of what Jesus wants us to do as Christians.

Bible Study

Say, *In John 4:31-34, what kind of food is Jesus talking about? In verse 34, what does Jesus say that He is doing on earth? If Jesus followed God's will for His life, what should you do? In John 4:35-38, what kind of harvest does Jesus mean? How can you help do God's work on earth?* Ask students to share their memory verse, Psalm 143:10, with someone special. Suggestions for sharing the verse include saying it to another family member, saying it to someone by telephone, reciting it to a stuffed animal, or writing it to mail.

Key Idea: When you do God's will, you must trust Him for the harvest.

Corresponding Music

None this lesson

Learning the Basics

Focus: Language Arts and Math

Unit 11 - Day 5

Language Arts

On a markerboard or a piece of paper, write the following sentences leaving out the beginning capital letters and the ending punctuation marks: Thomas was eager to help the men as they worked. The frame of the house was starting to tip! Walk slowly. Who would help fix the frame? Thomas was as quick as a cat. He climbed the frame and slid it into place. Thomas saved the house! What will the men say about Thomas now? Say, *These sentences tell about the picture on p. 35 of* <u>American Pioneers and Patriots</u>. *Do you notice anything missing from the sentences? Let's add a capital letter to the beginning of each sentence. Let's decide which punctuation mark to add to the end of each sentence.*

<u>Key Idea</u>: Add capital letters and end punctuation to 4 types of sentences.

Reading Choices

Choose **one** of the reading options listed below (see Appendix for details).

★ A phonics program
★ *Scheduled Books for Emerging Readers*
★ *Drawn into the Heart of Reading Level 2/3*

<u>Key Idea</u>: Use a step-by-step program for reading instruction.

Math Exploration

Draw a large triangle on a piece of paper. Draw a circle at each point of the triangle. Choose three numbers that make a fact family (i.e. '5', '3', '8'). Write one number in each circle. Have students follow the lines on the triangle to find four number sentences that could be made using the three numbers in the circles (i.e. 5 + 3 = 8; 3 + 5 = 8; 8 - 3 = 5; 8 - 5 = 3). Remind students that the number sentences must make sense. For example, you could write '5 - 3 = 8' using those numbers, but it doesn't make sense. Repeat the activity using other numbers (i.e. '7', '2', '9').

✓ <u>Text Connection</u>: *Primary Mathematics Workbook 1A* p. 114

<u>Key Idea</u>: Introduce fact families.

Storytime

Read aloud a short portion of the historical fiction book that you selected. Give students a chance to retell today's story by using simple props to act out the story. If needed, you may read aloud parts of the text for students to act out.

<u>Key Idea</u>: Give students practice retelling a portion of a historical fiction book.

Learning Through History

Focus: Samoset and Squanto Help the Pilgrims

Unit 12 - Day 1

Reading About History

Read about history in the following resource:

★ *Stories of the Pilgrims* p. 116-120

Key Idea: As winter came, the Pilgrims worked hard to build a big log house. Many Pilgrims became sick and died. It was a long, hard winter.

Poetry and Rhymes

Read aloud the poem *"The Prayer Perfect"* (see Appendix) to the students. Do not share the title. Ask students to suggest some titles for the poem. Share the real title. Read the poem again with the students.

Key Idea: Read and appreciate a variety of classic poetry.

Science Exploration

Say, *Why did so many of the Pilgrims get sick? Let's do an experiment to see how germs spread.* Tear many small pieces of paper and place them in a glass. Pretend that the glass is a person's mouth, and the pieces of paper are germs. Pick up the glass. When I say, "Ah-choo!", shake the glass up. *What happened to the germs during the sneeze? Now, pick up all the little pieces of paper and put them back in the glass. This time when I say, "Ah-choo!", cover the mouth of the glass with your hand before you shake it up. What happened to the germs during the sneeze this time? How do you think germs are spread? Why is it important to cover your mouth when you sneeze or cough?*

Key Idea: Disease germs spread among the Pilgrims, killing many of them. Today, we are blessed to have ways to stop diseases from spreading.

Bible Study

Review the memory verse, Psalm 119:9-11, from Unit 7. Read the verse out loud. Say, *What does it mean to be 'clean' or 'pure'? Are you able to be pure all of the time? In Psalm 119:9, how does it say that you can cleanse your way or keep it pure? In Psalm 119:10-11, what does God say that you should do so that you do not sin against Him?* Say the verse together 3 times. Review the hand motions that go with the verse from Unit 7.

Key Idea: The Pilgrims kept their way pure by seeking God's will.

Corresponding Music

✔ *Hide 'Em in Your Heart Vol. 2*
CD - Track 21; Cassette - Side B
Song: *"I Have Hidden Your Word"*

Learning the Basics

Focus: Language Arts and Math

Unit 12 - Day 1

Language Arts

Choose **either** spelling list 1 **or** 2 (see Appendix for lists). Write each spelling word on a separate index card. Guide students to study each card one at a time, flip it over, write the word from memory on paper, flip the card back over to check the spelling, and erase and correct any mistakes.

<u>Copywork</u>: Have students copy part of the poem *"The Prayer Perfect"*.

<u>Key Idea</u>: Practice spelling words with long 'u', ending in silent 'e'.

Reading Choices

Choose **one** of the reading options listed below (see Appendix for details).

★ A phonics program
★ *Scheduled Books for Emerging Readers*
★ *Drawn into the Heart of Reading Level 2/3*

<u>Key Idea</u>: Use a step-by-step program for reading instruction.

Storytime

Say, *Name some things that have gone wrong in the story. What seems to be the biggest problem in the story right now? What are some different ways that the problem could be fixed? What would you choose to do?*

Read aloud the next portion of the historical fiction book that you selected. Pace your reading to complete the book during the next 5 days of plans.

<u>Key Idea</u>: Set a purpose for reading the next part of the historical fiction book.

Math Exploration

Place '8' items in one covered bowl and '7' items in another covered bowl. Make sure that students cannot see into the bowls. Write the total number of items in both bowls on a markerboard or a piece of paper ('15'). Allow students to choose one bowl and count the items in that bowl. Guide students to use that number to help them figure out how many items must be in the other bowl. For example, if there are '15' total items and there were '8' items in the bowl they chose, then there must be '7' items in the other bowl ('15 - 8 = 7' or '8 + 7 = 15').

✔ <u>Text Connection</u>: *Primary Mathematics Workbook 1A* p. 115

<u>Key Idea</u>: Add and subtract to '20'.

Learning Through History

Focus: Samoset and Squanto Help the Pilgrims

Unit 12 - Day 2

Reading About History

Read about history in the following resource:

★ *Stories of the Pilgrims* p. 121-126

Key Idea: In the spring, an Indian named Samoset came to visit the Pilgrims. He could speak English and was friendly. The Pilgrims were not sure they could trust Samoset.

Poetry and Rhymes

Read aloud the poem *"The Prayer Perfect"* (see Appendix) with the students. Discuss the poem's meaning. If you choose, photocopy the poem, cut it apart, and have the students put it in order.

Key Idea: Read classic poetry.

Science Exploration

Set a flashlight upright in the middle of a table to be the sun. Use a ball to be the Earth. Place a sticker on the top of the ball to be the North Pole. Tape a tinfoil star in one corner of the room to be the North Star. Have students slowly walk around the table to show the Earth orbiting the sun. As students walk, direct them to always keep the North Pole pointing to the North Star. As the Earth orbits the sun, watch where the light shines on the Earth. The Equator gets the most light. The Northern Hemisphere is warmest when the North Pole is towards the sun, and coldest when the North Pole is away from the sun.

✔ Text Connection: *God's Wonderful Works* p. 68-69

Key Idea: The Pilgrims had a cold winter. The ground was frozen, and they couldn't find food. They were relieved when spring finally arrived.

Bible Study

Review the memory verse from Unit 8, 1 Thessalonians 5:11, by saying it while the students join in on the parts they know. Ask, *When are some times that you have needed comforting? What does it mean to edify or encourage someone? Name some people that encourage you. How can you encourage others?* Next, have students do windmills by touching their right hand to their right foot, and then their left hand to their left foot. After every 5 windmills, have the students recite the Bible verse.

Key Idea: The Pilgrims encouraged each other during hard times.

Corresponding Music

✔ *Hide 'Em in Your Heart Vol. 2*
CD - Track 2; Cassette - Side A
Song: "Encourage One Another"

Learning the Basics

Focus: Language Arts and Math

Unit 12 - Day 2

Language Arts

Use the spelling list from Day 1. Say the first spelling word. Use it in a sentence. Repeat the word. Ask students to write the word on a markerboard or a piece of paper from memory. Give students the matching word card from Day 1 to compare with their spelling. Guide students to correct any mistakes. Repeat the activity with all 10 words.
<u>Copywork</u>: Have students copy part of the poem *"The Prayer Perfect"*.

<u>Key Idea</u>: Practice spelling words with long 'u' ending in silent 'e'.

Reading Choices

Choose **one** of the reading options listed below (see Appendix for details).

★ A phonics program
★ *Scheduled Books for Emerging Readers*
★ *Drawn into the Heart of Reading Level 2/3*

<u>Key Idea</u>: Use a step-by-step program for reading instruction.

Storytime

Read aloud the next portion of the historical fiction book that you selected. Ask students to retell or narrate what you read today. Remind students to tell the most important parts and to include details from the story in the retelling. As students work together to retell the story, write, type, or tape record the students' narration. When the students are finished, read the narration out loud. Highlight, circle, or underline one main idea from the narration for the students to copy.

<u>Key Idea</u>: Keep a sample of the students' narrations for the genre: *Historical Fiction*.

Math Exploration

These are the concepts that are covered in this review: writing numbers up to '20', fact families, number patterns, greater and smaller numbers, ordinal numbers, missing addends, and word problems. Review any concepts that students had difficulty understanding. In addition, complete the assigned review in the workbook listed below.

✔ <u>Text Connection</u>: *Primary Mathematics Workbook 1A* p. 116-119

<u>Key Idea</u>: Review difficult concepts.

Learning Through History

Focus: Samoset and Squanto Help the Pilgrims

Unit 12 - Day 3

Reading About History

Read about history in the following resource:

★ *Stories of the Pilgrims* p. 127-132

Key Idea: The Indian chief, Massasoit, came to meet with Governor Carver. The Pilgrims and the Indians made a peace treaty. The treaty lasted for 50 years.

Poetry and Rhymes

Read aloud the poem *"The Prayer Perfect"* (see Appendix) with the students. Read the poem aloud a second time, pausing after each line or two for students to add actions to the poem. The actions should make sense with the poem.

Key Idea: Read classic poetry.

Geography

Give each student a piece of white paper. In the bottom corner make a box that says *Key*. Down the left side of the box, write the words *gate, fort,* and *street*. Say, *Maps often use symbols to stand for real things. A map key tells you what each symbol means. Draw your own symbol next to each word in the key. Follow my directions to make a map of the fort at Plymouth. Draw a large, flat diamond shape to be the wall. Using the symbol from your key, draw a street that goes from left to right across the diamond. Label the street Leyden Street. Now, draw a street that goes from top to bottom in the diamond. Label that street Main Street. Use the symbol from your key to make a gate at each corner of the diamond. Use the symbol from your key to draw a fort in the left corner of the diamond.*

Key Idea: The Pilgrims finished building their fort at Plymouth in 1623.

Bible Study

Review the memory verse, Colossians 3:23, from Unit 9, by saying it while the students join in on the parts they know. Next, have students squat down, hop up, and squat back down again. After the last squat, have the students recite the entire Bible verse. Prompt students as needed. Repeat the activity.

✓ Text Connection: *Morning Bells* p. 52-54

Key Idea: The Pilgrims trusted that God heard their prayers. The Holy Spirit comforted them, and God took care of them.

Corresponding Music

None this lesson

Learning the Basics

Focus: Language Arts and Math

Unit 12 - Day 3

Language Arts

Using the spelling list from Day 1, choose 3 or more words that the students need to practice. Guide students to use each of the words that you chose in a sentence. On a markerboard or a piece of paper, write down the sentences as the students dictate them to you. Underline the spelling word in each sentence. Have the students copy the sentences on a piece of paper. Help students check their sentences and correct any mistakes.
Copywork: Have students copy part of the poem *"The Prayer Perfect"*.

Key Idea: Practice spelling words.

Reading Choices

Choose **one** of the reading options listed below (see Appendix for details).

★ A phonics program
★ *Scheduled Books for Emerging Readers*
★ *Drawn into the Heart of Reading Level 2/3*

Key Idea: Use a step-by-step program for reading instruction.

Storytime

Say, *As you listen to a story being read, the words paint a picture in your mind. As I'm reading to you today, whenever you hear a part of the story with good description that you can picture, hold up an imaginary camera and say, "Click".* Read aloud the next portion of the historical fiction book that you selected. After the reading, say, *Describe something from your own life that reminds you of one of the scenes in the story.*

Key Idea: Focus on the story element: *setting*.

Math Exploration

These are the concepts that are covered in this review: addition and subtraction to '20', number patterns, comparing sets, missing numbers in equations, and word problems. Review any concepts that students had difficulty understanding. Also, complete the assigned review in the workbook listed below.

✔ Text Connection: *Primary Mathematics Workbook 1A* p. 120-123

Key Idea: Review difficult concepts.

Learning Through History

Focus: Samoset and Squanto Help the Pilgrims

Unit 12 - Day 4

Reading About History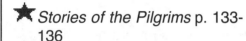

Read about history in the following resource:

★ *Stories of the Pilgrims* p. 133-136

<u>Key Idea</u>: Squanto came to live with the Pilgrims. His tribe had died. He taught the Pilgrims how to trap, fish, and plant corn. God used Squanto to help the Pilgrims survive.

History Activity

Draw a large circle on a piece of white paper. Make sure to leave room around the outside of the circle for students to draw small pictures. Say, *Many Indian tribes used a form of picture writing to tell stories. They wrote their stories in a circle using symbols or pictures to stand for words. Practice using your own form of picture writing. Draw symbols around the outside of the circle on your paper to tell a story. Write a few words under each symbol to help you remember the story. Tell me the story when you are finished drawing.*

<u>Key Idea</u>: Squanto helped Edward Winslow learn to speak the Indian language. Edward Winslow taught Squanto to read and write.

Poetry and Rhymes

Read aloud the poem *"The Prayer Perfect"* (see Appendix) with the students. Have students draw pictures that reflect the poem's meaning on either a photocopy of the poem or on their copywork. File the finished poem in a special place.

<u>Key Idea</u>: Read classic poetry.

Bible Study

Say, *When you become a Christian, God promises to put His Holy Spirit within you. What does that mean? How will the Holy Spirit help you?* Review the memory verse, Psalm 118:1, from unit 10 by saying it while the students join in on the parts they know. Next, have students hop backward 5 times. After every 5 hops, have the students recite the entire Bible verse.

<u>Key Idea</u>: God loves you so much that He sent the gift of His Holy Spirit to be with you. The Pilgrims were thankful for God's gifts.

Corresponding Music

✔ *Hide 'Em in Your Heart Vol. 2*
CD - Track 14; Cassette - Side B
Song: *"Give Thanks to the Lord"*

Learning the Basics

Focus: Language Arts and Math

Unit 12 - Day 4

Language Arts

Use the spelling list from Day 1. Say each word and use it in a sentence. Have students write each word and check it with the matching word card from Day 1. Guide students to correct any mistakes. Direct students to write each missed word with fingerpaint or sidewalk chalk.

Copywork: Have students copy part of *"The Prayer Perfect"*.

Key Idea: Practice spelling words with long 'u', ending in silent 'e'.

Reading Choices

Choose **one** of the reading options listed below (see Appendix for details).

★ A phonics program
★ *Scheduled Books for Emerging Readers*
★ *Drawn into the Heart of Reading Level 2/3*

Key Idea: Use a step-by-step program for reading instruction.

Storytime

Say, *Faith is having a strong belief that stands firm in the face of trouble.* Read aloud the key verse 2 Corinthians 4:18. Read aloud the next portion of the historical fiction book that you selected. Ask, *Did the book characters usually show faith or unbelief? Explain. Are you usually faithful to God?* Draw a picture showing one way that you could be more faithful. Post your picture in a place where you will see it often.

Key Idea: Focus on the Godly character trait: *faith*.

Math Exploration

In a column down the left side of a piece of paper, draw a rectangle, a circle, a square, a triangle, and a diamond. Walk through the house to find at least one example of each shape. Have students trace the outline of each shape they find with their fingers. Next, have students use a marker to add a colored dot to each corner of the shapes on the paper. Tell students to use the colored dots to help guide them as they draw their own shape next to the one that is already on the paper.

✔ Text Connection: *Primary Mathematics Workbook 1A* p. 124-125

Key Idea: Recognize and draw basic shapes.

Learning Through History

Focus: Samoset and Squanto Help the Pilgrims

Unit 12 - Day 5

Reading About History

Read the following passage from your own Bible:

 John 14:23-31

Key Idea: The Pilgrims needed God's comfort and guidance in a new place. They trusted the Bible and wanted to obey God. God sends the Holy Spirit to be our comfort and guide, just as Jesus promised.

Poetry and Rhymes

Have students get out the poems that they saved from the previous units. Ask students to select one or more poems to review. Read aloud the selected poems with the students.

Key Idea: Read classic poetry.

Artistic Expression

Cut a heart out of a coffee filter or a paper towel. Write "PEACE" on the heart in permanent marker. Have students fold up the heart. Place a small amount of water into 3 different cups. Add several drops of blue food coloring to the first cup. Add red food coloring to the second cup. Add yellow food coloring to the third cup. Guide students to dip one corner of the folded heart in the blue water, a different corner in the red water, and the last corner in the yellow water. Help students unfold the heart to see the colors bleed into one another. Lay the heart flat to dry. Read John 14:27 out loud.

Key Idea: The Lord floods our hearts with peace through the Holy Spirit, if we believe in Him. God is with us through good and bad times.

Bible Study

Ask, *In John 14:23 what does Jesus say you will do if you love Him? In John 14:26, who does Jesus promise God will send? What will the Holy Spirit do? In John 14:27, what does Jesus promise to leave with you? How can you have peace when you have times of trouble?* Ask students to share their memory verse, Psalm 143:10, with someone special. Suggestions for sharing the verse include saying it to another family member, saying it to someone by telephone, reciting it to a stuffed animal, or writing it to mail.

Key Idea: The Pilgrims had many troubled times. But, they trusted God and obeyed his teaching through it all.

Corresponding Music

None this lesson

Learning the Basics

Focus: Language Arts and Math

Unit 12 - Day 5

Language Arts

Say, *All people and many things have names. What is your name? What is the name of your town? What is the name of your favorite color? Words that name people, places, or things are called nouns.* At the top of a markerboard or a piece of paper write the following 3 headings: People, Places, Things. Direct students to walk through the house and look for nouns. Help students list each noun under the proper heading on the markerboard or paper. Ask, *Which heading seems to have the most nouns under it? Why might it have the most?*

<u>Key Idea</u>: Introduce nouns.

Reading Choices

Choose **one** of the reading options listed below (see Appendix for details).

★ *A phonics program*
★ *Scheduled Books for Emerging Readers*
★ *Drawn into the Heart of Reading Level 2/3*

<u>Key Idea</u>: Use a step-by-step program for reading instruction.

Storytime

Read aloud the final portion of the historical fiction book that you selected. You will need to select a fantasy book to read aloud next. Remind students about what you've read in the historical fiction book by showing them any pictures in the book and reading them some of the chapter titles. Say, *Retell your favorite part of the story. Why did you like that part of the book best?*

<u>Key Idea</u>: Give students practice retelling a portion of a historical fiction book.

Math Exploration

Set out an example of each solid (i.e. cylinder = can or a paper towel roll, cube = dice or a block, rectangular prism = aluminum foil box or a tissue box, cone = candy kiss or a party hat). Review the names of each solid shape. Place each solid on a piece of paper and trace one of its sides or faces. Notice the shape that was traced (cylinder = circle, cube = square, rectangular solid = rectangle or a square, cone = circle). Compare the solid shapes (i.e. number of corners, edges, and faces).

✔ <u>Text Connection</u>: *Primary Mathematics Workbook 1A* p. 126

<u>Key Idea</u>: Compare plane and solid shapes.

Learning Through History

Focus: The First Thanksgiving at Plymouth

Unit 13 - Day 1

Reading About History

Read about history in the following resource:

★ *Stories of the Pilgrims* p. 137-140

Key Idea: When spring came, the captain of the *Mayflower* offered to take the Pilgrims back to England for free. Even though the winter had been hard and there had been many deaths, the Pilgrims stayed.

Poetry and Rhymes

Read aloud the poem *"We Plough the Fields, and Scatter"* (see Appendix) to the students. Do not share the title. Ask students to suggest some titles for the poem. Share the real title. Read the poem again with the students.

Key Idea: Read and appreciate a variety of classic poetry.

Science Exploration

Draw lines to divide a strip of white paper into 4 sections. Write, *Spring,* at the top of section 1, *Summer,* at the top of section 2, *Fall,* at the top of section 3, and *Winter,* at the top of section 4. Say, *Use a brown colored pencil or crayon to draw a bare bush in each section. In the spring section, dot green paint on the bush to be leaves. In the summer section, dot green and pink paint on the bush to be leaves and flowers. In the fall section, dot red, orange, and yellow paint on the bush and on the ground to be falling leaves. For the winter section, dot white paint on the bush to be snow.*

✔ Text Connection: *God's Wonderful Works* p. 65-66

Key Idea: The Pilgrims were thankful to see spring. God has a special reason for each season.

Bible Study

Romans 8:28 is the memory verse for this unit. Read the verse out loud. Ask, *In Romans 8:28, what does it say that God uses for good? Does that mean that everything that happens to you will be good? Why not? God promises to work all things together for good for whom? What is a purpose? Whose purpose is God fulfilling?* Say the verse together 3 times. Add hand motions to help students remember the words.

Key Idea: Even in sad times God works all things together for good for those that love Him.

Corresponding Music

✔ *Hide 'Em in Your Heart Vol. 2* CD - Track 19; Cassette - Side B Song: *"All Things Work Together..."*

Learning the Basics

Focus: Language Arts and Math

Unit 13 - Day 1

Language Arts

Get out the spelling words on index cards that you saved from Unit 8 and Unit 9. Guide students to study each card one at a time, flip it over, write the word from memory on paper, flip the card back over to check the spelling, and erase and correct any mistakes. <u>Copywork</u>: Have students copy part of the poem *"We Plough the Fields, and Scatter"*.

<u>Key Idea</u>: Review spelling words from Unit 8 and Unit 9.

Reading Choices

Choose **one** of the reading options listed below (see Appendix for details).

★ A phonics program
★ *Scheduled Books for Emerging Readers*
★ *Drawn into the Heart of Reading Level 2/3*

<u>Key Idea</u>: Use a step-by-step program for reading instruction.

Storytime

Choose at least one fantasy to read aloud for the next 20 days of plans (see Appendix for suggested titles). Say, *A fantasy is a fictional or made-up story that is not limited to things that could really happen.* To introduce the genre, *Fantasy*, write a fantasy sentence. Have the students help you rewrite the fantasy sentence as a realistic sentence. For example, the fantasy sentence, "The purple cat talked to the dog", could be rewritten as the realistic sentence, "The striped cat meowed at the dog". Continue writing and rewriting sentences for additional practice. Read a portion of the fantasy you chose out loud.

<u>Key Idea</u>: Introduce the genre: *Fantasy*.

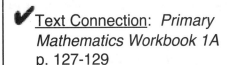

Math Exploration

Complete the assigned lesson in the workbook listed below.

✔ <u>Text Connection</u>: *Primary Mathematics Workbook 1A* p. 127-129

<u>Key Idea</u>: Match plane shapes with solid figures.

Learning Through History

Focus: The First Thanksgiving at Plymouth

Unit 13 - Day 2

Reading About History

Read about history in the following resource:

★ *Stories of the Pilgrims* p. 141-143

Key Idea: The Pilgrims spent the summer planting and storing food for the winter. After the good harvest, the Pilgrims honored God with a feast of Thanksgiving. They invited their Indian friends.

Poetry and Rhymes

Read aloud the poem *"We Plough the Fields, and Scatter"* (see Appendix) with the students. Discuss the poem's meaning. If you choose, photocopy the poem, cut it apart, and have the students place it in the correct order.

Key Idea: Read classic poetry.

Science Exploration

Cut a leaf with a long stem out of a paper towel. Draw veins on the leaf with a green watercolor marker. Fill a glass partway full of water. Hang the stem of the leaf over the edge and into the glass of water, and lay the leaf on a plate. Watch the stem "suck up the water" and carry it to the leaf. Explain that this is how plant roots carry water from the ground, up the stem, and to the leaves of a plant. Try the experiment again, but this time don't add water to the glass. Point out that when the leaf doesn't get any water, it dries up. Blow on the dry leaf and watch it fall to the ground. This is what happens in the fall.

✔ Text Connection: *God's Wonderful Works* p. 56-57 and 67

Key Idea: The Pilgrims were blessed with a bountiful harvest. They praised God for His goodness.

Bible Study

Say Romans 8:28 while the students join in on the parts they know. Use the hand motions you added on Day 1. Say, *What are some blessings that God has given you? Do you remember to thank God for His blessings? How can God turn harm into good? Where are all Christians' greatest blessings waiting for them?* Next, have students do 5 jumping jacks. After every 5 jumping jacks, have the students recite the entire verse. Prompt students as needed.

Key Idea: The Pilgrims didn't forget to thank God for His blessings.

Corresponding Music

✔ *Hide 'Em in Your Heart Vol. 2* CD - Track 19; Cassette - Side B Song: *"All Things Work Together..."*

Learning the Basics

Focus: Language Arts and Math

Unit 13 - Day 2

Language Arts

Get out the spelling cards that you saved from Unit 10. Say the first spelling word. Use it in a sentence. Repeat the word. Ask students to write the word on a markerboard or a piece of paper from memory. Give students the matching word card to compare with their spelling. Guide students to correct any mistakes. Repeat the activity with all 10 words. <u>Copywork</u>: Have students copy part of the poem *"We Plough the Fields, and Scatter"*.

<u>Key Idea</u>: Review spelling words from Unit 10.

Reading Choices

Choose **one** of the reading options listed below (see Appendix for details).

★ A phonics program
★ *Scheduled Books for Emerging Readers*
★ *Drawn into the Heart of Reading Level 2/3*

<u>Key Idea</u>: Use a step-by-step program for reading instruction.

Storytime

Read aloud the next portion of the fantasy that you selected. Without looking back at the story, model retelling or narrating the part of the fantasy that you read today to the students. Remember to tell the most important points and to add details from the story to the retelling without overwhelming the students. After the retelling, ask, *What feelings do you have as you listen to this story? Explain.* On paper, write a one-sentence summary of the students' answers for the students to copy.

<u>Key Idea</u>: Model retelling a story from a single reading.

Math Exploration

Complete the assigned lesson in the workbook listed below.

 <u>Text Connection</u>: *Primary Mathematics Workbook 1A* p. 130-132

<u>Key Idea</u>: Create pictures using the provided shapes.

Learning Through History

Focus: The First Thanksgiving at Plymouth

Unit 13 - Day 3

Reading About History

Read about history in the following resource:

★ *Stories of the Pilgrims* p. 144 - half of p. 147

Key Idea: The Pilgrims hunted, cooked, and baked to get ready for the feast. Massasoit came with many Indians. The Pilgrims began the day with prayers of Thanksgiving.

Poetry and Rhymes

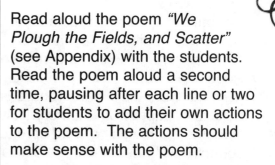

Read aloud the poem *"We Plough the Fields, and Scatter"* (see Appendix) with the students. Read the poem aloud a second time, pausing after each line or two for students to add their own actions to the poem. The actions should make sense with the poem.

Key Idea: Read classic poetry.

Artistic Expression

On pink or grey paper, draw the simple outline of a clam. Have students cut out the clam and trace around it to make another clam the same size. Make different colors of corn syrup paint by adding drops of food coloring to white corn syrup. You may also add glitter to the paint if you choose. Have students use Q-Tips to paint different-colored stripes of corn syrup paint on the clam. Make sure to keep the paint stripes thin, since the paint will take a long time to dry. When the paint is dry, staple the two sides of the clam together. Glue a popcorn seed inside the clam to be a pearl.

✔ Text Connection: *God's Wonderful Works* p. 78

Key Idea: The Pilgrim children dug for clams for the Thanksgiving feast. Clams are part of the mollusk family.

Bible Study

Say Romans 8:28 with the students. Use the hand motions you added on Day 1. Next, have students hop on their left foot until you say, *Freeze*. After they 'freeze', have the students recite the entire Bible verse. Prompt students as needed. Have students switch to the right foot, and repeat the activity.

✔ Text Connection: *Morning Bells* p. 25-27

Key Idea: The Pilgrims rejoiced and offered their hearts with glad thanksgiving to the Lord.

Corresponding Music

✔ *Hide 'Em in Your Heart Vol. 2* CD - Track 19; Cassette - Side B Song: *"All Things Work Together..."*

Learning the Basics

Focus: Language Arts and Math

Unit 13 - Day 3

Language Arts

Get out the spelling word cards from Unit 11. Choose 3 or more words that the students need to practice. Guide students to use each of the words that you chose in a sentence. On a markerboard or a piece of paper, write down the sentences as the students dictate them to you. Underline the spelling word in each sentence. Have the students copy the sentences on a piece of paper. Help students check their sentences and correct any mistakes.
<u>Copywork</u>: Have students copy part of the poem *"We Plough the Fields, and Scatter".*

<u>Key Idea</u>: Review spelling words.

Reading Choices

Choose **one** of the reading options listed below (see Appendix for details).

★ A phonics program
★ *Scheduled Books for Emerging Readers*
★ *Drawn into the Heart of Reading Level 2/3*

<u>Key Idea</u>: Use a step-by-step program for reading instruction.

Storytime

Say, *The mood is the feelings created by a story. How are you feeling today?* (i.e. happy, mad, silly, sad, excited). *Then, we would say that you are in a _____ mood today. Let's read to see how the characters in the fantasy are feeling.* Read aloud the next portion of the fantasy that you selected. After reading, ask, *What moods were the characters feeling in today's reading? How can you tell?*

<u>Key Idea</u>: Introduce the story element: *mood.*

Math Exploration

Set out round lids of various sizes. Have students trace the edges of the lids with their fingers as they place the lids in order from largest to smallest. Repeat the activity using rectangular pans of various sizes and square pans or lids of various sizes.

✔ <u>Text Connection</u>: *Primary Mathematics Workbook 1A* p. 133-134

<u>Key Idea</u>: Compare the sizes of various shapes.

Learning Through History

Focus: The First Thanksgiving at Plymouth

Unit 13 - Day 4

Reading About History

Read about history in the following resource:

★ *Stories of the Pilgrims* p. 147-151

<u>Key Idea</u>: At the feast, the Indians and Pilgrims played games. The Indians showed their skills, and the soldiers did a drill. The cannons and gunfire frightened the Indians. There was a lot of good food to eat.

Poetry and Rhymes

Read aloud the poem *"We Plough the Fields, and Scatter"* (see Appendix) with the students. Have students draw pictures that reflect the poem's meaning on either a photocopy of the poem or on their copywork. File the finished poem.

<u>Key Idea</u>: Read classic poetry.

History Activity

Say, *Let's play some games like the Pilgrims and Indians played at the first Thanksgiving.* Have students stand behind a masking tape line and jump as far as they can. Mark the place where they land with a small piece of tape. Allow the students to jump again and try to beat their previous jump. Give students a rolled-up pair of socks to toss into a bowl several feet away. Each time the students get the socks in the bowl, move it further away. Have students march around like soldiers and fire off imaginary guns. If it is nice weather, go outdoors and have students run from one mark to another. Time them. Allow students to run again to beat their first time.

<u>Key Idea</u>: The Indians and the Pilgrims played games to celebrate a good harvest. They gave thanks for the Lord's blessing.

Bible Study

Say Romans 8:28 with the students. Use the hand motions you added on Day 1. Say, *Name some things that you can offer to God. Explain what it means to offer yourself willingly. How can your hands gladly help others? What things can your lips say to serve God? How can you work for God's purpose, instead of your own?* Next, have the students do 5 sit-ups. After 5 sit-ups, have the students recite the entire Bible verse.

<u>Key Idea</u>: Even after so much sorrow and sadness, the Pilgrims willingly offered their thanks to God.

Corresponding Music

✓ *Hide 'Em in Your Heart Vol. 2*
CD - Track 19; Cassette - Side B
Song: *"All Things Work Together..."*

Learning the Basics

Focus: Language Arts and Math

Unit 13 - Day 4

Language Arts

Get out the spelling word cards from Unit 12. Say each word and use it in a sentence. Have students write each word and check it with the matching word card. Guide students to correct any mistakes. For each missed word, have students trace it in dry cornmeal, oatmeal, or sand on a plate.

Copywork: Have students copy part of the poem *"We Plough the Fields, and Scatter"*.

Key Idea: Review spelling words.

Reading Choices

Choose **one** of the reading options listed below (see Appendix for details).

★ A phonics program

★ *Scheduled Books for Emerging Readers*

★ *Drawn into the Heart of Reading Level 2/3*

Key Idea: Use a step-by-step program for reading instruction.

Storytime

Say, *Brotherly love means sincerely caring for others regardless of the circumstance.* Read aloud the key verse Philippians 1:9 to illustrate *brotherly love.* List some loving things that you do for others. Now, have students list ways that they show love.

Read aloud the next portion of the fantasy that you selected. Then, ask, *How do the characters show love? What could the characters do differently to be more loving?*

Key Idea: Introduce the Godly character trait: *brotherly love.*

Math Exploration

Use silverware to make a pattern (i.e. spoon, fork, knife, spoon, fork, knife). Point to each piece of silverware and have students name it as you go down the row. Ask, *What is the pattern?* Explain that the repeat of the pattern is ... (i.e. spoon, fork, knife). Cup your hands around the repeat throughout the pattern to "mark it off". Do the activity again with a different pattern. Ask students to name the repeat of the pattern. Then, ask students to cup their hands around the repeat to mark it off. Next, begin a pattern without finishing it (i.e. knife, fork, spoon, knife...). Have students continue the pattern and cup their hands around the repeat to mark it off.

✔ Text Connection: *Primary Mathematics Workbook 1A* p. 135

Key Idea: Complete a pattern.

Learning Through History

Focus: The First Thanksgiving at Plymouth

Unit 13 - Day 5

Reading About History

Read the following passage from your own Bible:

★ 1 Chronicles 29:10-20

Key Idea: Just like David and the Israelites, the Pilgrims offered their thanks to God. They knew that all things come from God and belong to Him. Like David, they wanted to serve God with their whole hearts.

Poetry and Rhymes

Have students get out the poems that they saved from the previous units. Ask students to select one or more poems to review. Read aloud the selected poems with the students.

Key Idea: Read classic poetry.

Geography

In the corner of a paper, draw a compass rose with the following directions on it: *N, NE, E, SE, S, SW, W,* and *NW*. Give students the following directions to draw a map of Jerusalem in Solomon's time: *In the upper right hand corner, draw a square. Label it, 'The Temple'. Several inches to the left of the temple, draw a rectangle. Label it, 'Solomon's Palace'. Halfway down the left side of the paper, draw a small house. Label it, 'David's House'. At the bottom of the paper in the center, draw a circle. Label it, 'David's Grave'.* Ask students directional questions like these: *If you are at Solomon's Palace, which direction must you go to get to the Temple? If you are at the Temple, which direction must you go to get to David's house?*

Key Idea: We need to give back to God what is His.

Bible Study

Ask, *In 1 Chronicles 29:11, what does King David say belongs to God? Why does 1 Chronicles 29:14 tell you to give generously to God? How does 1 Chronicles 29:17-18 say that you should give to God? Describe a time that you willingly offered something.* Ask students to share their memory verse, Romans 8:28, with someone special. Suggestions for sharing the verse include saying it to another family member, saying it to someone by telephone, reciting it to a stuffed animal, or writing it to mail.

Key Idea: The Pilgrims willingly offered what they had to the Lord.

Corresponding Music

✔ *Hide 'Em in Your Heart Vol. 2*
CD - Track 19; Cassette - Side B
Song: *"All Things Work Together..."*

Learning the Basics

Focus: Language Arts and Math

Unit 13 - Day 5

Language Arts

On a markerboard or a piece of paper, write a sentence using your child's first name (i.e. Cole likes to draw.). Ask, *Which word in the sentence is a name? What kind of letter do you notice at the beginning of the name? Nouns that tell the special name of a person, place, or thing are called proper nouns. Proper names begin with a capital letter.* Ask students to help make a list of the first names of their family members. Help students share a telling sentence for each family member's name. <u>Copywork</u>: Have students copy the sentence with their own name in it.

<u>Key Idea</u>: Introduce proper names.

Reading Choices

Choose **one** of the reading options listed below (see Appendix for details).

★ A phonics program
★ *Scheduled Books for Emerging Readers*
★ *Drawn into the Heart of Reading Level 2/3*

<u>Key Idea</u>: Use a step-by-step program for reading instruction.

Storytime

Read aloud a short portion of the fantasy that you selected. Guide students to retell the important events in today's story along with sound effects. Possible ideas for sound effects include using different voices for different characters, tapping thighs with hands for walking, clapping to show a door slamming, rubbing palms together to show running, etc.

<u>Key Idea</u>: Give students practice retelling a portion of a fantasy.

Math Exploration

Give students three different kinds of snacks (i.e. raisins, crackers, marshmallows). Ask students to make a pattern for you to continue. Name the repeat of the pattern and cup your hands around it to mark it off as you continue the pattern. Next, make a pattern that contains a mistake for the students to find (i.e. raisin, cracker, raisin, cracker, raisin, raisin). In order to find the mistake, ask students to name the repeat and cup their hands around it to mark it off as they go down the row. Vary the activity with other patterns.

✔ <u>Text Connection</u>: *Primary Mathematics Workbook 1A* p. 136

<u>Key Idea</u>: Complete a given pattern.

Learning Through History

Focus: More Problems for the Pilgrims at Plymouth

Unit 14 - Day 1

Reading About History

Read about history in the following resource:

★ *Stories of the Pilgrims* p. 152-154

Key Idea: An Indian came to warn the Pilgrims that a ship was coming. The Pilgrims hoped it was not a French ship coming to capture Plymouth. The red cross on the flag showed it was an English ship.

Poetry and Rhymes

Read aloud the poem *"The Arrow and the Song"* (see Appendix) to the students. Do not share the title. Ask students to suggest some titles for the poem. Share the real title. Read the poem again with the students.

Key Idea: Read and appreciate a variety of classic poetry.

Geography

Say, *An English ship sailed into Plymouth Harbor. Find England on a map or globe. On which continent is England located? Is Europe found north or south of the Equator? On which continent did the Pilgrims settle? Is North America north or south of the Equator? France was an enemy of England at the time of the Pilgrims. Find France on the map or globe. On which continent is France located? What are the names of the 7 continents? Which continents are located north of the Equator? Which continents are located south of the Equator?*

Key Idea: The Pilgrims were relieved to discover the ship was an English ship. Now, they would not have to fight to keep Plymouth an English settlement.

Bible Study

John 14:1-2 is the memory verse for this unit. Read the verse out loud. Ask, *What does it mean to be troubled? Why shouldn't your heart be troubled? Who does John 14:1 say you should trust? Why should you trust in God and His Son, Jesus?* Say the verse together 3 times. Add hand motions to help students remember the words.

Key Idea: The Pilgrims were relieved that the ship was from England. God was watching over them.

Corresponding Music

✔ *Hide 'Em in Your Heart Vol. 2* CD - Track 8; Cassette - Side A Song: *"In My Father's House"*

Learning the Basics

Focus: Language Arts and Math

Unit 14 - Day 1

Language Arts

Choose **either** spelling list 1 **or** 2 (see Appendix for lists). Write each spelling word on a separate index card. Guide students to study each card one at a time, flip it over, write the word from memory on paper, flip the card back over to check the spelling, and erase and correct any mistakes.

<u>Copywork</u>: Have students copy part of the poem *"The Arrow and the Song"*.

<u>Key Idea</u>: Practice spelling words with the 'or' sound as in 'horn'.

Reading Choices

Choose **one** of the reading options listed below (see Appendix for details).

★ A phonics program
★ *Scheduled Books for Emerging Readers*
★ *Drawn into the Heart of Reading Level 2/3*

<u>Key Idea</u>: Use a step-by-step program for reading instruction.

Storytime

Say, *What makes this story a fantasy?* (i.e. Have students give examples of things from the book that could not happen in real life). *Are all of the characters in the book people? If not, how would the story be different if they were all people?* Read aloud the next portion of the fantasy that you selected. Pace your reading to complete the fantasy during the next 15 days of plans.

<u>Key Idea</u>: Preread to build anticipation for the next part of the fantasy.

Math Exploration

Complete the assigned lesson in the workbook listed below.

✔ <u>Text Connection</u>: *Primary Mathematics Workbook 1A* p. 137

<u>Key Idea</u>: Use triangle tangrams to form other shapes.

Learning Through History

Focus: More Problems for the Pilgrims at Plymouth

Unit 14 - Day 2

Reading About History

Read about history in the following resource:

★ *Stories of the Pilgrims* p. 155-158

Key Idea: The ship from England brought new passengers. The ship did not bring enough food. So, the Pilgrims had to share their food with all the passengers and the sailors. There was hardly enough for winter.

Poetry and Rhymes

Read aloud the poem *"The Arrow and the Song"* (see Appendix) with the students. Discuss the poem's meaning. If you choose, photocopy the poem, cut it apart, and have students put it order.

Key Idea: Read classic poetry.

Artistic Expression

Give students a white piece of paper to color or paint like the English flag that was flown on the English ships. The Cross of Saint George was the flag that was flown on the *Mayflower* and on other English ships that arrived at Plymouth. The Cross of Saint George' flag is white with a red cross on it that divides the flag into 4 equal parts. Even after King James designed the "Union Jack" flag in 1603, to signify the union of Scotland and England, the English merchant ships still flew the Cross of Saint George on their foremast.

✔ Text Connection: *God's Wonderful Works* p. 21-23

Key Idea: The Pilgrims watched the sky to catch a glimpse of the ship's flag as it came over the horizon. More people arrived from England to settle in the new land.

Bible Study

Say John 14:1-2 while the students join in on the parts they know. Use the hand motions you added on Day 1. Say, *What are some things that trouble or worry you? How can trusting in God, and His Son Jesus, help you to worry less? What does Jesus promise you in John 14:2? How can that promise help you not to be troubled?* Next, have students do 3 push-ups. After 3 push-ups, have the students recite the entire Bible verse. Repeat the activity several times.

Key Idea: The Pilgrims had many troubles, but they still trusted in God.

Corresponding Music

✔ *Hide 'Em in Your Heart Vol. 2* CD - Track 8; Cassette - Side A Song: *"In My Father's House"*

Learning the Basics

Focus: Language Arts and Math

Unit 14 - Day 2

Language Arts

Use the spelling list from Day 1. Say the first spelling word. Use it in a sentence. Repeat the word. Ask students to write the word on a piece of paper or a markerboard from memory. Give students the matching word card from Day 1 to compare with their spelling. Guide students to correct any mistakes. Repeat the activity with all 10 words.
Copywork: Have students copy part of *"The Arrow and the Song"*.

Key Idea: Practice spelling words with the 'or' sound as in 'horn'.

Reading Choices

Choose **one** of the reading options listed below (see Appendix for details).

★ A phonics program
★ *Scheduled Books for Emerging Readers*
★ *Drawn into the Heart of Reading Level 2/3*

Key Idea: Use a step-by-step program for reading instruction.

Storytime

Read aloud the next portion of the fantasy that you selected. Without looking back at the story, begin retelling or narrating the part of the fantasy that you read today. After a short time, tap the student and say, *Your turn.* The student should pick up the narration where you left off. After a short time, the student should tap you and say, *Your turn.* Continue taking turns narrating in this manner until today's reading has been retold. Then, say, *Name one thing that you learned about the main character today.* Write it on paper for the students to copy.

Key Idea: Take turns retelling a story from a single reading.

Math Exploration

Say, *I wonder how tall you are compared to other objects? Let's walk through the house and find something taller than you. Then, let's find something that is shorter than you. Last, we'll find something about the same height as you.* After completing the walk through the house, use yarn or string to measure the length of each child's leg, arm, foot, neck, and hand. Cut pieces of string to match each measurement and label them with the body part. Tell students to compare the lengths of string and place them in order from shortest to longest. Say, *Which body part is the longest? Which is the shortest? How can you tell?*

Key Idea: Compare lengths using the terms 'longer', 'shorter', and 'taller'.

Learning Through History

Focus: More Problems for the Pilgrims at Plymouth

Unit 14 - Day 3

Reading About History

Read about history in the following resource:

★ *Stories of the Pilgrims* p. 159-162

Key Idea: An Indian messenger came with a snakeskin of arrows. The Indians meant to attack the Pilgrims. Governor Bradford filled the skin with gun powder and sent it to the chief as a warning. So, the Indians did not attack.

Poetry and Rhymes

Read aloud the poem *"The Arrow and the Song"* (see Appendix) with the students. Read the poem aloud a second time, pausing after each line or two for students to add their own actions to the poem. The actions should make sense with the poem.

Key Idea: Read classic poetry.

Science Exploration

Say, *Snakes belong to the reptile family. Reptiles are cold-blooded. Their skin is covered with scales. A snake's skin is not slimy to touch.* Guide students to cut a small snake out of paper. Help students use a hole-punch to punch circles out of brown, tan, and black paper. Have students use the colored paper circles as scales. Show students how to glue the scales onto the snake, slightly overlapping each circle with the one before it. Students may wish to make a colorful pattern with the scales as they glue them on the snake.

✔ Text Connection: *God's Wonderful Works* p. 114-115

Key Idea: The snakeskin of powder was returned to Plymouth after being passed among the Indian tribes.

Bible Study

Say John 14:1-2 with the students. Use the hand motions you added on Day 1. Next, have students skip around the room until you say, *Freeze.* After they 'freeze', have the students recite the entire Bible verse. Have students repeat the activity.

✔ Text Connection: *Morning Bells* p. 55-57

Key Idea: The Pilgrims trusted God to fight for them and show them what to do. You can trust the Lord to help you conquer your troubles too.

Corresponding Music

✔ *Hide 'Em in Your Heart Vol. 2* CD - Track 8; Cassette - Side A Song: *"In My Father's House"*

Learning the Basics

Focus: Language Arts and Math

Unit 14 - Day 3

Language Arts

Choose 3 or more words from the spelling list from Day 1. Ask students to use each of the words that you chose in a sentence. On a paper or a markerboard, write down the sentences as the students dictate them. Underline the spelling word in each sentence. Tell students to copy the sentences on paper and check their work. <u>Copywork</u>: Have students copy part of *"The Arrow and the Song"*.

<u>Key Idea</u>: Practice spelling words.

Reading Choices

Choose **one** of the reading options listed below (see Appendix for details).

★ A phonics program
★ *Scheduled Books for Emerging Readers*
★ *Drawn into the Heart of Reading Level 2/3*

<u>Key Idea</u>: Use a step-by-step program for reading instruction.

Storytime

Say, *Draw 4 circles on a piece of paper to be faces. In the first circle, draw eyes and a smile to be a happy face. In the second circle, draw eyes and a frown to be a sad face. In the third circle, draw eyes and a squiggly line for a mouth to be a mad face. In the fourth circle, draw eyes and an 'O' shape for a mouth to be a surprised or scared face.* Discuss times when the students have felt the mood shown by each face. Read aloud the next portion of the fantasy that you selected. As you read, stop periodically to have students point to the face that best shows the mood in the story at that time.

<u>Key Idea</u>: Focus on the story element: *mood*.

Math Exploration

Complete the assigned lesson in the workbook listed below.

✔ <u>Text Connection</u>: *Primary Mathematics Workbook 1A* p. 138-141

<u>Key Idea</u>: Compare lengths and heights of items using the terms 'longer', 'shorter', and 'taller'.

Learning Through History

Focus: More Problems for the Pilgrims at Plymouth

Unit 14 - Day 4

Reading About History

Read about history in the following resource:

★ *Stories of the Pilgrims* p. 163-168

Key Idea: Chief Massasoit was sick. He sent a messenger to the Pilgrims for help. Edward Winslow went to help Massasoit. The Indians learned that broth, fresh air, water, and quiet rest worked better than the medicine men.

Poetry and Rhymes

Read aloud the poem *"The Arrow and the Song"* (see Appendix) with the students. Have students draw pictures that reflect the poem's meaning on either a photocopy of the poem or on their copywork. File the finished poem in a special place.

Key Idea: Read classic poetry.

Science Exploration

Say, *Winslow prepared broth for Massasoit. Let's see why broth is digested more quickly than regular food.* Place a coffee filter over a glass. The filter is the stomach. The glass is the small intestine. In a bowl, mix 1/2 cup of water with 2 tablespoons salt to be broth. Pour half of the broth into the filter. Ask, *What happens to the broth? Why is it able to drip quickly from the stomach into the intestine?* Crumble a cracker and add it to the remaining broth in the bowl. Pour the rest of the broth into the filter. Ask, *What happens to the food now? Why is it taking more time for the food to be digested?*

✓ Text Connection: *God's Wonderful Works* p. 26

Key Idea: Edward Winslow made broth for Massasoit to drink.

Bible Study

Say John 14:1-2 with the students. Use the hand motions from Day 1. Say, *Name some sins that you are trying to conquer or stop doing. How can the Lord help you fight those sins? What do you need to do if you want the Lord to help you? Why does the Lord want you to ask for help and trust Him?* Next, have students run in place. When you say, *Freeze,* have the students stop and recite the verse. Repeat the activity.

Key Idea: The Indians found that the medicine men did not have the power they thought they did.

Corresponding Music

✓ *Hide 'Em in Your Heart Vol. 2*
CD - Track 8; Cassette - Side A
Song: *"In My Father's House"*

Learning the Basics

Focus: Language Arts and Math

Unit 14 - Day 4

Language Arts

Use the spelling list from Day 1. Say each word and use it in a sentence. Have students write each word and check it with the matching word card from Day 1. Guide students to correct any mistakes. Use a dark marker to write each missed word very largely on paper. Help students trace each missed word with glue. Allow the glue to dry in order to feel the words.
Copywork: Have students copy part of the poem *"The Arrow and the Song"*.

Key Idea: Practice spelling words with the 'or' sound as in 'horn'.

Reading Choices

Choose **one** of the reading options listed below (see Appendix for details).

★ A phonics program
★ *Scheduled Books for Emerging Readers*
★ *Drawn into the Heart of Reading Level 2/3*

Key Idea: Use a step-by-step program for reading instruction.

Storytime

Say, *Brotherly love means sincerely caring for others regardless of the circumstance.* Read aloud the key verse Philippians 1:9. Read aloud Acts 10:23-36. Ask, *How did Peter's actions show brotherly love?* Read aloud the next portion of the fantasy that you selected. Then, ask, *How do the main characters in the fantasy show brotherly love? What would the Biblical character, Peter, do differently from the characters in your book?*

Key Idea: Focus on the Godly character trait: *brotherly love*.

Math Exploration

Choose three objects for students to use as measuring tools (i.e. crayons, toothpicks, clothespins, markers, paperclips, or buttons). Choose **one** item for students to measure (i.e. notebook, pan, fork, or cookie sheet). Have students measure the length of the same item three times using the three different measuring tools. Write down the number of each measuring tool that it took to equal the length of the item. Compare the results. Ask, *Why aren't all of the measurements the same?*

✔ Text Connection: *Primary Mathematics Workbook 1A* p. 142-144

Key Idea: Measure with nonstandard units of measurement.

Learning Through History

Focus: More Problems for the Pilgrims at Plymouth

Unit 14 - Day 5

Reading About History

Read the following passage from your own Bible:

★ Exodus 14:5-31

<u>Key Idea</u>: In this Bible passage, the Lord fought for the Israelites and saved them from the Egyptians. The Lord watches over all of His people. He had a plan for the Pilgrims to settle in America. He has a plan for you too.

Poetry and Rhymes

Have students get out the poems that they saved from the previous units. Ask students to select one or more poems to review. Read aloud the selected poems with the students.

<u>Key Idea</u>: Read classic poetry.

History Activity

Say, *God made a path for the Israelites across the Red Sea. Let's do a fun experiment that will remind you of the parting of the Red Sea. Fill a bowl partway with water. Sprinkle pepper across the surface of the water. Hold the tip of a bar of soap in the center of the water. Watch what happens to the pepper. Were you surprised to see the pepper part and move toward the sides of the bowl? Can you imagine how amazed the Israelites must have been to see the waters of the Red Sea part?*

<u>Key Idea</u>: God did a miracle when He parted the Red Sea. He showed the Israelites that He is the one true God. The God of the Israelites is also the God of the Pilgrims and God over you.

Bible Study

Ask, *In Exodus 14:13-14 what does Moses tell the Israelites? What can you learn from Moses? In Exodus 14:31, what did the people do after God saved them? Why should you trust God? How do you know that God can help you?* Ask students to share their memory verse, John 14:1-2, with someone special. Suggestions for sharing the verse include saying it to another family member, saying it to someone by telephone, reciting it to a stuffed animal, or writing it to mail.

<u>Key Idea</u>: The God you serve today is the same God that saved the Israelites. Trust Him to help you.

Corresponding Music

✓ *Hide 'Em in Your Heart Vol. 2*
CD - Track 8; Cassette - Side A
Song: *"In My Father's House"*

Learning the Basics

Focus: Language Arts and Math

Unit 14 - Day 5

Language Arts

Say, *Your full name includes your first, middle, and last name. Your first and middle names are special names that were chosen for you. Your last name is your family name.* Write each student's full name on a piece of paper. Ask, *What kind of letter do you notice at the beginning of each name word? Nouns that tell the special name of a person, place, or thing are called proper nouns. Proper names begin with a capital letter.* Ask students to help make a list of the full names of their family members. Save the list for Unit 15 - Day 5.
Copywork: Have students copy their full name.

Key Idea: Write proper names.

Reading Choices

Choose **one** of the reading options listed below (see Appendix for details).

★ A phonics program

★ *Scheduled Books for Emerging Readers*

★ *Drawn into the Heart of Reading Level 2/3*

Key Idea: Use a step-by-step program for reading instruction.

Storytime

Read aloud a short portion of the fantasy that you selected. Prompt students to retell today's part of the story with the following ideas: *Describe the time of day or night and what the weather was like in the story. Explain the mood of the story by telling how the characters are feeling. What did the characters say to each other? What problem is there in the story?*

Key Idea: Give students practice retelling a portion of a fantasy.

Math Exploration

Tape a strip of masking tape on the table and label it from left to right 'lighter', 'as heavy as', 'heavier'. Find one can that weighs about a half a pound (i.e. 8 oz. can). Set out items to compare with the weight of the can (i.e. a spoon, a jug of milk or juice, a box of crackers, a bag of flour or sugar, a glass, a small can of food, a tissue box, a can of soda, or a bottle of water). Hold the 8 oz. can and pick up one other item at a time. Decide how the weight of each item compares to the can. Put each item under the correct column of the masking tape strip.

✓ Text Connection: *Primary Mathematics Workbook 1A* p. 145 (p. 146 is optional)

Key Idea: Compare weights of items.

Learning Through History

Focus: Dutch Pioneers Settle New Amsterdam

Unit 15 - Day 1

Reading About History

Read about history in the following resource:

★ *American Pioneers and Patriots* p. 42 and 50

Key Idea: Pioneers from Holland settled at New Amsterdam in America. A fort and a few houses were there already. Later, Dutch ships brought cows, sheep, and pigs. This meant there would be milk and butter for the pioneers.

Poetry and Rhymes

Read aloud the poem *"The Cow"* (see Appendix) to the students. Do not share the title. Ask students to suggest some titles for the poem. Share the real title. Read the poem again with the students.

Key Idea: Read and appreciate a variety of classic poetry.

Geography

Say, *The pioneers unloaded their cows on an island near New York City. An island is a small body of land surrounded by water. Why were the cows safer on an island?* Next, use masking tape to outline an island on the floor. Scatter cotton balls on the island to be cows. Say, *It is your job to keep the cows on the island. We will each use one index card as a canoe. I will load one cow at a time on my canoe, slide it across the floor to another place off the island, and unload the cow. Once, I've unloaded the cow, you can use your canoe to take the cow back to the island. At the end of 3 minutes, let's see if the cows are all on the island.*

Key Idea: The city of New Amsterdam later became New York City.

Bible Study

Matthew 25:21 is the memory verse for this unit. Read the verse out loud. Ask, *In Matthew 25:21, what does the master say to his servant? Explain what it means to be faithful. How can you be faithful to Jesus? What reward did the master give the servant for being faithful? If you are faithful to the Lord, how will He reward you?* Say the verse together 3 times. Add hand motions to help students remember the words.

Key Idea: The pioneers were faithful with what God gave them. You need to be faithful with what God has given you.

Corresponding Music

None this lesson

Learning the Basics

Focus: Language Arts and Math

Unit 15 - Day 1

Language Arts

Choose **either** spelling list 1 **or** 2 (see Appendix for lists). Write each spelling word on a separate index card. Guide students to study each card one at a time, flip it over, write the word on paper, flip the card back over to check the spelling, and erase and correct any mistakes.
<u>Copywork</u>: Have students copy part of the poem *"The Cow"*.

<u>Key Idea</u>: Practice spelling words with the 'er' sound as in 'her'.

Reading Choices

Choose **one** of the reading options listed below (see Appendix for details).

★ A phonics program
★ *Scheduled Books for Emerging Readers*
★ *Drawn into the Heart of Reading Level 2/3*

<u>Key Idea</u>: Use a step-by-step program for reading instruction.

Storytime

Choose one picture or a very descriptive passage from the next part of the fantasy book that you will read today. Do not show the students the page you have chosen. Read the passage or describe the picture to the students. Direct students to listen and follow the directions that you give them to draw the scene you are describing. When the drawings are complete, compare them to the page that you chose in the fantasy. Read aloud the next portion of the fantasy that you selected. Pace your reading to complete the book during the next 10 days of plans.

<u>Key Idea</u>: Set a purpose for reading the next part of the fantasy.

Math Exploration

Place an empty paper or plastic bag on a kitchen or a bathroom scale. Choose one kind of item to fill the bag until it weighs one pound (i.e. potatoes, shoes, cans of soup, heavy books, apples, or blocks). Write down how many of the item it took to make a pound. Test other kinds of items to see how many of each kind it takes to make a pound. Compare the results. Ask, *Why aren't the amounts the same?*

✔ <u>Text Connection</u>: *Primary Mathematics Workbook 1A* p. 147-148

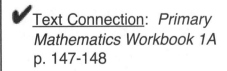

<u>Key Idea</u>: Measure items that equal one pound.

Learning Through History

Focus: Dutch Pioneers Settle New Amsterdam

Unit 15 - Day 2

Reading About History

Read about history in the following resource:

★ *American Pioneers and Patriots* p. 43-44

Key Idea: Peter took care of his special cow, Trinka, on the ship to New Amsterdam. When the ship arrived, Trinka didn't want to get off. Trinka got scared and accidentally dunked Peter in the water.

Poetry and Rhymes

Read aloud the poem *"The Cow"* (see Appendix) with the students. Discuss the poem's meaning. If you choose, photocopy the poem, cut it apart, and have the students place it in the correct order.

Key Idea: Read classic poetry.

Science Exploration

Help students make ice cream in a bag. Add 1/2 cup milk to a small ziplock bag. You may use skim, 1%, 2%, or whole milk. Add 1/2 tsp. vanilla and 1 T. sugar to the milk. Squeeze the air out of the bag and seal it tightly. In a large ziplock bag place 10-12 large ice cubes and 1/2 cup regular salt. Place the small ziplock bag, top side up, inside the large ziplock bag. Zip the large bag closed. Wrap the bag in a dish towel to absorb the moisture. Give the bag to the students to gently knead for 5 minutes. When the ice cream is firm, open the large bag over the sink and remove the small bag. Wipe it clean.

✔ Text Connection: *God's Wonderful Works* p. 104

Key Idea: Ice cream is a famous dairy product made from cow's milk.

Bible Study

Say Matthew 25:21 while the students join in on the parts they know. Use the hand motions you added on Day 1. Say, *Name some small tasks that you have been faithful in doing. Name some tasks that you need to be more faithful in doing. If you do not do a good job with the small things, will you be trusted with large things? Why not?* Next, have students do 5 toe touches. After 5 toe touches, have the students recite the entire Bible verse. Prompt the students as needed. Repeat the activity several times.

Key Idea: Peter was faithful with the task of caring for the cow, Trinka.

Corresponding Music

None this lesson

Learning the Basics

Focus: Language Arts and Math

Unit 15 - Day 2

Language Arts

Use the spelling list from Day 1. Say the first spelling word. Use it in a sentence. Repeat the word. Ask students to write the word on a markerboard or a piece of paper from memory. Give students the matching word card from Day 1 to compare with their spelling. Guide students to correct any mistakes. Repeat the activity with all 10 words.
<u>Copywork</u>: Have students copy part of the poem *"The Cow"*.

<u>Key Idea</u>: Practice spelling words with the 'er' sound as in 'her'.

Reading Choices

Choose **one** of the reading options listed below (see Appendix for details).

★ A phonics program

★ *Scheduled Books for Emerging Readers*

★ *Drawn into the Heart of Reading Level 2/3*

<u>Key Idea</u>: Use a step-by-step program for reading instruction.

Storytime

Read aloud the next portion of the fantasy book that you selected. Without looking back at the story, write a retelling of the part of the fantasy that you read today leaving blanks in place of key words (i.e. Chester was a _____ who lived in _____. He met a young boy named _____ at the _____ stand. _____ had a special talent. He could play beautiful _____.). Key words can be names, places, descriptive words, times of day, seasons, etc. Work with the students to reread the written narration and fill in the missing words.

<u>Key Idea</u>: Model retelling a story from a single reading.

Math Exploration

Set out packages of food items to compare (i.e. package of spaghetti, can of vegetables, bottle of ketchup, jar of peanut butter, bottle of cooking oil, box of oatmeal, can of soda, bag of chocolate chips, jar of mustard, bag of marshmallows, jar of jelly, jug of juice, or a can of soup). Guide students to check the labels of the items to find the packages' weights. Have students place the items in order from lightest to heaviest. Say, *Find the item that weighs closest to one pound. Compare the items using the words 'heavier' and 'lighter'*.

✓ <u>Text Connection</u>: *Primary Mathematics Workbook 1A* p. 149-150

<u>Key Idea</u>: Compare weights of items.

Learning Through History

Focus: Dutch Pioneers Settle New Amsterdam

Unit 15 - Day 3

Reading About History

Read about history in the following resource:

★ *American Pioneers and Patriots* p. 45-46

Key Idea: The cows, pigs, and horses needed to be moved off the island to find more grass. Trinka was being stubborn. Peter had a hard time getting her on the boat.

Poetry and Rhymes

Read aloud the poem *"The Cow"* (see Appendix) with the students. Read the poem aloud a second time, pausing after each line or two for students to add their own actions to the poem. The actions should make sense with the poem.

Key Idea: Read and appreciate a variety of classic poetry.

Science Exploration

Help students separate milk into curds and whey. Say, *Fill a glass 2/3 full of milk. Add 1 and 1/2 T. vinegar to the milk. Wait 5 minutes for the milk to separate. The clumps of milk that form are curds. The leftover liquid is whey. To strain out the curds, lay a paper towel over a bowl, and pour the milk over the paper towel. Do not drink the whey. It is sour milk. Rinse the curds with cold water. Then, squeeze the curds between dry paper towels to remove the moisture. Add a little salt to the curds and taste them. You may add a little plain yogurt or evaporated milk to the curds to make ricotta or cottage cheese.*

✔ Text Connection: *God's Wonderful Works* p. 88 and 110

Key Idea: The pioneers made their own cheese from cow's milk.

Bible Study

Say Matthew 25:21 with the students. Use the hand motions you added on Day 1. Next, have students lay on their backs and peddle their feet in the air like they are riding a bicycle. When you say, *Freeze,* the students should stop and recite the entire Bible verse. Repeat the activity.

✔ Text Connection: *Morning Bells* p. 28-30

Key Idea: Peter stayed on the boat to be near Trinka and to faithfully watch over her. He went with her to New Amsterdam.

Corresponding Music

None this lesson

Learning the Basics

Focus: Language Arts and Math

Unit 15 - Day 3

Language Arts

Using the spelling list from Day 1, choose 3 or more words that the students need to practice. Guide students to use each of the words that you chose in a sentence. On a markerboard or a piece of paper, write down the sentences as the students dictate them to you. Underline the spelling word in each sentence. Have the students copy the sentences on a piece of paper. Help students check their sentences and correct any mistakes.
<u>Copywork</u>: Have students copy part of the poem *"The Cow"*.

<u>Key Idea</u>: Practice spelling words with the 'er' sound as in 'her'.

Reading Choices

Choose **one** of the reading options listed below (see Appendix for details).

★ A phonics program
★ *Scheduled Books for Emerging Readers*
★ *Drawn into the Heart of Reading Level 2/3*

<u>Key Idea</u>: Use a step-by-step program for reading instruction.

Storytime

Read aloud the next portion of the fantasy book that you selected. Down the left side of a piece of paper, draw 4 rectangles. Ask students to list 4 main characters from the fantasy. Write one character's name in each rectangle. Draw an arrow next to each rectangle. At the end of each arrow, draw a circle to be a face. Ask students to add eyes and a mouth to each face to show the mood of that character in today's reading.

<u>Key Idea</u>: Focus on the story element: *mood*.

Math Exploration

These are the concepts that are covered in this review: writing numbers up to '20'; adding and subtracting; comparing sizes, lengths, and heights; using addition and subtraction in word problems. Review any concepts that students had difficulty understanding. In addition, complete the assigned review in the workbook listed below.

✔ <u>Text Connection</u>: *Primary Mathematics Workbook 1A* p. 151-154

<u>Key Idea</u>: Review difficult concepts.

Learning Through History

Focus: Dutch Pioneers Settle New Amsterdam

Unit 15 - Day 4

Reading About History

Read about history in the following resource:

★ *American Pioneers and Patriots* p. 47-49

<u>Key Idea</u>: Some of the cows ate poisonous weeds and died. But, Trinka was safe. Later, English warships came and took over New Amsterdam. The English changed the city's name to New York.

Poetry and Rhymes

Read aloud the poem *"The Cow"* (see Appendix) with the students. Have students draw pictures that reflect the poem's meaning on either a photocopy of the poem or on their copywork. File the finished poem in a special place.

<u>Key Idea</u>: Read classic poetry.

Artistic Expression

Cut a piece of green paper in half the long way. Have students cut fringes along the long side of the paper to be grass. Glue the green paper on top of the bottom half of a piece of blue paper. Do not put any glue on the fringe part of the grass. Cut out a brown or black circle that is the size of an orange. Cut out a brown or black oval that is the size of a pineapple. The two shapes will be used as a cow's head and body. Glue the small oval partway under the grass to be the cow's head. Glue the large oval partway under the grass, next to the head, to be the cow's body. Cut out and glue 2 white horns on the cow's head. Use markers to add a face and tail to the cow.

<u>Key Idea</u>: Watching over the cows while they grazed in the pasture was an important job for the young boys.

Bible Study

Say Matthew 25:21 with the students. Use the hand motions you added from Day 1. Ask, *How do you know if you have been faithful with the jobs you are given? Who is watching you all of the time? If you have not been faithful in your tasks, what should you do? Why does it help to ask the Lord to forgive you?* Next, have students gallop by leading with their left foot until you say, *Freeze*. After they 'freeze', have the students recite the entire Bible verse. Have students switch to the right foot and repeat the activity.

<u>Key Idea</u>: Peter stayed with Trinka all night when the cows were sick.

Corresponding Music

None this lesson

Learning the Basics

Focus: Language Arts and Math

Unit 15 - Day 4

Language Arts

Use the spelling list from Day 1. Say each word and use it in a sentence. Have students write each word and check it with the matching word card from Day 1. Guide students to correct any mistakes. For each missed word, have students hop on one foot and spell the word out loud, hopping each time they say a letter. <u>Copywork</u>: Have students copy part of *"The Cow"*.

<u>Key Idea</u>: Practice spelling words with the 'er' sound as in 'her'.

Reading Choices

Choose **one** of the reading options listed below (see Appendix for details).

★ A phonics program
★ *Scheduled Books for Emerging Readers*
★ *Drawn into the Heart of Reading Level 2/3*

<u>Key Idea</u>: Use a step-by-step program for reading instruction.

Storytime

Say, *Brotherly love means sincerely caring for others regardless of the circumstance.* Read aloud Philippians 1:9. Say, *Name some ways that we care for others when it isn't easy* (i.e. care for the sick and elderly, care for those who are unkind, let others go first, forgive, give away a larger portion, share a precious item). Discuss, *How can we become even more loving* (i.e. be more Christ-like, show self-control, be an example to others)? Read aloud the next portion of the fantasy that you selected. Ask, *How do the book characters show loving care for others when it isn't easy? Do the characters show the opposite trait, hatred?*

<u>Key Idea</u>: Focus on the Godly character trait: *brotherly love*.

Math Exploration

These are the concepts that are covered in this review: writing number words up to 'twenty', counting with ordinal numbers, ordering numbers, completing number sentences, comparing lengths of items, patterning, completing a shape, and using addition and subtraction in word problems. Review any concepts that students had difficulty understanding. Also, complete the assigned review in the workbook listed below.

✓ <u>Text Connection</u>: *Primary Mathematics Workbook 1A* p. 155-158

<u>Key Idea</u>: Review difficult concepts.

Learning Through History

Focus: Dutch Pioneers Settle New Amsterdam

Unit 15 - Day 5

Reading About History

Read the following passage from your own Bible:

★ Matthew 25:14-30

Key Idea: In this parable, a master gave three men money. When the master came back, each man was judged by what he had done with what he had been given. When the Lord returns, you will be judged by how you use what you were given.

Poetry and Rhymes

Have students get out the poems that they saved from the previous units. Ask students to select one or more poems to review. Read aloud the selected poems with the students.

Key Idea: Read classic poetry.

History Activity

Get out 10 quarters or dimes, 4 nickels, and 1 penny to be the talents in today's parable. Read Matthew 25:14-30 out loud. As you read, have the students use the coins to act out the parable. Ask, *What did you learn from the parable? What does the Lord want you to do with your talents? If you don't use them to glorify God, which man in the parable are you like?* Next, have the students get out their timeline. Say, *Let's find the column that says 1600 on your timeline. Draw a small cow in that column. Write 'Dutch settle New Amsterdam, 1624' under it.*

Key Idea: Each of us is given certain talents and abilities. Many people forget that all talents come from God and should be used to glorify Him. Are you using your talents to glorify God?

Bible Study

Say, *In Matthew 25:14-23, what did the master say to the first two men? Why did he invite them to share in his happiness? In Matthew 25:24-30, what did the master say to the last man? What consequence did the man receive? Which man does Christ want you to be like? Why?* Ask students to share their memory verse, Matthew 25:21, with someone special. Suggestions for sharing the verse include saying it to another family member, saying it to someone by telephone, reciting it to a stuffed animal, or writing it to mail.

Key Idea: God gives you gifts to use for His glory. You must use your money, time, and gifts to honor God.

Corresponding Music

None this lesson

Learning the Basics

Focus: Language Arts and Math

Unit 15 - Day 5

Language Arts

Take out the list of names that you saved from Unit 14 - Day 5. Say, *A person's full name includes their first, middle, and last name. Proper names begin with a capital letter. Look at your full name. Color the capital letters you see in your name. Where do you notice that the capital letters are found? The beginning or first letter of each word is called the initial letter. So, the three initial letters of your full name would be...* (i.e. C.M.A.). Say, *A person's initials can be used as a short way of referring to their proper name. Color the capital letters in the names of your other family members on the list. Write each family member's initials beside their name on the list.*
Copywork: Have students copy their initials.

Key Idea: Practice writing initials for proper names.

Reading Choices

Choose **one** of the reading options listed below (see Appendix for details).

★ A phonics program
★ *Scheduled Books for Emerging Readers*
★ *Drawn into the Heart of Reading Level 2/3*

Key Idea: Use a step-by-step program for reading instruction.

Math Exploration

Set out two bowls that contain different-sized items (i.e. cereal pieces, small building bricks, coins, buttons, clothespins, or cotton balls). Have students choose one bowl. Tell them to estimate how many items they will be able to pick up in one handful. Allow students to take one handful from one bowl, count the items, and compare the result to their estimate. Have students repeat the activity with the items in the other bowl. Compare the results. Ask, *Were the number of items in the handfuls the same? Why not?*

✓ Text Connection: *Primary Mathematics Workbook 1B* p. 7

Key Idea: Compare groups of objects.

Storytime

Read aloud a short portion of the fantasy that you selected.

Guide students to retell today's reading by asking them to share 5 new things that happened in the story today.

Key Idea: Give students practice retelling a portion of a fantasy.

Learning Through History

Focus: King Philip Declares War on the Pilgrims

Unit 16 - Day 1

Reading About History

Read about history in the following resource:

★ *Stories of the Pilgrims* p. 169 - half of p. 171

Key Idea: Almost fifty years after the Pilgrims settled at Plymouth, Chief Massasoit died. Massasoit and the Pilgrims had always kept the peace. Massasoit's son, Philip, hated the colonists and declared war on them.

Poetry and Rhymes

Read aloud the poem *"God, Who Made the Earth"* (see Appendix) to the students. Do not share the title. Ask students to suggest some titles for the poem. Share the real title. Read the poem again with the students.

Key Idea: Read and appreciate a variety of classic poetry.

Artistic Expression

Help students "weave" an Indian blanket using strips of paper. Give each student a 9" x 12" piece of red paper. Fold the paper in half the long way and cut slits starting at the fold about half an inch apart. Do not cut the slits all the way to the edge. Leave a 1/2" border all the way around the red paper. Open the red paper and lay it flat. Tell students to cut strips of equal widths of different colored construction paper to weave into their red blankets. Show students how to weave each strip of paper up, over, and under the slits in the red paper. Tape the colored strips of paper to the border around the red paper at the end of each row.

Key Idea: The Indians traded their land for beads, buttons, knives, and red blankets. They were beginning to feel cheated out of their land.

Bible Study

Proverbs 15:3 is the memory verse for this unit. Read the verse out loud. Ask, *Can the Lord always see you? How do you know? What does Proverbs 15:3 tell you that the Lord is watching or beholding? Does the Lord have a plan for what is happening in this world? How do you know?* Say the verse together 3 times. Add hand motions to help students remember the words.

Key Idea: The Lord had a plan for the Pilgrims. He watched over them and helped them settle at Plymouth.

Corresponding Music

✔ *Hide 'Em in Your Heart Vol. 2*
CD - Track 15; Cassette - Side B
Song: *"The Eyes of the Lord"*

Learning the Basics

Focus: Language Arts and Math

Unit 16 - Day 1

Language Arts

Choose **either** spelling list 1 **or** 2 (see Appendix for lists). Write each spelling word on a separate index card. Guide students to study each card one at a time, flip it over, write the word from memory on paper, flip the card back over to check the spelling, and erase and correct any mistakes.

Copywork: Have students copy part of the poem *"God, Who Made the Earth"*.

Key Idea: Practice spelling words with the 'ir' sound as in 'girl'.

Reading Choices

Choose **one** of the reading options listed below (see Appendix for details).

★ A phonics program

★ *Scheduled Books for Emerging Readers*

★ *Drawn into the Heart of Reading Level 2/3*

Key Idea: Use a step-by-step program for reading instruction.

Storytime

Say, *Name some of the characters in the fantasy story. If you were a character in this story, what would you like best about what's happening? What would you change in the story if you could? Why would you change this?*

Read aloud the next portion of the fantasy that you selected. Pace your reading to complete the fantasy book during the next 5 days of plans.

Key Idea: Set a purpose for reading the next part of the fantasy.

Math Exploration

Draw a hill with a valley on a white piece of paper. Give students 10 cotton balls, marshmallows, or white chocolate chips to be snowballs. Place 10 snowballs at the top of the mountain. Tell students to roll 1 snowball down the hill into the valley. Say, *10 - 1 = 9*. Roll another snowball into the valley. Say, *9 - 1 = 8*. Continue until no snowballs are left on the hill. Next, place 1 snowball in the valley. Roll 1 more snowball down the hill into the valley. Say, *1 + 1 = 2*. Continue untill all 10 snowballs are in the valley.

✓ Text Connection: *Primary Mathematics Workbook 1B* p. 8-9

Key Idea: Create sets with one more or one less.

Learning Through History

Focus: King Philip Declares War on the Pilgrims

Unit 16 - Day 2

Reading About History

Read about history in the following resource:

★ *Stories of the Pilgrims* p. 171-174

Key Idea: King Philip and his Indians began attacking the colonists. They burned houses, took women and children, and killed many people. It was a dangerous time for the colonists.

Poetry and Rhymes

Read aloud the poem *"God, Who Made the Earth"* (see Appendix) with the students. Discuss the poem's meaning. If you choose, photocopy the poem, cut it apart, and have the students put it in order.

Key Idea: Read classic poetry.

Geography

Say, *A field is flat land that has been cleared for planting or to be a pasture. A forest is land where many trees grow.* Scatter stuffed animals on one side of a room to be colonists. On the other side of the room, push together several chairs to be a forest. Say, *I will hide in the forest like an Indian. My job is to sneak into the field, grab a colonist, and run back to the forest. Your job is to chase me and tap me before I get to the forest. If you tap me before I get to the forest, you may take the colonist back to the field. If I get to the forest without being tapped, I will keep the colonist in the forest.*

Key Idea: The problems between the Indians and the colonists got worse. Indians hid in the forest and attacked the colonists.

Bible Study

Say Proverbs 15:3 while the students join in on the parts they know. Use the hand motions you added on Day 1. Say, *If you do something sneaky and no one catches you, does that mean God didn't see it? If you do something good, but no one notices, does God notice? Are you ever really alone? Why is God always watching you?* Next, have students do windmills by touching their right hand to their right foot, and then their left hand to their left foot. After every 5 windmills, have the students recite the Bible verse.

Key Idea: God sees everything.

Corresponding Music

✓ *Hide 'Em in Your Heart Vol. 2* CD - Track 15; Cassette - Side B
Song: *"The Eyes of the Lord"*

Learning the Basics

Focus: Language Arts and Math

Unit 16 - Day 2

Language Arts

Use the spelling list from Day 1. Say the first spelling word. Use it in a sentence. Repeat the word. Ask students to write the word on a markerboard or a piece of paper from memory. Give students the matching word card from Day 1 to compare with their spelling. Guide students to correct any mistakes. Repeat the activity with all 10 words.
<u>Copywork</u>: Have students copy part of the poem *"God, Who Made the Earth"*.

<u>Key Idea</u>: Practice spelling words with the 'ir' sound as in 'girl'.

Reading Choices

Choose **one** of the reading options listed below (see Appendix for details).

★ A phonics program

★ *Scheduled Books for Emerging Readers*

★ *Drawn into the Heart of Reading Level 2/3*

<u>Key Idea</u>: Use a step-by-step program for reading instruction.

Storytime

Read aloud the next portion of the fantasy that you selected. Ask students to retell or narrate what you read today. Remind students to tell the most important parts and to include details from the story in the retelling. As students work together to retell the story, write, type, or tape record the students' narration. When the students are finished, read the narration out loud. Highlight, circle, or underline one main idea from the narration for the students to copy.

<u>Key Idea</u>: Keep a sample of the students' narrations for the genre: *Fantasy*.

Math Exploration

Set out groups of different numbers of items (i.e. forks, spoons, cups, plates, napkins, glasses, bowls). Choose two groups of items to compare (i.e. plates and spoons). Show students how to match items from the two groups one-to-one to see which group has more. Next, point out that the leftover items don't have a match. Ask, *How many leftover items are there? How many more items does one group have than the other?* For example, there are 5 plates and 8 spoons. There are 3 more spoons than plates. Ask, *Which group has fewer items? Which group has more?*

<u>Key Idea</u>: Match items one-to-one to see which group has more and which group has less.

Learning Through History

Focus: King Philip Declares War on the Pilgrims

Unit 16 - Day 3

Reading About History

Read about history in this resource:

★ *Stories of the Pilgrims* p. 175 - half of p. 178

Key Idea: Two little girls named Prudence and Endurance were left alone one day while their parents went to the village. An Indian tribe lived nearby in the forest. They seemed friendly.

Poetry and Rhymes

Read aloud the poem *"God Who Made the Earth"* (see Appendix) with the students. Read the poem aloud a second time, pausing after each line or two for students to add actions to the poem. The actions should make sense.

Key Idea: Read classic poetry.

Science Exploration

Say, *Let's experiment with shadows. Turn off the lights. Hold a flashlight directly over top of a stuffed animal's head like the sun when it is noon. Describe the shadow that's formed. How big is it? Next, hold the flashlight at an angle pointing to the stuffed animal like the sun in the late afternoon. How is the shadow that's formed different from the shadow you saw before? Last, hold the flashlight straight out to the side of the stuffed animal like the sun as its going down. How does the shadow look now? Why did the shadows get longer and larger as the sun went down?*

✔ Text Connection: *God's Wonderful Works* p. 130-131

Key Idea: As the sun was going down, the girls prepared their lanterns and hid in the potato pit to surprise the Indians.

Bible Study

Say Proverbs 15:3 with the students. Use the hand motions you added on Day 1. Next, have students squat down, hop up, and squat back down again. After the last squat, have the students recite the entire Bible verse. Prompt students as needed. Repeat the activity.

✔ Text Connection: *Morning Bells* p. 97-99

Key Idea: Prudence and Endurance were not scared. They believed they were safe. Jesus protects and cares for you. He saves you from your enemies and gives you eternal life.

Corresponding Music

✔ *Hide 'Em in Your Heart Vol. 2* CD - Track 15; Cassette - Side B
Song: *"The Eyes of the Lord"*

Learning the Basics

Focus: Language Arts and Math

Unit 16 - Day 3

Language Arts

Using the spelling list from Day 1, choose 3 or more words that the students need to practice. Guide students to use each of the words that you chose in a sentence. On a markerboard or a piece of paper, write down the sentences as the students dictate them to you. Underline the spelling word in each sentence. Have the students copy the sentences on a piece of paper. Help students check their sentences and correct any mistakes.

Copywork: Have students copy part of the poem *"God, Who Made the Earth"*.

Key Idea: Practice spelling words with the 'ir' sound as in 'girl'.

Reading Choices

Choose **one** of the reading options listed below (see Appendix for details).

★ A phonics program
★ *Scheduled Books for Emerging Readers*
★ *Drawn into the Heart of Reading Level 2/3*

Key Idea: Use a step-by-step program for reading instruction.

Storytime

Read aloud the next portion of the fantasy that you selected.

Say, *What is the problem in the story? How does that problem seem to make the characters feel? Would the mood be different if the problem was solved or fixed? How would solving the problem change the mood of the story?*

Key Idea: Focus on the story element: *mood*.

Math Exploration

Complete the assigned lesson in the workbook listed below.

✓ Text Connection: *Primary Mathematics Workbook 1B* p. 10-11

Key Idea: Match items one-to-one to see which group has more and which group has less.

Learning Through History

Focus: King Philip Declares War on the Pilgrims

Unit 16 - Day 4

Reading About History

Read about history in the following resource:

★ *Stories of the Pilgrims* p. 178-181

Key Idea: Indians came to the farm while the girls' parents were gone. Prudence and Endurance hid in the potato pit with their lighted lanterns. At night when the Indians came back, the girls jumped up and scared them.

Poetry and Rhymes

Read aloud the poem *"God, Who Made the Earth"* (see Appendix) with the students. Have students draw pictures that reflect the poem's meaning on either a photocopy of the poem or on their copywork. File the finished poem in a special place.

Key Idea: Read classic poetry.

Science Exploration

Say, *Light reflects best off of smooth, flat surfaces. Let's use a bouncy ball to show how light rays bounce off of flat surfaces.* Either stand facing a partner or in a circle several feet apart. Take turns bouncing the ball to one another. *What do you notice about how the ball bounces? Back up two steps.* Take turns bouncing the ball to one another again. *What do you notice about how the ball bounces now? Back up two more steps and repeat the experiment. Why is the ball bouncing lower and at a wider angle? This is how light rays bounce off of flat surfaces.*

✔ Text Connection: *God's Wonderful Works* p. 13 and 15

Key Idea: The girls used lighted lanterns to surprise the Indians. The reflection of the lanterns scared the Indians, and they ran away.

Bible Study

Say Proverbs 15:3 with the students. Use the hand motions from Day 1. Say, *Name some things that you are tempted to do that are wrong. What is a shield? How does Jesus act like a shield against temptation for you? Who is stronger, Satan or Jesus?* Next, have students hop backward 5 times. After every 5 hops, have the students recite the entire Bible verse.

Key Idea: Jesus took care of Prudence and Endurance. He sees everything. Jesus can be your shield too, if you ask Him to help you.

Corresponding Music

✔ *Hide 'Em in Your Heart Vol. 2* CD - Track 15; Cassette - Side B Song: *"The Eyes of the Lord"*

Learning the Basics

Focus: Language Arts and Math

Unit 16 - Day 4

Language Arts

Use the spelling list from Day 1. Say each word and use it in a sentence. Have students write each word and check it with the matching word card from Day 1. Guide students to correct any mistakes. For each missed word, have students trace the word with their finger on a patch of carpet.

Copywork: Have students copy part of the poem *"God, Who Made the Earth"*.

Key Idea: Practice spelling words with the 'ir' sound as in 'girl'.

Reading Choices

Choose **one** of the reading options listed below (see Appendix for details).

★ A phonics program
★ *Scheduled Books for Emerging Readers*
★ *Drawn into the Heart of Reading Level 2/3*

Key Idea: Use a step-by-step program for reading instruction.

Storytime

Say, *Brotherly love means sincerely caring for others regardless of the circumstance.* Read aloud the key verse Philippians 1:9. Read aloud the next portion of the fantasy that you selected. Ask, *Did the main character usually show love or hate? Explain. Are you usually loving or unloving? Draw a picture showing one way that you could be more loving. Post your picture in a place where you will see it often.*

Key Idea: Focus on the Godly character trait: *brotherly love*.

Math Exploration

Draw a fence across the bottom of a piece of paper. Give students cereal pieces to be brown birds and raisins or chocolate chips to be black birds. Have students use their birds to act out stories comparing the numbers of the two kinds of birds on their papers (i.e. 4 black birds were on the fence. 3 brown birds came along. How many fewer brown birds are there? How many more black birds than brown birds are there?). Repeat the activity using different numbers of black birds and brown birds.

✓ Text Connection: *Primary Mathematics Workbook 1B* p. 12-13

Key Idea: Compare the numbers of two sets of items using subtraction.

Learning Through History

Focus: King Philip Declares War on the Pilgrims

Unit 16 - Day 5

Reading About History

Read the following passage from your own Bible:

★ 2 Samuel 22:26-36

Key Idea: The eyes of the Lord see all things. He is a shield to those that trust in Him. Many colonists turned to God in times of trouble, since the Indians were against them.

Poetry and Rhymes

Have students get out the poems that they saved from the previous units. Ask students to select one or more poems to review. Read aloud the selected poems with the students.

Key Idea: Read classic poetry.

History Activity

Have students act out the verses from 2 Samuel 22, as you read them aloud. Read verse 29. Have students walk through a dark room with a flashlight. Read verse 30. Have students crawl across the floor alternating their right hand and right leg with their left hand and left leg like they are scaling a wall. Read verse 31. Have students use a plastic lid as a shield to deflect rolled up socks or beanbags that you toss at them. Read verse 32. Place a piece of tape on the floor to be a rock. Have students stand on one foot on the 'rock' and count to five. Read verses 34. Have students run in place on their tiptoes like a deer. Read verse 35. Have students throw up a ball and catch it 5 times, using their hands and arms. Read verse 36. Stoop down, give the students a hug, and tell them they did great.

Key Idea: God watches over us from heaven to give us what we need.

Bible Study

Ask, *In 2 Samuel 22:26, what does it say God does for those that are faithful? Are you able to be faithful all of the time? Why not? Is God always faithful? In 2 Samuel 22:31, who does the Lord shield? What does it mean for God to be your rock?* Ask students to share their memory verse, Proverbs 15:3, with someone special. Suggestions for sharing the verse include saying it to another family member, saying it to someone by telephone, reciting it to a stuffed animal, or writing it to mail.

Key Idea: God is your rock and shield in times of trouble.

Corresponding Music

✓ *Hide 'Em in Your Heart Vol. 2*
CD - Track 15; Cassette - Side B
Song: *"The Eyes of the Lord"*

Learning the Basics

Focus: Language Arts and Math

Unit 16 - Day 5

Language Arts

On a markerboard or a paper, write the following sentences using your child's name: ___ played outside. Can ___ have dessert? ___ read a good book. ___ went swimming. ___ can't wait for the birthday party. ___will have fun at the park. Will ___ get to go to the zoo? Ask, *What name do you see in the sentences? What kind of letter is at the beginning of each name? When you are talking about yourself, what word do you use instead of your name?* (i.e. I played outside.) *Since 'I' takes the place of your name, it needs to begin with a capital letter.* Give each student an index card with the word 'I' on it. Have students read each sentence, place their 'I' card over their name in the sentence, and then read it again.

<u>Key Idea</u>: Point out that 'I' is always capitalized.

Reading Choices

Choose **one** of the reading options listed below (see Appendix for details).

★ A phonics program
★ *Scheduled Books for Emerging Readers*
★ *Drawn into the Heart of Reading Level 2/3*

<u>Key Idea</u>: Use a step-by-step program for reading instruction.

Storytime

Read aloud the final portion of the fantasy that you selected. You will need to select a mystery book to read aloud next. Guide students to use their toys to set up an important scene from today's reading. Then, have students use the scene to retell what happened in the story.

<u>Key Idea</u>: Give students practice retelling a portion of a fantasy.

Math Exploration

Complete the assigned lesson in the workbook listed below.

✔ <u>Text Connection</u>: *Primary Mathematics Workbook 1B* p. 14-17

<u>Key Idea</u>: Decide whether to add or subtract for each word problem.

Learning Through History

Focus: Two Pilgrim Children Become Captives

Unit 17 - Day 1

Reading About History

Read about history in the following resource:

⭐ *Stories of the Pilgrims* p. 183 - half of p. 186

Key Idea: Two little boys named Isaac and Joseph were taken captive by some Indians near the village of Haverhill. The boys hoped that someone would save them.

Poetry and Rhymes

Read aloud the poem *"Evening"* (see Appendix) to the students. Do not share the title. Ask students to suggest some titles for the poem. Share the real title. Read the poem again with the students.

Key Idea: Read and appreciate a variety of classic poetry.

Science Exploration

Say, *Fish have slimy skin that is covered with scales. The scales protect the fish by reflecting its surroundings like a mirror as it swims. This helps camouflage or hide the fish.* Cut a fish shape out of aluminum foil. To make the foil easier to cut, place it between 2 sheets of newspaper, and then cut out the fish. Give each student a fish to demonstrate how camouflage works. Have students make their fish swim to different areas of the house, stopping to see how the fish reflects its surroundings along the way.

✔ Text Connection: *God's Wonderful Works* p. 72 and 76

Key Idea: Isaac and Joseph planned to go fishing once they finished cutting the corn. The Indians captured the two boys as they were drinking from the stream.

Bible Study

1 Peter 5:7 is the memory verse for this unit. Read the verse out loud. Ask, *What does the word 'cast' mean? In 1 Peter 5:7, what does it tell you to cast upon the Lord? Explain the meaning of anxiety or cares. Why should you cast your cares or anxiety upon the Lord?* Say the verse together 3 times. Add hand motions to help students remember the words.

Key Idea: Isaac and Joseph were very scared. When you are scared or worried, the Lord tells you to cast your cares upon Him and trust Him.

Corresponding Music

None this lesson

Learning the Basics

Focus: Language Arts and Math

Unit 17 - Day 1

Language Arts

Choose **either** spelling list 1 **or** 2 (see Appendix for lists). Write each spelling word on a separate index card. Guide students to study each card one at a time, flip it over, write the word from memory on paper, flip the card back over to check the spelling, and erase and correct any mistakes.

Copywork: Have students copy part of the poem *"Evening"*.

Key Idea: Practice spelling words with the 'ar' sound as in 'farm'.

Reading Choices

Choose **one** of the reading options listed below (see Appendix for details).

★ A phonics program
★ *Scheduled Books for Emerging Readers*
★ *Drawn into the Heart of Reading Level 2/3*

Key Idea: Use a step-by-step program for reading instruction.

Storytime

Choose at least one mystery to read aloud for the next 20 days of plans (see Appendix for suggested titles). Say, *A mystery is a story that has a puzzling problem to be solved.* To introduce the genre, Mystery, secretly choose one item and place it in a box. Give clues to the contents of the box. Have students guess what item is in the box. Next, have students secretly place an item in the box. Have them give you clues to guess the contents of the box. Read a portion of the mystery you chose.

Key Idea: Introduce the genre: *Mystery*.

Math Exploration

Complete the assigned lesson in the workbook listed below.

✓ Text Connection: *Primary Mathematics Workbook 1B* p. 18-20

Key Idea: Practice reading picture graphs.

Learning Through History

Focus: Two Pilgrim Children Become Captives

Unit 17 - Day 2

Reading About History

Read about history in the following resource:

⭐ *Stories of the Pilgrims* p. 186 - half of p. 190

Key Idea: The Indians took Isaac and Joseph to their camp. The boys knew their fathers could not find them there. They were obedient and worked hard, so the Indians would trust them.

Poetry and Rhymes

Read aloud the poem *"Evening"* (see Appendix) with the students. Discuss the poem's meaning. If you choose, photocopy the poem, cut it apart, and have the students place it in the correct order.

Key Idea: Read and appreciate a variety of classic poetry.

Artistic Expression

Read aloud the last paragraph on p. 186 - top of p. 187 of *Stories of the Pilgrims*. Guide students to make a picture to show the setting described in that paragraph. Have students brush watercolor paints across the top half of a piece of white paper to look like a sunset. Guide students to glue a strip of tinfoil across the bottom of the paper to be the lake. Help students cut out a line of jagged trees from black paper and glue them between the lake and the sunset.

Key Idea: As the sun went down, Isaac and Joseph saw the Indian camp by the lake. This would be their home for awhile. The Indians taught the boys to grind corn, carry water from the spring, gather wood for the fire, and tan deer skins.

Bible Study

Say 1 Peter 5:7 while the students join in on the parts they know. Use the hand motions you added on Day 1. Say, *Name some cares or worries that you have. How can you cast those worries on Jesus? Why does Jesus want you to turn to Him for help? How will it help to cast your cares on Him?* Next, have students do 5 jumping jacks. After 5 jumping jacks, have the students recite the entire Bible verse. Prompt the students as needed. Repeat the activity several times.

Key Idea: The boys were not sure what would happen to them in the Indian camp. They hoped to escape.

Corresponding Music

None this lesson

Learning the Basics

Focus: Language Arts and Math

Unit 17 - Day 2

Language Arts

Use the spelling list from Day 1. Say the first spelling word. Use it in a sentence. Repeat the word. Ask students to write the word on a markerboard or a piece of paper from memory. Give students the matching word card from Day 1 to compare with their spelling. Guide students to correct any mistakes. Repeat the activity with all 10 words.
<u>Copywork</u>: Have students copy part of the poem *"Evening"*.

<u>Key Idea</u>: Practice spelling words with the 'ar' sound as in 'farm'.

Reading Choices

Choose **one** of the reading options listed below (see Appendix for details).

★ A phonics program

★ *Scheduled Books for Emerging Readers*

★ *Drawn into the Heart of Reading Level 2/3*

<u>Key Idea</u>: Use a step-by-step program for reading instruction.

Storytime

Read aloud the next portion of the mystery that you selected. Without looking back at the story, model retelling or narrating the part of the mystery that you read today to the students. Remember to tell the most important points and to add details from the story to the retelling without overwhelming the students. After the retelling, ask, *What things seem mysterious or strange in the story?* On paper, write a one-sentence summary of the students' answers to the question. Have the students copy the sentence.

<u>Key Idea</u>: Model retelling a story from a single reading.

Math Exploration

Tape a long strip of masking tape on the table. Draw a diamond, a club, a spade, and a heart on the masking tape. Give students a deck of playing cards with the Jokers removed. Have them flip over the top card and place it above the matching suit on the masking tape strip (i.e. a 10 of hearts would be placed above the heart on the masking tape strip). Continue flipping over 15 more cards and placing them in a column above the matching suit on the strip to create a graph. Discuss the graph.

✔ <u>Text Connection</u>: *Primary Mathematics Workbook 1B* p. 21-22

<u>Key Idea</u>: Read and interpret picture graphs.

Learning Through History

Focus: Two Pilgrim Children Become Captives

Unit 17 - Day 3

Reading About History

Read about history in the following resource:

 Stories of the Pilgrims p. 190-194

<u>Key Idea</u>: Joseph and Isaac lived with the Indians all winter. They learned many new things. The Indians talked about going to Canada in the spring.

Poetry and Rhymes

Read aloud the poem *"Evening"* (see Appendix) with the students. Read the poem aloud a second time, pausing after each line or two for students to add their own actions to the poem. The actions should make sense with the poem.

<u>Key Idea</u>: Read and appreciate a variety of classic poetry.

Geography

Say, *The Indians planned to take the boys up the river to Canada in the spring. The beginning of a river is called the source. The bottom of a river is called the river bed. The sides of the river are called the river bank. The place where the river runs into another body of water is called the mouth.* Use 4 strips of paper to make labels for 'source', 'bed', 'bank', and 'mouth'. Have students use playdough or clay to make a model in a cake pan of a river running into a lake. Give students the labels to place at the correct spots on their model. Carefully add water to the model.

<u>Key Idea</u>: Joseph and Isaac could understand most of what the Indians said. They heard the Indians talk about traveling up the river to Canada.

Bible Study

Say 1 Peter 5:7 with the students. Use the hand motions you added on Day 1. Next, have students hop on their left foot until you say, *Freeze*. After they 'freeze', have the students recite the entire Bible verse. Prompt students as needed. Have students switch to the right foot, and repeat the activity.

✔ <u>Text Connection</u>: *Morning Bells* p. 61-63

<u>Key Idea</u>: Joseph and Isaac must have felt all alone. You are never alone. God cares for you and watches over you all of the time.

Corresponding Music

None this lesson

Learning the Basics

Focus: Language Arts and Math

Unit 17 - Day 3

Language Arts

Using the spelling list from Day 1, choose 3 or more words that the students need to practice. Guide students to use each of the words that you chose in a sentence. On a markerboard or a piece of paper, write down the sentences as the students dictate them to you. Underline the spelling word in each sentence. Have the students copy the sentences on a piece of paper. Help students check their sentences and correct any mistakes.

Copywork: Have students copy part of the poem *"Evening"*.

Key Idea: Practice spelling words with the 'ar' sound as in 'farm'.

Reading Choices

Choose **one** of the reading options listed below (see Appendix for details).

★ A phonics program

★ *Scheduled Books for Emerging Readers*

★ *Drawn into the Heart of Reading Level 2/3*

Key Idea: Use a step-by-step program for reading instruction.

Storytime

Read aloud the next portion of the mystery that you selected.

Say, *Who are some of the characters in the mystery? Explain what is happening in the mystery. Predict means to guess what will happen next using the clues in the story. Predict what will happen next in the mystery. How did you make your guess about what will happen?*

Key Idea: Introduce the story element: *prediction*.

Math Exploration

Provide a grouping of four different types of snacks for students to graph (i.e. crackers, raisins, cereal pieces, fruit, or pretzels). Tape a long strip of masking tape to the table. Write the names of the four types of snacks on the masking tape. Direct students to choose one snack and place it above its matching title on the masking tape. Continue placing the snacks one at a time in the correct column of the graph. Discuss the results of the graph.

✔ Text Connection: *Primary Mathematics Workbook 1B* p. 23-24

Key Idea: Represent data using a graph.

Learning Through History

Focus: Two Pilgrim Children Become Captives

Unit 17 - Day 4

Reading About History

Read about history in this resource:

★ *Stories of the Pilgrims* p. 195 - top of p. 198

Key Idea: Since the Indians planned to sell Isaac and Joseph to the French in Canada, the boys escaped in the night. The Indians came looking for them, but they didn't find them.

Poetry and Rhymes

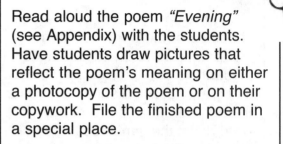

Read aloud the poem *"Evening"* (see Appendix) with the students. Have students draw pictures that reflect the poem's meaning on either a photocopy of the poem or on their copywork. File the finished poem in a special place.

Key Idea: Read and appreciate a variety of classic poetry.

Science Exploration

Show students a book up close. Walk 15-20 feet away. Ask, *Does the book look smaller to you now? Did the size of the book change? Why does it look smaller?* Say, *This is like the sun. It is really very large, but we are so far away from it that it looks small.* Show students a flashlight beam up close. Next, walk 15-20 feet away to a place. Ask, *Does the flashlight beam look dimmer to you now? Did the brightness of the flashlight change? Why does the flashlight beam seem dimmer?* Say, *This is like the sun. It is really very bright and hot, but we are so far away from it that it only warms the Earth instead of burning it.*

✔ Text Connection: *God's Wonderful Works* p. 63

Key Idea: When the boys escaped, they followed the stars at night and the sun during the day.

Bible Study

Say 1 Peter 5:7 with the students. Use the hand motions you added on Day 1. Say, *Name some people that love you. How do you know that they love you? What do they do to take care of you? How does God care for you?* Next, have the students do 5 sit-ups. After 5 sit-ups, have the students recite the entire Bible verse.

Key Idea: As Isaac and Joseph were escaping through the forest, God was watching over them. He watches over you too.

Corresponding Music

None this lesson

Learning the Basics

Focus: Language Arts and Math

Unit 17 - Day 4

Language Arts

Use the spelling list from Day 1. Say each word and use it in a sentence. Have students write each word and check it with the matching word card from Day 1. Guide students to correct any mistakes. For each missed word, have students spell the word out loud, clapping once each time they say a letter.

Copywork: Have students copy part of the poem *"Evening"*.

Key Idea: Practice spelling words with the 'ar' sound as in 'farm'.

Reading Choices

Choose **one** of the reading options listed below (see Appendix for details).

★ A phonics program
★ *Scheduled Books for Emerging Readers*
★ *Drawn into the Heart of Reading Level 2/3*

Key Idea: Use a step-by-step program for reading instruction.

Storytime

Say, *Loyalty means showing firm, faithful support even in times of trouble.* Read aloud the key verse Proverbs 19:11 to illustrate *loyalty*. List some people that you feel loyalty toward. Now, have students list people that they feel loyalty toward.

Read aloud the next portion of the mystery that you selected. Then, ask, *Which characters show loyalty? To whom do they show loyalty? What could the characters do to be more loyal?*

Key Idea: Introduce the Godly character trait: *loyalty*.

Math Exploration

Give students a set of up to 40 items (i.e. dry cereal pieces, buttons, cotton balls, or dry macaroni). Tell students to count their items to get a total. Next, provide cups or bowls for students to place groups of 10 items into as they count. Direct students to make as many groups of 10 as possible. Demonstrate how much easier it is to count by tens and then count on to add the leftovers, instead of counting all of the items one at a time.

✔ Text Connection: *Primary Mathematics Workbook 1B* p. 25

Key Idea: Count up to '40' by placing items in groups of ten.

Learning Through History

Focus: Two Pilgrim Children Become Captives

Unit 17 - Day 5

Reading About History

Read the following passage from your own Bible:

 1 Peter 5:5-11

Key Idea: This Bible passage gives hope to those that are suffering. Isaac and Joseph felt scared and alone, yet God had His mighty hand over them. God is stronger than any evil in the world.

Poetry and Rhymes

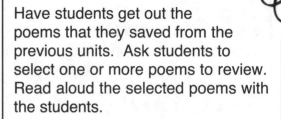

Have students get out the poems that they saved from the previous units. Ask students to select one or more poems to review. Read aloud the selected poems with the students.

Key Idea: Read and appreciate a variety of classic poetry.

History Activity

Read 1 Peter 5:6-9. Say, *Let's go on a short journey. As you go on your journey, you will need the Lord's help to protect you from your enemy, the lion. You will start in the laundry room and tiptoe to the living room. Every time you hear me roar like a lion, you must stop and recite 1 Peter 5:7 before continuing on your journey. When you reach the end of your journey, say a prayer of thanks to God for keeping you safe.* Repeat the activity using different movements like galloping, hopping, or skipping. Then, have students get out their timeline. Say, *Let's find the column that says 1600. Draw a small hatchet in that column. Write 'King Philip's War, 1675' under it.*

Key Idea: Isaac and Joseph needed God's help and protection.

Bible Study

Ask, *What does 1 Peter 5:6 tell you about God? In 1 Peter 5:9, how does it say that you can resist the devil? In 1 Peter 5:10, what does God promise Christians who are suffering? How can you trust God even when you are suffering?* Ask students to share their memory verse, 1 Peter 5:7, with someone special. Suggestions for sharing the verse include saying it to another family member, saying it to someone by telephone, reciting it to a stuffed animal, or writing it to mail.

Key Idea: God promises to help you if you call upon Him.

Corresponding Music

None this lesson

Learning the Basics

Focus: Language Arts and Math

Unit 17 - Day 5

Language Arts

Get out 7 index cards. Say, *Nouns that tell the special name of a person, place, or thing are called proper nouns. Proper names begin with a capital letter.* Ask, *How many days are in a week? Since each day has its own special name, what kind of letter should be at the beginning of each day? Help me list the days of the week on index cards, starting with Sunday* (i.e. Sunday, Monday, Tuesday, Wednesday, Thursday, Friday, Saturday). Say, *Mix the cards up and put them in order. Color the capital letter at the beginning of each day of the week.* Copywork: Have students copy the names of the days of the week.

Key Idea: Capitalize the names of the days of the week.

Reading Choices

Choose **one** of the reading options listed below (see Appendix for details).

★ *A phonics program*

★ *Scheduled Books for Emerging Readers*

★ *Drawn into the Heart of Reading Level 2/3*

Key Idea: Use a step-by-step program for reading instruction.

Storytime

Read aloud a short portion of the mystery that you selected. Give students a chance to orally retell the portion of today's story that you read aloud. Use the following prompts as needed: *What happened in the beginning of the part that we read today? What happened during the middle of the part we read today? Explain what happened at the end.*

Key Idea: Give students practice retelling a portion of a mystery.

Math Exploration

Say, *I will call out a number between '1' and '35'. Next, I will start clapping. Your job is to begin at the number that I called out and count up by ones for each clap that you hear. When I stop clapping, call out the ending number. Last, write that number on a markerboard or a piece of paper. Let's practice. If I say, '29' and clap three times like this..clap...clap...clap. What number will you call out? ('32'). Now, write '32". Let's play again.*

✔ Text Connection: *Primary Mathematics Workbook 1B* p. 26-27

Key Idea: Practice counting and writing numbers up to '40'.

Learning Through History

Focus: Trouble in the New Land

Unit 18 - Day 1

Reading About History

Read about history in the following resource:

★ *Stories of the Pilgrims* p. 198-202

Key Idea: Joseph and Isaac became tired and hungry as they traveled for days. Finally, Joseph became too weak to go any further. Isaac carried him until they came to a fort. The boys were finally safe.

Poetry and Rhymes

Read aloud the poem *"Jesus Bids Us Shine"* (see Appendix) to the students. Do not share the title. Ask students to suggest some titles for the poem. Share the real title. Read the poem with the students.

Key Idea: Read and appreciate a variety of classic poetry.

Science Exploration

Choose one scent (i.e vanilla, almond, or peppermint extract, or lemon juice) to put on 8-10 cotton balls. Place the cotton balls in a trail for the students to follow. Have the trail end at a tub or a sink partway filled with water. Place the last cotton ball in the water. Put a different scent on 6 other cotton balls. Scatter those cotton balls randomly around the trail. Say, *The dogs followed Isaac and Joseph's scent, until they lost it at the river.* Give students the first cotton ball with the scent you want them to follow. Have students sniff each cotton ball for the scent and try to follow the trail. Discuss how the scent was lost in the water.

✔ Text Connection: *God's Wonderful Works* p. 95

Key Idea: God gave dogs a very good sense of smell.

Bible Study

Review the memory verse, Romans 8:28, from Unit 13. Read the verse out loud. Say, *In Romans 8:28, how does it say that God works? What is a purpose? Whose purpose are Christians called to fulfill? Do all people on earth have a Godly purpose? How can you discover God's purpose for you?* Say the verse together 3 times. Review the hand motions that go with the verse from Unit 13.

Key Idea: God brought Isaac and Joseph back safely. God has a plan for everything that happens to us.

Corresponding Music

✔ *Hide 'Em in Your Heart Vol. 2*
CD - Track 19; Cassette - Side B
Song: *"All Things Work Together..."*

Learning the Basics

Focus: Language Arts and Math

Unit 18 - Day 1

Language Arts

Get out the spelling words on index cards that you saved from Unit 14. Guide students to study each card one at a time, flip it over, write the word from memory on paper, flip the card back over to check the spelling, and erase and correct any mistakes.

<u>Copywork</u>: Have students copy part of the poem *"Jesus Bids Us Shine"*.

<u>Key Idea</u>: Review spelling words from Unit 14.

Reading Choices

Choose **one** of the reading options listed below (see Appendix for details).

★ A phonics program
★ *Scheduled Books for Emerging Readers*
★ *Drawn into the Heart of Reading Level 2/3*

<u>Key Idea</u>: Use a step-by-step program for reading instruction.

Storytime

Say, *How can you tell that a story is a mystery? Remember, a mystery is a story that has a puzzling problem to be solved. What is the mystery in this book? Who are some of the characters that seem important to the mystery? Listen for clues or important items as we read today. If you hear a clue or something that sounds puzzling, say, "Hmmmm" and rub your chin. I'll do it along with you!* Read aloud the next portion of the mystery that you selected. Pace your reading to complete the mystery during the next 15 days of plans.

<u>Key Idea</u>: Preread to build anticipation for the next part of the mystery.

Math Exploration

Give students up to 40 items (i.e. crayons, puzzle pieces, cotton balls, or small blocks). Provide ziplock bags for the students. Tell students to count and bag their items in groups of 10. Then, have students count by tens and add on the leftover items to find the total number of items. Direct students to write a number sentence on a markerboard or a piece of paper to describe their totals (i.e. 3 tens + 8 leftovers = 38, or 30 + 8 = 38). Repeat the activity with a different number of items.

<u>Key Idea</u>: Group items in tens for faster counting.

Learning Through History

Focus: Trouble in the New Land

Unit 18 - Day 2

Reading About History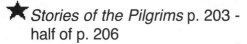

Read about history in the following resource:

★ *Stories of the Pilgrims* p. 203 - half of p. 206

Key Idea: A widow in the village of Swansea was kind to the Indians that lived nearby. She wouldn't give them hard cider because it would make them drunk. This made an Indian, named Warmsly, angry.

Poetry and Rhymes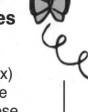

Read aloud the poem *"Jesus Bids Us Shine"* (see Appendix) with the students. Discuss the poem's meaning. If you choose, photocopy the poem, cut it apart, and have the students put it in order.

Key Idea: Read and appreciate a variety of classic poetry.

Artistic Expression

Say, *Mary and Benjamin hid a quill of powder inside a candle to make a sparkler candle. When the wick burned down to the quill, the powder would go off. Let's make a picture of the sparkler candle.* Give students a colored sheet of paper. Have them cut a candle out of white paper and glue it to the center of the colored paper. Help students cut designs out of the colored paper around the candle. Leave at least a 1/2" between cut-outs. Tape a sheet of tin foil to the back of the paper to shine or sparkle through the cut-outs.

✔ Text Connection: *God's Wonderful Works* p. 17

Key Idea: Mary and Benjamin made a sparkler candle to use at their special party. The war with the Indians seemed to be over.

Bible Study

Review the memory verse from Unit 14, John 14:1-2, by saying it while the students join in on the parts they know. Say, *What are some things that are troubling you right now? In John 14:1, what does it say you should do? How can John 14:2 comfort you or help you feel better?* Next, have students do 3 push-ups. After 3 push-ups, have the students recite the entire Bible verse. Repeat the activity several times.

Key Idea: The widow was troubled about Warmsly's anger. She had to trust God to protect her family.

Corresponding Music

✔ *Hide 'Em in Your Heart Vol. 2* CD - Track 8; Cassette - Side A Song: *"In My Father's House"*

Learning the Basics

Focus: Language Arts and Math

Unit 18 - Day 2

Language Arts

Get out the spelling cards that you saved from Unit 15. Say the first spelling word. Use it in a sentence. Repeat the word. Ask students to write the word on a markerboard or a piece of paper from memory. Give students the matching word card to compare with their spelling. Guide students to correct any mistakes. Repeat the activity with all 10 words. <u>Copywork</u>: Have students copy part of the poem *"Jesus Bids Us Shine"*.

<u>Key Idea</u>: Review spelling words.

Reading Choices

Choose **one** of the reading options listed below (see Appendix for details).

★ A phonics program
★ *Scheduled Books for Emerging Readers*
★ *Drawn into the Heart of Reading Level 2/3*

<u>Key Idea</u>: Use a step-by-step program for reading instruction.

Storytime

Read aloud the next portion of the mystery that you selected. Without looking back at the story, begin retelling or narrating the part of the mystery that you read today. After a short time, tap the student and say, *Your turn.* The student should pick up the narration where you left off. After a short time, the student should tap you and say, *Your turn.* Continue taking turns narrating in this manner until today's reading has been retold. Then, say, *Name one thing that you learned about the main character today.* Write it on paper for the students to copy.

<u>Key Idea</u>: Take turns retelling a story from a single reading.

Math Exploration

Complete the assigned lesson in the workbook listed below.

✓ <u>Text Connection</u>: *Primary Mathematics Workbook 1B* p. 28-30

<u>Key Idea</u>: Place items in groups of 10 to help find the sum.

Learning Through History

Focus: Trouble in the New Land

Unit 18 - Day 3

Reading About History

Read about history in the following resource:

⭐ *Stories of the Pilgrims* p. 206 - 211

Key Idea: The children made a sparkler candle for a special party. During the party, Warmsly came with several Indians and demanded cider. The candle went off and scared the Indians away.

Poetry and Rhymes

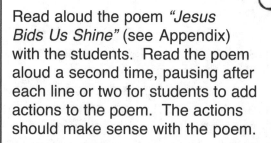

Read aloud the poem *"Jesus Bids Us Shine"* (see Appendix) with the students. Read the poem aloud a second time, pausing after each line or two for students to add actions to the poem. The actions should make sense with the poem.

Key Idea: Read and appreciate a variety of classic poetry.

History Activity

Say, *Let's pretend that we are at Mary and Benjamin's party waiting for the sparkler candle to go off.* Set a flashlight in the center of the room to be a sparkler candle. Give the students a snack of apples, lunch meat, or bread. Have the students sit on the floor around the candle while they eat their snack. Say, *when I flash the flashlight, it means the candle is going off. Whenever you see the light flashing, you must stop eating and run around the room in a circle until you get back to your spot. When you get to your spot, recite the memory verse Matthew 25:21.* Repeat the activity several times while the students are eating their snack.

Key Idea: God protected the widow and her family from the Indians.

Bible Study

Review the memory verse, Matthew 25:21, from Unit 15, by saying it while the students join in on the parts they know. Next, have students skip around the room until you say, *Freeze.* After they 'freeze', have the students recite the entire Bible verse. Have students repeat the activity.

✔ Text Connection: *Morning Bells* p. 16-18

Key Idea: The widow in Swansea was faithful to God. God promises to be with you. He wants you to trust Him and not be afraid.

Corresponding Music

None this lesson

Learning the Basics

Focus: Language Arts and Math

Unit 18 - Day 3

Language Arts

Choose 3 or more words from the spelling cards for Unit 16 that the students need to practice. Guide students to use each of the words that you chose in a sentence. On a paper or a markerboard, write down the sentences as the students dictate them. Underline the spelling word in each sentence. Tell students to copy the sentences on paper and check them. <u>Copywork</u>: Have students copy part of *"Jesus Bids Us Shine"*.

<u>Key Idea</u>: Review spelling words.

Reading Choices

Choose **one** of the reading options listed below (see Appendix for details).

★ A phonics program
★ *Scheduled Books for Emerging Readers*
★ *Drawn into the Heart of Reading Level 2/3*

<u>Key Idea</u>: Use a step-by-step program for reading instruction.

Storytime

Down the left side of a piece of paper write the following question starters: *Who, What, When, Where, Why, How*. Say, *Today you will be a story detective. Think of questions that will help you look for clues as we read today. Tell me one question you have about the mystery that starts with the word, "Who"*. Write the question down on the paper next to the word, *Who*. Continue asking students to share questions about the mystery for each of the remaining words on the paper. Save the list of questions for Unit 19 - Day 3. Read aloud the next portion of the mystery.

<u>Key Idea</u>: Focus on the story element: *prediction*.

Math Exploration

Use the '1' - '40' number chart on p. 32 of *Primary Mathematics Workbook 1B*. Cover several numbers in the same row of the chart with a small item (i.e. dry cereal piece, dime, raisin, or a small button). Ask students to name the numbers that are covered up. Students may check to see if they are correct by looking under each covered number. Repeat the activity by covering different numbers in the chart.

✔ <u>Text Connection</u>: *Primary Mathematics Workbook 1B* p. 31-32

<u>Key Idea</u>: Find the missing numbers in a counting pattern.

Learning Through History

Focus: Trouble in the New Land

Unit 18 - Day 4

Reading About History

Read about history in the following resource:

★ *Stories of the Pilgrims* p. 212-216

Key Idea: One day, a maid saw an Indian sneaking up on the house. She hid the children under two brass kettles. The Indian fired his gun at the kettles, but the children were safe. The Indian ran away.

Poetry and Rhymes

Read aloud the poem *"Jesus Bids Us Shine"* (see Appendix) with the students. Have students draw pictures that reflect the poem's meaning on either a photocopy of the poem or on their copywork. File the finished poem in a special place.

Key Idea: Read classic poetry.

Science Exploration

Use wrapping paper to cut out some butterflies. To make the cutting go more quickly, place the paper in a pile and cut out a stack of butterflies at the same time. Without letting the students see you, lay the butterflies on top of things throughout one room. Try to lay the butterflies in places where they are camouflaged by their background. Have students walk into the room where you have hidden the butterflies and point to the first one they see. Ask, *Why did you see that butterfly first?* Have students find the rest of the butterflies. Ask, *Which butterfly was the hardest to see? Why was the butterfly camouflaged?*

✔ Text Connection: *God's Wonderful Works* p. 121

Key Idea: One Sunday morning, as butterflies flitted by the window, an Indian snuck up to the house.

Bible Study

Say, *When you are afraid, what should you do? Can you trust God to help you? How do you know? God promises to help and strengthen you. What does God ask you to do?* Review the memory verse, Proverbs 15:3, from Unit 16 by saying it while the students join in on the parts they know. Next, have students run in place. Say, *Freeze,* and have the students stop and recite the entire Bible verse. Repeat the activity.

Key Idea: God protected the children from the Indians. You need to ask God for help and trust in Him.

Corresponding Music

✔ *Hide 'Em in Your Heart Vol. 2* CD - Track 15; Cassette - Side B Song: *"The Eyes of the Lord"*

Learning the Basics

Focus: Language Arts and Math

Unit 18 - Day 4

Language Arts

Get out the spelling word cards from Unit 17. Say each word and use it in a sentence. Have students write each word and check it with the matching word card. Guide students to correct any mistakes. For each missed word, have students "write" the word with their index finger in soapy water.

<u>Copywork</u>: Have students copy part of the poem *"Jesus Bids Us Shine"*.

<u>Key Idea</u>: Review the spelling words from Unit 17.

Reading Choices

Choose **one** of the reading options listed below (see Appendix for details).

★ *A phonics program*
★ *Scheduled Books for Emerging Readers*
★ *Drawn into the Heart of Reading Level 2/3*

<u>Key Idea</u>: Use a step-by-step program for reading instruction.

Storytime

Say, *Loyalty means showing firm, faithful support even in times of trouble.* Read aloud the key verse Proverbs 19:11. Read aloud 1 Samuel 1:21-28. Ask, *How did Hannah's actions show loyalty to God?*

Read aloud the next portion of the mystery that you selected. Then, ask, *How do the characters in the mystery show loyalty? What would the Biblical character, Hannah, do differently from the characters in your book?*

<u>Key Idea</u>: Focus on the Godly character trait: *loyalty*.

Math Exploration

Take all of the cards numbered '2' - '9' from a deck of playing cards. Place the cards you took in a pile facedown. Players will take turns drawing two cards at a time and placing them face-up on the table in front of themselves. Each player makes the greatest number they can with their two cards. All players compare their totals to see who has the highest number. The player with the highest number gets 1 point. Keep track of points until one player receives 5 points. That player is the winner.

✔ <u>Text Connection</u>: *Primary Mathematics Workbook 1B* p. 33

<u>Key Idea</u>: Compare numbers to see which are greater or smaller.

Learning Through History

Focus: Trouble in the New Land

Unit 18 - Day 5

Reading About History

Read the following passage from your own Bible:

Matthew 14:22-32

Key Idea: Jesus told the disciples not to be afraid. Jesus wanted the disciples to trust Him and know He is the Son of God. During colonial times, many colonists needed to trust God to keep them safe.

Poetry and Rhymes

Have students get out the poems that they saved from the previous units. Ask students to select one or more poems to review. Read aloud the selected poems with the students.

Key Idea: Read and appreciate a variety of classic poetry.

Geography

Say, *In Matthew 14:22-32, Jesus went up on a mountainside to pray. A mountain is a steeply rising chunk of land. As Jesus was praying, a storm came up on the lake. A lake is a body of water surrounded by land.* Build a mountain in the sink out of clay or playdough. Use a sponge or a washcloth soaked with water to be a cloud. Move the cloud over the mountain from west to east. As the cloud rises higher to go over the mountain, squeeze the cloud to drop rain on the west side of the mountain like a storm. The cold air above the mountains caused the clouds to drop their water as rain or snow.

✓ Text Connection: *God's Wonderful Works* p. 1-3

Key Idea: The disciples needed to trust that Jesus is the Son of God during the storm on the lake.

Bible Study

Ask, *In Matthew 14:27, what did Jesus say to the disciples?* Explain what it means to have courage. When might you need to have courage? What can you learn from Peter in Matthew 14:28-31? Should you doubt the Lord? Why not? Ask students to share their memory verse, 1 Peter 5:7, with someone special. Suggestions for sharing the verse include saying it to another family member, saying it to someone by telephone, reciting it to a stuffed animal, or writing it to mail.

Key Idea: Many colonists were Godly people that had faith in Jesus. Jesus wants us to believe and trust in Him.

Corresponding Music

None this lesson

Learning the Basics

Focus: Language Arts and Math

Unit 18 - Day 5

Language Arts

Get out the index cards of the days of the week that you made for Unit 17 - Day 5. Say, *Nouns that tell the special name of a person, place, or thing are called proper nouns. Proper nouns begin with a capital letter. The names of the days of the week are special names, so each day begins with a capital letter.* Tell students to mix the index cards and sequence the days or the week in order beginning with Sunday. Have the students use the order of the cards as a guide to sing the days of the week to the tune of *"Twinkle, Twinkle, Little Star"* or *"Clementine"*.
Copywork: Have students copy the names of the days of the week again.

Key Idea: Capitalize the names of the days of the week.

Reading Choices

Choose **one** of the reading options listed below (see Appendix for details).

★ *A phonics program*
★ *Scheduled Books for Emerging Readers*
★ *Drawn into the Heart of Reading Level 2/3*

Key Idea: Use a step-by-step program for reading instruction.

Storytime

Read aloud a short portion of the mystery that you selected. Have students use playdough or clay to build a scene from today's reading. Then, have students tell what is happening using the scene that they built as a way of retelling today's reading.

Key Idea: Give students practice retelling a portion of a mystery.

Math Exploration

Place pennies and dimes in a central location. Place a set of cards numbered '1' - '9' facedown. Direct students to draw a card. The number they drew tells how many dimes to take. Have students draw a second card. This number tells how many pennies to take. Tell students to count their dimes by tens and add on their pennies to get the total. Help students write a number sentence for their coins on a markerboard or a piece of paper (i.e. 6 dimes + 5 pennies = 65, or 60 + 5 = 65).

✔ Text Connection: *Primary Mathematics Workbook 1B* p. 34

Key Idea: Practice writing numbers with tens and ones.

Learning Through History

Focus: Life for the Puritans in Colonial Times

Unit 19 - Day 1

Reading About History

Read about history in the following resource:

★ *Boys and Girls of Colonial Days* p. 22-24 (old version, p. 20-22)

Key Idea: Remember Biddle was a Puritan girl living near Plymouth Rock. Her father was gone in Boston on business. Her mother left her alone to go help a sick neighbor.

Poetry and Rhymes

Read aloud the poem *"Monday's Child"* (see Appendix) to the students. Do not share the title. Ask students to suggest some titles for the poem. Share the real title. Read the poem again with the students.

Key Idea: Read and appreciate a variety of classic poetry.

Geography

Use the map on p. 52 of *American Pioneers and Patriots* for today's lesson. Say, *Trace your finger along the Atlantic Coast. Find Boston, Massachusetts on the map. Name the colonies that were settled by English people. Name the colony that was settled by Spanish people. Point to the French territory. Find the area of the country that was claimed by both England and France.*

Key Idea: Plymouth Rock was an English colony on the Atlantic coast near Boston. Remember Biddle and her family lived near Plymouth Rock in colonial times.

Bible Study

1 John 4:10-11 is the memory verse for this unit. Read the verse out loud. Say, *In 1 John 4:10, what does it say God did to show His love to you? Do you deserve God's love? What does 1 John 4:11 tell you to do? Why should we love one another?* Say the verse together 3 times. Add hand motions to help students remember the words.

Key Idea: Remember Biddle's mother showed love to her neighbor by traveling to care for her when she was sick. Remember had to stay home alone.

Corresponding Music

✓ *Hide 'Em in Your Heart Vol. 2* CD - Track 10; Cassette - Side A Song: *"We Love Him"*

Learning the Basics

Focus: Language Arts and Math

Unit 19 - Day 1

Language Arts

Choose **either** spelling list 1 **or** 2 (see Appendix for lists). Write each spelling word on a separate index card. Guide students to study each card one at a time, flip it over, write the word from memory on paper, flip the card back over to check the spelling, and erase and correct any mistakes.

<u>Copywork</u>: Have students copy part of the poem *"Monday's Child"*.

<u>Key Idea</u>: Practice spelling words with long 'a' spelled 'ay' as in 'day'.

Reading Choices

Choose **one** of the reading options listed below (see Appendix for details).

★ A phonics program

★ *Scheduled Books for Emerging Readers*

★ *Drawn into the Heart of Reading Level 2/3*

<u>Key Idea</u>: Use a step-by-step program for reading instruction.

Storytime

Give each student a notepad or a piece of paper. Say, *As I read the mystery today, each time you hear something mysterious or puzzling, make a checkmark on your paper.*

Read aloud the next portion of the mystery that you selected. Pace your reading to complete the mystery during the next 10 days of plans. After today's reading is finished, have students draw or write one way to solve the mystery.

<u>Key Idea</u>: Set a purpose for reading the next part of the mystery.

Math Exploration

Fold a sheet of paper in half to make two columns. Write 'tens' on the left side and 'ones' on the right side. Give students 9 dimes and 9 pennies. Remind students that one dime = 10 pennies. Say, *I want you to use your dimes and pennies to make the number '45'. Place the dimes on the 'tens' side and the pennies on the 'ones' side of your paper. Count the 'tens'. Write that number. Next, write the number of 'ones'. Read the total. Did you write the number '45'?* Repeat the activity with different numbers. Save the paper.

✔ <u>Text Connection</u>: *Primary Mathematics Workbook 1B* p. 35

<u>Key Idea</u>: Write numbers using 'tens' and 'ones'.

Learning Through History

Focus: Life for the Puritans in Colonial Times

Unit 19 - Day 2

Reading About History

Read about history in the following resource:

⭐ *Boys and Girls of Colonial Days* p.25-28 (old version, p. 23-25)

Key Idea: Remember spent her days alone cleaning the house. When the house was clean, she made soap. She comforted herself by singing hymns from church.

Poetry and Rhymes

Read aloud the poem *"Monday's Child"* (see Appendix) with the students. Discuss the poem's meaning. If you choose, photocopy the poem, cut it apart, and have the students place it in the correct order.

Key Idea: Read and appreciate a variety of classic poetry.

Artistic Expression

Say, *After Remember finished scrubbing the floor, she sprinkled sand on it in a pretty pattern. Let's make our own floor pattern.* Have students draw a simple pattern on a brown piece of paper. Outline the pattern with glue. Slowly shake sand or salt on the glue lines. Shake off the excess sand or salt in the garbage. To make the pictures more colorful, you may want to use food coloring to color the sand or salt various colors before sprinkling it on the paper.

Key Idea: Remember used her time to glorify God. She worked hard cleaning the house the way her mother had taught her. She chose to be cheerful while she worked.

Bible Study

Say 1 John 4:10-11 while the students join in on the parts they know. Use the hand motions you added on Day 1. Ask, *Who do you find it hard to love? Why? What reason does 1 John 4:11 give you for loving others? Do you think that you are difficult to love sometimes? Does God still love you? Why?* Next, have students do 5 toe touches. After every 5 toe touches, have the students recite the entire verse. Prompt students as needed.

Key Idea: Remember worked hard to show love to her mother.

Corresponding Music

✓ *Hide 'Em in Your Heart Vol. 2* CD - Track 10; Cassette - Side A Song: *"We Love Him"*

Learning the Basics

Focus: Language Arts and Math

Unit 19 - Day 2

Language Arts

Use the spelling list from Day 1. Say the first spelling word. Use it in a sentence. Repeat the word. Ask students to write the word on paper or markerboard from memory. Give students the matching word card from Day 1 to compare with their spelling. Guide students to correct any mistakes. Repeat the activity with all 10 words. <u>Copywork</u>: Have students copy part of *"Monday's Child"*.

<u>Key Idea</u>: Practice spelling words with long 'a' spelled 'ay' as in 'day'.

Reading Choices

Choose **one** of the reading options listed below (see Appendix for details).

★ A phonics program

★ *Scheduled Books for Emerging Readers*

★ *Drawn into the Heart of Reading Level 2/3*

<u>Key Idea</u>: Use a step-by-step program for reading instruction.

Storytime

Read aloud the next portion of the mystery that you selected. Without looking back at the story, write a retelling of the part of the mystery that you read today leaving blanks in place of key words (i.e. _____, _____, and _____ had a mystery to solve. _____ found a clue in the _____. She shared the clue with her _____. The clue was a _____. The kids were _____ about the clue.). Key words can be names, places, descriptive words, time of day, seasons, etc. Work with the students to reread the written narration and fill in the missing words.

<u>Key Idea</u>: Model retelling a story from a single reading.

Math Exploration

Use the 'tens' and 'ones' chart from Unit 19 - Day 1. Give students a set of cards numbered '1' - '9'. Say the following riddles for students to answer using their cards and their 'tens' and 'ones' chart: *I have a '3' in the 'tens' place and a '4' in the 'ones' place. What number am I? Now, show me one less than '34' with your cards. Show me '10' more than '33' with your cards. Here is a new riddle. I have a '6' in the 'tens' place and a '7' in the 'ones' place. What number am I? Show me one more than '67'. Now, show me '10' less than '68'.* Continue the activity with other riddles. Save the chart.

<u>Key Idea</u>: Practice using the 'tens' and 'ones' place to show various numbers up to '100'.

Learning Through History

Focus: Life for the Puritans in Colonial Times

Unit 19 - Day 3

Reading About History

Read about history in the following resource:

★ *Boys and Girls of Colonial Days* p. 29-33 (old version, p. 26-29)

<u>Key Idea</u>: After Remember finished making soap, an Indian came to her cabin. The Indian wanted to take Remember with him. Then, he saw the soap. Instead, the Indian traded 2 turkeys for the soap.

Poetry and Rhymes

Read aloud the poem *"Monday's Child"* (see Appendix) with the students. Read the poem aloud a second time, pausing after each line or two for students to add their own actions to the poem. The actions should make sense with the poem.

<u>Key Idea</u>: Read classic poetry.

Science Exploration

Get out a large ball to be the Earth. Tape a tiny, play person to the Earth. Ask, *When sunset comes, does the sun really go down? Let's do an experiment to find out. I will hold a flashlight directly over the ball to be the sun. Slowly spin the ball so the person is facing the sun. The sun looks like it is directly over the person right now. This is what it looks like at noon. Now, slowly spin the person away from the sun. As the Earth turns away from the sun, it looks like the sun is going down in the sky. Is the sun really moving? What is moving instead of the sun?*

✔ Text Connection: *God's Wonderful Works* p. 6 and 19

<u>Key Idea</u>: As the sun was beginning to set, Remember saw an Indian.

Bible Study

Say 1 John 4:10-11 with the students. Use the hand motions you added on Day 1. Next, have students lay on their backs and peddle their feet in the air like they are riding a bicycle. When you say, *Freeze,* the students should stop and recite the entire Bible verse. Repeat the activity.

✔ Text Connection: *Morning Bells* p. 58-60

<u>Key Idea</u>: Remember was kind to the Indian. She had stored God's words in her heart to comfort her when she was afraid.

Corresponding Music

✔ *Hide 'Em in Your Heart Vol. 2* CD - Track 10; Cassette - Side A Song: *"We Love Him"*

Learning the Basics

Focus: Language Arts and Math

Unit 19 - Day 3

Language Arts

Using the spelling list from Day 1, choose 3 or more words that the students need to practice. Guide students to use each of the words that you chose in a sentence. On a markerboard or a piece of paper, write down the sentences as the students dictate them to you. Underline the spelling word in each sentence. Have the students copy the sentences on a piece of paper. Help students check their sentences and correct any mistakes.
<u>Copywork</u>: Have students copy part of the poem *"Monday's Child"*.

<u>Key Idea</u>: Practice spelling words.

Reading Choices

Choose **one** of the reading options listed below (see Appendix for details).

★ A phonics program
★ *Scheduled Books for Emerging Readers*
★ *Drawn into the Heart of Reading Level 2/3*

<u>Key Idea</u>: Use a step-by-step program for reading instruction.

Storytime

Read aloud the next portion of the mystery that you selected. Get out the questions from Unit 18 - Day 3 that the students asked about the mystery. Reread each question out loud to the students. Ask students to circle any questions that can be answered now. Have students share the answers to those questions after they circle them. Guide students to make predictions of how the remaining questions might be answered.

<u>Key Idea</u>: Focus on the story element: *prediction*.

Math Exploration

Complete the assigned lesson in the workbook listed below.

✔ <u>Text Connection</u>: *Primary Mathematics Workbook 1B* p. 36-38

<u>Key Idea</u>: Practice using the 'tens' and 'ones' place to show various numbers up to '100'.

Learning Through History

Focus: Life for the Puritans in Colonial Times

Unit 19 - Day 4

Reading About History

Read about history in the following resource:

★ *Stories of the Pilgrims* p. 220-228

Key Idea: The Puritans knew the Sabbath day was the Lord's Day. They did not work on the Sabbath. Instead, they went to church and worshiped the Lord.

Poetry and Rhymes

Read aloud the poem *"Monday's Child"* (see Appendix) with the students. Have students draw pictures that reflect the poem's meaning on either a photocopy of the poem or on their copywork. File the finished poem in a special place.

Key Idea: Read classic poetry.

Science Exploration

Say, *The Puritans were called to worship on the Sabbath day by the beating of a drum. Let's see how sound travels.* Blindfold the students. Stand across the room and lightly beat a drum or tap a wooden spoon against a bowl. Have the students point in the direction that the sound is coming from. Repeat the activity by quietly moving to different parts of the room and beating the drum again. Have students plug their ears and try the activity again. Ask, *Was it harder to decide which direction the sound was coming from when your ears were plugged? When your ears were plugged, the sound waves were being blocked by your fingers.*

✔ Text Connection: *God's Wonderful Works* p. 132 and 137

Key Idea: The Puritans set aside the Sabbath Day for the Lord just like we should do.

Bible Study

Say 1 John 4:10-11 with the students. Use the hand motions from Day 1. Say, *How does God speak to Christians today? Why did God give us His word, the Bible? When you read the Bible, how does God speak to you? What does the Lord expect you to do when you hear His words?* Have students gallop leading with their left foot until you say, *Freeze*. After they 'freeze', have the students recite the verse. Have students switch to the right foot and repeat the activity.

Key Idea: The Puritans carefully listened to God's word.

Corresponding Music

✔ *Hide 'Em in Your Heart Vol. 2* CD - Track 10; Cassette - Side A Song: *"We Love Him"*

Learning the Basics

Focus: Language Arts and Math

Unit 19 - Day 4

Language Arts

Use the spelling list from Day 1. Say each word and use it in a sentence. Have students write each word and check it with the matching word card from Day 1. Guide students to correct any mistakes. For each missed word, have students jump in place and spell the word out loud jumping each time they say a letter.
<u>Copywork</u>: Have students copy part of the poem *"Monday's Child"*.

<u>Key Idea</u>: Practice spelling words.

Reading Choices

Choose **one** of the reading options listed below (see Appendix for details).

★ A phonics program
★ *Scheduled Books for Emerging Readers*
★ *Drawn into the Heart of Reading Level 2/3*

<u>Key Idea</u>: Use a step-by-step program for reading instruction.

Storytime

Say, *Loyalty means showing firm, faithful support even in times of trouble.* Read aloud the key verse Proverbs 19:11. Say, *Name some ways that we show loyalty in times of trouble* (i.e. don't gossip, comfort someone who has made a mistake, stand up for someone, help those who are sick). Discuss, *How can we be more loyal?* (i.e. wait to hear their side of the story, don't judge others, listen). Read aloud the next portion of the mystery that you selected. Ask, *How do the book characters show loyalty in times of trouble? Do the characters show the opposite trait, disloyalty?*

<u>Key Idea</u>: Focus on the Godly character trait: *loyalty*.

Math Exploration

Complete the assigned lesson in the workbook listed below.

✔ <u>Text Connection</u>: *Primary Mathematics Workbook 1B* p. 39-40

Note: Remind students to start with the larger number and count up or back. You may need to point out the number patterns and explain the pictures.

<u>Key Idea</u>: Use number patterns to help with addition and subtraction of greater numbers.

Learning Through History

Focus: Life for the Puritans in Colonial Times

Unit 19 - Day 5

Reading About History

Read the following passage from your own Bible:

★ Psalm 119:105-112

Key Idea: The Puritans knew that they needed God's word, the Bible, to show them how to live. They set aside time to study God's word and tried to follow it.

Poetry and Rhymes

Have students get out the poems that they saved from the previous units. Ask students to select one or more poems to review. Read aloud the selected poems with the students.

Key Idea: Read classic poetry.

History Activity

Say, *The Puritans followed God's word closely. God's word provided a light for them to follow in a dark and sinful world. Let's practice having you follow a light. As we walk, let's keep God's word with us.* Open the Bible to Psalm 119:105-112. Carry the open Bible while you lead the students with a flashlight. Point the flashlight beam on the floor and move it slowly as you walk. Have the students follow the light closely, so they don't run into anything. You may choose to read the Bible passage out loud while you are leading the students through the house.

Key Idea: God uses His word to lead us. The Bible will show us how to live, if we read it and follow it. Do you read and study God's word?

Bible Study

Say, *What does Psalm 119:105 mean? How is God's word a light for your path? In Psalm 119:110-112, how does it say you can stay on the right path and stay away from wicked things? Why is it so important to read the Bible daily?* Ask students to share their memory verse, 1 John 4:10-11, with someone special. Suggestions for sharing the verse include saying it to another family member, saying it to someone by telephone, reciting it to a stuffed animal, or writing it to mail.

Key Idea: The Puritans knew it was important to study God's word.

Corresponding Music

✓ *Hide 'Em in Your Heart Vol. 2*
CD - Track 10; Cassette - Side A
Song: *"We Love Him"*

Learning the Basics

Focus: Language Arts and Math

Unit 19 - Day 5

Language Arts

Get out 12 index cards. Ask, *How many months are in a year? Since each month has its own special name, what kind of letter should be at the beginning of each month?* Help me list the names of the months of the year on index cards, starting with January. Mix the cards up and put the months in order. Color the capital letter at the beginning of each month. <u>Copywork</u>: Have students begin copying the names of the months of the year.

<u>Key Idea</u>: Capitalize the names of the months of the year.

Reading Choices

Choose **one** of the reading options listed below (see Appendix for details).

★ *A phonics program*
★ *Scheduled Books for Emerging Readers*
★ *Drawn into the Heart of Reading Level 2/3*

<u>Key Idea</u>: Use a step-by-step program for reading instruction.

Storytime

Read aloud a short portion of the mystery that you selected. Guide students to retell today's reading by dictating a note to you about the mystery. The note should be a retelling of today's reading. Begin the note as follows:
Dear _____,
    We are reading a mystery about...
          Love,
          _____

Have the students sign the note and give it to another person.

<u>Key Idea</u>: Give students practice retelling a portion of a mystery.

Math Exploration

Use the 'tens' and 'ones' chart from Unit 19 - Day 1. Write '22 + 6 = ___' on a markerboard or a piece of paper. Say, *Use dimes and pennies to show the numbers '22' and '6' on the 'tens' and 'ones' chart. Leave a space between the two groups of coins on the chart. Push the pennies together to add the 'ones'. Push the dimes together to add the 'tens'. Count to get the total number of 'tens' and 'ones'.* Write the total in the blank on the markerboard or piece of paper. Repeat the activity with these equations: '54 + 3 = ___', '72 + 7 = ___', '35 + 4 = ___'.

✔ <u>Text Connection</u>: *Primary Mathematics Workbook 1B* p. 41-42

<u>Key Idea</u>: Add greater numbers.

Learning Through History

Focus: Colonial Schools

Unit 20 - Day 1

Reading About History

Read about history in the following resource:

Stories of the Pilgrims p. 217-219

Key Idea: The children in the colonies were schooled either at home or in a schoolhouse. They were taught to read and write. Little girls stitched samplers.

Poetry and Rhymes

Read aloud the poem *"Against Idleness and Mischief"* (see Appendix) to the students. Do not share the title. Ask students to suggest some titles for the poem. Share the real title. Read the poem again with the students.

Key Idea: Read and appreciate a variety of classic poetry.

Geography

Say, *In colonial times, children were often schooled at home by their mother or a neighbor. At the end of their lesson time, they stood with their toes on a crack in the floor and recited what they had learned. Stand with your toes on a crack in the floor. Recite your memory verse, Proverbs 12:24. Read aloud today's poem, "Against Idleness...". Recall and recite the meaning of some past geography terms that we have studied. What is a continent? A country? A city? An ocean? A bay? A harbor? An island? The source of a river? A river bed? The mouth of a river? A forest? A field?*

Key Idea: Many colonial children were schooled at home. Later, schoolhouses were built. Wood to heat the school was sent by the parents. Teachers were paid with food or clothing.

Bible Study

Proverbs 12:24 is the memory verse for this unit. Read the verse out loud. Ask, *What does it mean to be diligent?* Explain what it means to be lazy or slothful. *Why do you think that diligent hands will rule? Describe what this verse says will happen to the lazy or slothful man.* Say the verse together 3 times. Add hand motions to help students remember the words.

Key Idea: In colonial schools, lazy children sat in the corner with a dunce hat. Children of parents who were too lazy to bring wood for the stove sat in the cold part of the room.

Corresponding Music

None this lesson

Learning the Basics

Focus: Language Arts and Math

Unit 20 - Day 1

Langugage Arts

Choose **either** spelling list 1 **or** 2 (see Appendix for lists). Write each spelling word on a separate index card. Guide students to study each card one at a time, flip it over, write the word on paper, flip the card back over to check the spelling, and erase and correct any mistakes.
<u>Copywork</u>: Have students copy part of *"Against Idleness and Mischief"*.

<u>Key Idea</u>: Practice spelling words.

Reading Choices

Choose **one** of the reading options listed below (see Appendix for details).

★ A phonics program
★ *Scheduled Books for Emerging Readers*
★ *Drawn into the Heart of Reading Level 2/3*

<u>Key Idea</u>: Use a step-by-step program for reading instruction.

Storytime

Choose one important picture from the mystery book. You may need to use the cover, if there are no other pictures in the book. Tell students that they have one minute to look at the picture and remember as much of what they see as possible. After one minute, put the picture out of sight. Have students tell you as much as they can remember about the picture. Prompt students as needed by asking the following questions: *Which characters were in the picture? What place did you see? Which mysteri-ous things did you notice?* Read aloud the next portion of the mystery that you selected. Pace your reading to complete the mystery during the next 5 days of plans.

<u>Key Idea</u>: Set a purpose for reading the next part of the mystery.

Math Exploration

Either use a meterstick as a number line or tape a long strip of masking tape on the floor and number it '1' - '40' to be a number line. Say a number between '1' and '40' for the students to find and point to on the number line. Then, have students find the number +1, +2, +3, and -1, -2, -3. Students should move their finger up and back on the number line to add or subtract the numbers. Keep the number line out for students to refer to as they complete today's workbook assignment.

✓ <u>Text Connection</u>: *Primary Mathematics Workbook 1B* p. 43

<u>Key Idea</u>: Count up or back to add or subtract.

Learning Through History

Focus: Colonial Schools

Unit 20 - Day 2

Reading About History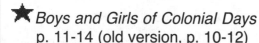

Read about history in the following resource:

★ *Boys and Girls of Colonial Days* p. 11-14 (old version, p. 10-12)

Key Idea: Percival and his mother were home alone while his father was in Boston. Percival's mother was worried about the Indians.

Poetry and Rhymes

Read aloud the poem *"Against Idleness and Mischief"* (see Appendix) with the students. Discuss the poem's meaning. If you choose, photocopy the poem, cut it apart, and have the students put it in order.

Key Idea: Read classic poetry.

Artistic Expression

Say, *Ribbons were given each month in Puritan schools to show how well the students had learned their lessons. Colorful ribbons were given for good conduct. Black ribbons were given for lazy behavior.* Have students design and create their own red ribbon for good conduct. Provide a variety of craft items for the students to use to make their ribbon (i.e. paper, paint, yarn, crepe paper, or ribbon).

Key Idea: Percival's mother wanted him to get a ribbon for good conduct in school. Persival had worked hard at learning his lessons all month. This was the day the ribbons were being awarded.

Bible Study

Say Proverbs 12:24 while the students join in on the parts they know. Use the hand motions you added on Day 1. Say, *Name some things you do diligently in school. Name some things you are lazy or slothful with in school. Should you only be diligent if you like the task? Why not?* Next, have students do windmills by touching their right hand to their right foot, and then their left hand to their left foot. After 5 windmills, have the students recite the Bible verse. Repeat the activity.

Key Idea: Percival worked diligently to learn his lessons. He hoped to earn a red ribbon of merit. Lazy students earned black ribbons.

Corresponding Music

None this lesson

Learning the Basics

Focus: Language Arts and Math

Unit 20 - Day 2

Language Arts

Use the spelling list from Day 1. Say the first spelling word. Use it in a sentence. Repeat the word. Ask students to write the word on a markerboard or a piece of paper from memory. Give students the matching word card from Day 1 to compare with their spelling. Guide students to correct any mistakes. Repeat the activity with all 10 words.

Copywork: Have students copy part of the poem *"Against Idleness and Mischief"*.

Key Idea: Practice spelling words with long 'a' spelled 'ai' as in 'sail'.

Reading Choices

Choose **one** of the reading options listed below (see Appendix for details).

★ A phonics program
★ *Scheduled Books for Emerging Readers*
★ *Drawn into the Heart of Reading Level 2/3*

Key Idea: Use a step-by-step program for reading instruction.

Storytime

Read aloud the next portion of the mystery that you selected. Ask students to retell or narrate what you read today. Remind students to tell the most important parts and to include details from the story in the retelling. As students work together to retell the story, write, type, or tape record the students' narration. When the students are finished, read the narration out loud. Highlight, circle, or underline one main idea from the narration for the students to copy.

Key Idea: Keep a sample of the students' narrations for the genre: *Mystery*.

Math Exploration

Complete the assigned lesson in the workbook listed below.

✔ Text Connection: *Primary Mathematics Workbook 1B* p. 44

Note: Use the number line from Unit 20 - Day 1 as needed for help with this assignment.

Key Idea: Count on or backward to add or subtract numbers to '40'.

Learning Through History

Focus: Colonial Schools

Unit 20 - Day 3

Reading About History

Read about history in the following resource:

★ *Boys and Girls of Colonial Days* p. 15-17 (old version, p. 13-15)

Key Idea: Percival earned a red ribbon at school for hard work and good behavior. It was dusk when he began walking home from school with Deliverance, his neighbor.

Poetry and Rhymes

Read aloud the poem *"Against Idleness and Mischief"* (see Appendix) with the students. Read the poem aloud a second time, pausing after each line or two for students to add their own actions to the poem. The actions should make sense with the poem.

Key Idea: Read classic poetry.

Science Exploration

Tape a white piece of paper to the wall. Turn off the lights. Stand back several feet. Shine a flashlight on the paper. Have a student hold a small ball between the flashlight and the paper to be Earth. Ask, *What colors do you see on the paper? Toward evening, the Earth turns away from the sun, and the sun begins to set. The light from the sun must travel further to reach Earth at that time of day. As the light travels, some of the colors are scattered. Let's see which colors reach Earth.* Fill a clear glass full of water. Add several drops of milk. Hold the glass between the flashlight and the Earth. Say, *Notice which colors you see now.*

✔ Text Connection: *God's Wonderful Works* p. 18

Key Idea: The sun was setting in the sky as Percival walked home.

Bible Study

Say Proverbs 12:24 with the students. Use the hand motions you added on Day 1. Next, have students squat down, hop up, and squat back down again. After the last squat, have the students recite the entire Bible verse. Prompt students as needed. Repeat the activity.

✔ Text Connection: *Morning Bells* p. 43-45

Key Idea: Deliverance was sorry she'd done a foolish prank at school. Each of us are tempted to do things that are wrong. We need to be diligent and do the right thing, like Percival.

Corresponding Music

None this lesson

Learning the Basics

Focus: Language Arts and Math

Unit 20 - Day 3

Language Arts

Using the spelling list from Day 1, choose 3 or more words that the students need to practice. Guide students to use each of the words that you chose in a sentence. On a markerboard or a piece of paper, write down the sentences as the students dictate them to you. Underline the spelling word in each sentence. Have the students copy the sentences on a piece of paper. Help students check their sentences and correct any mistakes.

Copywork: Have students copy part of the poem *"Against Idleness and Mischief"*.

Key Idea: Practice spelling words with long 'a' spelled 'ai' as in 'sail'.

Reading Choices

Choose **one** of the reading options listed below (see Appendix for details).

★ A phonics program

★ *Scheduled Books for Emerging Readers*

★ *Drawn into the Heart of Reading Level 2/3*

Key Idea: Use a step-by-step program for reading instruction.

Storytime

Read aloud the next portion of the mystery that you selected.

Say, *Who are the main characters in the story? What are the characters doing to solve the mystery? How do you predict that the story will end? What clues helped you make that prediction or guess?*

Key Idea: Focus on the story element: *prediction*.

Math Exploration

Fold a sheet of paper in half to make two columns. Write 'tens' on the left side and 'ones' on the right side. Say, *We are going to play a game. Each player will roll a die and place that number of cereal pieces in the 'ones' column. Continue taking turns rolling and adding pieces to the 'ones' column. Once there are '10' cereal pieces in the 'ones' column, trade them for one pretzel stick or licorice stick. Place the stick in the 'tens' column. One stick = 10 cereal pieces. Continue playing until one player has 5 sticks.*

✓ Text Connection: *Primary Mathematics Workbook 1B* p. 45

Key Idea: Use manipulatives to practice regrouping with 'tens'.

Learning Through History

Focus: Colonial Schools

Unit 20 - Day 4

Reading About History

Read about history in the following resource:

★ *Boys and Girls of Colonial Days* p. 18-21 (old version, p. 16-19)

Key Idea: On their way home, Percival and Deliverance met Chief Big Hawk. Big Hawk wanted to take Deliverance and attack their cabins. Instead, Percival gave Big Hawk his red ribbon.

Poetry and Rhymes

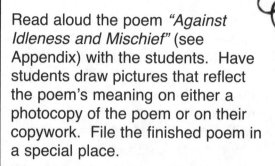

Read aloud the poem *"Against Idleness and Mischief"* (see Appendix) with the students. Have students draw pictures that reflect the poem's meaning on either a photocopy of the poem or on their copywork. File the finished poem in a special place.

Key Idea: Read classic poetry.

Science Exploration

Say, *After Chief Big Hawk left with Percival's ribbon, Percival told Deliverance they should "run like rabbits". Rabbits are known for their quickness. God made each animal special. Rabbits can also twitch their ears. Let's see if you can twitch your ears. A kangaroo can jump up to 40 feet in one jump. Let's measure how far you can jump. A sperm whale can hold its breath an hour, as its diving underwater. Let's time you to see how long you can hold your breath. A small hummingbird can flap its wings 700 times in 10 seconds. Let's count how many times you can flap your arms in 10 seconds.*

✔ Text Connection: *God's Wonderful Works* p. 102

Key Idea: Percival and Deliverance ran home quickly, like rabbits.

Bible Study

Say Proverbs 12:24 with the students. Use the hand motions from Day 1. Say, *Have you ever earned any rewards? Explain. Is it more important to get a reward or to please Jesus by doing what is right? How is pleasing Jesus a reward?* Next, have students hop backward 5 times. After 5 hops, have the students recite the entire Bible verse. Repeat the activity several times.

Key Idea: Percival gladly gave up his red ribbon to save Deliverance. He knew that earthly rewards are not as important as doing the right thing.

Corresponding Music

None this lesson

Learning the Basics

Focus: Language Arts and Math

Unit 20 - Day 4

Language Arts

Use the spelling list from Day 1. Say each word and use it in a sentence. Have students write each word and check it with the matching word card from Day 1. Guide students to correct any mistakes. For each missed word, have students write the word on paper and trace around it 3 times using 3 different colors.

Copywork: Have students copy part of the poem *"Against Idleness and Mischief"*.

Key Idea: Practice spelling words with long 'a' spelled 'ai' as in 'sail'.

Reading Choices

Choose **one** of the reading options listed below (see Appendix for details).

★ A phonics program
★ *Scheduled Books for Emerging Readers*
★ *Drawn into the Heart of Reading Level 2/3*

Key Idea: Use a step-by-step program for reading instruction.

Storytime

Say, *Loyalty means showing firm, faithful support even in times of trouble.* Read aloud the key verse Proverbs 19:11. Read aloud the next portion of the mystery that you selected. Ask, *Was the main character usually loyal or disloyal? Explain. Are you usually loyal? Draw a picture showing one way that you could be more loyal. Post your picture in a place where you will see it often.*

Key Idea: Focus on the Godly character trait: *loyalty*.

Math Exploration

Complete the assigned lesson in the workbook listed below.

✔ Text Connection: *Primary Mathematics Workbook 1B* p. 46-48

Key Idea: Practice regrouping in addition using 'tens' and 'ones'.

Learning Through History

Focus: Colonial Schools

Unit 20 - Day 5

Reading About History

Read the following passage from your own Bible:

★ 2 Thessalonians 3:6-15

Key Idea: Paul showed by example how to work diligently. He warned the Thessalonians not to be idle. The Puritans followed this example. They worked diligently during the week and rested on the Sabbath.

Poetry and Rhymes

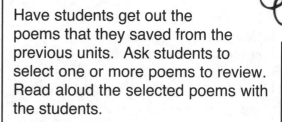

Have students get out the poems that they saved from the previous units. Ask students to select one or more poems to review. Read aloud the selected poems with the students.

Key Idea: Read classic poetry.

History Activity

Say, *Let's practice working diligently to help earn the food you eat. I will give you a task. Work diligently at the task. When you are done, come and tell me. I will inspect to see how well you did the task. Then, I will give you another task.* Some possible tasks include the following: unloading the dishwasher, folding towels or clothes, wiping the bathroom counters and sinks clean, taking out the garbages, scrubbing out a drawer, scrubbing the refrigerator, washing the inside shelves of a cupboard, picking up toys, or making beds. If the students are idle while doing their task, read them 2 Thessalonians 3:11-15.

✓ Text Connection: *God's Wonderful Works* p. 138 and 140

Key Idea: Paul warned against idleness. He expected everyone to do their share of the work.

Bible Study

Ask, *In 2 Thessalonians 3:7-9, what example did Paul set for the Thessalonians? What does Paul say in 2 Thessalonians 3:10-12 about those who are idle? How do you please Christ when you work diligently? Is all work pleasing to the Lord? Why not? Is there a time to rest? When?* Ask students to share their memory verse, Proverbs 12:24, with someone special. Suggestions for sharing the verse include saying it to another family member, saying it to someone by telephone, reciting it to a stuffed animal, or writing it to mail.

Key Idea: The Puritans followed the Bible as their guide for how to work.

Corresponding Music

None this lesson

Learning the Basics

Focus: Language Arts and Math

Unit 20 - Day 5

Language Arts

Get out the index cards of the months from Unit 19 - Day 5. Say, *Nouns that tell the special name of a person, place, or thing are called proper nouns. The names of the months are proper nouns.* Tell students to mix the index cards and sequence the months from January to December. Next, have students stand facing you several feet away. Using a soft ball, take turns with the students throwing and catching the ball and saying the names of the months in order.
<u>Copywork</u>: Have students finish copying the names of the months.

<u>Key Idea</u>: Capitalize the names of the months.

Reading Choices

Choose **one** of the reading options listed below (see Appendix for details).

★ A phonics program
★ *Scheduled Books for Emerging Readers*
★ *Drawn into the Heart of Reading Level 2/3*

<u>Key Idea</u>: Use a step-by-step program for reading instruction.

Storytime

Read aloud the final portion of the mystery that you selected. You will need to select a nonfiction book to read aloud next. Give students 5 minutes to find three items that have something to do with today's reading. After the students collect the items, have them tell you what each item has to do with the story. Prompt students to retell any important details they missed by asking, *Who?, What? When? Where? Why? How?* questions.

<u>Key Idea</u>: Give students practice retelling a portion of a mystery.

Math Exploration

Fold a piece of paper in half. Give students counters (i.e. clothespins, paperclips, cotton balls, or paper fasteners). Say, *Use the counters to show the addition problems on Workbook 1B p. 49. For example, to show '7 + 8 = ___', place '7' counters on the left half of the paper and '8' counters on the right half of the paper. Move the counters to make 'ten' on one side. Then, count on from 'ten' to find the total.* Repeat the activity for the other problems.

✔ <u>Text Connection</u>: *Primary Mathematics Workbook 1B* p. 49

<u>Key Idea</u>: Use counters to practice addition facts with sums up to '18'.

Learning Through History

Focus: Pioneers from France Settle Detroit

Unit 21 - Day 1

Reading About History

Read about history in the following resource:

★ *American Pioneers and Patriots* p. 54 and 63

<u>Key Idea</u>: The French explored the middle part of America. They traded with the Indians. Frenchmen learned to use Indian canoes to travel. Most of the French pioneers got along well with the Indians.

Artistic Expression

Make clay using the following recipe: Mix 1 cup of flour and 1 cup of salt. Add water and knead it until the mixture feels like clay. If the dough becomes too hard, add a little water. If it is too sticky, add a little flour. Have students use the clay and some toothpicks to build a small canoe. Refer to p. 54 of *American Pioneers and Patriots* for a picture of a canoe. Let the canoe dry. Once it is dry, students may choose to paint their canoe.

<u>Key Idea</u>: The French used Indian canoes to travel up the river to Fort Detroit. The pioneers could carry the canoes from one river to another. They were light to carry, but very strong.

Poetry and Rhymes

Read aloud the poem *"A June Day"* (see Appendix) to the students. Do not share the title. Ask students to suggest some titles for the poem. Share the real title. Read the poem again with the students.

<u>Key Idea</u>: Read and appreciate a variety of classic poetry.

Bible Study

Philippians 4:8 is the memory verse for this unit. Read the verse out loud. Ask, *In Philippians 4:8, what kinds of things does Paul say you should think about? What does 'virtuous' or 'excellent' mean? Why should you fill your mind with those things? How does your mind control you?* Say the verse together 3 times. Add hand motions to help students remember the words.

<u>Key Idea</u>: The French tried to have a friendly relationship with the Indians. French priests shared their religion with the Indians.

Corresponding Music

✓ *Hide 'Em in Your Heart Vol. 2*
CD - Track 13; Cassette - Side B
Song: *"Think About Such Things"*

Learning the Basics

Focus: Language Arts and Math

Unit 21 - Day 1

Language Arts

Choose **either** spelling list 1 **or** 2 (see Appendix for lists). Write each spelling word on a separate index card. Guide students to study each card one at a time, flip it over, write the word from memory on paper, flip the card back over to check the spelling, and erase and correct any mistakes.

<u>Copywork</u>: Have students copy part of the poem *"A June Day"*.

<u>Key Idea</u>: Practice spelling words with long 'e' spelled 'ee' as in 'keep'.

Reading Choices

Choose **one** of the reading options listed below (see Appendix for details).

★ A phonics program
★ *Scheduled Books for Emerging Readers*
★ *Drawn into the Heart of Reading Level 2/3*

<u>Key Idea</u>: Use a step-by-step program for reading instruction.

Storytime

Choose at least one nonfiction book to read aloud for the next 20 days of plans (see Appendix for suggested titles). To introduce the genre, *Nonfiction*, read through the table of contents or the summary of the book you selected. Say, *What is this book about? Does it have pictures, charts, maps, or photographs? Choose one to study. Tell me what you found out. Nonfiction books give information and facts based on real people and events.* Read a portion of the nonfiction book you chose.

<u>Key Idea</u>: Introduce the genre: *Nonfiction*.

Math Exploration

Complete the assigned lesson in the workbook listed below.

✓ <u>Text Connection</u>: *Primary Mathematics Workbook 1B* p. 50-51

<u>Key Idea</u>: Notice addition patterns to help make adding easier.

Learning Through History

Focus: Pioneers from France Settle Detroit

Unit 21 - Day 2

Reading About History

Read about history in the following resource:

★ *American Pioneers and Patriots* p. 55-56

Key Idea: Marie traveled with her family and her special doll, Lady Claire, in a canoe.

Poetry and Rhymes

Read aloud the poem *"A June Day"* (see Appendix) with the students. Discuss the poem's meaning. If you choose, photocopy the poem, cut it apart, and have the students place it in the correct order.

Key Idea: Read classic poetry.

Science Exploration

Say, *Birds have different kinds of beaks to get the food they need.* Set out a tweezers, a clothespin, a slotted spoon, and a straw or an eyedropper. Set out grains of rice, sunflower or popcorn seeds, mini-marshmallows in a bowl of water, and yellow water in a glass. Try using each tool to pick up the various food items. Say, *A tweezers is like a woodpecker's beak. It is best for pulling insects out of cracks, like the grains of rice. A clothespin is like a sparrow's beak. It is best for cracking open seeds. A slotted spoon is like a pelican's beak. It is best for scooping creatures out of water, like the marshmallows. A straw or eyedropper is like a hummingbird's beak. It is best for sucking nectar out of flowers, like the yellow water.*

✔ Text Connection: *God's Wonderful Works* p. 71 and 82

Key Idea: Marie saw a hummingbird sipping nectar from a flower.

Bible Study

Say Philippians 4:8 with the students. Use the hand motions you added on Day 1. Say, *Where are the things you read, watch, and hear recorded? Are you careful about what you put into your mind? Why should you spend time reading and hearing God's word? How does your mind help you know right from wrong?* Next, have students do 5 jumping jacks. After 5 jumping jacks, have the students recite the entire Bible verse. Prompt the students as needed. Repeat the activity.

Key Idea: Marie was very careful with Lady Claire. How are you careful?

Corresponding Music

✔ *Hide 'Em in Your Heart Vol. 2*
CD - Track 13; Cassette - Side B
Song: *"Think About Such Things"*

Learning the Basics

Focus: Language Arts and Math

Unit 21 - Day 2

Language Arts

Use the spelling list from Day 1. Say the first spelling word. Use it in a sentence. Repeat the word. Ask students to write the word on a markerboard or a piece of paper from memory. Give students the matching word card from Day 1 to compare with their spelling. Guide students to correct any mistakes. Repeat the activity with all 10 words.

Copywork: Have students copy part of the poem *"A June Day"*.

Key Idea: Practice spelling words with long 'e' spelled 'ee' as in 'keep'.

Reading Choices

Choose **one** of the reading options listed below (see Appendix for details).

★ A phonics program

★ *Scheduled Books for Emerging Readers*

★ *Drawn into the Heart of Reading Level 2/3*

Key Idea: Use a step-by-step program for reading instruction.

Storytime

Read aloud the next portion of the nonfiction book that you selected. Without looking back at the story, model retelling or narrating the part of the nonfiction book that you read today to the students. Remember to tell the most important points and to add details from the book to the retelling without overwhelming the students. After the retelling, ask, *What was today's reading mostly about?* On paper, write the answer to the question as one sentence for the students to copy.

Key Idea: Model retelling a story from a single reading.

Math Exploration

Say, *Write a number between '10' and '20' on a markerboard or a piece of paper* (i.e. '15'). *After you have written your number, listen and count the number of times that I clap. Subtract the number of claps from the number you wrote down* (i.e. 15 - 5 claps = ___). *Count backward by ones for each clap that you heard to get the answer to your subtraction problem* (i.e. '14', '13', '12',, '11', '10'). *Write the answer on your markerboard or piece of paper* (i.e. 15 - 5 = 10). Repeat the activity with different numbers.

✔ Text Connection: *Primary Mathematics Workbook 1B* p. 52

Key Idea: Practice subtraction facts up to '20'.

Learning Through History

Focus: Pioneers from France Settle Detroit

Unit 21 - Day 3

Reading About History

Read about history in the following resource:

★ *American Pioneers and Patriots* p. 57-59

Key Idea: During their trip, one canoe hit a rock and was lost. There were Indians in the forest. The Frenchmen shared their campfire with them. Claire's father traded beads and blankets for a new canoe.

Poetry and Rhymes

Read aloud the poem *"A June Day"* (see Appendix) with the students. Read the poem aloud a second time, pausing after each line or two for students to add their own actions to the poem. The actions should make sense with the poem.

Key Idea: Read classic poetry.

Science Exploration

Divide a piece of waxed paper or blue paper into 4 sections. Use whipped cream or shaving cream on waxed paper, or cotton balls or white chalk on blue paper, to show 4 different types of clouds. Refer to the science text p. 30 to see pictures of puffy cumulus clouds; thin, whispy, cirrus clouds; thick, gray stratus clouds; or whispy, puffy cirro-cumulus clouds. Ask, *Which clouds are a sign of good weather? Describe cirrus and cirro-cumulus clouds. Which clouds can mean good weather if they are white, or bad weather if they are dark? Describe cumulus clouds. Which clouds are a sign of rainy weather? Describe stratus clouds.*

✓ Text Connection: *God's Wonderful Works* p. 30

Key Idea: It started to rain on Claire.

Bible Study

Say Philippians 4:8 with the students. Use the hand motions you added on Day 1. Next, have students hop on their left foot until you say, *Freeze*. After they 'freeze', have the students recite the entire Bible verse. Prompt students as needed. Have students switch to the right foot, and repeat the activity.

✓ Text Connection: *Morning Bells* p. 37-39

Key Idea: Claire's father was kind to the Indians. The Indians were kind in return.

Corresponding Music

✓ *Hide 'Em in Your Heart Vol. 2* CD - Track 13; Cassette - Side B Song: *"Think About Such Things"*

Learning the Basics

Focus: Language Arts and Math

Unit 21 - Day 3

Language Arts

Using the spelling list from Day 1, choose 3 or more words that the students need to practice. Guide students to use each of the words that you chose in a sentence. On a markerboard or a piece of paper, write down the sentences as the students dictate them to you. Underline the spelling word in each sentence. Have the students copy the sentences on a piece of paper. Help students check their sentences and correct any mistakes.

<u>Copywork</u>: Have students copy part of the poem *"A June Day"*.

<u>Key Idea</u>: Practice spelling words with long 'e' spelled 'ee' as in 'keep'.

Reading Choices

Choose **one** of the reading options listed below (see Appendix for details).

★ A phonics program

★ *Scheduled Books for Emerging Readers*

★ *Drawn into the Heart of Reading Level 2/3*

<u>Key Idea</u>: Use a step-by-step program for reading instruction.

Storytime

Say, *The details or information given in the book explain the main or big idea of the book. What is the author mostly showing or telling about in this book?* Hint: Use the book title for help in guessing the main idea. Page through the book and look at the pictures. Discuss the things that you notice.

Read aloud the next portion of the nonfiction book that you selected.

<u>Key Idea</u>: Introduce the story element: *main idea*.

Math Exploration

Get out four ziplock bags. Place 10 items in each bag (i.e. cotton balls, puzzle pieces, small blocks). Write a subtraction sentence for students to solve using the bags (i.e. 40 - 6 = ___). Say, *Each bag contains 10 items. Take 4 bags to equal the '40' items that you have before you subtract. To subtract '6', open one bag and take out 6 items. Set those 6 items aside because you're taking them away. Recount the full 'tens' bags and the remaining 4 items to find the answer to the problem* (i.e. 40 - 6 = 34).

✓ <u>Text Connection</u>: *Primary Mathematics Workbook 1B* p. 53-54

<u>Key Idea</u>: Practice subtraction with 'zeroes'.

Learning Through History

Focus: Pioneers from France Settle Detroit

Unit 21 - Day 4

Reading About History

Read about history in the following resource:

★ *American Pioneers and Patriots* p. 60-62

Key Idea: The French pioneers traveled by canoe with their new Indian friends to Fort Detroit. The Indians traded with the Frenchmen. An Indian woman gave Marie tiny moccasins for Lady Claire.

Poetry and Rhymes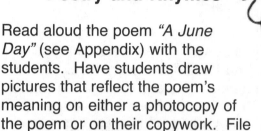

Read aloud the poem *"A June Day"* (see Appendix) with the students. Have students draw pictures that reflect the poem's meaning on either a photocopy of the poem or on their copywork. File the finished poem in a special place.

Key Idea: Read and appreciate a variety of classic poetry.

Geography

Say, *Use the map on p. 52 of American Pioneers and Patriots. Trace the Mississippi River with your finger. What are the names of the 5 Great Lakes? Find Detroit on the map. Which of the Great Lakes is nearest to Detroit? Starting in Montreal, Canada, trace the French explorer LaSalle's route. Trace the French explorer Marquette's route.*

Key Idea: Claire and her family finally arrived in Detroit. It was raining during the last part of their journey. The sun came out as their canoe landed.

Bible Study

Say Philippians 4:8 with the students. Use the hand motions you added on Day 1. Ask, *What is something special or beautiful that you have? Why is it special to you? Are you special to Jesus? Is it because you are so pure and good? How can you be pure and good in God's eyes?* Next, have the students do 5 sit-ups. After 5 sit-ups, have the students recite the entire Bible verse.

Key Idea: Lady Claire was special to Marie. You are special to Jesus.

Corresponding Music

✓ *Hide 'Em in Your Heart Vol. 2* CD - Track 13; Cassette - Side B Song: *"Think About Such Things"*

Learning the Basics

Focus: Language Arts and Math

Unit 21 - Day 4

Language Arts

Use the spelling list from Day 1. Say each word and use it in a sentence. Have students write each word and check it with the matching word card from Day 1. Guide students to correct any mistakes. Direct students to write each missed word with fingerpaint or sidewalk chalk. <u>Copywork</u>: Have students copy part of *"A June Day"*.

<u>Key Idea</u>: Practice spelling words with long 'e' spelled 'ee' as in 'keep'.

Reading Choices

Choose **one** of the reading options listed below (see Appendix for details).

★ A phonics program
★ *Scheduled Books for Emerging Readers*
★ *Drawn into the Heart of Reading Level 2/3*

<u>Key Idea</u>: Use a step-by-step program for reading instruction.

Storytime

Say, *Obedience is a willingness to do what is asked or required without complaint.* Read aloud the key verses Psalm 119:33-34 to illustrate *obedience*. List some ways that you are obedient. Now, have students list ways that they show obedience.

Read aloud the next portion of the nonfiction book that you selected. Then, ask, *What are some examples of obedience from your nonfiction book? How is obedience an important part of the topic that you are studying?*

<u>Key Idea</u>: Introduce the Godly character trait: *obedience*.

Math Exploration

Complete the assigned lesson in the workbook listed below.

✔ <u>Text Connection</u>: *Primary Mathematics Workbook 1B* p. 55-56

Note: Use counters as needed. Notice the patterns to help with subtraction.

<u>Key Idea</u>: Use subtraction patterns to help with subtracting numbers with 'tens' and 'ones'.

Learning Through History

Focus: Pioneers from France Settle Detroit

Unit 21 - Day 5

Reading About History

Read the following passage from your own Bible:

★ Phillipians 4:4-13

Key Idea: Paul knew that Jesus was always with him. That made him joyful, even in bad times. Paul prayed about everything. The early pioneers who trusted in God prayed about everything too. It helped them get through many hard times.

History Activity

Say, *Get out your timeline. We have read about the French people settling in Detroit. Let's find the column that says 1700. Draw a small rainbow in that column. Write 'French settle Detroit, 1701' under it.* Next, have students think of someone they know who could use some encouragement. Help students copy Philippians 4:13 to send to someone, or call someone and read the verse to encourage them.

Key Idea: Paul reminds Christians to encourage each other in times of need. It is important to think of someone beside ourselves.

Poetry and Rhymes

Have students get out the poems that they saved from the previous units. Ask students to select one or more poems to review. Read aloud the selected poems with the students.

Key Idea: Read classic poetry.

Bible Study

Ask, *In Philippians 4:6, what does Paul tell you to do when you are anxious or worried? What does Philippians 4:7 say God will give you when you pray? What does it mean to be content? In Philippians 4:11-13, what does Paul teach you about being content?* Ask students to share their memory verse, Philippians 4:8, with someone special. Suggestions for sharing the verse include saying it to another family member, saying it to someone by telephone, reciting it to a stuffed animal, or writing it to mail.

Key Idea: The early pioneers had to learn to be content with very little.

Corresponding Music

✓ *Hide 'Em in Your Heart Vol. 2* CD - Track 13; Cassette - Side B
Song: *"Think About Such Things"*

Learning the Basics

Focus: Language Arts and Math

Unit 21 - Day 5

Language Arts

Write your birthdate on a piece of paper or a markerboard (i.e. July 26, 1968). Read the date out loud and say, *This is my birthdate. In which month was I born? On what day of the month was I born? How is the day of the month written? In what year was I born? How is the year written? What mark separates the day of the month from the year? Why do we need a comma between the day of the month and the year?* Repeat the questions listed above with the birthdates of other family members. Then, write today's date.

<u>Copywork</u>: Have students copy their own birthdate.

<u>Key Idea</u>: Correctly capitalize and punctuate dates.

Reading Choices

Choose **one** of the reading options listed below (see Appendix for details).

★ A phonics program

★ *Scheduled Books for Emerging Readers*

★ *Drawn into the Heart of Reading Level 2/3*

<u>Key Idea</u>: Use a step-by-step program for reading instruction.

Math Exploration

On paper, write the following sentence: O + O + O = O (Make sure that the four circles are very large.) Give students fish crackers, dry cereal pieces, or dry marcaroni noodles to be fish. Have students place fish in the circles as you say this problem: *2 fish were swimming in the pond. 3 more fish swam over. Then, 4 fish swam up. How many fish are in the pond altogether? Place 2 fish in the first circle, 3 in the second, and 4 in the third circle. To add, slide all the fish together into the fourth circle. Count the fish.* Practice more problems.

✔ <u>Text Connection</u>: *Primary Mathematics Workbook 1B* p. 57-58

<u>Key Idea</u>: Add 3 or more numbers.

Storytime

Read aloud a short portion of the nonfiction book that you selected. Guide students to pantomime the important actions from today's reading, without using any words. After the pantomime is over, have students retell what they acted out.

<u>Key Idea</u>: Give students practice retelling a portion of a nonfiction book.

Learning Through History

Focus: Life in Colonial Philadelphia and Boston

Unit 22 - Day 1

Reading About History

Read about history in the following resource:

★ *Boys and Girls of Colonial Days* p. 34-39 (old version, p. 30-34)

Key Idea: The Arnolds were a Quaker family living in Philadelphia in colonial times. They were poor and very cold. Benjamin Franklin also lived in Philadelphia. He was an inventor and a writer.

Poetry and Rhymes

Read aloud the poem *"Little Things"* (see Appendix) to the students. Do not share the title. Ask students to suggest some titles for the poem. Share the real title. Read the poem again with the students.

Key Idea: Read and appreciate a variety of classic poetry.

Science Exploration

Say, *Lightning is a giant spark that gives off so much heat that it causes a booming sound like an explosion. The boom happens at the same time as the lightning. Since light travels faster than sound, we see lightning first and hear the thunder later.* Sit in a dark room. Give students a flashlight to flash on and off like lightning. Wait 5-15 seconds and then pound the floor like thunder. Have students count 1-1000, 2-1000, 3-1000, and so on to see how many seconds apart the thunder and the lightning were. To find out how many miles away a storm is, divide the number of seconds you counted by 5.

✓ Text Connection: *God's Wonderful Works* p. 28-29

Key Idea: Ben Franklin invented lightning rods.

Bible Study

2 Corinthians 9:7 is the memory verse for this unit. Read the verse out loud. Ask, *How does 2 Corinthians 9:7 say that you should give? What does it mean to do something grudgingly or reluctantly? Why doesn't God want you to give that way? What kind of giver does it say that God loves?* Say the verse together 3 times. Add hand motions to help students remember the words.

Key Idea: Benjamin Franklin enjoyed sharing his inventions with the people of Philadelphia.

Corresponding Music

✓ *Hide 'Em in Your Heart Vol. 2* CD - Track 9; Cassette - Side A Song: *"God Loves a Cheerful Giver"*

Learning the Basics

Focus: Language Arts and Math

Unit 22 - Day 1

Language Arts

Choose **either** spelling list **1 or** 2 (see Appendix for lists). Write each spelling word on a separate index card. Guide students to study each card one at a time, flip it over, write the word on paper, flip the card back over to check the spelling, and erase and correct any mistakes.
Copywork: Have students copy part of the poem *"Little Things"*.

Key Idea: Practice spelling words with long 'e' spelled 'ea' as in 'eat'.

Reading Choices

Choose **one** of the reading options listed below (see Appendix for details).

★ A phonics program
★ *Scheduled Books for Emerging Readers*
★ *Drawn into the Heart of Reading Level 2/3*

Key Idea: Use a step-by-step program for reading instruction.

Storytime

Say, *What can you tell me about the nonfiction book that we are reading?* On paper, list what the students share. Ask, *What questions do you have about the topic in our book?* On paper, list any questions the students share. If students are having a hard time coming up with questions, page through the book and show them some of the upcoming pictures or topics. Read aloud the next portion of the nonfiction book that you selected. Pace your reading to complete the book during the next 15 days of plans.

Key Idea: Preread to build anticipation for the next part of the nonfiction book.

Math Exploration

Use only cards numbered '2' - '9' from a deck of playing cards. Shuffle those cards and deal three to each player. Players should add the numbers on the three cards in their hand to get a total. The player with the total closest to '20' wins one token. Use coins, buttons, or other pieces as tokens. The first player to earn 5 tokens wins. Remind students to start with the largest number and count up to make adding three numbers easier.

✓ Text Connection: *Primary Mathematics Workbook 1B* p. 59

Key Idea: Practice adding three numbers.

Learning Through History

Focus: Life in Colonial Philadelphia and Boston

Unit 22 - Day 2

Reading About History

Read about history in the following resource:

★ *Boys and Girls of Colonial Days* p. 40-44 (old version, p. 35-38)

Key Idea: The Arnolds had to stay with a kind neighbor when it got too cold in their own home. Benjamin Franklin made an iron stove for the Arnolds to keep their house warm.

Geography

Say, *Today's story happened in the city of Philadelphia. Look on a map or globe or use the map on p. 165 of* American Pioneers and Patriots. *Find the state of Pennsylvania on the east coast of the United States. Then, find the city of Philadelphia. Name some other cities that are found in the state of Pennsylvania. Which of the Great Lakes does the state of Pennsylvania border? Which ocean is closest to the state of Pennsylvania?*

Key Idea: Benjamin Franklin lived in Philadelphia and had a workshop there. He invented many new things. Philadelphia is often referred to as "The City of Brotherly Love".

Poetry and Rhymes

Read aloud the poem *"Little Things"* (see Appendix) with the students. Discuss the poem's meaning. If you choose, photocopy the poem, cut it apart, and have the students place it in the correct order.

Key Idea: Read classic poetry.

Bible Study

Say 2 Corinthians 9:7 while the students join in on the parts they know. Use the hand motions you added on Day 1. Say, *Name some things that you give to others. Which is more important, how much you give or how you act when you give? Why does God look at the heart of a giver? How can you be more cheerful when you give?* Next, have students do 3 push-ups. After 3 push-ups, have the students recite the entire Bible verse. Repeat the activity several times.

Key Idea: Benjamin Franklin was a cheerful giver.

Corresponding Music

✔ *Hide 'Em in Your Heart Vol. 2* CD - Track 9; Cassette - Side A Song: *"God Loves a Cheerful Giver"*

Learning the Basics

Focus: Language Arts and Math

Unit 22 - Day 2

Language Arts

Use the spelling list from Day 1. Say the first spelling word. Use it in a sentence. Repeat the word. Ask students to write the word on a piece of paper or on a markerboard from memory. Give students the matching word card from Day 1 to compare with their spelling. Guide students to correct any mistakes. Repeat the activity with all 10 words.
Copywork: Have students copy part of the poem *"Little Things"*.

Key Idea: Practice spelling words with long 'e' spelled 'ea' as in 'eat'.

Reading Choices

Choose **one** of the reading options listed below (see Appendix for details).

★ A phonics program
★ *Scheduled Books for Emerging Readers*
★ *Drawn into the Heart of Reading Level 2/3*

Key Idea: Use a step-by-step program for reading instruction.

Storytime

Read aloud the next portion of the nonfiction book that you selected. Without looking back at the story, begin retelling or narrating the part of the nonfiction book that you read today. After a short time, tap the student and say, *Your turn.* The student should pick up the narration where you left off. After a short time, the student should tap you and say, *Your turn.* Continue taking turns narrating in this manner until today's reading has been retold. Then, say, *Name one thing that you learned from the nonfiction book today.* Write it on paper for the students to copy.

Key Idea: Take turns retelling a story from a single reading.

Math Exploration

These are the concepts that are covered in this review: counting and writing numbers to '40', continuing number patterns, ordering numbers, comparing sets, subtracting and adding greater numbers, interpreting graphs, adding and subtracting using number sentences. Review any concepts that students had difficulty understanding. Also, complete the assigned review in the workbook listed below.

✔ Text Connection: *Primary Mathematics Workbook 1B* p. 60-63

Key Idea: Review difficult concepts.

Learning Through History

Focus: Life in Colonial Philadelphia and Boston

Unit 22 - Day 3

Reading About History

Read about history in the following resource:

★ *Boys and Girls of Colonial Days* p. 45-49 (old version, p. 39-42)

Key Idea: Deacon Drowne was a coppersmith in colonial Boston. The children loved to see what he could create. Peter Faneuil was a wealthy man in Boston. He admired a large grasshopper the Deacon had made.

Poetry and Rhymes

Read aloud the poem *"Little Things"* (see Appendix) with the students. Read the poem aloud a second time, pausing after each line or two for students to add their own actions to the poem. The actions should make sense with the poem.

Key Idea: Read and appreciate a variety of classic poetry.

Science Exploration

Say, *Grasshoppers are insects. Insects have 6 legs and 3 body parts: head, thorax, and abdomen.* Choose one of the following recipes to make peanut butter playdough. Recipe 1: Mix together 1 cup peanut butter, 1/2 cup honey, and 2 cups of powdered sugar. Recipe 2: Mix together 1 cup peanut butter, 1 cup rolled oats, 1 cup non-fat dry milk, and 1/3 cup honey. Say, *Use playdough to make the grasshopper's head, thorax, and abdomen. Use yarn or pipecleaners for legs, wax paper for wings, and chocolate chips or raisins for eyes. Name the parts of the grasshopper as you eat them.*

✔ Text Connection: *God's Wonderful Works* p. 118-120

Key Idea: Deacon Drowne made a grasshopper out of copper.

Bible Study

Say 2 Corinthians 9:7 with the students. Use the hand motions you added on Day 1. Next, have students skip around the room until you say, *Freeze.* After they 'freeze', have the students recite the entire Bible verse. Have students repeat the activity.

✔ Text Connection: *Morning Bells* p. 22-24

Key Idea: Many people in colonial times worked to help one another. God expects you to use your gifts and talents to help others.

Corresponding Music

✔ *Hide 'Em in Your Heart Vol. 2* CD - Track 9; Cassette - Side A Song: *"God Loves a Cheerful Giver"*

Learning the Basics

Focus: Language Arts and Math

Unit 22 - Day 3

Language Arts

Using the spelling list from Day 1, choose 3 or more words that the students need to practice. Guide students to use each of the words that you chose in a sentence. On a markerboard or a piece of paper, write down the sentences as the students dictate them to you. Underline the spelling word in each sentence. Have the students copy the sentences on a piece of paper. Help students check their sentences and correct any mistakes.
<u>Copywork</u>: Have students copy part of the poem *"Little Things"*.

<u>Key Idea</u>: Practice spelling words with long 'e' spelled 'ea' as in 'eat'.

Reading Choices

Choose **one** of the reading options listed below (see Appendix for details).

★ A phonics program
★ *Scheduled Books for Emerging Readers*
★ *Drawn into the Heart of Reading Level 2/3*

<u>Key Idea</u>: Use a step-by-step program for reading instruction.

Storytime

In the center of a piece of paper, write the next topic that you will read about in the nonfiction book. Draw a box in each of the 4 corners of the same paper. Then, draw a line from the topic in the center to each of the 4 boxes. Read aloud the next portion of the nonfiction book that you selected. After today's reading, have students list one thing in each box about the topic listed in the center of the paper. Ask students to color the box with the most important idea.

<u>Key Idea</u>: Focus on the story element: *main idea*.

Math Exploration

On paper, draw five brown circles to be muffins. Give students chocolate chips, raisins, or dried fruit bits to use as counters. Have students use their counters to act out multiplication problems (i.e. I have 5 muffins. There are 3 chocolate chips in each muffin. How many chocolate chips are there altogether?). Write the problem on a markerboard or a piece of paper, so students can see that multiplication is repeated addition (i.e. $3 + 3 + 3 + 3 + 3 = 15$ or 5 three's = 15). Repeat the activity with different numbers of counters.

✓ <u>Text Connection</u>: *Primary Mathematics Workbook 1B* p. 64-65

<u>Key Idea</u>: Introduce multiplication as repeated addition.

Learning Through History

Focus: Life in Colonial Philadelphia and Boston

Unit 22 - Day 4

Reading About History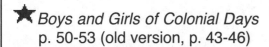

Read about history in the following resource:

★ *Boys and Girls of Colonial Days* p. 50-53 (old version, p. 43-46)

Key Idea: Mr. Faneuil wanted to give the city of Boston a new public hall. He wanted to build a meeting room above a market. At last the city decided to accept his gift. Deacon Drowne's grasshopper was placed on top as a weathervane.

Poetry and Rhymes

Read aloud the poem *"Little Things"* (see Appendix) with the students. Have students draw pictures that reflect the poem's meaning on either a photocopy of the poem or on their copywork. File the finished poem in a special place.

Key Idea: Read classic poetry.

Artistic Expression

Say, *Use the picture on p. 52 of Boys and Girls of Colonial Days (old version, p. 44) to make a model of Faneuil Hall. Cover a small block or Jello, pudding, or rice box with brown paper. Use a black marker to add details to the building. Attach a toothpick to the top of the building to be the weathervane. Cut out a small brown grasshopper and tape it to the top of the weathervane.*

Key Idea: As a boy, Samuel Adams often passed Deacon Drowne's shop on the way to school. He saw many of the Deacon's copper creations. Later, Samuel Adams voted to let Peter Faneuil build a public hall in Boston and put Deacon Drowne's grasshopper on top.

Bible Study

Say 2 Corinthians 9:7 with the students. Use the hand motions from Day 1. Say, *Name some ways that you help others. What are some jobs that you could do without being asked? When you help without being asked, what does it show God about your heart? How should you act as you help?* Next, have students run in place. Say, *Freeze,* and have the students stop and recite the Bible verse. Repeat the activity several times.

Key Idea: Mr. Faneuil gave a heartfelt gift to the city of Boston.

Corresponding Music

✔ *Hide 'Em in Your Heart Vol. 2* CD - Track 9; Cassette - Side A Song: *"God Loves a Cheerful Giver"*

Learning the Basics

Focus: Language Arts and Math

Unit 22 - Day 4

Language Arts

Use the spelling list from Day 1. Say each word and use it in a sentence. Have students write each word and check it with the matching word card from Day 1. Guide students to correct any mistakes. For each missed word, have students trace it in dry cornmeal, oatmeal, or sand on a plate.

<u>Copywork</u>: Have students copy part of the poem *"Little Things"*.

<u>Key Idea</u>: Practice spelling words with long 'e' spelled 'ea' as in 'eat'.

Reading Choices

Choose **one** of the reading options listed below (see Appendix for details).

★ A phonics program

★ *Scheduled Books for Emerging Readers*

★ *Drawn into the Heart of Reading Level 2/3*

<u>Key Idea</u>: Use a step-by-step program for reading instruction.

Storytime

Say, *Obedience is a willingness to do what is asked or required without complaint.* Read aloud the key verses Psalm 119:33-34. Read aloud Genesis 4:2-7. Ask, *How did Abel's actions show obedience?*

Read aloud the next portion of the nonfiction book that you selected. Then, ask, *What is an example of obedience from your nonfiction book? What does the Biblical character, Abel, teach us about obedience?*

<u>Key Idea</u>: Focus on the Godly character trait: *obedience*.

Math Exploration

Set out four index cards or small pieces of paper to be donut boxes. Give students 'O'-shaped cereal pieces or other round items to be donuts. Have students use their donuts to act out multiplication problems (i.e. There are 4 donut boxes. Each box has 5 donuts. How many donuts are there in all?). Write the problem on paper so that students can see that multiplication is repeated addition (i.e. 5 + 5 + 5 + 5 = 20). Repeat the activity using different numbers of donuts.

✔ <u>Text Connection</u>: *Primary Mathematics Workbook 1B* p. 66-67

<u>Key Idea</u>: Introduce multiplication as repeated addition.

Learning Through History

Focus: Life in Colonial Philadelphia and Boston

Unit 22 - Day 5

Reading About History

Read the following passage from your own Bible:

 2 Corinthians 9:6-15

Key Idea: God wants you to give generously with a cheerful heart. Everything comes from God and should be used to serve Him. Many colonists were Godly people that used what they had to serve God.

Poetry and Rhymes

Have students get out the poems that they saved from the previous units. Ask students to select one or more poems to review. Read aloud the selected poems with the students.

Key Idea: Read classic poetry.

History Activity

Say, *Get out your timeline. We have been reading about Faneiul Hall in Boston. Let's find the column that says 1700. Draw a small grasshopper in that column. Write 'Faneuil Hall, Boston, 1742' under it. Earlier, we also read about Benjamin Franklin. Let's find the column that says 1700. Draw a small pair of spectacles in that column. Write 'Benjamin Franklin, 1706-1790' under it.*

Key Idea: It is important to share the gifts and talents God has given you with others. Benjamin Franklin, Deacon Drowne, and Peter Faneuil shared their inventions, creations, and money with others.

Bible Study

Ask, *In 2 Corinthians 9:6, what do the words sparingly and generously or bountifully mean? What might it mean to reap what you sow? In 2 Corinthians 9:11-12, what kind of riches is God talking about? What does God tell you in 2 Corinthians 9:13-14?* Ask students to share their memory verse, 2 Corinthians 9:7, with someone special. Suggestions for sharing the verse include saying it to another family member, saying it to someone by telephone, reciting it to a stuffed animal, or writing it to mail.

Key Idea: God expects you to be generous with what He gives you.

Corresponding Music

✔ *Hide 'Em in Your Heart Vol. 2*
CD - Track 9; Cassette - Side A
Song: *"God Loves a Cheerful Giver"*

Learning the Basics

Focus: Language Arts and Math

Unit 22 - Day 5

Language Arts

Say, *Common nouns are **not** special. They name common places or things. Have you ever been to the zoo? 'Zoo' is a common noun because there are many zoos. What was the special name of the zoo that you visited? The proper name of a place is capitalized because it is a special name.* Write the proper name of the zoo on paper or on a markerboard. Don't forget to capitalize the name. Repeat the questioning above with the students to write the special name of a restaurant, church, grocery store, and gas station.

<u>Copywork</u>: Have students copy one or more of the special names from today's lesson.

<u>Key Idea</u>: Introduce the difference between common and proper nouns.

Reading Choices

Choose **one** of the reading options listed below (see Appendix for details).

★ A phonics program

★ *Scheduled Books for Emerging Readers*

★ *Drawn into the Heart of Reading Level 2/3*

<u>Key Idea</u>: Use a step-by-step program for reading instruction.

Storytime

Read aloud a short portion of the nonfiction book that you selected. Say, *Choose one picture, diagram, map, or chart from today's reading. Use the picture you chose to help you retell some of the important facts from today's reading.*

<u>Key Idea</u>: Give students practice retelling a portion of a nonfiction book.

Math Exploration

Complete the assigned lesson in the workbook listed below.

✔ <u>Text Connection</u>: *Primary Mathematics Workbook 1B* p. 68-69

<u>Key Idea</u>: Use multiplication to find the product.

Learning Through History

Focus: Trouble Before the Revolutionary War

Unit 23 - Day 1

Reading About History

Read about history in the following resource:

★ *Boys and Girls of Colonial Days* p. 86-91 (old version, p. 73-77)

Key Idea: Eli and his mother lived in the wilderness by the Blue Ridge Mountains. George was a young surveyor who came to spend the night.

Poetry and Rhymes

Read aloud the poem *"North-West Passage'* (see Appendix) to the students. Do not share the title. Ask students to suggest some titles for the poem. Share the real title. Read the poem again with the students.

Key Idea: Read and appreciate a variety of classic poetry.

Science Exploration

In the 13 colonies, a British system of describing land was used to outline a person's property. Here is a colonial property description: From the junction of Muddy and Indian Creek, north 400 yards to the standing rock, west to the oak tree, south to the bank of Muddy Creek, and back to the starting point. Help students write a description of their backyard using details of the land. 66 foot chains with 100 links were used to measure the land. 80 chains equaled 1 mile. Help students use yarn to cut a 3 foot "chain" length. Allow the students to experiment with the chain to measure a room. Help the students write their room measurements in chains.

✔ Text Connection: *God's Wonderful Works* p. 37

Key Idea: The Indians were upset with the measuring of their land.

Bible Study

Proverbs 15:1 is the memory verse for this unit. Read the verse out loud. Ask, *What is wrath? How does Proverbs 15:1 say that you can turn away wrath? What happens if you speak harshly or grievously to someone? Why do those kinds of words stir up anger?* Say the verse together 3 times. Add hand motions to help students remember the words.

Key Idea: Eli and his mother tried to live peacefully with the Indians. They also wanted to be kind to the young boy, George. The Indians were very angry.

Corresponding Music

None this lesson

Learning the Basics

Focus: Language Arts and Math

Unit 23 - Day 1

Language Arts

Choose **either** spelling list **1 or** 2 (see Appendix for lists). Write each spelling word on a separate index card. Guide students to study each card one at a time, flip it over, write the word from memory on paper, flip the card back over to check the spelling, and erase and correct any mistakes.

Copywork: Have students copy part of the poem *"Northwest Passage"*.

Key Idea: Practice spelling words with final 'y' that says long 'e' as in 'baby'.

Reading Choices

Choose **one** of the reading options listed below (see Appendix for details).

★ A phonics program
★ *Scheduled Books for Emerging Readers*
★ *Drawn into the Heart of Reading Level 2/3*

Key Idea: Use a step-by-step program for reading instruction.

Storytime

Ask, *What did you find out that you didn't know before we began reading this book? Is the information in the book told as a story or listed as a series of facts? How is this nonfiction book different from the other kinds of books that we've read for storytime?*

Read aloud the next portion of the nonfiction book that you selected. Pace your reading to complete the nonfiction book during the next 10 days of plans.

Key Idea: Set a purpose for reading the next part of the nonfiction book.

Math Exploration

Set out 5 bowls. Give students 40 snacks (i.e. pretzels, chips, crackers, or popcorn). On a paper or a markerboard, write "___ groups of ___ in each group = ___ (total)". Under that, write "___ x ___ = ___". Have students act out multiplication problems using their snacks and bowls (i.e. There are 5 bowls. Each bowl has 3 snacks. How many snacks are there altogether?). Help students fill in the blanks on the markerboard or paper to complete the multiplication sentences. Repeat the activity with different numbers of snacks.

✓ Text Connection: *Primary Mathematics Workbook 1B* p. 70-71

Key Idea: Practice multiplication.

Learning Through History

Focus: Trouble Before the Revolutionary War

Unit 23 - Day 2

Reading About History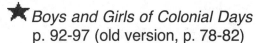

Read about history in the following resource:

★ *Boys and Girls of Colonial Days* p. 92-97 (old version, p. 78-82)

Key Idea: The Indians planned to burn Eli's cabin. Eli bravely came out to face the angry Indians. He reminded the Chief of the way they had taken care of his daughter, Laughing Brook. Eli helped the Indians accept George.

Poetry and Rhymes

Read aloud the poem *"Northwest Passage"* (see Appendix) with the students. Discuss the poem's meaning. If you choose, photocopy the poem, cut it apart, and have the students put it in order.

Key Idea: Read classic poetry.

History Activity

Read aloud the first half of p. 93 of *Boys and Girls of Colonial Days* (old version, p. 77). Ask students to act out an Indian war dance from the description that was just read. Drum loudly while students dance in a circle with wild whoops and yells. Then, read aloud the third paragraph on p. 95 of *Boys and Girls of Colonial Days* (old version, p. 81). Have students act out an Indian dance of welcome. Drum slowly while students walk with slow, stately steps in a circle. After the dance has ended, quietly put your things away.

Key Idea: After Eli spoke to the Chief, the Indians welcomed the surveyor, George Washington. Washington later became a great general in the American Revolution.

Bible Study

Say Proverbs 15:1 while the students join in on the parts they know. Use the hand motions you added on Day 1. Ask, *Describe an argument that you have had with someone. How did the argument end? What kind of a voice did you use when you were arguing? If you had spoken gently or softly, what might have happened instead? How can you remember to speak gently?* Next, have students do 5 toe touches. After 5 toe touches, have the students recite the entire Bible verse. Prompt students as needed. Repeat the activity.

Key Idea: Eli spoke kindly to the Chief. He was careful not to argue.

Corresponding Music

None this lesson

Learning the Basics

Focus: Language Arts and Math

Unit 23 - Day 2

Language Arts

Use the spelling list from Day 1. Say each word and use it in a sentence. Ask students to write each word on a piece of paper or on a markerboard from memory. Give students the matching word cards from Day 1 to compare with their spelling and correct any mistakes.
Copywork: Have students copy part of the poem *"Northwest Passage"*.

Key Idea: Practice words with final 'y' that says long 'e' as in 'baby'.

Reading Choices

Choose **one** of the reading options listed below (see Appendix for details).

★ A phonics program
★ *Scheduled Books for Emerging Readers*
★ *Drawn into the Heart of Reading Level 2/3*

Key Idea: Use a step-by-step program for reading instruction.

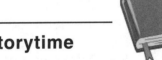

Storytime

Read aloud the next portion of the nonfiction book that you selected. Without looking back at the story, write a retelling of the part of the nonfiction book that you read today leaving blanks in place of key words (i.e. Pioneers began traveling west _____ years ago. They often traveled in _____ wagons. To keep their _____ from breaking on the trip, they placed them in barrels of _____. The journey west was very _____.). Key words can be names, places, descriptive words, times of day, seasons, etc. Work with the students to reread the written narration and fill in the missing words.

Key Idea: Model retelling a story from a single reading.

Math Exploration

On paper, draw 6 black semi-circles to be ant hills. Give students raisins or chocolate chips to be ants. On a paper or a markerboard, write "___ groups of ___ in each group = ___ (total)". Under that, write "___ x ___ = ___". Have students act out multiplication problems using their ants and anthills (i.e. There are 5 anthills. Each hill has 6 ants. How many ants are there in all?). Help students fill in the blanks on the markerboard or paper to complete the multiplication sentences. Repeat the activity with different numbers of ants.

✓ Text Connection: *Primary Mathematics Workbook 1B* p. 72

Key Idea: Practice multiplication.

Learning Through History

Focus: Trouble Before the Revolutionary War

Unit 23 - Day 3

Reading About History

Read about history in the following resource:

★ *Boys and Girls of Colonial Days* p. 54-top half of 57 (old version, p. 47-49)

Key Idea: Patience Arnold lived near Lexington with her family. Her mother went to a neighbor's and left Patience in charge of the key to the barn. While Patience was stitching, a group of soldiers came to the door.

Poetry and Rhymes

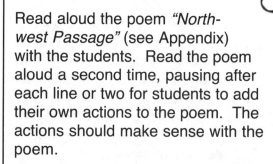

Read aloud the poem *"Northwest Passage"* (see Appendix) with the students. Read the poem aloud a second time, pausing after each line or two for students to add their own actions to the poem. The actions should make sense with the poem.

Key Idea: Read classic poetry.

Artistic Expression

Read aloud the description of the garden on the top half of p. 56 of *Boys and Girls of Colonial Days* (old version, p. 48). Cut a strip of green paper that is about 6" high. Sketch a zigzag line across the top of the strip to be grass. Have students cut on the line. Fold back the bottom 1" of the strip to make a platform for the grass to stand on. Set the grass up on a flat surface. Provide students with colored paper to use for adding other items to the grass strip. Students may want to cut out and glue on a variety of items that go with today's story such as pink apple blossoms, bees, robins, bluebirds, and flowers.

Key Idea: Patience longed to run in the garden. But, she obediently kept stitching her sampler instead.

Bible Study

Say Proverbs 15:1 with the students. Use the hand motions you added on Day 1. Next, have students lay on their backs and peddle their feet in the air like they are riding a bicycle. When you say, *Freeze*, the students should stop and recite the entire Bible verse. Repeat the activity.

✓ Text Connection: *Morning Bells* p. 46-48

Key Idea: Patience wanted to play outside, but she didn't become angry when her mother told her to keep working on her sampler. She tried to be content as she stitched.

Corresponding Music

None this lesson

Learning the Basics

Focus: Language Arts and Math

Unit 23 - Day 3

Language Arts

Using the spelling list from Day 1, choose 3 or more words that the students need to practice. Guide students to use each of the words that you chose in a sentence. On a markerboard or a piece of paper, write down the sentences as the students dictate them to you. Underline the spelling word in each sentence. Have the students copy the sentences on a piece of paper. Help students check their sentences and correct any mistakes.

<u>Copywork</u>: Have students copy part of the poem *"Northwest Passage"*.

<u>Key Idea</u>: Practice spelling words with final 'y' that says long 'e' as in 'baby'.

Reading Choices

Choose **one** of the reading options listed below (see Appendix for details).

★ A phonics program
★ *Scheduled Books for Emerging Readers*
★ *Drawn into the Heart of Reading Level 2/3*

<u>Key Idea</u>: Use a step-by-step program for reading instruction.

Storytime

Say, *Let's look through the next part of our nonfiction book to see if the author used pictures, maps, charts, or photographs. Take time to study these pages. From looking at them, what do you think today's reading is mostly about?*

Read aloud the next portion of the nonfiction book that you selected.

<u>Key Idea</u>: Focus on the story element: *main idea*.

Math Exploration

Complete the assigned lesson in the workbook listed below.

✓ <u>Text Connection</u>: *Primary Mathematics Workbook 1B* p. 73-75

<u>Key Idea</u>: Practice multiplication as repeated addition. Write the corresponding addition and multiplication sentences.

Learning Through History

Focus: Trouble Before the Revolutionary War

Unit 23 - Day 4

Reading About History

Read about history in the following resource:

★ *Boys and Girls of Colonial Days* p. 57-63 (old version, p. 50-54)

Key Idea: Patience didn't give the soldiers the key to the barn. She bravely kept stitching as the soldiers searched the house. When the Captain questioned her about the key, she answered him softly.

Poetry and Rhymes

Read aloud the poem *"Northwest Passage"* (see Appendix) with the students. Have students draw pictures that reflect the poem's meaning on either a photocopy of the poem or on their copywork. File the finished poem in a special place.

Key Idea: Read classic poetry.

Science Exploration

Guide students to make a scented, herb garden picture. Draw 3 large squares to be garden signs down the left side of a piece of paper. Next to the garden signs, help students draw an outline of 3 rows of grassy-looking herb plants. Have students use a glue and water mixture to "paint" glue over one row of the herb garden at a time. Choose a different dried herb to sprinkle on each row. Write the name of the herb on the garden sign at the beginning of each row. Possible suggestions for dried herbs that you might have in your spice cabinet are oregano leaves, leaf thyme, parsley flakes, dill weed, or basil.

✔ Text Connection: *God's Wonderful Works* p. 54

Key Idea: The soldiers trampled Mrs. Arnold's herb garden.

Bible Study

Say Proverbs 15:1 with the students. Use the hand motions from Day 1. Say, *Explain what it means to be content. What is the opposite of being content? How do you usually act when something happens that you do not like? Describe how you can practice being content with what the Lord has planned for you.* Next, have students gallop by leading with their left foot until you say, *Freeze*. After they 'freeze', have the students recite the entire Bible verse. Have students switch to the right foot and repeat the activity.

Key Idea: Patience acted content, even though the soldiers scared her.

Corresponding Music

None this lesson

Learning the Basics

Focus: Language Arts and Math

Unit 23 - Day 4

Language Arts

Use the spelling list from Day 1. Say each word and use it in a sentence. Have students write each word and check it with the matching word card from Day 1. Guide students to correct any mistakes. Use a dark marker to write each missed word very largely on paper. Help students trace each missed word with glue. Allow the glue to dry in order to feel the words.
<u>Copywork</u>: Have students copy part of the poem *"Northwest Passage"*.

<u>Key Idea</u>: Practice words with final 'y' that says long 'e' as in 'baby'.

Reading Choices

Choose **one** of the reading options listed below (see Appendix for details).

★ A phonics program
★ *Scheduled Books for Emerging Readers*
★ *Drawn into the Heart of Reading Level 2/3*

<u>Key Idea</u>: Use a step-by-step program for reading instruction.

Storytime

Say, *Obedience is a willingness to do what is asked or required without complaint.* Read aloud Psalm 119:33-34. Say, *What are some things that you are asked to do without complaint? How do you know that God expects you to be obedient to Him?* Read aloud the next portion of the nonfiction book. Ask, *How can you see obedience to God in the topics you are studying in your nonfiction book?* (i.e. laws of nature, governments and laws patterned after the Bible, punishment for wrong, families with Godly standards, consequences for Godless societies).

<u>Key Idea</u>: Focus on the Godly character trait: *obedience*.

Math Exploration

Place 7 cracker squares on blue paper to be rafts in water. Give students items to be people (i.e. small blocks, coins, play people, or macaroni noodles). On a paper or a markerboard, write "___ groups of ___ in each group = ___ (total)". Under that, write "___ x ___ = ___". Have students act out multiplication problems using their people and rafts (i.e. There are 7 rafts. Each raft has 3 people. How many people are there in all?). Help students complete the multiplication sentences on the paper or markerboard. Repeat the activity.

✓ <u>Text Connection</u>: *Primary Mathematics Workbook 1B* p. 76-78

<u>Key Idea</u>: Practice multiplication.

Learning Through History

Focus: Trouble Before the Revolutionary War

Unit 23 - Day 5

Reading About History

Read the following passage from your own Bible:

★ Genesis 13:1-18

Key Idea: In the history stories we read this week, the children turned away wrath by speaking softly. In this Bible passage, Abram gave Lot first choice of the land to stop the quarreling. Lot took the best land.

Poetry and Rhymes

Have students get out the poems that they saved from the previous units. Ask students to select one or more poems to review. Read aloud the selected poems with the students.

Key Idea: Read classic poetry.

Geography

Read Genesis 13:11-17 out loud. Say, *Length means how long something is, and breadth means how wide something is. Let's use your feet to measure the length and breadth of this room.* Show students how to count how many "feet" long the room is, by placing one foot directly in front of the other foot. Then, have students measure the breadth or width of the room the same way. Help students make a map of their measurements using a scale. Write 'scale' in the bottom right hand corner. Draw a 1" line segment and write 1 inch = 1 foot. Help students use a ruler to draw an outline of the room's walls using the map scale.

Key Idea: The Lord blessed Abram by giving him the length and breadth of the land.

Bible Study

Say, *In Genesis 13:8-9, how did Abram stop the quarreling? Did Abram have to let Lot choose first? In Genesis 13:10-12, what did Lot do? In Genesis 13:13, what problem can you see is coming for Lot? How did God bless Abram in Genesis 13:14-18? What can you learn from Abram and Lot?* Ask students to share their memory verse, Proverbs 15:1, with someone special. Suggestions for sharing the verse include saying it to another family member, saying it to someone by telephone, reciting it to a stuffed animal, or writing it to mail.

Key Idea: God had consequences for Abram's and Lot's choices. Your choices have consequences too.

Corresponding Music

None this lesson

Learning the Basics

Focus: Language Arts and Math

Unit 23 - Day 5

Language Arts

Write your child's name and address on paper. Say, *This is the special address of the place where you live. On what street do you live?* There are street signs that say the special name of each street. We'll watch for them when we go out. *What is the number of your house?* The number of your house should be on the outside of it. Let's look. *In what city do you live?* Each city has a sign with its special name on it as you enter the city. We'll watch for city signs when we go out. *What state do you live in?* Let's look on the globe or map to find your special state. *What punctuation mark do you notice between the city and state? What capital letters do you see in your address?* Copywork: Have students copy their address.

Key Idea: Correctly capitalize and punctuate an address.

Storytime

Read aloud a short portion of the nonfiction book that you selected. Guide students to retell today's reading by saying, *Tell me what you can remember from today's reading. Name some new things that you learned.*

Key Idea: Give students practice retelling a portion of a nonfiction book.

Reading Choices

Choose **one** of the reading options listed below (see Appendix for details).

★ A phonics program
★ *Scheduled Books for Emerging Readers*
★ *Drawn into the Heart of Reading Level 2/3*

Key Idea: Use a step-by-step program for reading instruction.

Math Exploration

These are the concepts that are covered in this review: writing numbers up to '40'; solving story problems using addition, subtraction, and multiplication; reading graphs; and choosing the correct operation to use to solve a story problem. Review any concepts that students had difficulty understanding. Also, complete the assigned review in the workbook listed below.

✔ Text Connection: *Primary Mathematics Workbook 1B* p. 79-82

Key Idea: Review difficult concepts.

Learning Through History

Focus: The Time of the American Revolution

Unit 24 - Day 1

Reading About History

Read about history in the following resource:

★ *Boys and Girls of Colonial Days* p. 64-69 (old version, p. 55-59)

Key Idea: Tabitha lived in Philadelphia at the time of the Revolution. She wrote to her cousin John about George Washington's visit to Betsy Ross. He wanted Betsy to stitch a new flag for the colonies.

Poetry and Rhymes

Read aloud the poem *"The Star-Spangled Banner"* (see Appendix) to the students. Do not share the title. Ask students to suggest some titles for the poem. Share the real title. Read the poem with the students.

Key Idea: Read and appreciate a variety of classic poetry.

Science Exploration

Say, *Many trees grow fruit. Apples, and other fruits, are made mostly of water. Do a test to check if a food is made mostly of water or fat. Divide a paper into 4 parts. Choose 4 foods to test (i.e. a sliced apple, orange, or grape, potato chip, cracker, bologna, or cheese). Press a different piece of food on each section of the paper, leaving them there for 4 minutes. Label each section with the name of the food. Remove the food. Let the paper set for 8-10 minutes. Hold the paper up to a light. If a greasy spot is left, the food is mostly fat. If a spot was there, but has evaporated, the food is mostly water.*

✔ Text Connection: *God's Wonderful Works* p. 8 and 49

Key Idea: Tabitha gathered apples to send to her cousin, John.

Bible Study

Review the memory verse, 1 John 4:9-11, from Unit 19. Read the verse out loud. Ask, *How does God show that He loves you? What does 1 John 4:11 say you should do because God loves you? Name some people you know that are sad, lonely, or hurting. How can you show God's love to those people?* Say the verse together 3 times. Review the hand motions that go with the verse from Unit 19.

Key Idea: Betsy was a widow, and Tabitha was lonely. So, Tabitha and Betsy were kind to one another.

Corresponding Music

✔ *Hide 'Em in Your Heart Vol. 2* CD - Track 10; Cassette - Side A Song: *"We Love Him"*

Learning the Basics

Focus: Language Arts and Math

Unit 24 - Day 1

Language Arts

Get out the spelling words on index cards that you saved from Unit 19 and Unit 20. Guide students to study each card one at a time, flip it over, write the word from memory on paper, flip the card back over to check the spelling, and erase and correct any mistakes.

<u>Copywork</u>: Have students copy part of the poem *"The Star-Spangled Banner"*.

<u>Key Idea</u>: Review spelling words from Unit 19 and Unit 20.

Reading Choices

Choose **one** of the reading options listed below (see Appendix for details).

★ A phonics program
★ *Scheduled Books for Emerging Readers*
★ *Drawn into the Heart of Reading Level 2/3*

<u>Key Idea</u>: Use a step-by-step program for reading instruction.

Storytime

Read aloud the next portion of the nonfiction book that you selected. Pace your reading to complete the book during the next 5 days of plans.

Ask, *Has this book been easy to understand? Show me one of the most interesting parts in the book. What made that part interesting? Does this book remind you of any other book? Explain.*

<u>Key Idea</u>: Set a purpose for reading the next part of the nonfiction book.

Math Exploration

These are the concepts that are covered in this review: completing addition patterns, comparing sets using 'more' and 'fewer', writing missing numbers in number sentences, and adding and subtracting with 'tens' and 'ones'. Review any concepts that students had difficulty understanding. Also, complete the assigned review in the workbook listed below.

✔ <u>Text Connection</u>: *Primary Mathematics Workbook 1B* p. 83-84

<u>Key Idea</u>: Review difficult concepts.

Learning Through History

Focus: The Time of the American Revolution

Unit 24 - Day 2

Reading About History

Read about history in the following resource:

★ *Boys and Girls of Colonial Days* p. 70-74 (old version, p. 60-63)

Key Idea: Tabitha's letter told John how Betsy Ross designed a new flag for the colonies. She explained what the colors stood for and how the flag was going to be adopted by Congress.

Poetry and Rhymes

Read aloud the poem *"The Star-Spangled Banner"* (see Appendix) with the students. Discuss the poem's meaning. If you choose, photocopy the poem, cut it apart, and have the students put it in order.

Key Idea: Read classic poetry.

Science Exploration

Say, *The stars in the sky are always shining. But, during the day they cannot be seen as easily as at night, because it is so bright.* Leave the lights on like day. Shine a flashlight up on the ceiling to be a star. Ask, *Is it easy to see the star shining? Why, or why not?* While the flashlight is still shining on the ceiling, turn the lights off like night. Ask, *Is it easier to see the star shining now? Why, or why not?*

✔ Text Connection: *God's Wonderful Works* p. 62

Key Idea: George Washington wanted the new flag to have stars. Betsy Ross sewed thirteen, five-point stars on the new flag, one for each of the colonies. The flag also had thirteen red and white stripes.

Bible Study

Review the memory verse Proverbs 12:24, from Unit 20, by saying it while the students join in on the parts they know. Say, *Explain what it means to be diligent. If you do not learn diligence as a child, what kind of adult might you become? What does God think about laziness? What are some of the consequences of laziness?* Next, have students do windmills by touching their right hand to their right foot and then their left hand to their left foot. After 5 windmills, have the students recite the Bible verse. Repeat the activity.

Key Idea: Betsy Ross worked diligently at the task she was given by General Washington.

Corresponding Music

None this lesson

Learning the Basics

Focus: Language Arts and Math

Unit 24 - Day 2

Language Arts

Get out the spelling cards that you saved from Unit 21. Say the first spelling word. Use it in a sentence. Repeat the word. Ask students to write the word on a markerboard or a piece of paper from memory. Give students the matching word card to compare with their spelling. Guide students to correct any mistakes. Repeat the activity with all 10 words.

<u>Copywork</u>: Have students copy part of the poem *"The Star-Spangled Banner"*.

<u>Key Idea</u>: Review spelling words from Unit 21.

Reading Choices

Choose **one** of the reading options listed below (see Appendix for details).

★ A phonics program

★ *Scheduled Books for Emerging Readers*

★ *Drawn into the Heart of Reading Level 2/3*

<u>Key Idea</u>: Use a step-by-step program for reading instruction.

Storytime

Read aloud the next portion of the nonfiction book that you selected. Ask students to retell or narrate what you read today. Remind students to tell the most important parts and to include details from the story in the retelling. As students work together to retell the story, write, type, or tape record the students' narration. When the students are finished, read the narration out loud. Highlight, circle, or underline one main idea from the narration for the students to copy.

<u>Key Idea</u>: Keep a sample of the students' narrations for the genre: *Nonfiction*.

Math Exploration

Use a muffin tin to be holes in the ground. Give students macaroni noodles or pieces of string or yarn to be snakes. Have students use their snakes to act out the following story problems: *There were 5 holes. Each hole had 1 snake in it. 3 snakes crawled out. How many are left?* (i.e. 5 - 3 = 2). *5 snakes crawled into a hole. 2 more crawled in. How many are there in all?* (i.e. 5 + 2 = 7). *There were 6 holes. Each hole had 3 snakes in it. How many snakes are there altogether?* (i.e. 6 x 3 = 18). Continue with other examples.

✓ <u>Text Connection</u>: *Primary Mathematics Workbook 1B* p. 85-86

<u>Key Idea</u>: Decide when to multiply, add, or subtract in story problems.

Learning Through History

Focus: The Time of the American Revolution

Unit 24 - Day 3

Reading About History

Read about history in the following resource:

★ *Boys and Girls of Colonial Days* p. 75-80 (old version, p. 64-68)

Key Idea: Prudence lived in Philadelphia during the Revolution. She stitched a flag just like the flags Betsy Ross had made. Prudence's neighbor, William, heard that the Redcoats were coming soon.

Poetry and Rhymes

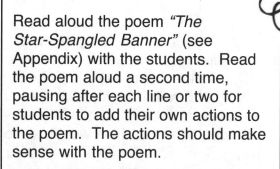

Read aloud the poem *"The Star-Spangled Banner"* (see Appendix) with the students. Read the poem aloud a second time, pausing after each line or two for students to add their own actions to the poem. The actions should make sense with the poem.

Key Idea: Read classic poetry.

Artistic Expression

Help students create an edible, flag snack. Make a spreadable frosting by mixing 1/3 cup softened butter or margarine, 1/2 tsp. vanilla, a pinch of salt, 2 cups of powdered sugar, and a little milk. Leave 1/3 of the frosting white. Add food coloring to make 1/3 of the frosting red and 1/3 of the frosting blue. Give each student a large graham cracker on a piece of waxed paper to frost. Say, *Spread a blue frosting square in the top left corner of the cracker. Then, alternate spreading thin red and white stripes across the cracker. Start and end with a red stripe. Use a toothpick to dot 13 white dots in a circle in the blue square to be stars. Eat your flag.*

Key Idea: The colors of the flag each have a meaning. The white stands for purity, the red stands for bravery, and the blue stands for justice.

Bible Study

Review the memory verse, Philippians 4:8, from Unit 21, by saying it while the students join in on the parts they know. Next, have students squat down, hop up, and squat back down again. After the last squat, have the students recite the entire Bible verse. Prompt students as needed. Repeat the activity.

✓ Text Connection: *Morning Bells* p. 76-78

Key Idea: Prudence wanted to make a flag to show her loyalty to the Continental Army.

Corresponding Music

✓ *Hide 'Em in Your Heart Vol. 2* CD - Track 13; Cassette - Side B Song: *"Think About Such Things"*

Learning the Basics

Focus: Language Arts and Math

Unit 24 - Day 3

Language Arts

Get out the spelling word cards from Unit 22. Choose 3 or more words that the students need to practice. Guide students to use each of the words that you chose in a sentence. On a markerboard or a piece of paper, write down the sentences as the students dictate them to you. Underline the spelling word in each sentence. Have the students copy the sentences on a piece of paper. Help students check their sentences and correct any mistakes.
<u>Copywork</u>: Have students copy part of *"The Star-Spangled Banner"*.

<u>Key Idea</u>: Review spelling words.

Reading Choices

Choose **one** of the reading options listed below (see Appendix for details).

★ A phonics program
★ *Scheduled Books for Emerging Readers*
★ *Drawn into the Heart of Reading Level 2/3*

<u>Key Idea</u>: Use a step-by-step program for reading instruction.

Storytime

Read aloud the next portion of the nonfiction book that you selected. Discuss with the students the main theme or overall idea of the book. At the top of a piece of paper, write one or two sentences that summarize the theme of the book. Allow students to show the theme of the book by choosing one of these options: draw a picture, a map, or a chart; write words; or select an appropriate photograph. Students should place their work on the paper under the written summary of the theme.

<u>Key Idea</u>: Focus on the story element: *main idea*.

Math Exploration

These are the concepts that are covered in this review: fact families, multiplication, shapes, ordinal numbers, length, and weight. Review any concepts that students had difficulty understanding. Also, complete the assigned review in the workbook listed below.

✔ <u>Text Connection</u>: *Primary Mathematics Workbook 1B* p. 87-88

<u>Key Idea</u>: Review difficult concepts.

Learning Through History

Focus: The Time of the American Revolution

Unit 24 - Day 4

Reading About History

Read about history in the following resource:

★ *Boys and Girls of Colonial Days* p. 81-85 (old version, p. 69-72)

Key Idea: When the Redcoats came to Philadelphia, Prudence and William drummed and waved their flag. The British general was surprised by their bravery.

Poetry and Rhymes

Read aloud the poem *"The Star-Spangled Banner"* (see Appendix) with the students. Have students draw pictures that reflect the poem's meaning on either a photocopy of the poem or on their copywork. File the finished poem in a special place.

Key Idea: Read classic poetry.

History Activity

Say, *Let's practice some military commands. 'To salute', hold the fingers of your right hand together, bring it over your right eye, palm down, like the brim of a hat. 'To the right flank', means turn and march right. 'To the left flank', means turn and march left. 'To the rear', means turn and march the opposite direction. 'Wheel', means curve around a center point. 'Attention', means stand silent and motionless, waiting for a command. 'At ease', means keep your right foot in place, remain silent, but movement is allowed.* Have students get out their timeline. Say, *Let's find the column that says 1700. Draw a small flag in that column. Write 'Revolutionary War, 1776'.*

Key Idea: The British general spoke kindly to the children and ordered his troops to march on.

Bible Study

Review the memory verse, 2 Corinthians 9:7, from unit 22 by saying it while the students join in on the parts they know. Say, *Why do people carry flags or banners? What might it mean to carry a banner for Jesus? How can you show others that you live for Jesus?* Next, have students hop backward 5 times. After every 5 hops, have the students recite the entire Bible verse.

Key Idea: Prudence cheerfully helped her mother. She bravely waved her flag to save their home.

Corresponding Music

✔ *Hide 'Em in Your Heart Vol. 2* CD - Track 9; Cassette - Side A Song: *"God Loves a Cheerful Giver"*

Learning the Basics

Focus: Language Arts and Math

Unit 24 - Day 4

Language Arts

Get out the spelling word cards from Unit 23. Say each word and use it in a sentence. Have students write each word and check it with the matching word card. Guide students to correct any mistakes. For each missed word, have students hop on one foot and spell the word out loud, hopping each time they say a letter.

<u>Copywork</u>: Have students copy part of the poem *"The Star-Spangled Banner"*.

<u>Key Idea</u>: Review spelling words.

Reading Choices

Choose **one** of the reading options listed below (see Appendix for details).

★ A phonics program
★ *Scheduled Books for Emerging Readers*
★ *Drawn into the Heart of Reading Level 2/3*

<u>Key Idea</u>: Use a step-by-step program for reading instruction.

Storytime

Say, *Obedience is a willingness to do what is asked or required without complaint.* Read aloud the key verses Psalm 119:33-34. Read aloud the next portion of the nonfiction book that you selected. Ask, *How could the nonfiction book have done a better job of showing the trait obedience in connection with God's word? Explain. How could you do a better job of being obedient? Draw a picture showing one way that you could be more obedient. Post your picture in a place where you will see it often.*

<u>Key Idea</u>: Focus on the Godly character trait: *obedience*.

Math Exploration

These are the concepts that are covered in this review: multiplication, addition, and subtraction stories. Review any concepts that students had difficulty understanding. Also, complete the assigned review in the workbook listed below.

✔ <u>Text Connection</u>: *Primary Mathematics Workbook 1B* p. 89-90

<u>Key Idea</u>: Review difficult concepts.

Learning Through History

Focus: The Time of the American Revolution

Unit 24 - Day 5

Reading About History

Read the following passage from your own Bible:

 1 Samuel 24:1-22

Key Idea: Saul was trying to kill David, yet David spared Saul's life. David trusted God to guide him. During the Revolution, many colonists trusted in God's will. They prayed for God to guide them.

Poetry and Rhymes

Have students get out the poems that they saved from the previous units. Ask students to select one or more poems to review. Read aloud the selected poems with the students.

Key Idea: Read classic poetry.

Geography

Read aloud 1 Samuel 24:1-3. Place an inch of damp sand, oatmeal, or cornmeal in the bottom of a pan. Say, *Saul heard that David was hiding in the Desert of En Gedi. A desert is a dry, sandy wilderness. Mold a desert in your pan. Saul went to look for David near the Crags of the Wild Goats. A crag is a steep, rough rock. Form a crag in your pan. David was hiding in a cave. A cave is a hollow place in a hill or underground. Make a cave in your pan.* Ask, *Why didn't David kill Saul when he had the chance? Who was more important to David, his men or God? How can you tell?*

Key Idea: David knew God had chosen Saul, and he trusted God to deal with him. David placed his trust in God and not in men.

Bible Study

Ask, *In 1 Samuel 24:4-7, what can you learn from David's actions? In 1 Samuel 24:9-11, how can you see that it is more important to listen to the Lord than to listen to what others tell you? In 1 Samuel 24:12-13, who does David say will judge Saul? How can you follow David's example?* Ask students to share their memory verse, Proverbs 15:1, with someone special. Suggestions for sharing the verse include saying it to another family member, saying it to someone by telephone, reciting it to a stuffed animal, or writing it to mail.

Key Idea: David chose not to listen to his men. He turned his anger away from Saul and trusted God.

Corresponding Music

None this lesson

Learning the Basics

Focus: Language Arts and Math

Unit 24 - Day 5

Language Arts

Say, *Common nouns are **not** special. They name common places or things. I'm going to make a list of a few of my favorite things* (i.e. babies, teaching, hot baths, eating out, sunny days, and chocolate). *The things on my list are all common nouns. Now, I'd like you to tell me some of your favorite things. I will write them down as you say them. Are the things on your list common nouns? Why? How can we change one of the common nouns to a proper noun?*
Copywork: Have students copy some of their favorite things off of their list.

Key Idea: Practice listing common things.

Reading Choices

Choose **one** of the reading options listed below (see Appendix for details).

★ A phonics program
★ *Scheduled Books for Emerging Readers*
★ *Drawn into the Heart of Reading Level 2/3*

Key Idea: Use a step-by-step program for reading instruction.

Storytime

Read aloud the final portion of the nonfiction book that you selected. You will need to select a humorous book to read aloud next. Give students a chance to orally retell the portion of the book that you read aloud today. Prompt students after the retelling to fill in missing details by using leading questions that begin with these words: *Who? What? When? Where? Why? How?*

Key Idea: Give students practice retelling a portion of a nonfiction book.

Math Exploration

Set out 4 stuffed toys. Give students 16 treats (i.e. marshmallows, crackers, dry cereal pieces, or raisins). Say, *Divide the 16 treats equally among the 4 stuffed toys. How many treats will each toy receive?* (i.e. Each toy receives 4 treats). Repeat the acivity using different numbers of stuffed toys and treats. Remember to use numbers of treats that can be divided equally without any left over (i.e. 20 treats divided among 5 stuffed toys).

✔ Text Connection: *Primary Mathematics Workbook 1B* p. 91

Key Idea: Introduce division as sharing items equally.

Learning Through History

Focus: Young Soldiers in the Continental Army

Unit 25 - Day 1

Reading About History

Read about history in the following resource:

★ *Boys and Girls of Colonial Days* p. 98-103 (old version, p. 83-87)

Key Idea: Richard was 10 years old when he signed up to march with the Continental Army. His job was to play the fife for the troops. Later, his division was taken captive by the British.

Poetry and Rhymes

Read aloud the poem *"A Child's Prayer"* (see Appendix) to the students. Do not share the title. Ask students to suggest some titles for the poem. Share the real title. Read the poem again with the students.

Key Idea: Read and appreciate a variety of classic poetry.

Science Exploration

Say, *Lay a paper flat on the table. Lift up a corner of the paper and roll it diagonally to form a cone. The small hole on one end should be an inch across. Hold the cone to your mouth. Speak into it. What happens to your voice? Hold the small end of the cone against one ear. Point the other end of the cone toward different sounds (i.e. talking, music, birds chirping).* Ask, *Were you able to hear sounds better with the cone? What does the cone do? How does it gather sound into one place? Cup a hand around one ear. Your outer ear gathers the sounds that you hear.*

✔ Text Connection: *God's Wonderful Works* p. 132

Key Idea: The troops loved hearing Richard play his fife.

Bible Study

John 15:13 is the memory verse for this unit. Read the verse out loud. Ask, *What does John 15:13 say shows the greatest love? Who gave His life for all men? Did Christ have to die for you and me? Why did He choose to die for our sins?* Say the verse together 3 times. Add hand motions to help students remember the words.

Key Idea: Richard knew he might be killed when he signed up to march with the army. He was willing to lay down his life for his country. Christ laid down His life for you.

Corresponding Music

✔ *Hide 'Em in Your Heart Vol. 2*
CD - Track 3; Cassette - Side A
Song: *"Greater Love"*

Learning the Basics

Focus: Language Arts and Math

Unit 25 - Day 1

Language Arts

Choose **either** spelling list 1 **or** 2 (see Appendix for lists). Write each spelling word on a separate index card. Guide students to study each card one at a time, flip it over, write the word on paper, flip the card back over to check the spelling, and erase and correct any mistakes.
<u>Copywork</u>: Have students copy part of the poem *"A Child's Prayer"*.

<u>Key Idea</u>: Practice spelling words with long 'o' spelled 'ow' as in 'grow'.

Reading Choices

Choose **one** of the reading options listed below (see Appendix for details).

★ A phonics program
★ *Scheduled Books for Emerging Readers*
★ *Drawn into the Heart of Reading Level 2/3*

<u>Key Idea</u>: Use a step-by-step program for reading instruction.

Storytime

Choose at least one humorous book to read aloud for the next 20 days of plans (see Appendix for suggested titles). To introduce the genre, *Humor*, help students write a humorous alliteration using their own name. An alliteration is repeating the same letter sound at the beginning of each word in a sentence. Alliterations are often called tongue twisters, like "Peter Piper picked a peck of pickled peppers..." Repeat each student's alliteration quickly 3 or more times. Say, *Humor includes stories, jokes, or poems that cause laughter and are very entertaining.* Read a portion of the humorous book you chose.

<u>Key Idea</u>: Introduce the genre: *Humor*.

Math Exploration

Set out 3 cups to represent cups of hot chocolate. Give students 15 toppings to divide equally among the 3 cups (i.e. marshmallows, red hots, or other counters). Ask, *How many toppings are in each cup?* Repeat the activity using different numbers of cups and toppings. Make sure the toppings can be divided equally among the cups with none left over (i.e. 12 toppings divided equally among 4 cups).

✔ <u>Text Connection</u>: *Primary Mathematics Workbook 1B* p. 92

<u>Key Idea</u>: Divide items into equal groups.

Learning Through History

Focus: Young Soldiers in the Continental Army

Unit 25 - Day 2

Reading About History

Read about history in the following resource:

★ *Boys and Girls of Colonial Days* p. 104-107 (old version, p. 88-91)

Key Idea: After he was captured, Richard had a fist fight with an English boy. Richard was weak and tired, but he fought with bravery. Due to his bravery, the British officer let Richard and his colonol go.

Poetry and Rhymes

Read aloud the poem *"A Child's Prayer"* (see Appendix) with the students. Discuss the poem's meaning. If you choose, photocopy the poem, cut it apart, and have the students place it in the correct order.

Key Idea: Read classic poetry.

Geography

Help students use a United States map to find the following battle sites of American victories during the Revolutionary War: (1) Concord, New Hampshire (2) Trenton, New Jersey (3) Saratoga, New York (4) Valley Forge, Pennsylvania (5) Yorktown, Virginia (on the Chesapeake Bay). Say, *British General Cornwallis surrendered in Yorktown to American General George Washington in 1781. In which part of America were all of the key battles fought? Why weren't any battles fought in the middle or the western part of America?* Look on the map on p. 52 of <u>American Pioneers and Patriots</u> to see America at the time of the Revolution.

Key Idea: Richard was with the army during many important battles.

Bible Study

Say John 15:13 while the students join in on the parts they know. Use the hand motions you added on Day 1. Say, *Explain what it means to be self-centered. Name some things you do that are self-centered. What can you give up or sacrifice to show love to someone else? How do others sacrifice themselves for you?* Next, have students do 5 jumping jacks. After 5 jumping jacks, have the students recite the entire Bible verse. Prompt the students as needed. Repeat the activity.

Key Idea: Richard made many sacrifices to march with the army.

Corresponding Music

✔ *Hide 'Em in Your Heart Vol. 2*
CD - Track 3; Cassette - Side A
Song: *"Greater Love"*

Learning the Basics

Focus: Language Arts and Math

Unit 25 - Day 2

Language Arts

Use the spelling list from Day 1. Say the first spelling word. Use it in a sentence. Repeat the word. Ask students to write the word on a markerboard or a piece of paper from memory. Give students the matching word card from Day 1 to compare with their spelling. Guide students to correct any mistakes. Repeat the activity with all 10 words.

Copywork: Have students copy part of the poem *"A Child's Prayer"*.

Key Idea: Practice spelling words with long 'o' spelled 'ow' as in 'grow'.

Reading Choices

Choose **one** of the reading options listed below (see Appendix for details).

★ A phonics program
★ *Scheduled Books for Emerging Readers*
★ *Drawn into the Heart of Reading Level 2/3*

Key Idea: Use a step-by-step program for reading instruction.

Storytime

Read aloud the next portion of the humorous book that you selected. Without looking back at the story, model retelling or narrating the part of the book that you read today to the students. Remember to tell the most important points and to add details from the story to the retelling without overwhelming the students. After the retelling, say, *Name one funny thing that happened in the story.* On paper, write the event as one sentence for the students to copy.

Key Idea: Model retelling a story from a single reading.

Math Exploration

Give students 18 'O'-shaped cereal pieces to be cows, or 18 cotton balls to be sheep. Say, *You are the farmer. Your job is to herd these 18 animals into 3 equal groups. How many animals will be each group?* If needed, demonstrate how to place animals one at a time into 3 groups until all 18 animals are divided. Write the following corresponding division sentence on a markerboard or piece of paper: 18 animals divided into 3 groups = 6 animals in each group. Repeat the activity using different numbers.

✔ Text Connection: *Primary Mathematics Workbook 1B* p. 93-94

Key Idea: Divide items equally among groups.

Learning Through History

Focus: Young Soldiers in the Continental Army

Unit 25 - Day 3

Reading About History

Read about history in the following resource:

★ *Boys and Girls of Colonial Days* p. 122-130 (old version, p. 105-112)

Key Idea: Levi was a young boy who fought at Lexington and Bunker Hill. Later, he was chosen to watch over General Washington's bodyguards. Even though it wasn't as exciting as fighting, Levi quietly did his job well.

Poetry and Rhymes

Read aloud the poem *"A Child's Prayer"* (see Appendix) with the students. Read the poem aloud a second time, pausing after each line or two for students to add their own actions to the poem. The actions should make sense with the poem.

Key Idea: Read classic poetry.

Science Exploration

Say, *Your nose and your tongue work together. Take a bite of an apple or a banana. Taste it while you chew it and swallow it. Take a sniff of cinnamon or vanilla. Take another bite of the same fruit. Did you notice anything different about how the fruit tastes now? Did it taste like the flavor you sniffed before taking a second bite? Plug your nose and take a third bite of the fruit. Did the fruit seem to have as much taste? Your sense of smell affects how things taste to you. That is why you can't taste as well when your nose is plugged.*

✔ Text Connection: *God's Wonderful Works* p. 134-135

Key Idea: Levi helped the General give a dinner party in the mess tent for some important guests.

Bible Study

Say John 15:13 with the students. Use the hand motions you added on Day 1. Next, have students hop on their left foot until you say, *Freeze*. After they 'freeze', have the students recite the entire Bible verse. Prompt students as needed. Have students switch to the right foot, and repeat the activity.

✔ Text Connection: *Morning Bells* p. 79-81

Key Idea: Levi chose to be a soldier in the Continental Army. Christ wants you to be a soldier for Him and stand up for what you believe.

Corresponding Music

✔ *Hide 'Em in Your Heart Vol. 2* CD - Track 3; Cassette - Side A Song: *"Greater Love"*

Learning the Basics

Focus: Language Arts and Math

Unit 25 - Day 3

Language Arts

Use the spelling list from Day 1. Say each word and use it in a sentence. Have students write each word and check it with the matching word card from Day 1. Guide students to correct any mistakes. For each missed word, have students trace the word with their finger on a patch of carpet.

<u>Copywork</u>: Have students copy part of the poem *"A Child's Prayer"*.

<u>Key Idea</u>: Practice spelling words with long 'o' spelled 'ow' as in 'grow'.

Reading Choices

Choose **one** of the reading options listed below (see Appendix for details).

★ A phonics program

★ *Scheduled Books for Emerging Readers*

★ *Drawn into the Heart of Reading Level 2/3*

<u>Key Idea</u>: Use a step-by-step program for reading instruction.

Storytime

Say, *Usually there is a reason that something happens. This is called a cause. What happens as a result of the cause is called an effect.* Ask the students to tell you a joke. Say, *You told a joke, and I laughed. The joke was the cause. The laughter was the effect. As we read today, listen for causes and effects.* Read aloud the next portion of the humorous book that you selected. At the end of the reading, say, *Tell me one thing that happened in the story. What happened next? Why? What caused that to happen?*

<u>Key Idea</u>: Introduce the story element: *cause* and *effect*.

Math Exploration

On paper, outline 5 red barns. Give students cotton balls or raisins to be sheep. Have students use their sheep to act out the following division problems: *There are 12 sheep. You can fit 4 sheep in each barn. How many barns are filled?* (12 sheep divided into groups of 4 would fill 3 barns). *There are 15 sheep. They must be divided equally into 5 barns. How many sheep are in each barn?* (15 sheep divided into 5 barns equals 3 sheep in each barn).

✔ <u>Text Connection</u>: *Primary Mathematics Workbook 1B* p. 95

<u>Key Idea</u>: Divide items equally among groups.

Learning Through History

Focus: Young Soldiers in the Continental Army

Unit 25 - Day 4

Reading About History

Read about history in the following resource:

⭐ *Boys and Girls of Colonial Days* p. 118-121 (old version, p. 101-104)

Key Idea: George Washington was a great general. Even though he was in charge, he set an example of serving others. He was never too great to help those in need.

Poetry and Rhymes

Read aloud the poem *"A Child's Prayer"* (see Appendix) with the students. Have students draw pictures that reflect the poem's meaning on either a photocopy of the poem or on their copywork. File the finished poem in a special place.

Key Idea: Read classic poetry.

History Activity

Have students get out their timeline. Say, *British General Cornwallis surrendered to American General Washington at Yorktown, Pennsylvania in 1781. Let's find the column that says 1700. Find the small flag that you drew in that column. Under the flag, it should say, 'Revolutionary War, 1776'. After the year 1776, add a dash and the year '1781' to show when the war ended.* Say, *General Washington set an example of serving others. Even though he was the General, he was always willing to help his men. Watch for ways that you can help others today.*

Key Idea: The corporal in today's story thought he was too important to help his men. Jesus shows us that we are never too great to help others.

Bible Study

Say John 15:13 with the students. Use the hand motions you added on Day 1. Ask, *If you are a Christian, you are part of what army? When you are in Christ's army, what are you fighting against? How can you stand up for Jesus? Why is your life safe with Jesus?* Next, have the students do 5 sit-ups. After 5 sit-ups, have the students recite the entire Bible verse.

Key Idea: Washington's men loved and respected him. They followed his example. You can show love to Jesus by following His example.

Corresponding Music

✔ *Hide 'Em in Your Heart Vol. 2* CD - Track 3; Cassette - Side A Song: *"Greater Love"*

Learning the Basics

Focus: Language Arts and Math

Unit 25 - Day 4

Language Arts

Use the spelling list from Day 1. Say each word and use it in a sentence. Have students write each word and check it with the matching word card from Day 1. Guide students to correct any mistakes. For each missed word, have students trace the word with their finger on a patch of carpet.
<u>Copywork</u>: Have students copy part of the poem *"A Child's Prayer"*.

<u>Key Idea</u>: Practice spelling words with the long 'o' spelled 'ow' as in 'grow'.

Reading Choices

Choose **one** of the reading options listed below (see Appendix for details).

★ A phonics program
★ *Scheduled Books for Emerging Readers*
★ *Drawn into the Heart of Reading Level 2/3*

<u>Key Idea</u>: Use a step-by-step program for reading instruction.

Storytime

Say, *Joy means rejoicing, even in times of trouble, because God is with you no matter what happens to you.* Read aloud the key verse 1 Chronicles 16:10-11 to illustrate *joy*. List some ways that you can show joy. Now, have students share some things that have made them joyful.

Read aloud the next portion of the humorous book that you selected. Then, ask, *How do the characters show joy? What could the characters do differently to be more joyful?*

<u>Key Idea</u>: Introduce the Godly character trait: *joy*.

Math Exploration

Complete the assigned lesson in the workbook listed below.

✓ <u>Text Connection</u>: *Primary Mathematics Workbook 1B* p. 96-98

<u>Key Idea</u>: Practice sharing items equally to divide them into groups.

Learning Through History

Focus: Young Soldiers in the Continental Army

Unit 25 - Day 5

Reading About History

Read the following passage from your own Bible:

★ Ephesians 6:10-20

Key Idea: Paul encourages Christians to be brave in the fight against evil. We must trust in the Lord and in the Lord's power. The Continental Army needed to be brave to overcome many hard times. They trusted their General. General Washington trusted in God.

Poetry and Rhymes

Have students get out the poems that they saved from the previous units. Ask students to select one or more poems to review. Read aloud the selected poems with the students.

Key Idea: Read classic poetry.

Artistic Expression

Have students create pieces of armor to dress a small, stuffed animal with the "armor of God". Help them use gray paper to make each piece of armor. Say, *Make a belt and write 'Truth' on it. Tape it around the animal's waist. Make a breastplate to protect the animal's chest. Write 'Righteousness' on it. Tape it to the animal's chest. Make 2 feet coverings. Write 'Peace' on them. Tape them to the tops of the animal's feet. Cut out a shield. Write 'Faith' on it. Tape it to the animal's paw. Make a helmet. Write 'Salvation' on it. Tape it around the animal's head. Make a sword. Write 'Spirit' on it. Tape it to the animal's empty paw.*

Key Idea: When you are scared, you need to trust God to protect you.

Bible Study

Ask, *In Ephesians 6:10-11, what does Paul tell you? In Ephesians 6:14-15, find 3 parts of armor that God gives you. In Ephesians 6:16-17, find 3 more pieces of armor that the Lord gives you. What does Paul say in Ephesians 6:18? How can you pray throughout the day?* Ask students to share their memory verse, John 15:13, with someone special. Suggestions for sharing the verse include saying it to another family member, saying it to someone by telephone, reciting it to a stuffed animal, or writing it to mail.

Key Idea: You can be strong in the Lord and in His power.

Corresponding Music

✔ *Hide 'Em in Your Heart Vol. 2* CD - Track 3; Cassette - Side A
Song: *"Greater Love"*

Learning the Basics

Focus: Language Arts and Math

Unit 25 - Day 5

Language Arts

Say, *The word for one thing by itself is 'single'. So, a 'singular noun' means one of something. 'Dog' is a singular noun. The word for more than one thing is 'plural'. 'Dogs' is a plural noun. To make 'dog' plural, we added an '-s'. This is one way to make a singular noun plural.* Write the following list of singular nouns on paper: crayon, marker, scissor, paint, pencil, eraser, paper, book. Say, *These are all singular nouns. Circle any nouns on the list that you have. If you have more than one of the circled items, cross out the singular word and write the plural instead* (i.e. 'crayon' becomes 'crayons'). <u>Copywork</u>: Have students copy the plural nouns from the list.

<u>Key Idea</u>: Write plural nouns.

Reading Choices

Choose **one** of the reading options listed below (see Appendix for details).

★ A phonics program
★ *Scheduled Books for Emerging Readers*
★ *Drawn into the Heart of Reading Level 2/3*

<u>Key Idea</u>: Use a step-by-step program for reading instruction.

Storytime

Read aloud a short portion of the humorous book that you selected. Give students a chance to orally retell the portion of today's story that you read aloud. Use the following prompts as needed: *Wasn't it funny when... Tell me about it. What happened next? Describe some other funny parts in today's reading.*

<u>Key Idea</u>: Give students practice retelling a portion of a humorous book.

Math Exploration

Give each student a lump of playdough or clay. Have students roll out or flatten the lump into a circle. Give students a plastic or a butter knife to use to cut the circle in half. Direct students to check if their two halves are equal by laying them on top of one another. Show students how to write one-half as 1/2. Next, help students cut their halves into fourths. Direct students to check if their fourths are equal by laying them on top of each other. Show students how to write one-fourth as 1/4.

✔ <u>Text Connection</u>: *Primary Mathematics Workbook 1B* p. 99-100

<u>Key Idea</u>: Make halves and quarters.

Learning Through History

Focus: The Beginning of the United States of America

Unit 26 - Day 1

Reading About History

Read about history in the following resource:

★ *American Pioneers and Patriots* p. 68

Key Idea: After the war ended, George Washington was chosen to be the first President of the United States. The President was going to live in New York City. The entire city welcomed the new President.

Poetry and Rhymes

Read aloud the poem *"The Flag Goes By"* (see Appendix) to the students. Do not share the title. Ask students to suggest some titles for the poem. Share the real title. Read the poem again with the students.

Key Idea: Read and appreciate a variety of classic poetry.

Geography

Say, *When George Washington was President, he lived in New York City. Find New York City on a map.* Later, a home was built for the next presidents in Washington, D.C. The house was painted white after the War of 1812, when the British tried to burn it. Then, people started calling it the White House. Find Washington, D.C. on a map. Ask, *Why do you think the White House was built on the eastern side of the United States, instead of in the middle of the country?* Look at the map on p. 52 of *American Pioneers and Patriots* to remind students that Washington D.C. was in the center of the United States at the time when the White House was built.

Key Idea: Later, the White House was built in Washington, D.C.

Bible Study

Galations 5:22-23 is the memory verse for this unit. Read the verse out loud. Say, *In Galations 5:22-23, what does it say that the Holy Spirit produces in you? Why would these things be called fruits of the Spirit? Explain how fruit grows. How can you have the fruit of the Spirit grow in you?* Say the verse together 3 times. Add hand motions to help students remember the words.

Key Idea: George Washington worked to develop the fruits of the Spirit. He followed God's word.

Corresponding Music

✓ *Hide 'Em in Your Heart Vol. 2* CD - Track 17; Cassette - Side B Song: *"The Fruit of the Spirit"*

Learning the Basics

Focus: Language Arts and Math

Unit 26 - Day 1

Language Arts

Choose **either** spelling list 1 **or** 2 (see Appendix for lists). Write each spelling word on a separate index card. Guide students to study each card one at a time, flip it over, write the word from memory on paper, flip the card back over to check the spelling, and erase and correct any mistakes.

Copywork: Have students copy part of the poem *"The Flag Goes By"*.

Key Idea: Practice spelling words with the 'ow' sound as in 'cow'.

Reading Choices

Choose **one** of the reading options listed below (see Appendix for details).

★ A phonics program
★ *Scheduled Books for Emerging Readers*
★ *Drawn into the Heart of Reading Level 2/3*

Key Idea: Use a step-by-step program for reading instruction.

Storytime

Say, *Watch for any funny parts in today's reading that make you laugh. Whenever you hear a funny part, hold your stomach with your hands and say, "Ha! Ha!"*

Read aloud the next portion of the humorous book that you selected. Pace your reading to complete the book during the next 15 days of plans.

Key Idea: Set the stage to build anticipation for the next part of the humorous book.

Math Exploration

Trace around the bottom of a glass to make three circles on a piece of paper. Help students divide each circle into '4' equal parts. Give the following directions for students to color each circle: *On the first circle, color 1/4 yellow, 1/4 pink, and 1/2 green. For the second circle, color 1/2 brown and the other half orange. On the third circle, color 1/4 blue, 1/4 purple, 1/4 black, and leave 1/4 white.* Point out to students that two-fourths is the same as one-half.

✔ Text Connection: *Primary Mathematics Workbook 1B* p. 101-102

Key Idea: Recognize halves and quarters of shapes.

Learning Through History

Focus: The Beginning of the United States of America

Unit 26 - Day 2

Reading About History

Read about history in the following resource:

★ *American Pioneers and Patriots* p. 69-71

Key Idea: Nathan lived on a farm near New York City. His father was killed in the War for Independence. Nathan rode his horse to the city to see George Washington become President. Washington had led the army through many hard times.

Poetry and Rhymes

Read aloud the poem *"The Flag Goes By"* (see Appendix) with the students. Discuss the poem's meaning. If you choose, photocopy the poem, cut it apart, and have the students put it in order.

Key Idea: Read classic poetry.

Science Exploration

Say, *Horses are measured in 'hands'. A hand is measured using the width of one hand with the fingers together placed sideways. Then, one hand is moved over top of the other from the ground up to the horse's withers, which is the lump above the arch of the horse's back. Average horses are 15 hands tall. That is the same as 60".* Practice measuring 15 hands on the wall to see how tall a horse is. Next, play a horse riding game. Set up several boxes or bowls in an obstacle course. Have students ride a mop or a yardstick like a horse and zig-zag around each obstacle.

✔ Text Connection: *God's Wonderful Works* p. 92-93

Key Idea: Nathan rode his horse through the streets of New York City.

Bible Study

Say Galations 5:22-23 while the students join in on the parts they know. Use the hand motions you added on Day 1. Say, *Let's read through the fruits of the Spirit in Galations 5:22-23. As we read each fruit, let's discuss some ways that we could show that trait. Which fruit of the Spirit do you need to work on the most?* Next, have students do 3 push-ups. After 3 push-ups, have the students recite the entire Bible verse. Repeat the activity several times.

Key Idea: The American people were ready for peace, which is a fruit of the Spirit.

Corresponding Music

✔ *Hide 'Em in Your Heart Vol. 2* CD - Track 17; Cassette - Side B Song: *"The Fruit of the Spirit"*

Learning the Basics

Focus: Language Arts and Math

Unit 26 - Day 2

Language Arts

Use the spelling list from Day 1. Say the first spelling word. Use it in a sentence. Repeat the word. Ask students to write the word on a markerboard or a piece of paper from memory. Give students the matching word card from Day 1 to compare with their spelling. Guide students to correct any mistakes. Repeat the activity with all 10 words. <u>Copywork</u>: Have students copy part of the poem *"The Flag Goes By"*.

<u>Key Idea</u>: Practice spelling words with the 'ow' sound as in 'cow'.

Reading Choices

Choose **one** of the reading options listed below (see Appendix for details).

★ A phonics program
★ *Scheduled Books for Emerging Readers*
★ *Drawn into the Heart of Reading Level 2/3*

<u>Key Idea</u>: Use a step-by-step program for reading instruction.

Storytime

Read aloud the next portion of the humorous book that you selected. Without looking back at the story, begin retelling or narrating the part of the book that you read today. After a short time, tap the student and say, *Your turn.* The student should pick up the narration where you left off. After a short time, the student should tap you and say, *Your turn.* Continue taking turns narrating in this manner until today's reading has been retold. Then, say, *Name one thing that you learned about the main character today.* Write it on paper for the students to copy.

<u>Key Idea</u>: Take turns retelling a story from a single reading.

Math Exploration

Complete the assigned lesson in the workbook listed below.

✓ <u>Text Connection</u>: *Primary Mathematics Workbook 1B* p. 103-104

Note: Remind students to find the repeat of the pattern first, and then answer the problems.

<u>Key Idea</u>: Complete the patterns using fractional shapes.

Learning Through History

Focus: The Beginning of the United States of America

Unit 26 - Day 3

Reading About History

Read about history in the following resource:

★ *American Pioneers and Patriots* p. 72-74

Key Idea: George Washington was sworn in as President in New York City. The city celebrated when he became President. Then, President Washington went to St. Paul's chapel to pray for help with the job he had to do.

History Activity

Discuss the meaning of the words in the *Pledge of Allegiance*. Have students place one hand on their hearts and say the Pledge.

*I pledge allegiance to the flag,
Of the United States of America,
And to the Republic,
For which it stands,
One nation, under God, indivisible,
With liberty, and justice for all.*

Have students get out their timeline. Say, *Let's find the column that says 1700. Draw a small blue circle to be the Presidential Seal in that column. Write 'Washington-1st U.S. President, 1789' under it.*

Key Idea: Many people died so that America could be free.

Poetry and Rhymes

Read aloud the poem *"The Flag Goes By"* (see Appendix) with the students. Read the poem aloud a second time, pausing after each line or two for students to add their own actions to the poem. The actions should make sense with the poem.

Key Idea: Read and appreciate a variety of classic poetry.

Bible Study

Say Galations 5:22-23 with the students. Use the hand motions you added on Day 1. Next, have students skip around the room until you say, *Freeze*. After they 'freeze', have the students recite the entire Bible verse. Have students repeat the activity.

✔ **Text Connection:** *Morning Bells* p. 82-84

Key Idea: George Washington gave hope to America. It was important to him to please God and to pray for God's help in all that he did.

Corresponding Music

✔ *Hide 'Em in Your Heart Vol. 2*
CD - Track 17; Cassette - Side B
Song: *"The Fruit of the Spirit"*

Learning the Basics

Focus: Language Arts and Math

Unit 26 - Day 3

Language Arts

Using the spelling list from Day 1, choose 3 or more words that the students need to practice. Guide students to use each of the words that you chose in a sentence. On a markerboard or a piece of paper, write down the sentences as the students dictate them to you. Underline the spelling word in each sentence. Have the students copy the sentences on a piece of paper. Help students check their sentences and correct any mistakes.
Copywork: Have students copy part of the poem *"The Flag Goes By"*.

Key Idea: Practice 'ow' words.

Reading Choices

Choose **one** of the reading options listed below (see Appendix for details).

★ A phonics program

★ *Scheduled Books for Emerging Readers*

★ *Drawn into the Heart of Reading Level 2/3*

Key Idea: Use a step-by-step program for reading instruction.

Storytime

Say, *Usually there is a reason that something happens. This is called a cause. What happens as a result of the cause is called an effect. Listen for examples of cause and effect as I read today. I will stop off and on as I read to mention events that I notice that cause another action to take place* (i.e. I noticed _____ happened. That might make _____ happen. I noticed _____ made _____ happen.) Read aloud the next portion of the humorous book that you selected.

Key Idea: Focus on the story element: *cause* and *effect*.

Math Exploration

Make cards numbered '1' - '12'. Spread the cards out in a circle with the '12' at the top like the face of a huge clock. Have a student lie down in the center of the circle to be the hands on the clock. Say, *Use your body to show me 5:00 on the clock. Your arms will be the minute hand. At 5:00, the minute hand would point to the '12'. Keep your arms together and point them at the '12'. Your legs will be the hour hand. At 5:00, the hour hand would point to the '5'. Keep your legs together and point them at the '5'.* Repeat the activity with different times.

Key Idea: Practice telling time to the hour on a clock.

Learning Through History

Focus: The Beginning of the United States of America

Unit 26 - Day 4

Reading About History

Read about history in the following resource:

★ *American Pioneers and Patriots* p. 75-77

Key Idea: As it grew dark, Nathan rode for home. He told his mother all about President Washington. He was excited to have seen the man that his father had served under. It was a day Nathan would always remember.

Poetry and Rhymes

Read aloud the poem *"The Flag Goes By"* (see Appendix) with the students. Have students draw pictures that reflect the poem's meaning on either a photocopy of the poem or on their copywork. File the finished poem in a special place.

Key Idea: Read classic poetry.

Science Exploration

Say, *When Washington became President, people celebrated with fireworks. Let's do an experiment to see the colors of the fireworks.* Add a 1/2 cup of milk to a shallow bowl. On one side of the bowl, along the bowl's edge, add 4 drops of red food coloring. 1/3 of the way further around the bowl, add 4 drops of blue coloring. 1/3 of the way further around the bowl, add 4 drops of yellow food coloring. Add 1 drop of liquid dish soap to the center of the milk. Watch several minutes as the colors begin to move. Wait 10-15 minutes to see the colors mix to make orange, green, and purple. Explain that milk has fat in it. As the soap begins to break down the fat, the food coloring moves across the surface and the colors mix together.

Key Idea: It was a time to celebrate.

Bible Study

Say Galations 5:22-23 with the students. Use the hand motions you added on Day 1. Say, *Name some things you do to please Jesus. Do you think that you ever make Jesus unhappy? When? What should you do if you sin? How can you try to please Jesus more?* Next, have students run in place. When you say, *Freeze,* have the students stop and recite the entire Bible verse. Repeat the activity several times.

Key Idea: It was a big job to be America's first President. President Washington wanted to do it well.

Corresponding Music

✔ *Hide 'Em in Your Heart Vol. 2* CD - Track 17; Cassette - Side B Song: *"The Fruit of the Spirit"*

Learning the Basics

Focus: Language Arts and Math

Unit 26 - Day 4

Language Arts

Use the spelling list from Day 1. Say each word and use it in a sentence. Have students write each word and check it with the matching word card from Day 1. Guide students to correct any mistakes. For each missed word, have students spell the word out loud, clapping once each time they say a letter.

<u>Copywork</u>: Have students copy part of the poem *"The Flag Goes By"*.

<u>Key Idea</u>: Practice spelling words with the 'ow' sound as in 'cow'.

Reading Choices

Choose **one** of the reading options listed below (see Appendix for details).

★ *A phonics program*
★ *Scheduled Books for Emerging Readers*
★ *Drawn into the Heart of Reading Level 2/3*

<u>Key Idea</u>: Use a step-by-step program for reading instruction.

Storytime

Say, *Joy means rejoicing, even in times of trouble, because God is with you no matter what happens to you.* Read aloud the key verse 1 Chronicles 16:10-11 to illustrate *joy*. Read aloud Genesis 21:1-7. Ask, *How did Sarah's actions show joy?*

Read aloud the next portion of the humorous book that you selected. Then, ask, *How does the main character in the humorous book show joy? What would the Biblical character, Sarah, do differently from the character in your book?*

<u>Key Idea</u>: Focus on the Godly character trait: *joy*.

Math Exploration

Complete the assigned lesson in the workbook listed below.

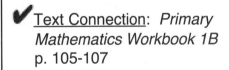
✔ <u>Text Connection</u>: *Primary Mathematics Workbook 1B* p. 105-107

<u>Key Idea</u>: Practice telling time to the hour.

Learning Through History

Focus: The Beginning of the United States of America

Unit 26 - Day 5

Reading About History

Read the following passage from your own Bible:

★ Colossians 3:12-17

Key Idea: God shows you how to live your life for Him. He expects you to love others and work with them. As America became a new nation, it was important to work together and to honor God for His goodness.

Poetry and Rhymes

Have students get out the poems that they saved from the previous units. Ask students to select one or more poems to review. Read aloud the selected poems with the students.

Key Idea: Read classic poetry.

Artistic Expression

Help students fold a paper to look like a shirt. Fold a white piece of paper in half the long way and open it up. Lay the paper flat on the table. Fold the left side of the paper in to touch the fold at the center. Fold the right side of the paper in to touch the fold at the center. Fold back the top corner of both sides from the center like a shirt collar. Have students color the outside of the shirt to look like the one that they have on. Read aloud Colossians 3:12-14. Have students listen for traits that God wants them to have inside their hearts. Open the flaps of the shirt, and have students write the following traits inside: *love, compassion, kindness, humility, gentleness,* and *patience.*

Key Idea: You are meant to glorify God with your life. Other people should be able to see Christ inside of you.

Bible Study

Ask, *In Colossians 3:13, what reason does the Lord give you for forgiving others? What does Colossians 3:14-15 say about love and peace? How can you honor God with your life? In Colossians 3:17, what does it say about honoring God?* Ask students to share their memory verse, Galations 5:22-23, with someone special. Suggestions for sharing the verse include saying it to another family member, saying it to someone by telephone, reciting it to a stuffed animal, or writing it to mail.

Key Idea: It is important to honor God with your life.

Corresponding Music

✔ *Hide 'Em in Your Heart Vol. 2* CD - Track 17; Cassette - Side B Song: *"The Fruit of the Spirit"*

Learning the Basics

Focus: Language Arts and Math

Unit 26 - Day 5

Language Arts

Write the following sentence on a markerboard or a piece of paper: *I like the colors purple, blue, and red.* Say, *What things are listed in this sentence? When we list three or more things of the same kind in a sentence, the words are called a series. How are purple, blue, and red alike? What mark do you see after each color in the series? Words in a series are separated using a comma.* Ask, *What are 3 colors that you like?* Write the students' answers. Leave out the commas. Give students macaroni noodles. Ask them to use the noodles as commas and place them where they belong in the sentence. <u>Copywork</u>: Copy the sentence from today's lesson.

<u>Key Idea</u>: Practice using commas in a series.

Reading Choices

Choose **one** of the reading options listed below (see Appendix for details).

★ A phonics program

★ *Scheduled Books for Emerging Readers*

★ *Drawn into the Heart of Reading Level 2/3*

<u>Key Idea</u>: Use a step-by-step program for reading instruction.

Storytime

Read aloud a short portion of the humorous book that you selected. Have students draw a picture of one funny part from today's reading. When the drawings are complete, ask students to tell you about their pictures as a way of retelling what happened in the story.

<u>Key Idea</u>: Give students practice retelling a portion of a humorous book.

Math Exploration

Give students clocks to use to practice telling time to the hour and the half-hour. If you do not have clocks available, you may repeat the activity from Unit 26 - Day 3. Say a time for students to show on their clock (i.e. 4:30). Have students show you the time and explain where the minute hand and hour hand are pointing (i.e. At 4:30, the hour hand is halfway between the '4' and the '5' and the minute hand is pointing to the '6'). Repeat the activity using different times.

✔ <u>Text Connection</u>: *Primary Mathematics Workbook 1B* p. 108

<u>Key Idea</u>: Practice telling time to the hour and the half-hour.

Learning Through History

Focus: The First American President

Unit 27 - Day 1

Reading About History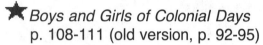

Read about history in the following resource:

⭐ *Boys and Girls of Colonial Days* p. 108-111 (old version, p. 92-95)

Key Idea: Betsy lived in Salisbury, North Carolina. The President was coming to visit her town. Betsy had planned to be a flower girl in the parade. But, she had to stay home to care for her grandmother instead.

Poetry and Rhymes

Read aloud the poem *"Pippa's Song"* (see Appendix) to the students. Do not share the title. Ask students to suggest some titles for the poem. Share the real title. Read the poem again with the students.

Key Idea: Read and appreciate a variety of classic poetry.

Artistic Expression

Guide students to trace around the bottom of a glass on a tissue or on tissue paper. Stack 4 layers of tissue or tissue paper and cut out 4 circles at once. Hold the tissues while the students cut a slit on both sides of the stack of circles, starting at the outside edge and stopping before reaching the center. Insert a piece of yarn or string through the slits, and gather the layers of tissue together as you gently pull the yarn or string and tie it into a knot. Help students gently pull apart the layers of tissue and twist them to look like flower petals. Instruct students to use a pink marker to color the tips of the petals pink.

Key Idea: Betsy was supposed to be a flower girl in the parade for the President. She had a new dress with pink flowers on it for the parade.

Bible Study

Luke 16:10 is the memory verse for this unit. Read the verse out loud. Say, *Explain what it means to be trustworthy or faithful. What does it mean to be dishonest or unjust? Describe what Luke 16:10 teaches you about caring for the things that God gives you.* Say the verse together 3 times. Add hand motions to help students remember the words.

Key Idea: Betsy was disappointed that she wouldn't get to wear her new dress or see the President. But, she obeyed her mother and did what her mother asked of her.

Corresponding Music

None this lesson

Learning the Basics

Focus: Language Arts and Math

Unit 27 - Day 1

Language Arts

Choose **either** spelling list 1 **or** 2 (see Appendix for lists). Write each spelling word on a separate index card. Guide students to study each card one at a time, flip it over, write the word from memory on paper, flip the card back over to check the spelling, and erase and correct any mistakes.

<u>Copywork</u>: Have students copy part of the poem *"Pippa's Song"*.

<u>Key Idea</u>: Practice spelling words with the 'oo' sound as in 'moon'.

Reading Choices

Choose **one** of the reading options listed below (see Appendix for details).

★ A phonics program

★ *Scheduled Books for Emerging Readers*

★ *Drawn into the Heart of Reading Level 2/3*

<u>Key Idea</u>: Use a step-by-step program for reading instruction.

Storytime

Say, *How is the book that we are reading humorous or funny? What is the difference between silly and realistic humor? Is the humor in this book mostly silly or realistic? Why is it important that humor be used in an appropriate way?*

Read aloud the next portion of the humorous book that you selected. Pace your reading to complete the humorous book during the next 10 days of plans.

<u>Key Idea</u>: Set a purpose for reading the next part of the humorous book.

Math Exploration

Have students check the time on the clock at the beginning of today's lesson and write it down on a piece of paper or a markerboard. At the middle of the students' math lesson, ask them to check the time again and write it below the first time. At the end of the math lesson, have students check the time a third time and write it below the other times on the piece of paper or markerboard. Discuss how much time has passed from the beginning of the lesson to the end.

✔ <u>Text Connection</u>: *Primary Mathematics Workbook 1B* p. 109-110

<u>Key Idea</u>: Write times to the hour, half-hour, and minute.

Learning Through History

Focus: The First American President

Unit 27 - Day 2

Reading About History

Read about history in the following resource:

★ *Boys and Girls of Colonial Days* p. 112-117 (old version, p. 96-100)

Key Idea: Betsy had a visitor while she was in charge of the house. She was very polite and served the guest cornbread and milk. Later, Betsy discovered that her guest was President Washington.

Poetry and Rhymes
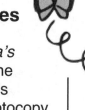

Read aloud the poem *"Pippa's Song"* (see Appendix) with the students. Discuss the poem's meaning. If you choose, photocopy the poem, cut it apart, and have the students place it in the correct order.

Key Idea: Read classic poetry.

History Activity

Use the following recipe to help students make a simple cornbread, just like Betsy served the President. Mix together 2 beaten eggs, 1/4 cup vegetable oil, 1 cup milk, 1 and 1/2 cups cornmeal, 1/4 cup sugar, 1 cup of flour, 2 and 1/4 tsp. baking powder, and 3/4 tsp. salt. You may also add raisins. Pour the mixture into a greased 8" x 8" or 9" x 9" pan. Bake at 450 degrees for 20-25 minutes. If you are using a glass pan, bake the cornbread at 425 degrees for 18 minutes instead. When the bread pulls away from the sides of the pan and a toothpick inserted into the center comes out clean, the bread is done. Serve it warm with butter and syrup or honey.

Key Idea: The President was pleased with Betsy and with the meal.

Bible Study

Say Luke 16:10 while the students join in on the parts they know. Use the hand motions you added on Day 1. Say, *Name some small things that you can be trusted with. How can you show that you can be trusted with larger things? Why is it important to be honest and work hard even when the job seems small and unimportant?* Next, have students do 5 toe touches. After 5 toe touches, have the students recite the entire Bible verse. Prompt the students as needed. Repeat the activity several times.

Key Idea: It seemed like Betsy was missing everything, but by doing her job well she pleased the President.

Corresponding Music

None this lesson

Learning the Basics

Focus: Language Arts and Math

Unit 27 - Day 2

Language Arts

Use the spelling list from Day 1. Say the first spelling word. Use it in a sentence. Repeat the word. Ask students to write the word on a markerboard or a piece of paper from memory. Give students the matching word card from Day 1 to compare with their spelling. Guide students to correct any mistakes. Repeat the activity with all 10 words.
Copywork: Have students copy part of the poem *"Pippa's Song"*.

Key Idea: Practice 'oo' words.

Reading Choices

Choose **one** of the reading options listed below (see Appendix for details).

★ A phonics program
★ *Scheduled Books for Emerging Readers*
★ *Drawn into the Heart of Reading Level 2/3*

Key Idea: Use a step-by-step program for reading instruction.

Storytime

Read aloud the next portion of the humorous book that you selected. Without looking back at the story, write a retelling of the part of the book that you read today leaving blanks in place of key words (i.e. _____ was a house painter. He had always been very interested in _____. Admiral _____ sent Mr. Popper a _____ in the mail. The _____ ate a lot of _____, _____, and _____.). Key words can be names, places, descriptive words, times of day, seasons, etc. Work with the students to reread the written narration and fill in the missing words.

Key Idea: Model retelling a story from a single reading.

Math Exploration

These are the concepts that are covered in this review: writing numbers, finding missing addends, continuing number patterns, comparing more or less, completing number sentences, and telling time to the hour and half-hour. Review any concepts that students had difficulty understanding. Also, complete the assigned review in the workbook listed below.

✓ Text Connection: *Primary Mathematics Workbook 1B* p. 111-112

Key Idea: Review difficult concepts.

Learning Through History

Focus: The First American President

Unit 27 - Day 3

Reading About History

Read about history in the following resource:

★ *Boys and Girls of Colonial Days*
   p. 131- top half of p. 135
   (old version, p. 113-117)

Key Idea: George Washington took great care in watching over Mount Vernon.

Poetry and Rhymes

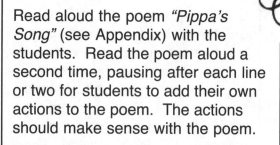

Read aloud the poem *"Pippa's Song"* (see Appendix) with the students. Read the poem aloud a second time, pausing after each line or two for students to add their own actions to the poem. The actions should make sense with the poem.

Key Idea: Read and appreciate a variety of classic poetry.

Geography

Give each student a piece of paper. Say, *Follow the directions I give you to draw a map of Mount Vernon's five farms on paper. Across the bottom, draw a river. Label it 'Potomac River. On the right side above the river, draw a tall rectangle. Label it 'River Farm, 1207 acres'. In the center above the river, draw a wide, thin rectangle. Label it 'Mansion House Farm'. Above the river on the left side, draw a medium rectangle. Label it 'Union Farm, 928 acres'. Above Union Farm, make a narrow rectangle up to the top of the paper. Label it 'Dogue Run Farm, 650 acres'. Above Mansion House Farm, write 'marsh and woodland'. Above River Farm make a triangle. Label it 'Muddy Hole Farm, 476 acres'.*

Key Idea: George Washington's home was Mount Vernon. He lived at Mansion House Farm on the Potomac River.

Bible Study

Say Luke 16:10 with the students. Use the hand motions you added on Day 1. Next, have students lay on their backs and peddle their feet in the air like they are riding a bicycle. When you say, *Freeze,* the students should stop and recite the entire Bible verse. Repeat the activity.

✓ Text Connection: *Morning Bells* p. 13-15

Key Idea: George Washington believed that it was important to live according to the Bible. He thought of others before himself.

Corresponding Music

None this lesson

Learning the Basics

Focus: Language Arts and Math

Unit 27 - Day 3

Language Arts

Choose 3 or more words from the spelling list from Day 1 that the students need to practice. Guide students to use each practice word in a sentence. On a markerboard or a piece of paper, write down the sentences as the students dictate them to you. Underline the spelling word in each sentence. Tell students to copy the sentences on paper, check them, and correct any mistakes. <u>Copywork</u>: Have students copy part of the poem *"Pippa's Song"*.

<u>Key Idea</u>: Practice 'oo' words.

Reading Choices

Choose **one** of the reading options listed below (see Appendix for details).

★ A phonics program
★ *Scheduled Books for Emerging Readers*
★ *Drawn into the Heart of Reading Level 2/3*

<u>Key Idea</u>: Use a step-by-step program for reading instruction.

Storytime

Say, *Usually there is a reason that something happens. This is called a cause. What happens as a result of the cause is called an effect.* Fold a piece of paper in half. Label the left side 'cause' and the right side 'effect'. Read aloud the next portion of the humorous book. As you read aloud, have students help you list the humorous events from the story on the 'cause' side of the paper. Draw an arrow from each cause over to the 'effect' side of the paper. When you are done reading, use a different color to write an effect next to each arrow from the 'cause' side of the paper.

<u>Key Idea</u>: Focus on the story element: *cause* and *effect*.

Math Exploration

These are the concepts that are covered in this review: addition sentences with two or more addends and story problems using addition and subtraction. Review any concepts that students had difficulty understanding. Also, complete the assigned review in the workbook listed below.

✔ <u>Text Connection</u>: *Primary Mathematics Workbook 1B* p. 113-114

<u>Key Idea</u>: Review difficult concepts.

Learning Through History

Focus: The First American President

Unit 27 - Day 4

Reading About History

Read about history in the following resource:

★ *Boys and Girls of Colonial Days* p. 135-140 (old version, p. 118-121)

Key Idea: George Washington provided corn and fish for the needy. He knew God expected him to share.

Poetry and Rhymes

Read aloud the poem *"Pippa's Song"* (see Appendix) with the students. Have students draw pictures that reflect the poem's meaning on either a photocopy of the poem or on their copywork. File the finished poem in a special place.

Key Idea: Read classic poetry.

Science Exploration

Make small signs that say *pasture, trees, cows, horses, pigs,* and *sheep.* Have students place the signs around the room to mark the parts of the farm. Give students the following directions to act out working on the farm: *Cut straw and feed the horses. Trim the branches on the trees. Lead the cows from the pasture to their stalls. Give the cows water and straw. Scoop out the pig stalls to clean them. Pour grain and water into the pig troughs. Gather leaves and weeds. Put them in the horse stalls. Gather leaves and cornstalks. Put them in the cow, pig, and sheep stalls. Walk the sheep in the sheep run.*

✓ Text Connection: *God's Wonderful Works* p. 87, 127, and 139

Key Idea: George Washington gave thoughtful directions for the care of his animals and farm.

Bible Study

Say Luke 16:10 with the students. Use the hand motions from Day 1. Say, *What are some things that you have given up to someone else that you really wanted for yourself? How can you remember to please Jesus, instead of pleasing yourself? If you never learn to please Jesus, but only please yourself, what kind of person will you become?* Have students gallop by leading with their left foot until you say, *Freeze.* After they 'freeze', have the students recite the verse. Have students switch to the right foot and repeat the activity.

Key Idea: George Washington was careful even with small things.

Corresponding Music

None this lesson

Learning the Basics

Focus: Language Arts and Math

Unit 27 - Day 4

Language Arts

Use the spelling list from Day 1. Say each word and use it in a sentence. Have students write each word and check it with the matching word card from Day 1. Guide students to correct any mistakes. Add several inches of soapy water to a sink. For each missed word, have students "write" the word with their index finger in the soapy water. <u>Copywork</u>: Have students copy part of *"Pippa's Song"*.

<u>Key Idea</u>: Practice 'oo' words.

Reading Choices

Choose **one** of the reading options listed below (see Appendix for details).

★ A phonics program

★ *Scheduled Books for Emerging Readers*

★ *Drawn into the Heart of Reading Level 2/3*

<u>Key Idea</u>: Use a step-by-step program for reading instruction.

Storytime

Say, *Joy means rejoicing, even in times of trouble, because God is with you no matter what happens to you.* Read aloud the key verse 1 Chronicles 16:10-11 to illustrate *joy*. List some troubles that have happened to you. Discuss, *What could you do in times of trouble to still be joyful?* (i.e. sing praises to God, pray, speak cheerful thoughts, smile, be positive). Read aloud the next portion of the humorous book that you selected. Ask, *What troubles did the book characters have? Did they show joy even in times of trouble? Do the characters show the opposite trait, despair or sadness?*

<u>Key Idea</u>: Focus on the Godly character trait: *joy*.

Math Exploration

Students will need an egg carton or a muffin tin with ten sections. Give students 100 items to use as counters (i.e. dry cereal pieces, small building blocks, dry macaroni noodles, or dry beans). Direct students to place 10 counters in each section. Students should continue counting by ones and filling sections until they reach '100'. Next, have students point to each section and count by 10's instead. Ask, *Which is a faster way to count, one at a time or by tens. Why do you think that we learn to count by 10's?*

✔ <u>Text Connection</u>: *Primary Mathematics Workbook 1B* p. 115

<u>Key Idea</u>: Count by 10's to '100'.

Learning Through History

Focus: The First American President

Unit 27 - Day 5

Reading About History

Read the following passage from your own Bible:

★ Luke 16:10-15

Key Idea: God tells us to serve Him instead of money. God is to be most important.

Poetry and Rhymes

Have students get out the poems that they saved from the previous units. Ask students to select one or more poems to review. Read aloud the selected poems with the students.

Key Idea: Read classic poetry.

Science Exploration

Read about fishing on p. 135-136 of *Boys and Girls of Colonial Days* (old version, p. 118). Say, *Herring live in the North Atlantic Ocean. They swim in schools. They grow to be 17" long. Herring are nicknamed "sawbellies" for the sharp scales on their belly. Listen to my directions to draw a herring on paper. Draw a fish with a single, dorsal fin on top of its back and a pointed tail. Make the jaw stick out in front. Draw sharp, jagged scales on its belly. Use a silver crayon to color silver patches on the fish. Use white to color its belly. Cut out the herring. Mix water with paint. Color wash blue and green on the top part of the fish. Color wash purple and green on the bottom of the fish.*

✔ Text Connection: *God's Wonderful Works* p. 75

Key Idea: George Washington was careful with what God had given him. He shared fish with those who had very little and was not greedy.

Bible Study

Say, *In Luke 16:11-12, what does it say will happen if you are not able to be trusted with what you are given? Who does Luke 16:13 say you should serve? How do people serve money instead of God? What does Luke 16:15 say that God knows? What do you want God to see when He looks inside your heart?* Ask students to share their memory verse, Luke 16:10, with someone special. Suggestions for sharing the verse include saying it to another family member, saying it to someone by telephone, reciting it to a stuffed animal, or writing it to mail.

Key Idea: God sees your heart. He knows who you serve.

Corresponding Music

None this lesson

Learning the Basics

Focus: Language Arts and Math

Unit 27 - Day 5

Language Arts

Write the following sentence on a markerboard or piece of paper: *Greyson jumps high.* Say, *Who is the subject of this sentence? What is Greyson doing? Words that tell what the subject of the sentence is doing are called verbs. Many verbs show action. I will say an action verb, and I want you to do it.* Say the following actions: *growl, sing, dance, squeal, smile, march, jump, spin, hop, jog, tiptoe, stomp. Now, think of 3 of your own actions to do.* <u>Copywork</u>: Use each student's 3 actions in a sentence for them to copy. Place a comma between each action as you list them in a series.

<u>Key Idea</u>: Introduce action verbs.

Reading Choices

Choose **one** of the reading options listed below (see Appendix for details).

★ A phonics program
★ *Scheduled Books for Emerging Readers*
★ *Drawn into the Heart of Reading Level 2/3*

<u>Key Idea</u>: Use a step-by-step program for reading instruction.

Storytime

Read aloud a short portion of the humorous book that you selected. Guide students to retell the important events in today's reading. Prompt students as needed with the following ideas: *At first, _____ (the main character) felt _____ (mood). Tell me about that part. Next, _____ felt _____. Explain that part to me. Last, _____ felt _____. Tell me how that part ended.*

<u>Key Idea</u>: Give students practice retelling a portion of a humorous book.

Math Exploration

Set out the 10's from one or more decks of playing cards. Have students count each mark on the playing cards to find out how many marks there are in all. Then, have students count the same cards by 10's. Ask, *Which was a faster way to find out how many marks were on the cards altogether? Why is it a good idea to learn to count by 10's?* Repeat the activity using different numbers of cards.

✓ <u>Text Connection</u>: *Primary Mathematics Workbook 1B* p. 116-117

<u>Key Idea</u>: Count by 10's and write the corresponding number.

Learning Through History

Focus: Pioneers Go West on the Wilderness Road

Unit 28 - Day 1

Reading About History

Read about history in the following resource:

★ *American Pioneers and Patriots* p. 82

Key Idea: Daniel Boone was a brave pioneer that made a trail to Kentucky called the Wilderness Road. People traveled west on this road. It was a hard trip.

Poetry and Rhymes

Read aloud the poem *"Farewell to the Farm"* (see Appendix) to the students. Do not share the title. Ask students to suggest some titles for the poem. Share the real title. Read the poem with the students.

Key Idea: Read and appreciate a variety of classic poetry.

Geography

Say, *In 1775, Daniel Boone marked a path 1,000 miles long called "The Wilderness Road" for pioneers to use as they traveled west. At first, the path was only a rough, muddy trail. It was so narrow that only a horse or a person could travel on it. The path used part of an old, Indian trail. 35 axmen cleared the path with Daniel Boone as he marked it.* Practice marking a path through our house. Make a red 'X' on 15 or more sticky notes. Choose a starting point for your path. Place a sticky note at the start on the floor. Every 3-4 feet, place another sticky note on the floor. See if another person can follow your path. If time allows, gather the sticky notes and set up a different path for the students to follow.

Key Idea: Travel on the Wilderness Road was long and hard.

Bible Study

Proverbs 22:6 is the memory verse for this unit. Read the verse out loud. Ask, *What does it mean to train yourself to do something? Is this an easy job? Who is supposed to train you when you are a child? What are your parents supposed to train you to do? In Proverbs 22:6, what does it say will happen if a child is trained in making good choices?* Say the verse together 3 times. Add hand motions to help students remember the words.

Key Idea: Pioneer families trained their children to be hard workers.

Corresponding Music

✔ *Hide 'Em in Your Heart Vol. 2*
CD - Track 1; Cassette - Side A
Song: *"Train Up a Child"*

Learning the Basics

Focus: Language Arts and Math

Unit 28 - Day 1

Language Arts

Choose **either** spelling list 1 **or** 2 (see Appendix for lists). Write each spelling word on a separate index card. Guide students to study each card one at a time, flip it over, write the word from memory, flip the card back over to check the spelling, and erase and correct any mistakes.

<u>Copywork</u>: Have students copy part of the poem *"Farewell to the Farm"*.

<u>Key Idea</u>: Practice spelling words with the 'oo' sound as in 'book'.

Reading Choices

Choose **one** of the reading options listed below (see Appendix for details).

★ A phonics program
★ *Scheduled Books for Emerging Readers*
★ *Drawn into the Heart of Reading Level 2/3*

<u>Key Idea</u>: Use a step-by-step program for reading instruction.

Storytime

Say, *Name the character in the story that is your favorite. Why did you choose this character? What problems has this character had?*

Read aloud the next portion of the humorous book that you selected. Pace your reading to complete the book during the next 5 days of plans. After reading, ask, *Which part of the story was the funniest?*

<u>Key Idea</u>: Set a purpose for reading the next part of the humorous book.

Math Exploration

Fold a piece of paper in half. Label the left half 'tens' and the right half 'ones'. From two decks of playing cards, take out all the 10's and one set of cards numbered '2' - '9'. Say, *We will use your cards and your 'tens' and 'ones' paper to show the number '42'. How many 10's cards do you need on the 'tens' side?* ('4'). *What card do you need on the 'ones' side?* ('2'). *To check if you are right, count your 10's and then count on to add your 'ones'* ('10', '20', '30', '40', '41', '42'). Repeat the activity with other numbers from '1' - '100'. Save the mat for later use.

✓ <u>Text Connection</u>: *Primary Mathematics Workbook 1B* p. 118

<u>Key Idea</u>: Form 2-digit numbers.

Learning Through History

Focus: Pioneers Go West on the Wilderness Road

Unit 28 - Day 2

Reading About History

Read about history in the following resource:

★ *American Pioneers and Patriots* p. 83-84 and 91

Key Idea: Molly's family was getting ready to travel on the Wilderness Road to Kentucky. They had heard that the land was good for farming.

Poetry and Rhymes

Read aloud the poem *"Farewell to the Farm"* (see Appendix) with the students. Discuss the poem's meaning. If you choose, photocopy the poem, cut it apart, and have the students put it in order.

Key Idea: Read classic poetry.

Science Exploration

Say, *Molly's father sheared sheep to get wool for Molly's dress. It took a long time to make the dress.* Give each student a cotton ball to be their "wool". Say, *Pretend to pick out any sticks or burrs to clean your wool. Comb your wool with a comb. Roll the wool quickly between your hands to make a long, strong piece of "yarn". Add blue food coloring to water. Dip your yarn in the water to dye it. Hang your yarn to dry over a hanger. Place a piece of wax paper under the hanger to catch any drips of dye.* Next, have students look at the tags of their clothes to see if they have any clothes made of linen or wool. Ask, *What are most clothes made of today?* (cotton)

✓ Text Connection: *God's Wonderful Works* p. 106

Key Idea: Molly's mother made her a new, blue dress for the journey.

Bible Study

Say Proverbs 22:6 while the students join in on the parts they know. Use the hand motions you added on Day 1. Say, *What are some things that you have been trained to do? Why is it hard work to learn something new? How can you help make learning new things easier?* Next, have students do windmills by touching their right hand to their right foot, and then their left hand to their left foot. After every 5 windmills, have the students recite the Bible verse.

Key Idea: The pioneers worked hard to learn to do many new things.

Corresponding Music

✓ *Hide 'Em in Your Heart Vol. 2* CD - Track 1; Cassette - Side A Song: *"Train Up a Child"*

Learning the Basics

Focus: Language Arts and Math

Unit 28 - Day 2

Language Arts

Use the spelling list from Day 1. Say the first spelling word. Use it in a sentence. Repeat the word. Ask students to write the word on a markerboard or a piece of paper from memory. Give students the matching word card from Day 1 to compare with their spelling. Guide students to correct any mistakes. Repeat the activity with all 10 words.

Copywork: Have students copy part of the poem *"Farewell to the Farm"*.

Key Idea: Practice spelling words with the 'oo' sound as in 'book'.

Reading Choices

Choose **one** of the reading options listed below (see Appendix for details).

★ A phonics program
★ *Scheduled Books for Emerging Readers*
★ *Drawn into the Heart of Reading Level 2/3*

Key Idea: Use a step-by-step program for reading instruction.

Storytime

Read aloud the next portion of the humorous book that you selected. Ask students to retell or narrate what you read today. Remind students to tell the most important parts and to include details from the story in the retelling. As students work together to retell the story, write, type, or tape record the students' narration. When the students are finished, read the narration out loud. Highlight, circle, or underline one main idea from the narration for the students to copy.

Key Idea: Keep a sample of the students' narrations for the genre: *Humor*.

Math Exploration

Complete the assigned lesson in the workbook listed below.

✓ Text Connection: *Primary Mathematics Workbook 1B* p. 119-121

Key Idea: Practice writing and showing numbers to '100' using 'tens' and 'ones'.

Learning Through History

Focus: Pioneers Go West on the Wilderness Road

Unit 28 - Day 3

Reading About History

Read about history in the following resource:

★ *American Pioneers and Patriots* p. 85-87

Key Idea: Molly and her family packed carefully for the long trip over the mountains. They were finally ready to leave. It was exciting at first, but as the trip went on the pioneers grew more and more tired.

Poetry and Rhymes

Read aloud the poem *"Farewell to the Farm"* (see Appendix) with the students. Read the poem aloud a second time, pausing after each line or two for students to add actions to the poem. The actions should make sense with the poem.

Key Idea: Read classic poetry.

History Activity

Say, *Use a map of the United States to follow the Wilderness Road. Begin at Richmond, VA. Follow the border of West Virginia down along the Shenandoah Valley. Find the place where the borders of Tennessee, Kentucky, and Virginia meet. This is called the Cumberland Gap. It is a break in the Appalachian Mountain chain, where you can get through the mountains. Look on p. 66 of* American Pioneers and Patriots. *Did the U.S. own the land covered by the Wilderness Road? Why was the Cumberland Gap so important?* Next, have students get out their timeline. Say, *Let's find the column that says 1700. Draw a red 'X' in that column. Write 'Daniel Boone, Wilderness Road, 1775' under it.*

Key Idea: From 1775-1810, 250,000 people traveled the Wilderness Road.

Bible Study

Say Proverbs 22:6 with the students. Use the hand motions you added on Day 1. Next, have students squat down, hop up, and squat back down again. After the last squat, have the students recite the entire Bible verse. Prompt students as needed. Repeat the activity.

✔ Text Connection: *Morning Bells* p. 19-21

Key Idea: Molly and her brothers did all they could to help their parents prepare for the journey. They worked hard to help bear each other's burdens.

Corresponding Music

✔ *Hide 'Em in Your Heart Vol. 2* CD - Track 1; Cassette - Side A Song: *"Train Up a Child"*

Learning the Basics

Focus: Language Arts and Math

Unit 28 - Day 3

Language Arts

Using the spelling list from Day 1, choose 3 or more words that the students need to practice. Guide students to use each of the words that you chose in a sentence. Write down the sentences as the students dictate them to you. Underline the spelling word in each sentence. Have the students copy the sentences on a piece of paper. Help students check their sentences and correct any mistakes. <u>Copywork</u>: Have students copy part of *"Farewell to the Farm"*.

<u>Key Idea</u>: Practice 'oo' words.

Reading Choices

Choose **one** of the reading options listed below (see Appendix for details).

★ A phonics program
★ *Scheduled Books for Emerging Readers*
★ *Drawn into the Heart of Reading Level 2/3*

<u>Key Idea</u>: Use a step-by-step program for reading instruction.

Storytime

Read aloud the next portion of the humorous book. Fold a paper in half. Ask students to draw a picture on the left side of the paper that shows something funny that happened in the story. On the right side of the paper, make 2 headings. The first heading should say 'cause'. The second heading should say 'effect'. Help students list any causes and effects that are shown in the pictures that they drew. Say, *Remember a cause is the reason something happens. What happens because of the cause is an effect.*

<u>Key Idea</u>: Focus on the story element: *cause* and *effect*.

Math Exploration

Complete the assigned lesson in the workbook listed below.

✓ <u>Text Connection</u>: *Primary Mathematics Workbook 1B* p. 122-123

<u>Key Idea</u>: Match number words and numbers up to '100'. Practice writing numbers up to '100'.

Learning Through History

Focus: Pioneers Go West on the Wilderness Road

Unit 28 - Day 4

Reading About History

Read about history in the following resource:

★ *American Pioneers and Patriots* p. 88-90

Key Idea: Molly's family had hard times on their journey. Once their horse slipped and dropped its load. Another time, a wildcat almost jumped on the girls. The family finally reached the fort in Kentucky.

Poetry and Rhymes

Read aloud the poem *"Farewell to the Farm"* (see Appendix) with the students. Have students draw pictures that reflect the poem's meaning on either a photocopy of the poem or on their copywork. File the finished poem in a special place.

Key Idea: Read classic poetry.

Science Exploration

Say, *Johnny shot a wildcat to protect his sisters. The long rifles used on the frontier were 4 feet long. Tape a 12" ruler to the end of a yardstick. Hold it to your shoulder to see how long the rifles were. Look at the rifle on p. 80 of* American Pioneers and Patriots*. Point to the parts of the rifle as we discuss them. The rifles had 3 parts: the lock, stock, and barrel. The lock was the firing mechanism (trigger, pan, hammer, and springs). The stock was the wooden part of the gun that held the lock and barrel. The barrel was the long tube that the bullet passed through.*

✔ Text Connection: *God's Wonderful Works* p. 94

Key Idea: Johnny shot a wildcat and saved his sisters. He earned a gun.

Bible Study

Say Proverbs 22:6 with the students. Use the hand motions you added on Day 1. Say, *What is a burden? How can you help bear someone else's burden? Why should Christians bear one another's burdens? Name some little ways that you can help at home.* Next, have students hop backward 5 times. After 5 hops, have the students recite the entire Bible verse. Repeat the activity several times.

Key Idea: Molly and her brothers were trained to think of others and watch for ways to be helpful.

Corresponding Music

✔ *Hide 'Em in Your Heart Vol. 2* CD - Track 1; Cassette - Side A Song: *"Train Up a Child"*

Learning the Basics

Focus: Language Arts and Math

Unit 28 - Day 4

Language Arts

Use the spelling list from Day 1. Say each word and use it in a sentence. Have students write each word and check it with the matching word card from Day 1. Guide students to correct any mistakes. For each missed word, have students jump in place and spell the word out loud, jumping each time they say a letter.

Copywork: Have students copy part of the poem *"Farewell to the Farm"*.

Key Idea: Practice spelling words with the 'oo' sound as in 'book'.

Reading Choices

Choose **one** of the reading options listed below (see Appendix for details).

★ A phonics program

★ *Scheduled Books for Emerging Readers*

★ *Drawn into the Heart of Reading Level 2/3*

Key Idea: Use a step-by-step program for reading instruction.

Storytime

Say, *Joy means rejoicing, even in times of trouble, because God is with you no matter what happens to you.* Read aloud the key verse 1 Chronicles 16:10-11. Read aloud the next portion of the humorous book that you selected. Ask, *Were the book characters usually joyful or sad? Explain. Are you usually joyful or sad? Draw a picture showing one way that you could be more joyful. Post your picture in a place where you will see it often.*

Key Idea: Focus on the Godly character trait: *joy*.

Math Exploration

Use the 'tens' and 'ones' mat from Unit 28 - Day 1. Give students 9 dimes and 9 pennies. Say, *Let's add 5 dimes and 4 pennies. Should you put the '5' dimes in the 'tens' column or the 'ones' column?* ('tens'). *Should you put the '4' pennies in the 'tens' column or the 'ones' column?* ('ones'). *Let's count the dimes by 10's and add on the pennies to find the total* ('10', '20', '30', '40', '50', '51', '52', '53', '54'). *Write a number sentence to show how you added the 'tens' and 'ones'* (i.e. 50 + 4 = 54). Repeat the activity with different numbers.

✓ Text Connection: *Primary Mathematics Workbook 1B* p. 124-125

Key Idea: Add 'tens' and 'ones'.

Learning Through History

Focus: Pioneers Go West on the Wilderness Road

Unit 28 - Day 5

Reading About History

Read the following passage from your own Bible:

Galations 6:2-10

Key Idea: Christians need to help one another to please Jesus. We must continue doing good even when no one seems to notice. The pioneers had to work hard to help one another without expecting anything in return.

Poetry and Rhymes

Have students get out the poems that they saved from the previous units. Ask students to select one or more poems to review. Read aloud the selected poems with the students.

Key Idea: Read classic poetry.

Artistic Expression

Read aloud Galations 6:7-9 about sowing, reaping, and harvesting. Say, *Pretty flowers remind of us of what happens when we sow good things in our lives. Weeds remind us of what happens when we sow bad things in our lives.* On a piece of colored paper, have the students draw the simple outline of a flower with a stem and several leaves. Guide students to outline the flower with glue. Then, have students place sunflower seeds, popcorn seeds, dried beans, or other seeds on the glue outline one at at time. If you do not have any seeds, students may glue on raisins, or dry cereal pieces instead.

Key Idea: Are you trying to please yourself or the Holy Spirit with the things you 'sow' in your life?

Bible Study

Ask, *How does Galations 6:4-5 say you will know if you have done your part? What does Galations 6:7-8 say are the consequences of your actions? Why does Galations 6:9 say you shouldn't stop doing good things? Who does Galations 6:10 say should receive special care?* Ask students to share their memory verse, Proverbs 22:6, with someone special. Suggestions for sharing the verse include saying it to another family member, saying it to someone by telephone, reciting it to a stuffed animal, or writing it to mail.

Key Idea: Each member of Molly's family worked hard to do their part.

Corresponding Music

✔ *Hide 'Em in Your Heart Vol. 2*
CD - Track 1; Cassette - Side A
Song: *"Train Up a Child"*

Learning the Basics

Focus: Language Arts and Math

Unit 28 - Day 5

Language Arts

Write the following sentences on paper: *The dog is loud. The dogs are loud.* Say, *Why do we use 'is' in the first sentence and 'are' in the second sentence? Which word is used for talking about one dog, 'is' or 'are'? Which word is used for talking about more than one dog, 'is' or 'are'?* Give students an index card with 'is' written on one side and 'are' on the other. Ask students to show the correct side of the card to complete each of these sentences: *The tiger __ growling. The cheetahs __ running. That monkey __ swinging. The lions __ roaring. That parrot __ talking.*

<u>Key Idea</u>: Use 'is' and 'are' correctly.

Reading Choices

Choose **one** of the reading options listed below (see Appendix for details).

★ *A phonics program*

★ *Scheduled Books for Emerging Readers*

★ *Drawn into the Heart of Reading Level 2/3*

<u>Key Idea</u>: Use a step-by-step program for reading instruction.

Storytime

Read aloud the final portion of the humorous book that you selected. You will need to select a realistic fiction book to read aloud next. Have students retell today's reading to a stuffed toy. Don't interrupt the students during the retelling, just let them retell it in their own way. When the students are done with the retelling, ask, *What picture in the book is your favorite? Tell me why it is your favorite.*

<u>Key Idea</u>: Give students practice retelling a portion of a humorous book.

Math Exploration

Use a book that has pages numbered up to '100' or more. Open the book to a page between '1' and '100'. Say, *Tell me the page number of this page.* Repeat the activity, having students practice reading various page numbers. Then, say, *Tell me what the next page number will be.* Check students answers by turning to the page. Vary the activity by saying, *Tell me what page number comes before this one.* Check students answers by turning back one page.

✓ <u>Text Connection</u>: *Primary Mathematics Workbook 1B* p. 126

<u>Key Idea</u>: Identify number patterns while counting to '100'.

Learning Through History

Focus: Pioneers Travel West on the Ohio River

Unit 29 - Day 1

Reading About History

Read about history in the following resource:

★ *American Pioneers and Patriots* p. 96-99

Key Idea: Many settlers began moving west. This caused more problems with the Indians. The O'Neil family was getting ready to sail down the Ohio River to Indiana. Mary Jane met Johnny Appleseed.

Poetry and Rhymes

Read aloud the poem *"The Planting of the Apple-Tree"* (see Appendix) to the students. Do not share the title. Ask students to suggest some titles for the poem. Share the real title. Read the poem again with the students.

Key Idea: Read and appreciate a variety of classic poetry.

Geography

Say, *The mother of the O'Neil family had moved many times in her life. Let's use the map on p. 66 of* <u>American Pioneers and Patriots</u> *to find the different places that she lived. Mother grew up in Boston, Massachusetts. When she got married, she moved to a farm in Connecticut. Then, the O'Neils moved to New York. They traveled by stagecoach. After that, the family moved to Pennsylvania. They traveled by oxcart. Now, the family was packing to move to Indiana. They were planning to travel down the Ohio River by flatboat to get there. The father of the O'Neil family kept his family moving West bit by bit to more unsettled country.*

Key Idea: The O'Neil family had moved many times.

Bible Study

Deuteronomy 5:16 is the memory verse for this unit. Read the verse out loud. Ask, *What does it mean to honor someone? Who does Deut. 5:16 tell you to honor? Why are you supposed to honor your father and mother? Who commands you to honor your parents? What is a command?* Say the verse together 3 times. Add hand motions to help students remember the words.

Key Idea: Mary Jane and her brothers and sisters obeyed their parents. They did as they were told.

Corresponding Music

✓ *Hide 'Em in Your Heart Vol. 2* CD - Track 6; Cassette - Side A Song: *"Honor Your Father & Mother"*

Learning the Basics

Focus: Language Arts and Math

Unit 29 - Day 1

Language Arts

Choose **either** spelling list 1 **or** 2 (see Appendix for lists). Write each spelling word on a separate index card. Guide students to study each card one at a time, flip it over, write the word on paper, flip the card back over to check the spelling, and erase and correct any mistakes. <u>Copywork</u>: Have students copy part of *"The Planting of the Apple-Tree"*.

<u>Key Idea</u>: Practice 'aw' words.

Reading Choices

Choose **one** of the reading options listed below (see Appendix for details).

★ A phonics program
★ *Scheduled Books for Emerging Readers*
★ *Drawn into the Heart of Reading Level 2/3*

<u>Key Idea</u>: Use a step-by-step program for reading instruction.

Storytime

Choose at least one realistic fiction book to read aloud for the next 20 days of plans (see Appendix for suggested titles). To introduce the genre, *Realistic Fiction*, share the following problems one at a time: *Your neighbor's cat is missing. Your little brother is crying. You lost your favorite book. You are lost at the zoo. Your friend dares you to walk on the railroad tracks.* Have students name a realistic way that each problem could be solved. Say, *Even though those problems didn't really happen, they could happen. Realistic fiction is a made-up story that seems real and happens in modern times.* Read a portion of the realistic fiction book you chose.

<u>Key Idea</u>: Introduce the genre: *Realistic Fiction*.

Math Exploration

On a markerboard or a piece of paper, write two numbers between '50' and '100'. Leave a blank between the two numbers (i.e. 40 ___ 60). In the blank, have students write one number that could come between the 2 numbers (i.e. 40 <u>50</u> 60). Notice that there are many possible numbers that could fit in the blank. Accept any number that makes sense in the blank. Repeat the activity using different numbers.

✔ <u>Text Connection</u>: *Primary Mathematics Workbook 1B* p. 127

<u>Key Idea</u>: Sequence and order numbers between '1' - '100'.

Learning Through History

Focus: Pioneers Travel West on the Ohio River

Unit 29 - Day 2

Reading About History

Read about history in the following resource:

★ *American Pioneers and Patriots* p. 100-101

Key Idea: One night as the O'Neils were traveling down the Ohio River, they came near an Indian camp.

Poetry and Rhymes

Read aloud the poem *"The Planting of the Apple-Tree"* (see Appendix) with the students. Discuss the poem's meaning. If you choose, photocopy the poem, cut it apart, and have the students put it in order.

Key Idea: Read classic poetry.

Science Exploration

Each student needs 4 circle-shaped snacks (i.e. banana slices, cookies, crackers, or cucumber slices). Say, *We will use the circles to show the moon's 8 phases. Set out one circle to be the New Moon, which is completely dark. Pick up a second circle. Bite the left side to make a backward 'C'. This is a Waxing Crescent. 'Waxing' means growing. Pick up a third circle. Bite off the left half to show a First Quarter Moon. Pick up the fourth circle. Nibble the right side to make a Waxing Gibbous. Flip over the 4 circles. Put the circles in order to show the moon slowly disappearing. Now, you see a Full Moon, Waning Gibbous, Last Quarter Moon, and Waning Crescent. 'Waning' means shrinking.*

✔ Text Connection: *God's Wonderful Works* p. 61

Key Idea: No moon shone as the flatboats passed the Indians' camp.

Bible Study

Say Deuteronomy 5:16 while the students join in on the parts they know. Use the hand motions you added on Day 1. Ask, *How can you honor your parents when you are young? As you get older, how can you honor your parents? When your parents are very old, what can you do to honor them?* Next, have students do 5 jumping jacks. After 5 jumping jacks, have the students recite the entire Bible verse. Prompt the students as needed. Repeat the activity several times.

Key Idea: The O'Neil children did exactly what their parents told them.

Corresponding Music

✔ *Hide 'Em in Your Heart Vol. 2* CD - Track 6; Cassette - Side A Song: *"Honor Your Father & Mother"*

Learning the Basics

Focus: Language Arts and Math

Unit 29 - Day 2

Language Arts

Use the spelling list from Day 1. Say the first spelling word. Use it in a sentence. Repeat the word. Ask students to write the word on a markerboard or a piece of paper from memory. Give students the matching word card from Day 1 to compare with their spelling. Guide students to correct any mistakes. Repeat the activity with all 10 words. <u>Copywork</u>: Have students copy part of *"The Planting of the Apple-Tree"*.

<u>Key Idea</u>: Practice spelling words with the 'aw' sound as in 'saw'.

Reading Choices

Choose **one** of the reading options listed below (see Appendix for details).

★ A phonics program
★ *Scheduled Books for Emerging Readers*
★ *Drawn into the Heart of Reading Level 2/3*

<u>Key Idea</u>: Use a step-by-step program for reading instruction.

Storytime

Read aloud the next portion of the realistic fiction book that you selected. Without looking back at the story, model retelling or narrating the part of the book that you read today to the students. Remember to tell the most important points and to add details from the story to the retelling without overwhelming the students. After the retelling, ask, *What makes this story seem real?* On paper, write the students' answers in one sentence. Have students copy the sentence.

<u>Key Idea</u>: Model retelling a story from a single reading.

Math Exploration

Complete the assigned lesson in the workbook listed below.

✔ <u>Text Connection</u>: *Primary Mathematics Workbook 1B* p. 128-129

<u>Key Idea</u>: Count up or back by '1's' or 10's with numbers to '100'.

Learning Through History

Focus: Pioneers Travel West on the Ohio River

Unit 29 - Day 3

Reading About History

Read about history in the following resource:

★ *American Pioneers and Patriots* p. 102-103

Key Idea: Finally, the O'Neils made it to Indiana. They worked hard to build their log house. The girls went to school one day. They begged to do school at home instead.

Poetry and Rhymes

Read aloud the poem *"The Planting of the Apple-Tree"* (see Appendix) with the students. Read the poem aloud a second time, pausing after each line or two for students to add their own actions to the poem. The actions should make sense with the poem.

Key Idea: Read and appreciate a variety of classic poetry.

Science Exploration

Say, *Apple trees have 6 parts: the roots, stem or trunk, branches, crown, flowers,* and *fruit*. Make a picture to show the parts of the tree. On a white piece of paper, color black soil along the bottom. On top of the soil, paint a brown trunk with branches coming out of it. Sprinkle coffee or tea grounds on the tree to be bark. Use a paper towel to blot green paint on the branches to make the crown of the tree. Place bits of white or pink tissue on the crown of the tree to be flowers. Hole punch red circles to add to the tree as apples. Use yarn or string to glue roots in the soil coming out of the tree trunk.

✔ Text Connection: *God's Wonderful Works* p. 55

Key Idea: Mary Jane planted the apple seeds that Johnny Appleseed had given her.

Bible Study

Say Deuteronomy 5:16 with the students. Use the hand motions you added on Day 1. Next, have students hop on their left foot until you say, *Freeze*. After they 'freeze', have the students recite the entire Bible verse. Prompt students as needed. Have students switch to the right foot, and repeat the activity.

✔ Text Connection: *Morning Bells* p. 85-87

Key Idea: It is not always easy to obey, but God says to do it anyway.

Corresponding Music

✔ *Hide 'Em in Your Heart Vol. 2* CD - Track 6; Cassette - Side A
Song: *"Honor Your Father & Mother"*

Learning the Basics

Focus: Language Arts and Math

Unit 29 - Day 3

Language Arts

Using the spelling list from Day 1, choose 3 or more words that the students need to practice. Guide students to use each of the words that you chose in a sentence. Write down the sentences as the students dictate them to you. Underline the spelling word in each sentence. Tell students to copy the sentences on paper, check them, and correct any mistakes.
Copywork: Have students copy part of *"The Planting of the Apple-Tree"*.

Key Idea: Practice 'aw' words.

Reading Choices

Choose **one** of the reading options listed below (see Appendix for details).

★ *A phonics program*
★ *Scheduled Books for Emerging Readers*
★ *Drawn into the Heart of Reading Level 2/3*

Key Idea: Use a step-by-step program for reading instruction.

Storytime

Read aloud the next portion of your realistic fiction book. Say, *Point of view refers to how a person or a character looks at, or views, something. Our points of view can be very different. For example, which ice cream do you think has the best flavor?* Have students share their answers. Say, *My point of view is that _____ ice cream has the best flavor. So, we each have our own point of view about ice cream. What is different about you and your point of view from the character in the story?* (i.e. age, family size, gender, likes, dislikes, setting, time of year).

Key Idea: Introduce the story element: *point of view.*

Math Exploration

Use the chart numbered from '1'-'100' in *Workbook 1B* p.131. Cover several numbers in the chart with snacks (i.e. mini-marshmallows, raisins, or chocolate chips). Ask students to name the covered numbers. Have students lift the snacks to check their answers. Discuss any patterns in the chart (i.e. tens all end in '0', numbers in the ones column end in '1's, numbers in the two's column end in '2's', etc.). Then, say, *Point to the number that is one more than '76'. Find the number that is '10' less than '80'. Point to the number that is one less than '59'. Find the number that is '10' more than '61'.*

Key Idea: Count on or back to find numbers from '1'-'100'.

Learning Through History

Focus: Pioneers Travel West on the Ohio River

Unit 29 - Day 4

Reading About History

Read about history in the following resource:

★ *American Pioneers and Patriots* p. 104

Key Idea: The O'Neil girls visited the pioneer school. They had never been to school. It was different from learning at home. The teacher seemed strict. Everyone was expected to be obedient.

Poetry and Rhymes

Read aloud the poem *"The Planting of the Apple-Tree"* (see Appendix) with the students. Have students draw pictures that reflect the poem's meaning on either a photocopy of the poem or on their copywork. File the finished poem in a special place.

Key Idea: Read classic poetry.

Artistic Expression

Say, *Students in pioneer schools learned their letters using a hornbook. Look on p. 104 in box 2 of American Pioneers and Patriots to see a picture of a hornbook. Let's make our own hornbook.* On brown paper, draw a square frying pan-shape with a handle for the students to cut out. Cut out a square of white paper in the same shape. Have students write the alphabet in capital letters on the white paper. Glue the white paper to the brown paper. Cut a piece of waxed paper to fit over the white paper. Staple it to the top of the hornbook. Allow students to use a washable marker to trace over several letters on the waxed paper. Use a wet paper towel to wipe the waxed paper clean.

Key Idea: The O'Neil children begged to be schooled at home. They promised to work hard.

Bible Study

Say Deuteronomy 5:16 with the students. Use the hand motions from Day 1. Ask, *How do you know what is right and what is wrong? What is your conscience? When your parents ask you to do something, is it alright to do it your own way instead? Why? Who else are you obeying when you honor your parents?* Next, have the students do 5 sit-ups. After 5 sit-ups, have the students recite the entire Bible verse.

Key Idea: When you honor your parents, you are obeying Jesus.

Corresponding Music

✓ *Hide 'Em in Your Heart Vol. 2* CD - Track 6; Cassette - Side A Song: *"Honor Your Father & Mother"*

Learning the Basics

Focus: Language Arts and Math

Unit 29 - Day 4

Language Arts

Use the spelling list from Day 1. Say each word and use it in a sentence. Have students write each word and check it with the matching word card from Day 1. Guide students to correct any mistakes. For each missed word, have students write the word on paper and trace around it 3 times using 3 different colors. <u>Copywork</u>: Have students copy part of the poem *"The Planting of the Apple-Tree"*.

<u>Key Idea</u>: Practice spelling words with the 'aw' sound as in 'saw'.

Reading Choices

Choose **one** of the reading options listed below (see Appendix for details).

★ A phonics program

★ *Scheduled Books for Emerging Readers*

★ *Drawn into the Heart of Reading Level 2/3*

<u>Key Idea</u>: Use a step-by-step program for reading instruction.

Storytime

Say, *Integrity means being honest and doing what is right, even when no one else is watching, so that you may be blameless in the eyes of the Lord.* Read aloud the key verse Titus 2:11-12 to illustrate *integrity*. Describe some times that you have done what's right or been honest. Now, have students list ways that they have done what's right. Read aloud the next portion of the realistic fiction book that you selected. Then, ask, *How do the characters show honesty or integrity? What could the characters do to show more integrity?*

<u>Key Idea</u>: Introduce the Godly character trait: *integrity*.

Math Exploration

Complete the assigned lesson in the workbook listed below.

✔ <u>Text Connection</u>: *Primary Mathematics Workbook 1B* p. 130-132

<u>Key Idea</u>: Count on or back to add numbers up to '100'.

Learning Through History

Focus: Pioneers Travel West on the Ohio River

Unit 29 - Day 5

Reading About History

Read the following passage from your own Bible:

★ Deuteronomy 30:11-20

Key Idea: God expects us to love Him and obey His commands. It is the parents' job to train their children in God's ways. Many pioneer families were careful to train their children to follow God.

Poetry and Rhymes

Have students get out the poems that they saved from the previous units. Ask students to select one or more poems to review. Read aloud the selected poems with the students.

Key Idea: Read classic poetry.

History Activity

Say, *Let's practice traveling down the Ohio River. As you travel, keep God's word with you.* Tape two masking tape lines several feet apart that curve like a river on the floor. Give students a rectangular lid to use as a flatboat. Place the Bible on the flatboat. Set soup cans in places throughout the river to be boulders. Have the students pull the flatboat down the river, carefully maneuvering around the 'boulders'. Next, have students get out their timeline. Say, *Let's find the column that says 1800. Draw a small flatboat in that column. Write 'Flatboats, Ohio River, 1811' under it.*

Key Idea: It is important to keep God's word near you at all times, like the Pioneers who traveled west on the Ohio River did.

Bible Study

Discuss, *In Deuteronomy 30:11-14, what does God tell you about His commands? What does the Lord tell you to do in Deuteronomy 30:16? In Deuteronomy 30:19-20, Moses gave Israel a choice. Explain the choice they had. What choice will you make?* Ask students to share their memory verse, Deuteronomy 5:16, with someone special. Suggestions for sharing the verse include saying it to another family member, saying it to someone by telephone, reciting it to a stuffed animal, or writing it to mail.

Key Idea: It is very important to choose to obey God and follow Him.

Corresponding Music

✓ *Hide 'Em in Your Heart Vol. 2*
CD - Track 6; Cassette - Side A
Song: "*Honor Your Father & Mother*"

Learning the Basics

Focus: Language Arts and Math

Unit 29 - Day 5

Language Arts

Write the following sentences on paper: *The bird was white. The birds were white.* Say, *Why do we use 'was' in the first sentence and 'were' in the second sentence? Which word is used for talking about one bird, 'was' or 'were'? Which word is used for talking about more than one bird, 'was' or 'were'?* Give students an index card with 'was' written on one side and 'were' on the other. Ask students to show the correct side of the card to complete these sentences: The whale __ swimming. The dophins __ jumping. The lobsters __ pinching. Carl the Crab __ crawling.

<u>Key Idea</u>: Use 'was' and 'were'.

Reading Choices

Choose **one** of the reading options listed below (see Appendix for details).

★ A phonics program

★ *Scheduled Books for Emerging Readers*

★ *Drawn into the Heart of Reading Level 2/3*

<u>Key Idea</u>: Use a step-by-step program for reading instruction.

Storytime

Read aloud a short portion of your realistic fiction book. Say, *Pretend you are the main character in the story that we are reading. Dictate a letter to someone in our family, explaining what has been happening in the story. I will write the letter as you dictate it to me. Since you are the main character, you must say, "I did..." and "I went..." instead of using the character's name. Sign the character's name at the bottom.*

<u>Key Idea</u>: Give students practice retelling a portion of a realistic fiction book.

Math Exploration

Cut out the square chart numbered from '1' - '100' in *Workbook 1B* p. 131. Then, cut the chart into 15 - 20 puzzle pieces, making sure to stay on the lines while cutting. Have students put the chart back together by placing the numbers in order from '1' - '100'.

✔ <u>Text Connection</u>: *Primary Mathematics Workbook 1B* p. 133

<u>Key Idea</u>: Sequence and order numbers between '1' - '100'.

Learning Through History

Focus: Pioneers Go West by Covered Wagon

Unit 30 - Day 1

Reading About History

Read about history in the following resource:

★ *American Pioneers and Patriots* p. 108

Key Idea: More and more pioneers went west to make new homes. Often they traveled in groups of covered wagons called wagon trains. The trip was very long and hard. Many pioneers died on the way.

Poetry and Rhymes

Read aloud the poem *"Written in March"* (see Appendix) to the students. Do not share the title. Ask students to suggest some titles for the poem. Share the real title. Read the poem again with the students.

Key Idea: Read and appreciate a variety of classic poetry.

Geography

Say, *Let's look at the two longest rivers in the United States: The Mississippi River and the Missouri River. The name Mississippi means "Great River". Use a United States map to find the source of the Mississippi River at Lake Itasca in Minnesota. Trace the Mississippi River's route from north to south until you reach the river's mouth in the Gulf of Mexico near Louisiana. The Missouri River is nicknamed "Big Muddy". Find the source of the Missouri River in Three Forks, Montana. Trace the Missouri River's route across the country until it flows into the Mississippi River near St. Louis, Missouri. Which of these 2 rivers is nearest to where you live?*

Key Idea: Many pioneers crossed the Mississippi and the Missouri Rivers as they traveled west.

Bible Study

Review the memory verse, John 15:13, from Unit 25. Read the verse out loud. Ask, *What are some of your least favorite jobs to do? Why is it important to work to please Jesus and others instead of only pleasing yourself? Did Jesus have to give His life for you? In John 15:13, why does it say that He did it?* Say the verse together 3 times. Review the hand motions that go with the verse from Unit 25, if you remember them.

Key Idea: As the pioneers traveled west, they had to do many hard jobs without complaint.

Corresponding Music

✔ *Hide 'Em in Your Heart Vol. 2*
CD - Track 3; Cassette - Side A
Song: *"Greater Love"*

Learning the Basics

Focus: Language Arts and Math

Unit 30 - Day 1

Language Arts

Choose **either** spelling list 1 **or** 2 (see Appendix for lists). Write each spelling word on a separate index card. Guide students to study each card one at a time, flip it over, write the word from memory on paper, flip the card back over to check the spelling, and erase and correct any mistakes.

Copywork: Have students copy part of the poem *"Written in March"*.

Key Idea: Practice spelling words with 'oi' or 'oy' as in 'boil' or 'boy'.

Reading Choices

Choose **one** of the reading options listed below (see Appendix for details).

★ *A phonics program*
★ *Scheduled Books for Emerging Readers*
★ *Drawn into the Heart of Reading Level 2/3*

Key Idea: Use a step-by-step program for reading instruction.

Storytime

Say, *What clues to the story are given in the book title or in the next chapter title? What interesting details do you see on the cover or in the pictures from today's reading? What makes this book realistic? What is one problem that needs to be solved in this story?*

Read aloud the next portion of the realistic fiction book that you selected. Pace your reading to complete the book during the next 15 days of plans.

Key Idea: Preread to build anticipation for the next part of the realistic fiction book.

Math Exploration

Use a meterstick, a measuring tape, or a yardstick as a number line. Say, *Point to the number '25'. Now, add '5' to '25'. You'll need to count on from '25' as you move 5 spaces up the number line ('26', '27', '28', '29', '30').* On a paper or a markerboard, write '19 + 8 = ___' for the students to solve. Have students use the number line to start at '19' and count on '8' more from there. Then, ask students to write the final number in the blank ('27'). Repeat the exercise with different addition problems.

✔ Text Connection: *Primary Mathematics Workbook 1B* p. 134-135

Key Idea: Count on to add numbers to '100'.

Learning Through History

Focus: Pioneers Go West by Covered Wagon

Unit 30 - Day 2

Reading About History

Read about history in the following resource:

★ *American Pioneers and Patriots* p. 109-111

Key Idea: Dan's family was going west with the wagon train. Each morning they rushed to pack and get on the trail. One morning a herd of buffaloes came stampeding toward the camp. The mules and oxen scattered and had to be found.

Science Exploration

Say, *Bison are American buffalo.* Have students pretend to be bison. Direct them to wallow or roll on their sides and backs, horn trees, rub against trees, and forage under snow for grass. Bison grow to be 6' tall and 10' long. They are the largest land mammal. Make a 6' x 10' masking tape outline on the floor to show students the size of a bison. In 1870, there were 5 and 1/2 million bison in America. Bison were hunted for sport. By 1885, the 1500 remaining bison were placed in parks to save them. Wild bison were extinct. Now, bison are found in parks and on farms.

✓ Text Connection: *God's Wonderful Works* p. 105 and 107

Key Idea: On the trip west, Dan got caught in a buffalo stampede.

Poetry and Rhymes

Read aloud the poem *"Written in March"* (see Appendix) with the students. Discuss the poem's meaning. If you choose, photocopy the poem, cut it apart, and have the students place it in the correct order.

Key Idea: Read classic poetry.

Bible Study

Review the memory verse Galations 5:22-23, from unit 26, by saying it while the students join in on the parts they know. Say, *Whose help do you need to show the fruits of the Spirit listed in Galations 5:22-23? Which fruit of the Spirit do you need the most help in showing? How can you do a better job of showing it? Can you do it on your own? Why?* Next, have students do 3 push-ups. After 3 push-ups, have the students recite the entire Bible verse. Repeat the activity several times.

Key Idea: Dan was a good helper. The Holy Spirit is our special helper.

Corresponding Music

✓ *Hide 'Em in Your Heart Vol. 2* CD - Track 17; Cassette - Side B Song: *"The Fruit of the Spirit"*

Learning the Basics

Focus: Language Arts and Math

Unit 30 - Day 2

Language Arts

Use the spelling list from Day 1. Say the first spelling word. Use it in a sentence. Repeat the word. Ask students to write the word on a piece of paper or on a markerboard from memory. Give students the matching word card from Day 1 to compare with their spelling. Guide students to correct any mistakes. Repeat the activity with all 10 words.
<u>Copywork</u>: Have students copy part of the poem *"Written in March"*.

<u>Key Idea</u>: Practice spelling words with 'oi' or 'oy' as in 'boil' or 'boy'.

Reading Choices

Choose **one** of the reading options listed below (see Appendix for details).

★ A phonics program
★ *Scheduled Books for Emerging Readers*
★ *Drawn into the Heart of Reading Level 2/3*

<u>Key Idea</u>: Use a step-by-step program for reading instruction.

Storytime

Read aloud the next portion of the realistic fiction book that you selected. Without looking back at the story, begin retelling or narrating the part of the book that you read today. After a short time, tap the student and say, *Your turn.* The student should pick up the narration where you left off. After a short time, the student should tap you and say, *Your turn.* Continue taking turns narrating in this manner until today's reading has been retold. Then, say, *Name one thing that you learned about the main character today.* Write it on paper for the students to copy.

<u>Key Idea</u>: Take turns retelling a story from a single reading.

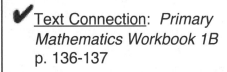

Math Exploration

Complete the assigned lesson in the workbook listed below.

✔ <u>Text Connection</u>: *Primary Mathematics Workbook 1B* p. 136-137

<u>Key Idea</u>: Count on to add numbers up to '100'.

Learning Through History

Focus: Pioneers Go West by Covered Wagon

Unit 30 - Day 3

Reading About History

Read about history in the following resource:

★ *American Pioneers and Patriots* p. 112-113

Key Idea: One night while they were hunting, Dan and his father found an abandoned wagon. They heard a strange sound. A baby was alone in the wagon. There was no sign of her parents. Dan's mother kept the baby as her own.

Poetry and Rhymes

Read aloud the poem *"Written in March"* (see Appendix) with the students. Read the poem aloud a second time, pausing after each line or two for students to add actions to the poem. The actions should make sense with the poem.

Key Idea: Read classic poetry.

Science Exploration

Say, *Vultures are birds that fly on a column of warm air. The draft of the warm air helps them lift into the sky. As they glide on the warm air, vultures swoop and dive in the sky. Let's see how vultures fly. Bend an index card to make an arc. Set the card in the middle of the table. Kneel in front of the table, so your mouth is even with the table's edge. Blow underneath the arc of the card. Did you see how the card rose on the air that you blew, just like a vulture rising on a column of warm air?*

✔ Text Connection: *God's Wonderful Works* p. 81, 84, and 126

Key Idea: Vultures were circling the broken-down wagon, when Dan and his father found the baby in it.

Bible Study

Review the memory verse, Luke 16:10, from Unit 27 by saying it while the students join in on the parts they know. Next, have students skip around the room until you say, *Freeze*. After they 'freeze', have the students recite the entire Bible verse. Have students repeat the activity.

✔ Text Connection: *Morning Bells* p. 73-75

Key Idea: Dan's mother did the right thing by taking the sickly baby to be her own. It is not always easy to care for others, but when you do, you are doing it for Jesus.

Corresponding Music

None this lesson

Learning the Basics

Focus: Language Arts and Math

Unit 30 - Day 3

Language Arts

Using the spelling list from Day 1, choose 3 or more words that the students need to practice. Guide students to use each of the words that you chose in a sentence. On a markerboard or a piece of paper, write down the sentences as the students dictate them to you. Underline the spelling word in each sentence. Have the students copy the sentences on a piece of paper. Help students check their sentences and correct any mistakes.
<u>Copywork</u>: Have students copy part of the poem *"Written in March"*..

<u>Key Idea</u>: Practice 'oi' or 'oy' words.

Reading Choices

Choose **one** of the reading options listed below (see Appendix for details).

★ A phonics program
★ *Scheduled Books for Emerging Readers*
★ *Drawn into the Heart of Reading Level 2/3*

<u>Key Idea</u>: Use a step-by-step program for reading instruction.

Storytime

Read aloud the next portion of the realistic fiction book that you selected. Say, *Point of view refers to how a person or a character looks at, or views, something. Dictate a letter from your point of view to one of the characters in the story. I will write the letter as you dictate it to me. Tell the character about yourself and your life. Ask the character any questions that you might have. Sign the letter with your name.* Save the students' letters for Unit 31 - Day 3.

<u>Key Idea</u>: Focus on the story element: *point of view.*

Math Exploration

Complete the assigned lesson in the workbook listed below.

✓ <u>Text Connection</u>: *Primary Mathematics Workbook 1B* p. 138-139

<u>Key Idea</u>: Practice double-digit addition with sums less than '100'.

Learning Through History

Focus: Pioneers Go West by Covered Wagon

Unit 30 - Day 4

Reading About History

Read about history in the following resource:

★ *American Pioneers and Patriots* p. 114-116

Key Idea: It began to snow and rain. The wagon train lost the trail in the mountains. Two peaceful Indians came and showed the wagons the way back to the trail. The pioneers were very grateful. They gave presents to the Indians. God protected Dan's family.

Artistic Expression

Help students make a mountain with 5 layers. Give each student a white piece of paper for the background. Each student will also need a sheet of light blue or gray paper, pink paper, lavender paper, dark purple paper, and black paper. Guide students to tear off the top several inches of the light blue or grey paper to outline the top of the mountains. Glue the mountain onto the white paper. Next, have students tear off the top of the pink paper, so it is lower than the light blue or gray paper. Glue the pink paper on next. Continue repeating the process to make the rest of the mountain layers with the lavender, dark purple, and black papers.

Key Idea: The wagon train was lost in the mountains. God saved them.

Poetry and Rhymes

Read aloud the poem *"Written in March"* (see Appendix) with the students. Have students draw pictures that reflect the poem's meaning on either a photocopy of the poem or on their copywork. File the finished poem in a special place.

Key Idea: Read classic poetry.

Bible Study

Review the memory verse, Proverbs 22:6, from Unit 28 by saying it while the students join in on the parts they know. Say, *Describe some times that you have helped someone who is poor, sick, hungry, or lonely. When you helped those people, who were you also serving? Why is it important to serve others?* Have students run in place. Say, *Freeze,* and have the students stop and recite the Bible verse. Repeat the activity.

Key Idea: The pioneers were lost. The Indians saved them.

Corresponding Music

✓ *Hide 'Em in Your Heart Vol. 2* CD - Track 1; Cassette - Side A
Song: *"Train Up a Child"*

Learning the Basics

Focus: Language Arts and Math

Unit 30 - Day 4

Language Arts

Use the spelling list from Day 1. Say each word and use it in a sentence. Have students write each word and check it with the matching word card from Day 1. Guide students to correct any mistakes. Direct students to write each missed word with fingerpaint or sidewalk chalk.

<u>Copywork</u>: Have students copy part of *"Written in March"*.

<u>Key Idea</u>: Practice spelling 'oi' or 'oy' words as in 'boil' or 'boy'.

Reading Choices

Choose **one** of the reading options listed below (see Appendix for details).

★ A phonics program

★ *Scheduled Books for Emerging Readers*

★ *Drawn into the Heart of Reading Level 2/3*

<u>Key Idea</u>: Use a step-by-step program for reading instruction.

Storytime

Say, *Integrity means being honest and doing what is right, even when no one else is watching, so that you may be blameless in the eyes of the Lord.* Read aloud the key verse Titus 2:11-12. Read aloud Daniel 6:6-23. Ask, *How did Daniel's actions show integrity?*

Read aloud the next portion of the realistic fiction book that you selected. Then, ask, *How do the characters in the realistic fiction book show integrity? What would the Biblical character, Daniel, do differently from the characters in your book?*

<u>Key Idea</u>: Focus on the Godly character trait: *integrity*.

Math Exploration

For each player, fold a piece of paper in half and label the left side 'tens' and the right side 'ones'. Say, *Each player will take a turn rolling the die. The player must choose whether to write the number rolled in the 'tens' column or the 'ones' column. If the number is written in the 'tens' column, then a '0' is written next to it in the 'ones' column. So, a '6' written in the 'tens' column would read '60'. After each player has rolled the die five times, the players add up their score. The player who is closest to '100' without going over wins.*

✓ <u>Text Connection</u>: *Primary Mathematics Workbook 1B* p. 140-141

<u>Key Idea</u>: Add with double-digits.

Learning Through History

Focus: Pioneers Go West by Covered Wagon

Unit 30 - Day 5

Reading About History

Read the following passage from your own Bible:

★ Matthew 25:31-46

Key Idea: Believers in Christ need to show mercy to those in need. When you serve others, you are serving Christ. Dan's family showed mercy to the baby they found in the wagon. The Indians showed mercy to the pioneers in the mountains.

Poetry and Rhymes

Have students get out the poems that they saved from the previous units. Ask students to select one or more poems to review. Read aloud the selected poems with the students.

Key Idea: Read classic poetry.

History Activity

Discuss and sing the words of "America the Beautiful" written by Katherine Lee Bates.

*O beautiful for spacious skies,
For amber waves of grain,
For purple mountain majesties
Above the fruited plain!
America! America!
God shed His grace on thee
And crowned thy good
With brotherhood
From sea to shining sea.*

Then, have students get out their timeline. Say, *Let's find the column that says 1800. Draw a small covered wagon in that column. Write 'Oregon Trail, 1842' under it.*

Key Idea: We are blessed that God shed His grace on America.

Bible Study

Ask, *In Matthew 25:34-40, what does Jesus say to the believers? What does it mean to show mercy to someone? Should Christians act differently than unbelievers? How? In Matthew 25:41-46, what does Jesus say to the unbelievers?* Ask students to share their memory verse, Deuteronomy 5:16, with someone special. Suggestions for sharing the verse include saying it to another family member, saying it to someone by telephone, reciting it to a stuffed animal, or writing it to mail.

Key Idea: Christians need to act differently from the rest of the world.

Corresponding Music

✔ *Hide 'Em in Your Heart Vol. 2*
CD - Track 6; Cassette - Side A
Song: *"Honor Your Father & Mother"*

Learning the Basics

Focus: Language Arts and Math

Unit 30 - Day 5

Language Arts

Write the following sentences on paper: *The frog has big eyes. The frogs have big eyes.* Say, *Why do we use 'has' in the first sentence and 'have' in the second sentence? Which word is used for talking about one frog, 'has' or 'have'? Which word is used for talking about more than one frog, 'has' or 'have'?* Give students an index card with 'has' written on one side and 'have' on the other. Ask students to show the correct side of the card to complete these sentences: The squirrel __ a long tail. The bears __ thick fur. A jackrabbit __ strong legs. Foxes __ pointed ears. Otters __ long bodies. <u>Copywork</u>: Copy one sentence.

<u>Key Idea</u>: Use 'has' and 'have'.

Reading Choices

Choose **one** of the reading options listed below (see Appendix for details).

★ A phonics program
★ *Scheduled Books for Emerging Readers*
★ *Drawn into the Heart of Reading Level 2/3*

<u>Key Idea</u>: Use a step-by-step program for reading instruction.

Storytime

Read aloud a short portion of the realistic fiction book that you selected. Give students a chance to orally retell today's reading. Prompt students as needed with the following questions: *What did the characters do? Then, what happened? After that what happened? Why did the characters do that?*

<u>Key Idea</u>: Give students practice retelling a portion of a realistic fiction book.

Math Exploration

Fold a piece of paper in half. Label the left side 'tens' and the right side 'ones'. Write "47 + 26 = ___" on a markerboard or a piece of paper. Give students dimes and pennies. Say, *To show '47', place 4 dimes in the 'tens' column' and '7' pennies in the 'ones' column. Leave a space below the coins. Below the space, show '26' by placing '2' dimes in the 'tens' column' and '6' pennies in the 'ones' column. Push the pennies together and count them. Since the total is '13', trade 10 pennies for 1 dime. Place the dime at the top of the 'tens' column. Push all the dimes together. You should have '7'.* Write the total in the blank. Repeat the activity with different numbers.

<u>Key Idea</u>: Add with double-digits.

Learning Through History

Focus: Pioneers on the Santa Fe Trail

Unit 31 - Day 1

Reading About History

Read about history in the following resource:

⭐ *American Pioneers and Patriots* p. 117

Key Idea: Pioneers lived in their covered wagons as they traveled west. When they stopped at night, the wagons made a circle.

Poetry and Rhymes

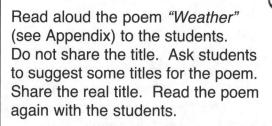

Read aloud the poem *"Weather"* (see Appendix) to the students. Do not share the title. Ask students to suggest some titles for the poem. Share the real title. Read the poem again with the students.

Key Idea: Read and appreciate a variety of classic poetry.

Science Exploration

Use a box or a laundry basket to be a wagon. Put several heavy items in the wagon (i.e. soup cans, books, or shoes). Give students a card with a red arrow drawn on it. Say, *After each command I give you, place the red arrow on the floor pointing in the direction you will push or pull. Pretend you are the oxen.* **Pull** *your wagon across a flat floor to be the prairie. Scatter pillows on the floor to be mud.* **Push** *your wagon through the mud. Lay a blanket on the floor to be a river.* **Pull** *your wagon across the river. Use stairs to be steep cliffs.* **Pull** *your wagon up the steep cliffs. Use a carpet or a rug as sand.* **Push** *your wagon through the sand.* **Pull** *your wagon into a circle and stop.*

Key Idea: Traveling by wagon was slow and difficult. It was hard work to push and pull the wagon through the tough spots on the trail. Precious items often had to be left behind.

Bible Study

Matthew 6:25-26 is the memory verse for this unit. Read the verse out loud. Discuss, *In Matthew 6:25, what does Jesus tell you about worry? What does Jesus say about the birds of the air in Matthew 6:26? Who is more valuable than the birds? Does worrying help anyone? Explain what Jesus says in Matthew 6:27.* Say the verse together 3 times. Add hand motions to help students remember the words.

Key Idea: The pioneers had many hardships. Jesus says to trust in Him and not worry about the hard times.

Corresponding Music

✔ *Hide 'Em in Your Heart Vol. 2*
CD - Track 4; Cassette - Side A
Song: *"Do Not Worry"*

Learning the Basics

Focus: Language Arts and Math

Unit 31 - Day 1

Language Arts

Get out the spelling words on index cards that you saved from Unit 25 and Unit 26. Guide students to study each card one at a time, flip it over, write the word from memory on paper, flip the card back over to check the spelling, and erase and correct any mistakes.

<u>Copywork</u>: Have students copy part of the poem *"Weather"*.

<u>Key Idea</u>: Review spelling words from Unit 25 and Unit 26.

Reading Choices

Choose **one** of the reading options listed below (see Appendix for details).

★ A phonics program
★ *Scheduled Books for Emerging Readers*
★ *Drawn into the Heart of Reading Level 2/3*

<u>Key Idea</u>: Use a step-by-step program for reading instruction.

Storytime

Say, *Is the setting, or place, in the story realistic? Explain. What place that you know of reminds you of the setting in the story? How are you the same as the main character? What good things does the main character do?*

Read aloud the next portion of the realistic fiction book that you selected. Pace your reading to complete the book during the next 10 days of plans.

<u>Key Idea</u>: Set a purpose for reading the next part of the realistic fiction book.

Math Exploration

Complete the assigned lesson in the workbook listed below.

✔ <u>Text Connection</u>: *Primary Mathematics Workbook 1B* p. 142-143

<u>Key Idea</u>: Add two or more numbers with double-digits.

Learning Through History

Focus: Pioneers on the Santa Fe Trail

Unit 31 - Day 2

Reading About History

Read about history in the following resource:

★ *American Pioneers and Patriots* p. 122

Key Idea: Independence, Missouri was the starting point for 3 different trails west: The Santa Fe Trail, The Oregon Trail, and the California Trail.

Poetry and Rhymes

Read aloud the poem *"Weather"* (see Appendix) with the students. Discuss the poem's meaning. If you choose, photocopy the poem, cut it apart, and have the students place it in the correct order.

Key Idea: Read classic poetry.

Geography

Read about the route of the Santa Fe Trail in paragraph 2 in the second column of p. 122 of *American Pioneers and Patriots*. Have students trace the Santa Fe Trail with their fingers on the map on p. 137. Ask, *Where does the trail start? Point to Independence, Missouri. A plain is a flat, open stretch of land. Where are the Great Plains? Point to the area before the mountains. Where would the Raton Pass be? A pass is a path or opening through the mountains. Point to the place where the trail crosses the mountains. Where is the Rio Grande? Point to the river near the bottom of the map. Start at the source of the Rio Grande and follow it to Santa Fe. The source of a river, is where it begins.*

Key Idea: The Santa Fe Trail went across the plains, through the mountains, and along the Rio Grande River to Santa Fe.

Bible Study

Say Matthew 6:25-26 while the students join in on the parts they know. Use the hand motions you added on Day 1. Ask, *Name some things that you worry about. Does God want you to spend your time worrying? Why shouldn't you worry? When you worry, are you trusting in God?* Next, have students do 5 toe touches. After 5 toe touches, have the students recite the entire Bible verse. Prompt the students as needed. Repeat the activity several times.

Key Idea: It is easy to worry, but it is better to trust God. He has a plan.

Corresponding Music

✓ *Hide 'Em in Your Heart Vol. 2* CD - Track 4; Cassette - Side A Song: *"Do Not Worry"*

Learning the Basics

Focus: Language Arts and Math

Unit 31 - Day 2

Language Arts

Get out the spelling cards that you saved from Unit 27. Say the first spelling word. Use it in a sentence. Repeat the word. Ask students to write the word on a markerboard or a piece of paper from memory. Give students the matching word card to compare with their spelling. Guide students to correct any mistakes. Repeat the activity with all 10 words. Copywork: Have students copy part of the poem *"Weather"*.

Key Idea: Review spelling words from Unit 27.

Reading Choices

Choose **one** of the reading options listed below (see Appendix for details).

★ A phonics program

★ *Scheduled Books for Emerging Readers*

★ *Drawn into the Heart of Reading Level 2/3*

Key Idea: Use a step-by-step program for reading instruction.

Storytime

Read aloud the next portion of the realistic fiction book that you selected. Without looking back at the story, write a retelling of the part of the book that you read today leaving blanks in place of key words (i.e. _____ was a young boy who was blinded by a _____. He had to learn how to _____, _____, and _____ all over again. This was very _____! Later, Jimmy went to _____ to learn how to use a guide _____.). Key words can be names, places, descriptive words, times of day, seasons, etc. Work with the students to reread the written narration and fill in the missing words.

Key Idea: Model retelling a story from a single reading.

Math Exploration

Use a meterstick, a measuring tape, or a yardstick as a number line. Say, *Point to the number '36'. Now, subtract '5' from '36'. You'll need to count back from '36' as you move 5 spaces back on the number line ('35', '34', '33', '32', '31').* On a paper or a markerboard, write "22 - 7 = ___" for the students to solve. Have students use the number line to start at '22' and count back '7' from there. Then, ask students to write the final number in the blank ('15'). Repeat the exercise with different subtraction problems.

✓ Text Connection: *Primary Mathematics Workbook 1B* p. 144-145

Key Idea: Count back to subtract numbers under '100'.

Learning Through History

Focus: Pioneers on the Santa Fe Trail

Unit 31 - Day 3

Reading About History

Read about history in the following resource:

★ *American Pioneers and Patriots* p. 123-124

Key Idea: Nick traveled with his father by wagon to Santa Fe. The mules that pulled the wagon were hard to handle. Nick lost his hat in a big windstorm on the way.

Poetry and Rhymes

Read aloud the poem *"Weather"* (see Appendix) with the students. Read the poem aloud a second time, pausing after each line or two for students to add their own actions to the poem. The actions should make sense with the poem.

Key Idea: Read classic poetry.

Science Exploration

Say, *Insects have 3 body parts, 6 legs, and 2 antennae. Some insects, like the firefly, have wings. Today we will do an activity about the firefly.* You will need a flashlight for yourself and a flashlight for each student. Students may share if needed. Go to a dark area of the house. Say, *Fireflies flash when they are looking for a mate. I will flash a series of long and short flashes by turning my flashlight on and off. You must flash the pattern back to me with your flashlight.* Start with 3 flashes in a series (i.e. long, short, short). Then, move onto 4 flashes in a series (i.e. short, short, long, short).

✓ Text Connection: *God's Wonderful Works* p. 122-124

Key Idea: Nick used his hat to fan away flies and mosquitos. There were many insects on the trip.

Bible Study

Say Matthew 6:25-26 with the students. Use the hand motions you added on Day 1. Next, have students lay on their backs and peddle their feet in the air like they are riding a bicycle. When you say, *Freeze,* the students should stop and recite the entire Bible verse. Repeat the activity.

✓ Text Connection: *Morning Bells* p. 40-42

Key Idea: Nick missed his hat. He wanted another one. God gives you many things to enjoy. It is important to thank Him for all His blessings.

Corresponding Music

✓ *Hide 'Em in Your Heart Vol. 2* CD - Track 4; Cassette - Side A Song: *"Do Not Worry"*

Learning the Basics

Focus: Language Arts and Math

Unit 31 - Day 3

Language Arts

Choose 3 or more words that the students need to practice from Unit 28. Guide students to use each of the words you chose in a sentence. Write down the sentences as the students dictate them to you. Underline the spelling word in each sentence. Tell the students to copy the sentences on paper, check them, and correct any mistakes.
Copywork: Have students copy part of the poem *"Weather"*.

Key Idea: Review spelling words.

Reading Choices

Choose **one** of the reading options listed below (see Appendix for details).

★ A phonics program
★ *Scheduled Books for Emerging Readers*
★ *Drawn into the Heart of Reading Level 2/3*

Key Idea: Use a step-by-step program for reading instruction.

Storytime

Read aloud the next portion of your realistic fiction book. Get out the letter from Unit 30 - Day 3 that the students dictated to the main character. Read it aloud to the students. Say, *Point of view refers to how a person or a character looks at, or views, something. Today you will dictate an answer to the letter that you wrote last week. I will write the letter as you dictate it to me. You must pretend to be the character in the story answering your letter. Use "I", "me", "my", and "mine" to show that you are the character. Sign the character's name at the bottom of the letter.*

Key Idea: Focus on the story element: *point of view*.

Math Exploration

Get out five ziplock bags. Place ten counters in each bag (i.e. cereal pieces, puzzle pieces, or macaroni noodles). Write '56' on a paper or a markerboard. Say, *Use the bags and counters to show '56'* (i.e. 5 bags of '10' and '6' loose counters). *Take away '3'. Count and write your total* ('53'). *Now, take away '8'. Since there are only '3' loose counters, you will need to open a 'tens' bag to get the remaining '5'. Count the full 'tens' bags and those left over. Write your new total.* Continue subtracting other numbers.

✔ Text Connection: *Primary Mathematics Workbook 1B* p. 146-147

Key Idea: Model double-digit subtraction with regrouping.

Learning Through History

Focus: Pioneers on the Santa Fe Trail

Unit 31 - Day 4

Reading About History

Read about history in the following resource:

★ *American Pioneers and Patriots* p. 125-126

Key Idea: Nick went looking for a hat. He tried to trade with a boy for an old black hat, but the boy didn't want to trade. Nick decided to offer his favorite thing, his mouth organ, for the hat. Just then, his father came with a new sombrero for him.

History Activity

Sing "Yankee Doodle" along with the words in the second column of p. 126 of American Pioneers and Patriots. If you have a harmonica or can whistle, do it to the tune of "Yankee Doodle". Then, place a hat in the middle of the floor and dance around it as you clap and sing "Yankee Doodle". Look at the picture on p. 125 to see how to dance around the hat, depending if you are a boy or a girl. Next, have students get out their timeline. Say, Let's find the column that says 1800. Draw a small Mexican hat in that column. Write 'Santa Fe Trail, 1825' under it.

Key Idea: Santa Fe was a Spanish city. The men wore sombreros and the women wore bright-colored skirts. The houses were made of adobe.

Poetry and Rhymes

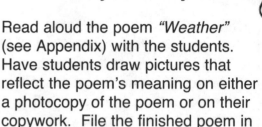

Read aloud the poem *"Weather"* (see Appendix) with the students. Have students draw pictures that reflect the poem's meaning on either a photocopy of the poem or on their copywork. File the finished poem in a special place.

Key Idea: Read classic poetry.

Bible Study

Say Matthew 6:25-26 with the students. Use the hand motions from Day 1. Ask, *How does God take care of you? Why does God give you all the things that you have? Does God want you to be happy? What do you need to remember to do when God blesses you?* Next, have students gallop by leading with their left foot until you say, *Freeze*. After they 'freeze', have the students recite the Bible verse. Have students switch to the right foot and repeat the activity.

Key Idea: God wants you to be glad for the things that He gives you.

Corresponding Music

✓ *Hide 'Em in Your Heart Vol. 2* CD - Track 4; Cassette - Side A Song: *"Do Not Worry"*

Learning the Basics

Focus: Language Arts and Math

Unit 31 - Day 4

Language Arts

Get out the spelling word cards from Unit 29 and Unit 30. Say each word and use it in a sentence. Have students write each word and check it with the matching word card. Guide students to correct any mistakes. For each missed word, have students trace it in dry cornmeal, oatmeal, or sand on a plate. <u>Copywork</u>: Have students copy part of *"Weather"*.

<u>Key Idea</u>: Review spelling words.

Reading Choices

Choose **one** of the reading options listed below (see Appendix for details).

★ A phonics program
★ *Scheduled Books for Emerging Readers*
★ *Drawn into the Heart of Reading Level 2/3*

<u>Key Idea</u>: Use a step-by-step program for reading instruction.

Storytime

Say, *Integrity means being honest and doing what is right, even when no one else is watching, so that you may be blameless in the eyes of the Lord.* Read aloud the key verse Titus 2:11-12. Say, *Name some times that you have done the right thing even though it was hard. List some ways to show self-control* (i.e. guard your thoughts, control your temper, delay a reaction, think through a decision, control your tongue, think before acting). Read aloud the next portion of the realistic fiction book that you selected. Ask, *How do the book characters do what's right even when it is hard? Do the characters ever show dishonesty or lack of self-control?*

<u>Key Idea</u>: Focus on the Godly character trait: *integrity*.

Math Exploration

Complete the assigned lesson in the workbook listed below.

✔ <u>Text Connection</u>: *Primary Mathematics Workbook 1B* p. 148-149

<u>Key Idea</u>: Practice double-digit subtraction with sums less than '100'.

Learning Through History

Focus: Pioneers on the Santa Fe Trail

Unit 31 - Day 5

Reading About History

Read the following passage from your own Bible:

★ Luke 12:22-34

<u>Key Idea</u>: Jesus doesn't want you to worry or be afraid. He wants you to trust God to take care of you. Nick's father took care of him. He bought Nick a new hat for the trip. Jesus tells you to trust God for all things.

Poetry and Rhymes

Have students get out the poems that they saved from the previous units. Ask students to select one or more poems to review. Read aloud the selected poems with the students.

<u>Key Idea</u>: Read classic poetry.

Artistic Expression

Draw the outline of a simple, treasure chest on yellow paper. Cut a small slit in the lid of the chest. Have the students cut out the chest. Allow students to decorate the chest with a variety of craft items (i.e. sequins, glitter, markers, or stickers). Make sure to leave the slit open. Put a line of glue around the outside of the treasure chest. Glue it to the center of a white piece of paper. Mix 1/4 cup warm water with 6 tsp. salt and 3 drops of yellow food coloring to make a salty solution. Have students paint the paper around the treasure chest with the solution to be a sandy beach. Last, help students cut out a small red heart. Write this scripture reference on the heart: *Luke 12:34*. Place the heart in the slit of the treasure chest.

<u>Key Idea</u>: Jesus wants your heart to belong to Him.

Bible Study

Discuss, *In Luke 12:29-30, why does Jesus say you shouldn't worry? In Luke 12:31, what does Jesus say you should do instead? How can you seek to make Jesus the King of your life? Where does Luke 12:34 say your heart will be? What does that mean?* Ask students to share their memory verse, Matthew 6:25-26, with someone special. Suggestions for sharing the verse include saying it to another family member, saying it to someone by telephone, reciting it to a stuffed animal, or writing it to mail.

<u>Key Idea</u>: Jesus wants you to spend your time seeking to please Him.

Corresponding Music

✓ *Hide 'Em in Your Heart Vol. 2*
CD - Track 4; Cassette - Side A
Song: *"Do Not Worry"*

Learning the Basics

Focus: Language Arts and Math

Unit 31 - Day 5

Language Arts

Write the following sentences on paper: *Beau is not sad. Beau isn't sad.* Say, *Do these two sentences mean the same thing? How are they different? What two words make up isn't? What letter is left out when is not is written as isn't? What takes the place of the missing letter? A contraction is two words that are put together to make one word. An apostrophe takes the place of any missing letters.* On paper, write *I am*. Next to it write *I'm*. Say, *Compare I am with I'm. Color the letters that are the same in both words. Which letter is left out of I'm? Why do we put an apostrophe in that spot?* Repeat the activity with it's, don't didn't, aren't, wasn't, and hasn't.

Key Idea: Introduce contractions.

Reading Choices

Choose **one** of the reading options listed below (see Appendix for details).

★ A phonics program

★ *Scheduled Books for Emerging Readers*

★ *Drawn into the Heart of Reading Level 2/3*

Key Idea: Use a step-by-step program for reading instruction.

Storytime

Read aloud a short portion of your realistic fiction book. Guide students to retell today's reading by saying, *Think of 5 questions that have to do with today's reading. Remember, questions begin with words such as 'who', 'what', 'when', 'where', 'why', 'how', and 'how much'. Ask me your questions to see if I can answer them.*

Key Idea: Give students practice retelling a portion of a realistic fiction book.

Math Exploration

Fold a piece of paper in half. Label the left side 'tens' and the right side 'ones'. Write "56 - 24 = ___" on a markerboard or a piece of paper. Give students dimes and pennies. Say, *To show '56', place 5 dimes in the 'tens' column' and '6' pennies in the 'ones' column. Below the coins, write the number to be subtracted, which is '24'. Write the '2' in the 'tens' column' and the '4' in the 'ones' column. Take away '4' pennies from the '6' pennies, which leaves '2'. Take away '2' dimes from the '5' dimes, which leaves '3'. Write the total in the blank.*

✓ Text Connection: *Primary Mathematics Workbook 1B* p. 150-151

Key Idea: Subtract larger numbers.

Learning Through History

Focus: The Oregon Trail and the California Trail

Unit 32 - Day 1

Reading About History

Read about history in the following resource:

★ *American Pioneers and Patriots* p. 127-128

Key Idea: Ten-year old Nell lived in a log cabin with her family. Her mother was sick. Nell's father, Jed, took her mother to the nearest town. Nell was left alone in the cabin to care for the twin babies.

Poetry and Rhymes

Read aloud the poem *"A Child's Prayer"* (see Appendix) to the students. Do not share the title. Ask students to suggest some titles for the poem. Share the real title. Read the poem again with the students.

Key Idea: Read and appreciate a variety of classic poetry.

Geography

Read about the route of the Oregon Trail in paragraph 3 in the second column of p. 122 of *American Pioneers and Patriots*. Have students trace the Oregon Trail with their fingers on the map on p. 120. Ask, *Where does the trail start? Point to St. Louis, Missouri. Where is the Platte River? Start at the source, which is the Mississippi River, and follow the Platte River across the Great Plains to the mountains. Where would the South Pass be? A pass is a path or opening through the mountains. Point to the place where the trail crosses the mountains. Where is the Snake River? Follow the Snake River to the mountains. Then, follow the Columbia River into Oregon City.*

Key Idea: Nell's family had traveled west on the Oregon Trail.

Bible Study

Proverbs 18:24 is the memory verse for this unit. Read the verse out loud and discuss its meaning with the students. Ask, *What does Proverbs 18:24 say about friends? Is it important to have a lot of friends? Who is the best friend you can have? How does Jesus show you that He is your best friend?* Say the verse together 3 times. Add hand motions to help students remember the words.

Key Idea: Even though Nell felt alone, Jesus was with her.

Corresponding Music

✓ *Hide 'Em in Your Heart Vol. 2* CD - Track 11; Cassette - Side B Song: *"There is a Friend"*

Learning the Basics

Focus: Language Arts and Math

Unit 32 - Day 1

Language Arts

Use the spelling list for Unit 32 (see Appendix for lists). Write each spelling word on a separate index card. Guide students to study each card one at a time, flip it over, write the word from memory on paper, flip the card back over to check the spelling, and erase and correct any mistakes.

Copywork: Have students copy part of the poem *"A Child's Prayer"*.

Key Idea: Practice spelling color words.

Reading Choices

Choose **one** of the reading options listed below (see Appendix for details).

★ A phonics program
★ *Scheduled Books for Emerging Readers*
★ *Drawn into the Heart of Reading Level 2/3*

Key Idea: Use a step-by-step program for reading instruction.

Storytime

Ask, *Which character would you choose as a friend? Why would you choose that character? Name some things that you like about the characters. What would you tell the characters to do to solve one of the problems in the story? What other story reminds you of this story? Explain.*

Read aloud the next portion of the realistic fiction book that you selected. Pace your reading to complete the book during the next 5 days of plans.

Key Idea: Set a purpose for reading the next part of the realistic fiction book.

Math Exploration

Complete the assigned lesson in the workbook listed below.

✔ Text Connection: *Primary Mathematics Workbook 1B* p. 152

Key Idea: Practice double-digit subtraction with regrouping.

Learning Through History

Focus: The Oregon Trail and the California Trail

Unit 32 - Day 2

Reading About History

Read about history in the following resource:

★ *American Pioneers and Patriots* p. 129-130

Key Idea: While the twins were sleeping, Nell fell asleep too. A bear smelled molasses and came in the open door.

Poetry and Rhymes

Read aloud the poem *"A Child's Prayer"* (see Appendix) with the students. Discuss the poem's meaning. If you choose, photocopy the poem, cut it apart, and have the students place it in the correct order.

Key Idea: Read classic poetry.

Science Exploration

Say, *Black bears can grow to be 10 feet tall and weigh up to 1,700 pounds! Bears have paws. What would it be like to have a paw, instead of a hand? Let's do an experiment to find out.* Have students fold their thumb into the palm of their hand. Then, wrap masking tape around the students hand to make a paw. Be careful not to wrap the tape too tightly. Have students try to pick up a variety of items with their paw (i.e. plastic bowl, book, pencil, paper, piece of fruit, or a paper clip). Ask, *Why do you think the bear swatted at the jug of molasses, rather than picking it up? Why would God give us hands instead of paws?*

✔ Text Connection: *God's Wonderful Works* p. 96

Key Idea: Nell got rid of the bear by throwing the molasses jug outside. Then, she shot the bear with the gun.

Bible Study

Say Proverbs 18:24 while the students join in on the parts they know. Use the hand motions you added on Day 1. Say, *What does a good friend do? Can your brothers or sisters be your friends? Who should be your best friend? Why can you trust Jesus to always be a good friend?* Next, have students do windmills by touching their right hand to their right foot, and then their left hand to their left foot. After every 5 windmills, have the students recite the Bible verse.

Key Idea: Nell loved her brothers and took good care of them.

Corresponding Music

✔ *Hide 'Em in Your Heart Vol. 2* CD - Track 11; Cassette - Side B Song: *"There is a Friend"*

Learning the Basics

Focus: Language Arts and Math

Unit 32 - Day 2

Language Arts

Use the spelling list from Day 1. Say the first spelling word. Use it in a sentence. Repeat the word. Ask students to write the word on a markerboard or a piece of paper from memory. Give students the matching word card from Day 1 to compare with their spelling. Guide students to correct any mistakes. Repeat the activity with all 10 words. <u>Copywork</u>: Have students copy part of the poem "*A Child's Prayer*".

<u>Key Idea</u>: Practice spelling color words.

Reading Choices

Choose **one** of the reading options listed below (see Appendix for details).

★ A phonics program
★ *Scheduled Books for Emerging Readers*
★ *Drawn into the Heart of Reading Level 2/3*

<u>Key Idea</u>: Use a step-by-step program for reading instruction.

Storytime

Read aloud the next portion of the realistic fiction book that you selected. Ask students to retell or narrate what you read today. Remind students to tell the most important parts and to include details from the story in the retelling. As students work together to retell the story, write, type, or tape record the students' narration. When the students are finished, read the narration out loud. Highlight, circle, or underline one main idea from the narration for the students to copy.

<u>Key Idea</u>: Keep a sample of the students' narration for the genre: *Realistic Fiction*.

Math Exploration

Complete the assigned lesson in the workbook listed below.

✓ <u>Text Connection</u>: *Primary Mathematics Workbook 1B* p. 153

<u>Key Idea</u>: Practice double-digit subtraction with regrouping.

Learning Through History

Focus: The Oregon Trail and the California Trail

Unit 32 - Day 3

Reading About History

Read about history in the following resource:

★ *American Pioneers and Patriots* p. 131-132

<u>Key Idea</u>: Ken was traveling to meet his father on the California Trail.

Poetry and Rhymes

Read aloud the poem *"A Child's Prayer"* (see Appendix) with the students. Read the poem aloud a second time, pausing after each line or two for students to add their own actions to the poem. The actions should make sense with the poem.

<u>Key Idea</u>: Read and appreciate a variety of classic poetry.

History Activity

Help students make a population bar graph to show how many people came to California during the Gold Rush. Tape a piece of masking tape in a large 'L' on the floor. Starting at the corner of the 'L', write the following numbers up the side of the tape to equal the **thousands** of people in California: 0, 50, 100, 150, 200, 250. Starting at the corner of the 'L', write the following years across the bottom of the tape: 1848, 1849, 1852. Tape a masking tape strip above each year to show the following populations: 1848=14,000; 1849=100,000; 1852= 250,000. Say, *Do you see the huge jump in population from 1848 to 1849? That is when gold was found in California. Get out your timeline. Let's find the column that says 1800. Draw a small gold nugget in that column. Write 'California Trail, 1849' under it.*

<u>Key Idea</u>: Ken's father had gone to look for gold. When he didn't find much, he started a store in San Jose.

Bible Study

Say Proverbs 18:24 with the students. Use the hand motions you added on Day 1. Next, have students squat down, hop up, and squat back down again. After the last squat, have the students recite the entire Bible verse. Prompt students as needed. Repeat the activity.

✔ <u>Text Connection</u>: *Morning Bells* p. 22-24

<u>Key Idea</u>: Ken gladly went west to help his father run the store in San Jose. He felt alone as he traveled. Always remember, Jesus is with you.

Corresponding Music

✔ *Hide 'Em in Your Heart Vol. 2* CD - Track 11; Cassette - Side B Song: *"There is a Friend"*

Learning the Basics

Focus: Language Arts and Math

Unit 32 - Day 3

Language Arts

Choose 3 or more words from the spelling list from Day 1 that the students need to practice. Guide students to use each of the practice words in a sentence. Write down the sentences as the students dictate them to you. Underline the spelling word in each sentence. Tell students to copy the sentences on paper, check them, and correct any mistakes. <u>Copywork</u>: Have students copy part of the poem *"A Child's Prayer"*.

<u>Key Idea</u>: Practice color words.

Reading Choices

Choose **one** of the reading options listed below (see Appendix for details).

★ A phonics program

★ *Scheduled Books for Emerging Readers*

★ *Drawn into the Heart of Reading Level 2/3*

<u>Key Idea</u>: Use a step-by-step program for reading instruction.

Storytime

Say, *Point of view can mean whose side of the story is being told. Let's figure out who the author is using to tell this story. Does it seem to be someone who is watching what is happening (like a reporter), or does it seem to be a character in the story? Listen while we read today to see if you can figure it out.* Read aloud the next portion of your realistic fiction book. Ask, *Did you notice who was telling the story? Was it one of the characters? If so, the character would be saying, "I" (as in the first person point of view). Or, was the writer reporting about the characters, (as in the third person point of view)?*

<u>Key Idea</u>: Focus on the story element: *point of view*.

Math Exploration

These are the concepts that are covered in this review: writing numbers with 'tens' and 'ones', finishing number patterns, ordering numbers from smallest to largest, working simple mulitplication and division problems, and completing story problems. Review any concepts that students had difficulty understanding. Also, complete the assigned review in the workbook listed below.

✔ <u>Text Connection</u>: *Primary Mathematics Workbook 1B* p. 154-157

<u>Key Idea</u>: Review difficult concepts.

Learning Through History

Focus: The Oregon Trail and the California Trail

Unit 32 - Day 4

Reading About History

Read about history in the following resource:

★ *American Pioneers and Patriots* p. 133-135

Key Idea: As Ken started west in the stagecoach, California became the thirty-first state. The governor got in Ken's coach to deliver the news to San Jose. Another coach started racing them to spread the news first.

Science Exploration

Have students pan for gold. Fill a sink or a tub 3/4 full with water. Place gold buttons or pennies in the water to be gold. Have students point to a spot in the water where they see gold. and push their finger straight down to see if the gold was where they pointed. Say, *The reflection of the water changes the appearance of where something actually is, which makes it hard to find objects in water.* Give students a slotted spoon, a strainer, or a collander to use as a pan. Have students scoop up the water and strain out the 'gold'.

✔ Text Connection: *God's Wonderful Works* p. 43-44

Key Idea: So many people moved to California to find gold that it became the 31st state in 1850.

Poetry and Rhymes

Read aloud the poem *"A Child's Prayer"* (see Appendix) with the students. Have students draw pictures that reflect the poem's meaning on either a photocopy of the poem or on their copywork. File the finished poem in a special place.

Key Idea: Read classic poetry.

Bible Study

Say Proverbs 18:24 with the students. Use the hand motions from Day 1. Say, *What are some things that you have to do all by yourself? Why is it important to learn to do some things alone? Name some chores you will learn as you get older. Why is it important to learn those things? Who is always there to help you?* Next, have students hop backward 5 times. After 5 hops, have the students recite the entire Bible verse. Repeat the activity several times.

Key Idea: Ken made the trip alone. His father met him at the station.

Corresponding Music

✔ *Hide 'Em in Your Heart Vol. 2* CD - Track 11; Cassette - Side B
Song: *"There is a Friend"*

Learning the Basics

Focus: Language Arts and Math

Unit 32 - Day 4

Language Arts

Use the spelling list from Day 1. Say each word and use it in a sentence. Have students write each word and check it with the matching word card from Day 1. Guide students to correct any mistakes. Use a dark marker to write each missed word very largely on paper. Help students trace each missed word with glue. Allow the glue to dry in order to feel the words.
Copywork: Have students copy part of the poem *"A Child's Prayer"*.

Key Idea: Practice color words.

Reading Choices

Choose **one** of the reading options listed below (see Appendix for details).

★ A phonics program
★ *Scheduled Books for Emerging Readers*
★ *Drawn into the Heart of Reading Level 2/3*

Key Idea: Use a step-by-step program for reading instruction.

Storytime

Say, *Integrity means being honest and doing what is right, even when no one else is watching, so that you may be blameless in the eyes of the Lord.* Read aloud the key verse Titus 2:11-12. Read aloud the next portion of the realistic fiction book that you selected. Ask, *Were the book characters usually showing integrity or dishonesty? Explain. Do you usually show integrity or dishonesty? Draw a picture showing one way that you could have more integrity. Post your picture in a place where you will see it often.*

Key Idea: Focus on the Godly character trait: *integrity*.

Math Exploration

Review the names of the coins and their values (penny = 1 cent, nickel = 5 cents, dime = 10 cents, quarter = 25 cents). Say, *You are going to play a game. Roll 1 die. Take that number of pennies. If you have 5 pennies, trade those for a nickel. Continue rolling the die and taking the matching number of pennies. Once you have 2 nickels, trade those for a dime. Keep trading pennies for nickels and nickels for dimes until you have twenty-five cents. When you have twenty-five cents, trade for one quarter. Then, the game is over.* Ask, *How many quarters are needed to make $1.00?*

Key Idea: Review the names and values of the coins.

Learning Through History

Focus: The Oregon Trail and the California Trail

Unit 32 - Day 5

Reading About History

Read the following passage from your own Bible:

★ Psalm 121:1-8

Key Idea: God is always there to help you. He watches over you all of the time. Even when the pioneers felt alone, God was watching over them. He never grows weary.

Poetry and Rhymes

Have students get out the poems that they saved from the previous units. Ask students to select one or more poems to review. Read aloud the selected poems with the students.

Key Idea: Read classic poetry.

Artistic Expression

Have students lay both of their hands, palm up with their fingers spread open on a piece of paper. Trace around the hands. Have the students cut them out and color them. Trace around a small plate or circular lid to be the Earth. Have students look at the globe or *God's Wonderful Works* p. 34 to color the Earth. Overlap the hands to look like they are holding something. Lay the Earth on top of the hands. Glue the Earth and the hands to a sheet of background paper. Copy Psalm 121:2 on the background paper.

Key Idea: God holds the Earth in His hands. He is always watching over His creation.

Bible Study

Ask, *In Psalm 121:1-2, where does it say that your help comes from? Read Psalm 121:3-4. Does the Lord ever sleep? How long does Psalm 121:7-8 say that the Lord will watch over you? Why should this Psalm make you trust in God? Are you ever alone?* Ask students to share their memory verse, Proverbs 18:24, with someone special. Suggestions for sharing the verse include saying it to another family member, saying it to someone by telephone, reciting it to a stuffed animal, or writing it to mail.

Key Idea: The Lord will never leave you alone. He is always there.

Corresponding Music

✔ *Hide 'Em in Your Heart Vol. 2*
CD - Track 11; Cassette - Side B
Song: *"There is a Friend"*

Learning the Basics

Focus: Language Arts and Math

Unit 32 - Day 5

Language Arts

Tape a long strip of masking tape to the floor. Write the letters of the alphabet in order on the strip. Leave several inches between letters. Get out the spelling word cards from **Unit 31.** Say, *Today we will put your spelling words in alphabetical order. Look at one of your spelling word cards. What is the first letter of the word? Place the word card above that letter on the alphabet strip. Continue placing the rest of your spelling word cards above the strip in the same way. After all cards have been placed, read the spelling words aloud in alphabetical order.*

Key Idea: Use alphabetical order.

Reading Choices

Choose **one** of the reading options listed below (see Appendix for details).

★ A phonics program
★ *Scheduled Books for Emerging Readers*
★ *Drawn into the Heart of Reading Level 2/3*

Key Idea: Use a step-by-step program for reading instruction.

Storytime

Read aloud the final portion of the realistic fiction book that you selected. You will need to select a folk tale to read aloud next. Ask students to retell today's reading. Prompt students with the following ideas as needed: *Tell me your favorite part of the story. What did you like best about the book? Were there any parts that you didn't like? Explain. Describe what happened at the end of the story.*

Key Idea: Give students practice retelling a portion of a realistic fiction book.

Math Exploration

Review the names of the coins and their values (penny = 1 cent, nickel = 5 cents, dime = 10 cents, quarter = 25 cents). Give students three different coins. Have them put the coins in order from least to greatest in value. Then, have students add the coins to see how much money they have. Repeat the activity using different coins. Increase the number of coins as students seem ready to add greater values.

✔ Text Connection: *Primary Mathematics Workbook 1B* p. 158

Key Idea: Count money with pennies, nickels, dimes, and quarters.

Learning Through History

Focus: Pioneers from Norway Settle on the Plains

Unit 33 - Day 1

Reading About History

Read about history in the following resource:

★ *American Pioneers and Patriots* p. 140-142

Key Idea: Hilda and her family came from Norway to live on the Great Plains. They had to live in a sod house. Hilda was homesick for Norway. She wanted to go back.

Poetry and Rhymes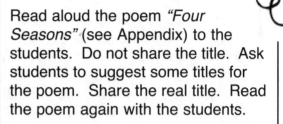

Read aloud the poem *"Four Seasons"* (see Appendix) to the students. Do not share the title. Ask students to suggest some titles for the poem. Share the real title. Read the poem again with the students.

Key Idea: Read and appreciate a variety of classic poetry.

Science Exploration

Have students use the map on p. 165 of *American Pioneers and Patriots* to find the states that have the following types of soil: (1) red desert soil: California, Arizona, and Nevada (2) gray soil: Idaho, Utah, and Nevada (3) white soil: New Mexico (4) red soil: Texas and Oklahoma (5) dark black or brown soil: Kansas, Nebraska, South Dakota, Iowa, and Missouri. Ask, *What color is the soil where you live?*

✔ Text Connection: *God's Wonderful Works* p. 39

Key Idea: Hilda's family moved to the Great Plains to have their own farmland. The soil on the Great Plains was dark black. It was excellent soil for growing crops.

Bible Study

Proverbs 17:22 is the memory verse for this unit. Read the verse out loud. Ask, *What does Proverbs 17:22 say a cheerful or merry heart is like? Explain what good medicine does. In Proverbs 17:22, what does a broken spirit do? Describe dry bones. After reading this Proverb, how do you think the Lord wants you to act?* Say the verse together 3 times. Add hand motions to help students remember the words.

Key Idea: Hilda was having a hard time being cheerful. Her mother tried to comfort her.

Corresponding Music

✔ *Hide 'Em in Your Heart Vol. 2* CD - Track 16; Cassette - Side B Song: *"A Joyful Heart"*

Learning the Basics

Focus: Language Arts and Math

Unit 33 - Day 1

Language Arts

Use the spelling list for Unit 33 (see Appendix for lists). Write each spelling word on a separate index card. Guide students to study each card one at a time, flip it over, write the word on paper, flip the card back over to check the spelling, and erase and correct any mistakes.

Copywork: Have students copy part of the poem *"Four Seasons"*.

Key Idea: Practice number words.

Reading Choices

Choose **one** of the reading options listed below (see Appendix for details).

★ A phonics program

★ *Scheduled Books for Emerging Readers*

★ *Drawn into the Heart of Reading Level 2/3*

Key Idea: Use a step-by-step program for reading instruction.

Storytime

Choose at least one folk tale to read aloud for the next 10 days of plans (see Appendix for suggested titles). To introduce the genre, *Folk Tale*, quietly tell a short folk tale to one student (i.e. *The Tortoise and the Hare, The Lion and the Mouse,* or *Belling the Cat*). Have that student quietly retell the folk tale to another student or to a stuffed toy until the folk tale has been retold several times. Repeat the last version of the folk tale out loud. Ask, *Is that exactly the same story as the one I told in the beginning? Why not? Folk tales often change as they are retold. That is why there are often several versions of the same story.* Read a part of the folk tale book you chose.

Key Idea: Introduce the genre: *Folk Tale*.

Math Exploration

Review the names of the coins and their values (penny = 1 cent, nickel = 5 cents, dime = 10 cents, quarter = 25 cents). Place a pile of pennies, nickels, dimes, and quarters in a bowl. Have students take one handful of coins. Direct students to place the coins on the table in order from highest to lowest in value. Have students point to each coin and say its name and its value. Guide students to add their coins to get a total amount of money. Repeat the activity with a different handful of coins.

✔ Text Connection: *Primary Mathematics Workbook 1B* p. 159

Key Idea: Determine how much money is in a set of coins.

Learning Through History

Focus: Pioneers from Norway Settle on the Plains

Unit 33 - Day 2

Reading About History

Read about history in the following resource:

★ *American Pioneers and Patriots* p. 143-145

Key Idea: Hilda's family had a long winter in the damp, sod house. Finally, father had to go to town to get supplies.

Poetry and Rhymes

Read aloud the poem *"Four Seasons"* (see Appendix) with the students. Discuss the poem's meaning. If you choose, photocopy the poem, cut it apart, and have the students place it in the correct order.

Key Idea: Read classic poetry.

Artistic Expression

Have students use white typing paper to make snowflakes. Start with a square piece of paper. Fold the paper in half diagonally to make a triangle. Fold the triangle in half again by making the pointed corners meet. Fold the next triangle into thirds by folding the right side to the center and the left side over top of the right side. The bottoms will not match up. Cut across the bottom of the paper, so it is straight. Then, have students cut pieces of the paper away to make a snowflake. The more paper that is cut away the more delicate the snowflake will look. Help students gently open the paper when they are done cutting.

Key Idea: On the way back from town, Father and Olaf got lost in a snowstorm. The oxen found the way back home. God was watching over Hilda's family.

Bible Study

Say Proverbs 17:22 while the students join in on the parts they know. Use the hand motions you added on Day 1. Say, *Name some people you know that are cheerful. How do you feel when you're with them? What are some ways you can be more cheerful? Will others want to be around you if you are always sad?* Next, have students do 5 jumping jacks. After 5 jumping jacks, have the students recite the entire Bible verse. Prompt the students as needed. Repeat the activity.

Key Idea: Hilda was not cheerful.

Corresponding Music

✓ *Hide 'Em in Your Heart Vol. 2*
CD - Track 16; Cassette - Side B
Song: *"A Joyful Heart"*

Learning the Basics

Focus: Language Arts and Math

Unit 33 - Day 2

Language Arts

Use the spelling list from Day 1. Say the first spelling word. Use it in a sentence. Repeat the word. Ask students to write the word on a markerboard or a piece of paper from memory. Give students the matching word card from Day 1 to compare with their spelling. Guide students to correct any mistakes. Repeat the activity with all 10 words.
Copywork: Have students copy part of the poem *"Four Seasons"*.

Key Idea: Practice number words.

Reading Choices

Choose **one** of the reading options listed below (see Appendix for details).

★ A phonics program

★ *Scheduled Books for Emerging Readers*

★ *Drawn into the Heart of Reading Level 2/3*

Key Idea: Use a step-by-step program for reading instruction.

Storytime

Read aloud the next portion of the folk tale that you selected. Without looking back at the story, begin retelling or narrating the part of the folk tale that you read today. After a short time, tap the student and say, *Your turn.* The student should pick up the narration where you left off. After a short time, the student should tap you and say, *Your turn.* Continue taking turns narrating in this manner until today's reading has been retold. Then, say, *What other story reminds you of the story that we read today? Explain.* Write a one sentence summary of the students' answers on paper for the students to copy.

Key Idea: Take turns retelling a story from a single reading.

Math Exploration

Write "25 cents" on a markerboard or a piece of paper. Give students pennies, nickels, dimes, and quarters. Guide students to find one or more ways to show '25 cents' (i.e. 25 pennies, 5 nickels, 2 dimes and 1 nickel, 1 quarter, etc.). Continue writing different amounts for students to use their coins to show in a variety of ways. Extend the activity by using one dollar bills and showing amounts of money over one dollar. It's not necessary to find all combinations for a given amount.

✔ Text Connection: *Primary Mathematics Workbook 1B* p. 160-161

Key Idea: Count dollars and coins to match given amounts of money.

Learning Through History

Focus: Pioneers from Norway Settle on the Plains

Unit 33 - Day 3

Reading About History

Read about history in the following resource:

★ *American Pioneers and Patriots* p. 146-147

Key Idea: In the spring, a group of wagons stopped at Hilda's house. Hilda was busy caring for the babies. Mother said Hilda could go back to Norway with another family. But, Hilda chose to stay instead.

Poetry and Rhymes

Read aloud the poem *"Four Seasons"* (see Appendix) with the students. Read the poem aloud a second time, pausing after each line or two for students to add actions to the poem. The actions should make sense with the poem.

Key Idea: Read classic poetry.

Geography

Have students use a world map or a globe to find Norway. Ask, *Norway is found on which continent? What countries are located around Norway? Which ocean would Hilda's family have to cross to get to the United States?* Read aloud the first paragraph in the second column on p. 140 of *American Pioneers and Patriots*. Ask, *What is the land like in Norway?* Read aloud the second and third paragraphs in the second column on p. 140 of *American Pioneers and Patriots*. Ask, *What is the land like on the Great Plains? Why would it be hard to come from Norway to live on the Great Plains?*

Key Idea: It was a big change for Hilda to move from Norway to the Great Plains. It was hard for Hilda to get used to her new life.

Bible Study

Say Proverbs 17:22 with the students. Use the hand motions you added on Day 1. Next, have students hop on their left foot until you say, *Freeze*. After they 'freeze', have the students recite the entire Bible verse. Prompt students as needed. Have students switch to the right foot, and repeat the activity.

✔ Text Connection: *Morning Bells* p. 31-33

Key Idea: Hilda was sorry for the way she had acted. She decided to stay and let the Lord help her be more content.

Corresponding Music

✔ *Hide 'Em in Your Heart Vol. 2* CD - Track 16; Cassette - Side B Song: *"A Joyful Heart"*

Learning the Basics

Focus: Language Arts and Math

Unit 33 - Day 3

Language Arts

Using the spelling list from Day 1, choose 3 or more words that the students need to practice. Guide students to use each of the words that you chose in a sentence. Write down the sentences as the students dictate them to you. Underline the spelling word in each sentence. Tell students to copy the sentences on a piece of paper. Help students check their sentences and correct any mistakes. <u>Copywork</u>: Have students copy part of *"Four Seasons"*.

<u>Key Idea</u>: Practice number words.

Reading Choices

Choose **one** of the reading options listed below (see Appendix for details).

★ A phonics program
★ *Scheduled Books for Emerging Readers*
★ *Drawn into the Heart of Reading Level 2/3*

<u>Key Idea</u>: Use a step-by-step program for reading instruction.

Storytime

Say, *Compare means to notice things that are the same between two items. Contrast means to notice things that are different between two items. As we read today, pay attention to the setting, or places, in the story. We will compare and contrast them to where you live.* Read aloud the next portion of the folk tale that you selected. Say, *How is the setting of the story the same as where you live? How is the setting of the story different from where you live?* Have students use playdough, or paints and paper, to "create" the setting of the story.

<u>Key Idea</u>: Introduce the story element: *compare* and *contrast*.

Math Exploration

Complete the assigned lesson in the workbook listed below.

✓ <u>Text Connection</u>: *Primary Mathematics Workbook 1B* p. 162-163

<u>Key Idea</u>: Compare two sets of money to see which is greater and which is less.

Learning Through History

Focus: Pioneers from Norway Settle on the Plains

Unit 33 - Day 4

Reading About History

Read about history in the following resource:

★ *American Pioneers and Patriots* p. 148

Key Idea: The Indians taught the pioneers how to grow corn. It could be grown in rocky ground. The pioneers also grew wheat. Wheat needed better ground to grow. It was hard work to make the corn into cornmeal and the wheat into flour.

Poetry and Rhymes

Read aloud the poem *"Four Seasons"* (see Appendix) with the students. Have students draw pictures that reflect the poem's meaning on either a photocopy of the poem or on their copywork. File the finished poem in a special place.

Key Idea: Read classic poetry.

Science Exploration

Have students use green playdough to make a model of a seed. You may choose to use the following recipe to make green playdough: Mix 1 cup flour and 1 cup salt with water until it is a playdough consistency. Add several drops of green food coloring. Refer to the picture of a seed on p. 51 of *God's Wonderful Works* as needed. Have students make 2 flat lima bean-shaped seed halves. Have students make a sprout out of playdough and add it inside the seed to be a new plant. Wrap the seed in saran wrap to be the seed coat.

✓ Text Connection: *God's Wonderful Works* p. 50-51

Key Idea: The pioneers learned how to grow crops from the Indians.

Bible Study

Say Proverbs 17:22 with the students. Use the hand motions you added on Day 1. Ask, *Do you ever do things that are wrong? Since Jesus forgives your sins, is it alright to keep doing wrong things? Why not? Why should Jesus' forgiveness make you want to try to do what's right?* Next, have the students do 5 sit-ups. After 5 sit-ups, have the students recite the entire Bible verse.

Key Idea: All people sin. Nobody deserves the Lord's forgiveness. His forgiveness should make you want to do your best.

Corresponding Music

✓ *Hide 'Em in Your Heart Vol. 2* CD - Track 16; Cassette - Side B
Song: *"A Joyful Heart"*

Learning the Basics

Focus: Language Arts and Math

Unit 33 - Day 4

Language Arts

Use the spelling list from Day 1. Say each word and use it in a sentence. Have students write each word and check it with the matching word card from Day 1. Guide students to correct any mistakes. For each missed word, have students hop on one foot and spell the word out loud, hopping each time they say a letter.
Copywork: Have students copy part of the poem *"Four Seasons"*.

Key Idea: Practice spelling number words.

Reading Choices

Choose **one** of the reading options listed below (see Appendix for details).

★ A phonics program
★ *Scheduled Books for Emerging Readers*
★ *Drawn into the Heart of Reading Level 2/3*

Key Idea: Use a step-by-step program for reading instruction.

Storytime

Say, *Virtue is listening to the Holy Spirit to do what is right and good so that you may follow God's law.* Introduce the key verse Proverbs 20:11 to illustrate *virtue*. Read aloud Luke 2:21-24, 39-40. Ask, *How did Mary and Joseph's actions show virtue?* Read aloud the next portion of the folk tale that you selected. Then, ask, *How do the characters in the folk tale show virtue? What would the Biblical characters, Mary and Joseph, do differently from the characters in your book?*

Key Idea: Focus on the Godly character trait: *virtue.*

Math Exploration

Say, *You have 50 cents to buy the letters in your name. Vowels cost 10 cents each and consonants cost 5 cents each. Let's find the total cost of your name to see if 50 cents is enough.* Write the letters of the student's name and the value of each letter underneath it. Add up the values. Say, *If 50 cents is not enough, how much more money is needed? If 50 cents is enough, how much change will you get back?* Use the names of other family members to see how much each name would cost.

✓ Text Connection: *Primary Mathematics Workbook 1B* p. 164

Key Idea: Decide whether you have enough money to buy an item.

Learning Through History

Focus: Pioneers from Norway Settle on the Plains

Unit 33 - Day 5

Reading About History

Read the following passage from your own Bible:

★ Philippians 2:3-15

Key Idea: Paul tells us not to be selfish, but to think of others instead. Jesus is the example of how we should act. Often we feel like complaining like Hilda did. But, if we believe in Jesus, we should act differently.

Poetry and Rhymes

Have students get out the poems that they saved from the previous units. Ask students to select one or more poems to review. Read aloud the selected poems with the students.

Key Idea: Read classic poetry.

History Activity

Say, *Hilda's family came to the Great Plains because of the Homestead Act, which gave away free farmland. Let's pretend you are racing to get free land. As you race, remember to put Jesus first.* Read Philippians 2:9-11. Give each student a frisbee or a lid and a small ball. Have students put the ball on the frisbee or the lid and carry it across the room like a waiter or a waitress. As students cross the room, whenever they hear you say the name *Jesus,* they need to stop, kneel, and say, *Jesus Christ is Lord.* Next, have students get out their timeline. Say, *Let's find the column that says 1800. Draw a small field in that column. Write 'Homestead Act: free land, 1862' under it.*

Key Idea: Jesus is our example of how we can live our lives to glorify our Father in heaven.

Bible Study

Ask, *In Philippians 2:3-5, how does Paul tell you to act? How does Philippians 2:6-8 describe Jesus? Why does Philippians 2:14-15 say you should do all things without complaining or arguing? If you are a Christian, why do others watch you to see if you're different?* Ask students to share their memory verse, Proverbs 17:22, with someone special. Suggestions for sharing the verse include saying it to another family member, saying it to someone by telephone, reciting it to a stuffed animal, or writing it to mail.

Key Idea: Do others see Christ in you?

Corresponding Music

✓ *Hide 'Em in Your Heart Vol. 2*
CD - Track 16; Cassette - Side B
Song: *"A Joyful Heart"*

Learning the Basics

Focus: Language Arts and Math

Unit 33 - Day 5

Language Arts

Tape a long strip of masking tape to the floor. Write the letters of the alphabet in order on the strip. Leave several inches between letters. Get out the spelling word cards from **Unit 32.** Say, *Let's put your spelling words in alphabetical order. Look at one of your spelling word cards. What is the first letter of the word?* Place the word card above that letter on the alphabet strip. Continue placing the rest of your spelling word cards above the strip in the same way. After all cards are placed, say, *Since three of the words begin with 'b', how can we decide which 'b' word would come first? When we look at the second letter, we see that 'blue' and 'black' would come before 'brown'. By looking at the third letter, we can see that 'black' would come before 'blue'. Read the words in order.*

<u>Key Idea</u>: Use alphabetical order.

Reading Choices

Choose **one** of the reading options listed below (see Appendix for details).

★ A phonics program
★ *Scheduled Books for Emerging Readers*
★ *Drawn into the Heart of Reading Level 2/3*

<u>Key Idea</u>: Use a step-by-step program for reading instruction.

Math Exploration

Complete the assigned lesson in the workbook listed below.

✔ <u>Text Connection</u>: *Primary Mathematics Workbook 1B* p. 165-166

Note: Discuss the problems and use coins and dollars as needed for additional help.

<u>Key Idea</u>: Decide whether you have enough money to buy an item that has an assigned price.

Storytime

Read aloud a short portion of the folk tale that you selected. Allow students to use a few props to help them retell today's reading. They may use the props to act out the story as they are retelling it.

<u>Key Idea</u>: Give students practice retelling a portion of a folk tale.

Learning Through History

Focus: The Transcontinental Railroad

Unit 34 - Day 1

Reading About History

Read about history in the following resource:

★ *American Pioneers and Patriots* p. 152-154

<u>Key Idea</u>: Abraham Lincoln was a poor pioneer boy born in Kentucky. His family moved many times. Later, he became our nation's 16th president. As president, Lincoln approved the building of a railroad that would cross America.

Poetry and Rhymes

Read aloud the poem *"Try Again"* (see Appendix) to the students. Do not share the title. Ask students to suggest some titles for the poem. Share the real title. Read the poem again with the students.

<u>Key Idea</u>: Read and appreciate a variety of classic poetry.

Geography

Say, *In 1862, the Transcontinental Railroad was built from the Missouri River to San Francisco, California.* Look at the map on p. 150 of *American Pioneers and Patriots*. Discuss the order by date that land was added to the United States. Ask, *What part of the map shows the United States in 1783? Which large purchase came next in the year 1803? After that in 1819-1821, which treaty came next? In 1845, which area was annexed? In 1846, which area was acquired through a deal with England? In 1848, which land was acquired by a treaty with Mexico? In 1853, which land was purchased from Mexico?*

<u>Key Idea</u>: Work began on the Transcontinental Railroad.

Bible Study

Philippians 3:13-14 is the memory verse for this unit. Read the verse out loud. Ask, *In Philippians 3:13, why must Paul forget what is behind him or in the past? Describe what it means to strain or reach toward something. What does Philippians 3:14, say that Paul is straining or pressing toward? Discuss the one thing Paul is saying you should do.* Say the verse together 3 times. Add hand motions to help students remember the words.

<u>Key Idea</u>: Lincoln did not have an easy life. Yet, he forgot the past and focused on what was ahead.

Corresponding Music

None this lesson

Learning the Basics

Focus: Language Arts and Math

Unit 34 - Day 1

Language Arts

Use the spelling list for Unit 34 (see Appendix for lists). Write each spelling word on a separate index card. Guide students to study each card one at a time, flip it over, write the word from memory on paper, flip the card back over to check the spelling, and erase and correct any mistakes.

<u>Copywork</u>: Have students copy part of the poem *"Try Again"*.

<u>Key Idea</u>: Practice spelling the names of the days of the week and the seasons.

Reading Choices

Choose **one** of the reading options listed below (see Appendix for details).

★ A phonics program
★ *Scheduled Books for Emerging Readers*
★ *Drawn into the Heart of Reading Level 2/3*

<u>Key Idea</u>: Use a step-by-step program for reading instruction.

Storytime

Say, *Folk tales are fables, fairy tales, legends and other tales that have been retold many times. They usually have a lesson or a moral. As I'm reading today, whenever I come to a problem in the story, I will stop and ask you to solve it. Next, we'll keep reading to see how the characters solve the problem. Watch for the moral or lesson that is taught in the story.* Read aloud the next portion of the folk tale that you selected. Pace your reading to complete the folk tale book during the next 5 days of plans.

<u>Key Idea</u>: Preread to build anticipation for the next part of the folk tale.

Math Exploration

These are the concepts that are covered in this review: counting money, comparing dollar amounts, and computing word problems that involve money. Review any concepts that students had difficulty understanding. Also, complete the assigned review in the workbook listed below.

✔ <u>Text Connection</u>: *Primary Mathematics Workbook 1B* p. 167-168

<u>Key Idea</u>: Review difficult concepts.

Learning Through History

Focus: The Transcontinental Railroad

Unit 34 - Day 2

Reading About History

Read about history in the following resource:

★ *American Pioneers and Patriots* p. 155-156

Key Idea: Mike and his father came from Ireland to America. They worked on the railroad starting at the Missouri River. Mike was a water boy. It was hot, dusty work.

Poetry and Rhymes

Read aloud the poem *"Try Again"* (see Appendix) with the students. Discuss the poem's meaning. If you choose, photocopy the poem, cut it apart, and have the students place it in the correct order.

Key Idea: Read and appreciate a variety of classic poetry.

Science Exploration

Fill a glass with hot water from the tap. Fill another glass with cold water from the tap. Without bumping the glasses, add 3 drops of food coloring to each glass. Watch the glasses carefully to see how the food coloring moves through the water. Ask, *In which glass of water did the food coloring move more quickly? Why might the food coloring have moved faster in that glass? When something is hot, the molecules move more quickly. So, the food coloring would move more quickly through the hot water than in the cold water.*

✔ Text Connection: *God's Wonderful Works* p. 27

Key Idea: The water the men drank as they worked in the desert was warm and stale. Yet, it was precious because water is hard to get in the desert.

Bible Study

Say Philippians 3:13-14 while the students join in on the parts they know. Use the hand motions you added on Day 1. Say, *Do you have any sins in your past that you are ashamed about? Have you asked Christ to forgive those sins? After asking for forgiveness, why can you forget about those sins? What does Philippians 3:13-14 say Christ wants you to do now?* Next, have students do 3 push-ups. After 3 push-ups, have the students recite the entire Bible verse. Repeat the activity.

Key Idea: Mike's family had a sad past in Ireland. He had to forget the past and work hard in America.

Corresponding Music

None this lesson

Learning the Basics

Focus: Language Arts and Math

Unit 34 - Day 2

Language Arts

Use the spelling list from Day 1. Say the first spelling word. Use it in a sentence. Repeat the word. Ask students to write the word on a markerboard or a piece of paper from memory. Give students the matching word card from Day 1 to compare with their spelling. Guide students to correct any mistakes. Repeat the activity with all 10 words.
<u>Copywork</u>: Have students copy part of the poem *"Try Again"*.

<u>Key Idea</u>: Practice spelling the names of the days of the week and the seasons.

Reading Choices

Choose **one** of the reading options listed below (see Appendix for details).

★ A phonics program
★ *Scheduled Books for Emerging Readers*
★ *Drawn into the Heart of Reading Level 2/3*

<u>Key Idea</u>: Use a step-by-step program for reading instruction.

Storytime

Read aloud the next portion of the folk tale that you selected. Ask students to retell or narrate what you read today. Remind students to tell the most important parts and to include details from the story in the retelling. As students work together to retell the story, write, type, or tape record the students' narration. When the students are finished, read the narration out loud. Highlight, circle, or underline one main idea from the narration for the students to copy.

<u>Key Idea</u>: Keep a sample of the students' narration for the genre: *Folk Tale*.

Math Exploration

These are the concepts that are covered in this review: word problems with subtraction, addition, and multiplication. Review any concepts that students had difficulty understanding. Also, complete the assigned review in the workbook listed below.

✔ <u>Text Connection</u>: *Primary Mathematics Workbook 1B* p. 169-170

Note: Have students draw pictures to help them solve problems 6-8 on p. 170.

<u>Key Idea</u>: Review difficult concepts.

Learning Through History

Focus: The Transcontinental Railroad

Unit 34 - Day 3

Reading About History

Read about history in the following resource:

★ *American Pioneers and Patriots* p. 157-159

Key Idea: As the two parts of the railroad track came closer to meeting, the Irish and the Chinese workers began to race. Each side tried to lay more track than the other. Mike rode the horse that pulled the loads of rails.

History Activity

Say, *Let's have a race like the men who were finishing the railroad track.* Place a laundry basket at one end of the room. Place a masking tape line to be the starting line at the other end of the room. Have the students stand behind the starting line. Give each student a bowl with 10 pairs of socks in it. Tell students they must take one pair of socks at a time out of their bowl and place them in the laundry basket. They may not throw the socks. Race to see who can get all 10 pairs of socks in the basket first. Then, have students get out their timeline. Say, *Let's find the column that says 1800. Draw a small railroad track in that column. Write 'Transcontinental Railroad, 1862' under it.*

Key Idea: The men raced to see who could lay the most track in one day.

Poetry and Rhymes

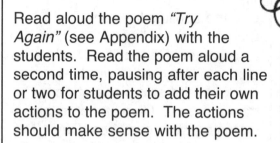

Read aloud the poem *"Try Again"* (see Appendix) with the students. Read the poem aloud a second time, pausing after each line or two for students to add their own actions to the poem. The actions should make sense with the poem.

Key Idea: Read classic poetry.

Bible Study

Say Philippians 3:13-14 with the students. Use the hand motions you added on Day 1. Next, have students skip around the room until you say, *Freeze.* After they 'freeze', have the students recite the entire Bible verse. Have students repeat the activity.

✓ Text Connection: *Morning Bells* p. 94-96

Key Idea: Even though the Irish didn't win the race, Mike needed to set aside his anger with the Chinese. Both sides had worked hard to finish the track. It hadn't been easy for either side.

Corresponding Music

None this lesson

Learning the Basics

Focus: Language Arts and Math

Unit 34 - Day 3

Language Arts

Using the spelling list from Day 1, choose 3 or more words that the students need to practice. Guide students to use each of the words you chose in a sentence. Write down the sentences as the students dictate them to you. Underline the spelling word in each sentence. Tell students to copy the sentences on paper, check them, and correct any mistakes. <u>Copywork</u>: Have students copy part of *"Try Again"*.

<u>Key Idea</u>: Practice spelling words.

Reading Choices

Choose **one** of the reading options listed below (see Appendix for details).

★ A phonics program
★ *Scheduled Books for Emerging Readers*
★ *Drawn into the Heart of Reading Level 2/3*

<u>Key Idea</u>: Use a step-by-step program for reading instruction.

Storytime

Say, *Compare means to notice things that are the same between two items. Contrast means to notice things that are different between two items. Look at the cover or find a picture in the book that shows one of the characters in the story. Compare and contrast yourself with the character in the picture. How are you the same? How are you different?* Read aloud the next portion of the folk tale that you selected. Say, *Name one problem in the story. What problem have you had that was similar? How did you solve the problem? How do you think the problem will be solved in the story?*

<u>Key Idea</u>: Focus on the story element: *compare* and *contrast*.

Math Exploration

These are the concepts that are covered in this review: adding and subtracting with 'tens' and 'ones', combining pieces to form a whole shape, coloring fractional parts including one-half and one-fourth, and reading a graph. Review any concepts that students had difficulty understanding. Also, complete the assigned review in the workbook listed below.

✔ <u>Text Connection</u>: *Primary Mathematics Workbook 1B* p. 171-172

<u>Key Idea</u>: Review difficult concepts.

Learning Through History

Focus: The Transcontinental Railroad

Unit 34 - Day 4

Reading About History

Read about history in the following resource:

★ *American Pioneers and Patriots* p. 160-162

Key Idea: When the railroad was finally finished, the nation was excited. Americans from all different backgrounds came together to celebrate. The railroad helped make travel easier across America.

Poetry and Rhymes

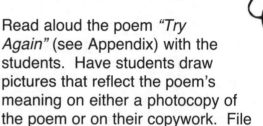

Read aloud the poem *"Try Again"* (see Appendix) with the students. Have students draw pictures that reflect the poem's meaning on either a photocopy of the poem or on their copywork. File the finished poem in a special place.

Key Idea: Read classic poetry.

Science Exploration

Guide students to make an edible model of the layers of the Earth. Give each student a clear glass. Use cooked vanilla pudding or a heated marshmallow as the deepest layer in the glass, which would be the Earth's core. On top of the core, add chocolate chips or raisins to be the Earth's rocky layer. On top of the rocky layer, sprinkle crushed graham crackers to be Earth's outer soil layer. Allow students to eat the model when it is finished.

✔ Text Connection: *God's Wonderful Works* p. 40-42

Key Idea: The Chinese railroad workers had to blast through mountains and cut through rock as they built the railroad.

Bible Study

Say Philippians 3:13-14 with the students. Use the hand motions you added on Day 1. Ask, *Name some things that get in the way of doing what Christ wants you to do. How can you put aside those things, so you can work harder for Christ? What race does Christ want you to run for Him? Describe the prize you will receive someday.* Next, have students run in place. When you say, *Freeze,* have the students stop and recite the entire Bible verse. Repeat the activity several times.

Key Idea: The railroad workers worked hard to finish the job.

Corresponding Music

None this lesson

Learning the Basics

Focus: Language Arts and Math

Unit 34 - Day 4

Language Arts

Use the spelling list from Day 1. Say each word and use it in a sentence. Have students write each word and check it with the matching word card from Day 1. Guide students to correct any mistakes. For each missed word, have students trace the word with their finger on a patch of carpet.

Copywork: Have students copy part of the poem *"Try Again"*.

Key Idea: Practice spelling words.

Reading Choices

Choose **one** of the reading options listed below (see Appendix for details).

★ A phonics program
★ *Scheduled Books for Emerging Readers*
★ *Drawn into the Heart of Reading Level 2/3*

Key Idea: Use a step-by-step program for reading instruction.

Storytime

Say, *Virtue is listening to the Holy Spirit to do what is right and good so that you may follow God's law.* Introduce the key verse Proverbs 20:11 to illustrate *virtue.* List some examples of times when you have done what is right and good. Ask your students to share times when they have done what is right and good (i.e. sharing, forgiving, praying, speaking respectfully, honoring your parents, reading your Bible, listening in church). Read aloud the next portion of the folk tale that you selected. Ask, *How do the characters do what is right and good? What could the characters do to show more virtue?*

Key Idea: Focus on the Godly character trait: *virtue.*

Math Exploration

These are the concepts that are covered in this review: adding money, comparing the cost of two differently-priced items, and solving word problems. Review any concepts that students had difficulty understanding. Also, complete the assigned review in the workbook listed below.

✔ Text Connection: *Primary Mathematics Workbook 1B* p. 173-174

Key Idea: Review difficult concepts.

Learning Through History

Focus: The Transcontinental Railroad

Unit 34 - Day 5

Reading About History

Read the following passage from your own Bible:

Philippians 3:12-4:1

Key Idea: Many of the pioneers needed faith in God as they started new lives in America. They wanted a different life from the one they knew. As Christians, others should see that we are different too. We need to try to be more like Christ each day as we wait for His return.

Artistic Expression

Read Philippians 3:20-21. Add food coloring to evaporated milk **or** condensed milk to make several different colors of paint. Have students use the milk-based paint to paint a picture of multi-colored clouds that remind them of heaven. Make sure that students do not apply the paint too thickly, as it will take a very long time to dry.

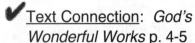Text Connection: *God's Wonderful Works* p. 4-5

Key Idea: Jesus Christ could return at any time. Are you ready for His return? If you've asked Jesus into your heart, you will have a home with Him in heaven someday.

Poetry and Rhymes

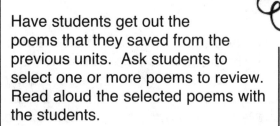

Have students get out the poems that they saved from the previous units. Ask students to select one or more poems to review. Read aloud the selected poems with the students.

Key Idea: Read classic poetry.

Bible Study

Ask, *In Philippians 3:12, what does Paul say you should 'take hold of' or follow? Have you asked Jesus into your heart? Once you have, how should you live your life? In Philippians 3:18-19, what does Paul warn you about? Where should your mind be instead of on earthly things? How can you stand up for Jesus?* Ask students to share their memory verse, Philippians 3:13-14, with someone special. Suggestions for sharing the verse include saying it to another family member, saying it to someone by telephone, reciting it to a stuffed animal, or writing it to mail.

Key Idea: Jesus wants to live in your heart. Ask Him in today.

Corresponding Music

None this lesson

Learning the Basics

Focus: Language Arts and Math

Unit 34 - Day 5

Language Arts

Write the following parts of a friendly letter on paper:

Today's Date

Dear ____, (**Greeting**)

I have been busy ... (**Body**)

        Sincerely, (**Closing**)
        Your name

Ask, *Which part comes first in a letter? What part is next? What punctuation mark do you see at the end of the greeting? What do you think the body of the letter contains? After the body, what comes last? Which punctuation mark do you see at the end of the closing?* Help students write a short friendly letter to someone.

<u>Key Idea</u>: Write a friendly letter.

Reading Choices

Choose **one** of the reading options listed below (see Appendix for details).

★ A phonics program

★ *Scheduled Books for Emerging Readers*

★ *Drawn into the Heart of Reading Level 2/3*

<u>Key Idea</u>: Use a step-by-step program for reading instruction.

Math Exploration

These are the concepts that are covered in this review: solving word problems using addition, subtraction, and multiplication, and solving word problems that involve money. Review any concepts that students had difficulty understanding. Also, complete the assigned review in the workbook listed below.

✔ <u>Text Connection</u>: *Primary Mathematics Workbook 1B* p. 175-176

Note: Use money or other manipulatives as needed to help solve the problems.

<u>Key Idea</u>: Review difficult concepts.

Storytime

Read aloud the final portion of the folk tale that you selected. Page through the book and show the students any pictures in the book to remind them of the different folk tales that you read. Ask, *Which folk tale or part of a folk tale was your favorite? Retell it. Why did you like that part best?*

<u>Key Idea</u>: Give students practice retelling a portion of a folk tale.

Appendix

Overview of Reading Choices

Note: For reading, decide which level best fits your child: beginning reader, emerging reader, or independent reader. Choose **one** of the reading options listed below that level.

If your child is a beginning reader, choose one of the phonics options below:

Reading Made Easy by Valerie Bendt:
This phonics program includes 108 lessons. The author recommends covering 3 lessons each week with review between lessons. This plan will allow a child to finish this phonics program in a typical school year consisting of 36 weeks. However, the author firmly emphasizes the necessity of pacing the program as needed to help the child be successful. The author's website is www.ReadingMadeEasy.net

The Reading Lesson by Michael Levin and Charan Langton:
This phonics program includes 20 lessons that are approximately 20 pages each. For children under the age of five, the authors recommend covering one page per day. For children between the ages of five and six, the authors recommend covering two to three pages per day. For children over the age of six, the authors recommend covering three or more pages per day. They suggest that no longer than five to seven minutes should be spent on a page and lessons should be under fifteen minutes in length. A companion CD-ROM that follows the book is also available. The authors' website is www.readinglesson.com

Your own phonics program:
Since I believe phonics instruction is a very personal decision for each family, I specifically designed *Beyond Little Hearts for His Glory* to work with any phonics program that you choose.

If your child is an emerging reader, choose to follow the *Scheduled Books for Emerging Readers* found in the Appendix, or use your own program.

Scheduled Books for Emerging Readers (in the Appendix):
This reading schedule is recommended if you have already completed most of your phonics instruction and feel that your child needs a year to strengthen that reading ability. The 14 books used in the schedule have been carefully chosen for their interest and gradually increase in reading difficulty throughout the year.

Overview of Reading Choices
(continued)

If your child is an independent reader, choose *Drawn into the Heart of Reading Teacher's Guide* and *Level 2/3 Student Book,* or use your own program.

> ***Drawn into the Heart of Reading* by Carrie Austin:**
> This reading program is multi-level and is designed to use with any books you choose. It is available for students in levels 2-8. It is divided into nine literature units which can be used in any order.
>
> *Drawn into the Heart of Reading* is based on instructions and activities that work with any literature. It can be used with one or more students of multiple ages at the same time because it is structured around daily plans that are divided into three levels of instruction.
>
> *Drawn into the Heart of Reading* is intended for use year after year as you move students through the various levels of instruction. It is designed to teach students to evaluate characters using a Christian standard based on Godly traits.
>
> In order to use *Drawn into the Heart of Reading* for your independent reader, you will need the *Teacher's Guide* and the *Level 2/3 Student Book.* You may also choose whether to purchase the optional *Sample Book Ideas List* and *Book Projects to Send Home: Grade 2.*

Scheduled Books for Emerging Readers

When to use this Emerging Reader's Schedule: This reading schedule is recommended if you have already completed most of your phonics instruction and feel that your child needs a year to strengthen that reading ability. The schedule listed below has been carefully planned to utilize interesting books that gradually increase in reading difficulty throughout the year. Each book has an approximate reading level noted next to it. Your child should read the assigned pages out loud to you.

Required Books for the Emerging Reader's Schedule:

Note: The books listed below are required in order to use the Emerging Reader's Schedule. For ease of use, Heart of Dakota Publishing sells the books listed below as a set on the website www.heartofdakota.com or by telephone at (605) 428-4068. Book descriptions are from the publisher or book reviewer.

Units 1-9: Choose **one** of the following Bibles:

The Early Reader's Bible by V. Gilbert Beers, 1995 Zonderkidz (Revised)
> ISBN 0310701392, Reading Level: 2.0
> This Bible features 64 easy-to-read Bible stories, based on the 250 most common words used in early reader books. It includes colorful illustrations, stimulating questions, and real-life applications to increase children's understanding of God's word. This Bible is easier than *The Beginner's Bible*.

The Beginner's Bible by Mission City Press, 2005 Zonderkidz (Revised)
> ISBN 0310709628, Reading Level: 2.4
> Written for early readers, *The Beginner's Bible* has a higher reading level than *The Early Reader's Bible*. Updated in 2005 with vibrant new illustrations, text, and stories, this version includes 90 favorite Bible stories that have been rewritten in a way that children can understand.

Unit 10:

Owl at Home by Arnold Lobel, 1982 Harper Trophy
> ISBN 0064440346, Reading Level: 2.7
> Owl lives by himself in a warm little house. One evening he invites Winter to sit by the fire. Another time he finds strange bumps in his bedroom. And when Owl goes for a walk one night, he makes a friend that follows him all the way home. This book relates 5 different adventures with Owl that leave you smiling.

Unit 11:

Frog and Toad All Year by Arnold Lobel, 1984 Harper Trophy Reprint Edition
> ISBN 0064440591, Reading Level: 2.7
> In winter, spring, summer, and fall, Frog and Toad are always together. Here is a wise and wonderful story for each season of the year and one for Christmas too. You will laugh along with Frog and Toad.

Scheduled Books for Emerging Readers
(continued)

Unit 12:

Frog and Toad Are Friends by Arnold Lobel, 1979 Harper Trophy
> ISBN 0064440206, Reading Level: 2.9
> Frog and Toad are best friends, participating in all elements of life together. The endearing pair hop along through five enchanting stories, looking for lost buttons, greeting the spring, and waiting for mail. Their genuine care for each other provides a heart-warming read.

Unit 13:

Wagon Wheels by Barbara Brenner, 1993 Harper Collins Reprint Edition
> ISBN 0064440524, Reading Level 2.5
> The Muldie boys and their father have come a long way to Kansas after the Civil War to take advantage of the free land offered through the Homestead Act. But when Daddy moves on to build them a home, the three boys must care for themselves. They must learn to care for one another and face the dangers of the wilderness alone.

Unit 14:

Amelia Bedelia by Peggy Parish, 1992 Harper Trophy
> ISBN 0064441555, Reading Level: 3.1
> Amelia Bedelia is a housekeeper who takes her instructions quite literally, which leads to some extremely funny messes. But older children know better, and they love the fact that they know better. Young readers will find this bumbling, charming, eager-to-please housekeeper as irresistible as her employers do.

Unit 15:

Buffalo Bill and the Pony Express by Eleanor Coerr, 1996 Harper Trophy
> ISBN 0064442209, Reading Level: 2.7
> This easy reader relates the aventures of 16-year-old Bill Cody, as he goes to work for the Pony Express. He is chased by thieves, caught in terrible weather, and stalked by wolves, none of which are mentioned in his letters home. The story is fast paced, exciting, and filled with terrific illustrations.

Unit 16:

Prairie School by Avi, 2003 Harper Trophy
> ISBN 0060513187, Reading Level: 2.9
> Nine-year-old Noah loves living on the Colorado prairie in the 1880's where he helps his parents with all the work. When Aunt Dora comes from the East in her wheelchair to teach him how to read, he sees no need to do so. However, his aunt refuses to give up. Impressed by her knowledge, Noah decides to learn to read and write. He realizes his aunt has opened a world beyond the prairie to him.

Scheduled Books for Emerging Readers
(continued)

Units 17-18:

First Flight: The Story of Tom Tate and The Wright Brothers by George Shea, 1997
    Harper Trophy, ISBN 006442152, Reading Level: 2.9
When twelve-year-old Tom Tate hears that Wilbur and Orville Wright are building a flying machine, he can't wait to try it. Tom's dad thinks it's dangerous. Some people think the Wrights are crazy. Can Tom help the brothers get their dream off the ground? This story chronicles the trial-and-error method of inventing and testing the airplane at Kitty Hawk in 1903.

Units 19-25:

Christian Liberty Nature Reader: Book 1 (Second Edition) by Julia Wright et al, 1996
    Christian Liberty Press (2nd revised edition), Reading Level: 3.0
    ISBN 1930092512
This is from a book series explaining the wonders of nature from a Christian perspective. Particular insects or animals are discussed in an old-fashioned but informative style. The growth and habits of creatures such as wasps, bees, spiders, prairie animals, oysters, snails and many others are discussed. Children increase their understanding and delight in God's creation as they read.

Units 26-27:

Tornado by Betsy Byars, 1997 Harper Trophy Reprint Edition
    ISBN 0064420639, Reading Level: 3.1
Through well-chosen incidents and details, this transitional novel captures the love between a boy and a dog. While waiting for a storm to pass, the family farmhand, Pete, tells stories of his childhood and his dog Tornado. The episodes are fairly short and the illustrations convey the story's drama, warmth, and occasional humor.

Units 28-30:

Animal Adventures (Little House Chapter Book) by Laura Ingalls Wilder, 1997
    Harper Trophy, ISBN 0064420507, Reading Level: 2.8
In the unsettled West, Laura Ingalls and her family are surrounded by wild animals. From bears and deer to badgers and panthers, Laura always manages to find herself caught up in animal adventures. Gentle adaptations of the original celebrated stories have been gathered in this exciting chapter book.

Unit 31-32:

The Bears on Hemlock Mountain by Alice Dalgliesh, 1992 Aladdin reissue edition
    ISBN 0689716044, Reading Level: 3.4
A young boy is sent on an errand over Hemlock Mountain. He's not so sure he likes going alone, because there may be bears on the mountain. With the help of the big iron pot he borrows, he completes his errand with more than a little excitement along the way.

Scheduled Books for Emerging Readers
(continued)

Units 33-34:
The Courage of Sarah Noble by Alice Dalgliesh, 1991 Aladdin 2nd edition
    ISBN 0689715404, Reading Level: 3.4
    In 1707, young Sarah Noble and her father traveled through wilderness to build a new home for their family. *Keep up your courage, Sarah Noble,* her mother had said, but Sarah found that it was not always easy to feel brave inside. The dark woods were full of animals and Indians, too, and Sarah was only eight! This true story is inspiring, as Sarah learns that to be afraid yet be brave is the greatest courage of all.

Emerging Reader's Schedule:

Questions: Questions for each day vary to include all the levels of Bloom's Taxonomy so that you have variety in what you ask your child each lesson. The level of the question is listed in parentheses following each question. Narration starters are also given for your child at least once each week.

Supplemental Book Titles: An additional supplemental title has been listed in the schedule each week to direct you to other excellent books that your child will enjoy reading again and again. These supplemental titles are considered optional but were very carefully selected for their content and listed in order to gradually increase in reading difficulty throughout the year. Feel free to supplement with any titles that you prefer or may have on hand.

Unit 1:
Supplemental title for Unit 1 (optional): *Floss* by Kim Lewis, 1994 Candlewick
    ISBN 1564022714, Reading Level: 1.8

Day 1: *The Early Reader's Bible* p. 3-9 (includes questions in text) **OR**
    The Beginner's Bible (2005 Edition) p. 7-17 (use questions below)
    Questions:
    What did God create on each day of creation? (knowledge)
    Why did God rest on the seventh day? (application)
    What can you say about Adam and Eve? (comprehension)

Day 2: *The Early Reader's Bible* p. 11-17 (includes questions in text) **OR**
    The Beginner's Bible (2005 Edition) p. 18-25 (use questions below)
    Questions:
    Describe the Garden of Eden. (knowledge)
    Explain what was happening at the end of today's story. (comprehension)
    Why do you think Adam and Eve had to leave the Garden of Eden? (analysis)

Scheduled Books for Emerging Readers
(continued)

Day 3: *The Early Reader's Bible* p. 19-25 (includes questions in text) **OR**
The Beginner's Bible (2005 Edition) p. 26-33 (use questions below)
Questions:
Explain what the world was like during Noah's time. (comprehension)
How did Noah know how to build the ark? (knowledge)
What might have happened if Noah hadn't listened to God? (synthesis)

Day 4: *The Early Reader's Bible* p. 27-33 (includes questions in text) **OR**
The Beginner's Bible (2005 Edition) p. 34-45 (use questions below)
Questions:
Why did God confuse the languages at Babel? (knowledge)
What can you tell me about Abraham? (comprehension)
Do you agree with what Lot did? What can you learn from what happened between Lot and Abraham? (evaluation)

Day 5: *The Early Reader's Bible* p. 35-49 (includes questions in text) **OR**
The Beginner's Bible (2005 Edition) p. 46-57 (use questions below)
Question:
Tell me about Isaac. (narration)

Unit 2:
Supplemental title for Unit 2 (optional): *Daniel's Duck* by Clyde Robert Bulla, 1982 Harper Trophy, ISBN 0064440311, Reading Level: 1.8
Day 1: *The Early Reader's Bible* p. 51-57 (includes questions in text) **OR**
The Beginner's Bible (2005 Edition) p. 58-65 (use questions below)
Questions:
What did Jacob do to trick Isaac and get the blessing? (knowledge)
Why do you think Esau was so angry with Jacob? (analysis)
How did God show Jacob that He was with him? (comprehension)

Day 2: *The Early Reader's Bible* p. 59-65 (includes questions in text) **OR**
The Beginner's Bible (2005 Edition) p. 66-77 (use questions below)
Questions:
How did God bless Jacob? (comprehension)
Have you ever needed to ask someone for forgiveness? Explain. (application)
What made Joseph's brothers upset with him? (analysis)

Day 3: *The Early Reader's Bible* p. 67-73 (includes questions in text) **OR**
The Beginner's Bible (2005 Edition) p. 78-91 (use questions below)
Questions:
When Joseph was in Egypt, what happened to him? (knowledge)

Scheduled Books for Emerging Readers
(continued)

Explain why the king needed Joseph. (comprehension)
How would the story change if Joseph hadn't forgiven his brothers? (synthesis)

Day 4: *The Early Reader's Bible* p. 75-81 (includes questions in text) **OR**
The Beginner's Bible (2005 Edition) p. 92-103 (use questions below)
Questions:
Why did Moses' mother hide him in a basket in the Nile River? (knowledge)
Tell how God saved Moses. (comprehension)
Would you have gone to Egypt if you were Moses? Explain. (synthesis)

Day 5: *The Early Reader's Bible* p. 83-97 (includes questions in text) **OR**
The Beginner's Bible (2005 Edition) p. 104-110 (use questions below)
Question:
Tell me all that you know about the plagues in Egypt. (narration)

Unit 3:

Supplemental title for Unit 3 (optional): *Clara and the Bookwagon* by Nancy Smiler Levinson, 1991 Harper Trophy, ISBN 006441342, Reading Level: 2.2

Day 1: *The Early Reader's Bible* p. 99-105 (includes questions in text) **OR**
The Beginner's Bible (2005 Edition) p. 111-123 (use questions below)
Questions:
How did God save the Israelites from Pharaoh's army? (knowledge)
Explain how God took care of the Israelites in the desert. (comprehension)
Why do you think God gave us His commandments? (analysis)

Day 2: *The Early Reader's Bible* p. 107-113 (includes questions in text) **OR**
The Beginner's Bible (2005 Edition) p. 124-135 (use questions below)
Questions:
Who told Moses that Israel could take the new land with God's help? (knowledge)
Why did God cause the Israelites to wander in the desert for 40 years? (comprehension)
Describe how God gave the Israelites the city of Jericho. (evaluation)

Day 3: *The Early Reader's Bible* p. 115-121 (includes questions in text) **OR**
The Beginner's Bible (2005 Edition) p. 136-145 (use questions below)
Questions:
Tell me about Deborah. (comprehension)
How did God use Gideon? (knowledge)
Do you think Gideon was afraid to do what God asked? Explain. (analysis)

Scheduled Books for Emerging Readers
(continued)

Day 4: *The Early Reader's Bible* p. 123-129 (includes questions in text) **OR**
The Beginner's Bible (2005 Edition) p. 146-155 (use questions below)
Questions:
When did Samson lose his strength? (knowledge)
How did Samson die? (comprehension)
In what ways did God bless Ruth for her faithfulness to Him? (analysis)

Day 5: *The Early Reader's Bible* p. 131-145 (includes questions in text) **OR**
The Beginner's Bible (2005 Edition) p. 156-163 (use questions below)
Question:
Tell me about Samuel. (narration)

Unit 4:
Supplemental title for Unit 4 (optional): *Katy and the Big Snow* by Virginia Lee Burton, 1974 Houghton Mifflin, ISBN 0395185629, Reading Level: 2.3

Day 1: *The Early Reader's Bible* p. 147-153 (includes questions in text) **OR**
The Beginner's Bible (2005 Edition) p. 164-172 (use questions below)
Questions:
What warning did God give His people when they asked for a king? (knowledge)
Can you guess why Saul wasn't a good king? (synthesis)
Why was Samuel surprised when God chose David to be the next king? (analysis)

Day 2: *The Early Reader's Bible* p. 155-161 (includes questions in text) **OR**
The Beginner's Bible (2005 Edition) p. 173-185 (use questions below)
Questions:
How did David beat Goliath? (comprehension)
Describe David's job at King Saul's house. (knowledge)
Was it right for King Saul to be jealous of David? Explain. (evaluation)

Day 3: *The Early Reader's Bible* p. 163-169 (includes questions in text) **OR**
The Beginner's Bible (2005 Edition) p. 186-200 (use questions below)
Questions:
Why didn't King Saul ever catch David? (knowledge)
What can you learn about King David by reading his songs? (analysis)
What things did King Solomon do that pleased God? (comprehension)

Scheduled Books for Emerging Readers
(continued)

Day 4: *The Early Reader's Bible* p. 171-177 (includes questions in text) **OR**
The Beginner's Bible (2005 Edition) p. 201-208 (use questions below)
Questions:
Can you think of a way that King Ahab could solve his problem with God? Explain. (application)
What did God do to take care of Elijah when there was no rain or food? (knowledge)
How can you tell that the lady Elijah talked to trusted God? (comprehension)

Day 5: *The Early Reader's Bible* p. 179-193 (includes questions in text) **OR**
The Beginner's Bible (2005 Edition) p. 209-221 (use questions below)
Question:
Tell me what you read about Elijah. (narration)

Unit 5:
Supplemental title for Unit 5 (optional): *Snowshoe Thompson* by Nancy Smiler Levinson, 1996 Harper Trophy, ISBN 0064442063, Reading Level: 2.2

Day 1: *The Early Reader's Bible* p.195-201 (includes questions in text) **OR**
The Beginner's Bible (2005 Edition) p. 222-234 (use questions below)
Questions:
How did God do a miracle with the oil to help the woman save her two sons? (knowledge)
Can you explain how God blessed the woman from Shunem for her kindness to Elisha? (comprehension)
What lesson did you learn from the story about Namaan? (application)

Day 2: *The Early Reader's Bible* p. 203-209 (includes questions in text) **OR**
The Beginner's Bible (2005 Edition) p. 235-246 (use questions below)
Questions:
Why did King Josiah fix God's temple? (knowledge)
Can you explain why God wanted Esther to be queen? (comprehension)
What made Haman hate the Jewish people? (synthesis)

Day 3: *The Early Reader's Bible* p. 211-217 (includes questions in text) **OR**
The Beginner's Bible (2005 Edition) p. 247-256 (use questions below)
Questions:
Would you have bowed down to the idol if you knew you would be thrown into a fiery furnace if you didn't? (evaluation)
How would you describe Daniel? (knowledge)
Explain how God saved Daniel. (comprehension)

Scheduled Books for Emerging Readers
(continued)

Day 4: *The Early Reader's Bible* p. 219-225 (includes questions in text) **OR**
The Beginner's Bible (2005 Edition) p. 257-264 (use questions below)
Questions:
Why do you think Jonah didn't want to go to Ninevah? (analysis)
How did Jonah know that God had sent the storm? (evaluation)
What happened to Jonah after the fish spit him out? (comprehension)

Day 5: *The Early Reader's Bible* p. 227-241 (includes questions in text) **OR**
The Beginner's Bible (2005 Edition) p. 266-281 (use questions below)
Question:
Tell me about baby Jesus' birth. (narration)

Unit 6:
Supplemental title for Unit 6 (optional): *Dolphins* by Sharon Bokoske, 1993 Random House Books, ISBN 0679844376, Reading Level: 2.4

Day 1: *The Early Reader's Bible* p. 243-249 (includes questions in text) **OR**
The Beginner's Bible (2005 Edition) p. 282-290 (use questions below)
Questions:
Who did Mary and Joseph meet at the temple? (knowledge)
What can you tell me about King Herod? (comprehension)
Why was it better that Mary and Joseph took Jesus to Egypt after He was born instead of to Nazareth? (evaluation)

Day 2: *The Early Reader's Bible* p. 251-257 (includes questions in text) **OR**
The Beginner's Bible (2005 Edition) p. 291-302 (use questions below)
Questions:
Why did Joseph know it was safe to go back to Nazareth? (knowledge)
Explain what happened to Jesus in Jerusalem. (comprehension)
How do you think others could see that Jesus was special? (analysis)

Day 3: *The Early Reader's Bible* p. 259-265 (includes questions in text) **OR**
The Beginner's Bible (2005 Edition) p. 303-313 (use questions below)
Questions:
Who was John the Baptist? (knowledge)
Tell what happened when Jesus came to John to be baptized. (evaluation)
Why did the disciples choose to follow Jesus? (evaluation)

Scheduled Books for Emerging Readers
(continued)

Day 4: *The Early Reader's Bible* p. 267-273 (includes questions in text) **OR**
The Beginner's Bible (2005 Edition) p. 314-323 (use questions below)
Questions:
What did Jesus do at the wedding feast? (knowledge)
What does Jesus say we can learn from the birds and the flowers? (analysis)
Can you explain what the Lord's Prayer is telling you? (synthesis)

Day 5: *The Early Reader's Bible* p. 275-281 (includes questions in text) **OR**
The Beginner's Bible (2005 Edition) p. 324-333 (use questions below)
Question:
Tell me what you remember that Jesus said and did. (narration)

Unit 7:
Supplemental title for Unit 7 (optional): *Dust for Dinner* by Ann Turner, 1997 Harper Trophy Reprint, ISBN 006444225X, Reading Level: 2.4
Day 1: *The Early Reader's Bible* p. 283-297 (includes questions in text) **OR**
The Beginner's Bible (2005 Edition) p. 334-350 (use questions below)
Questions:
Why wasn't Jesus afraid during the storm? (evaluation)
Can you explain why the disciples were amazed when Jesus calmed the storm? (comprehension)
How did Jesus know that the woman had touched Him? (knowledge)

Day 2: *The Early Reader's Bible* p. 299-313 (includes questions in text) **OR**
The Beginner's Bible (2005 Edition) p. 351-363 (use questions below)
Questions:
How are the fish in the net like the Kingdom of God? (knowledge)
Why were Jesus and His disciples tired? (analysis)
What miracle did Jesus do to feed 5,000 people? (comprehension)

Day 3: *The Early Reader's Bible* p. 315-329 (includes questions in text) **OR**
The Beginner's Bible (2005 Edition) p. 364-370 (use questions below)
Questions:
Tell why the disciples were in the boat without Jesus. (comprehension)
If you were one of the disciples in the boat, how would you have acted when you saw Jesus walking on the water? (application)
What did Peter do when he saw Jesus? (knowledge)

Scheduled Books for Emerging Readers
(continued)

Day 4: *The Early Reader's Bible* p. 331-345 (includes questions in text) **OR**
The Beginner's Bible (2005 Edition) p. 371-378 (use questions below)
Question:
Tell about the miracles that Jesus did in the stories that you read today. (narration)

Day 5: *The Early Reader's Bible* p. 347-361 (includes questions in text) **OR**
The Beginner's Bible (2005 Edition) p. 379-390 (use questions below)
Questions:
Tell the story Jesus told about being a good neighbor. (knowledge)
How were Mary and Martha different? (comprehension)
Are you more like Mary or Martha? (synthesis)

Unit 8:
Supplemental title for Unit 8 (optional): *A Weekend with Wendell* by Kevin Henkes, 1995 Harper Trophy, ISBN 0688140246, Reading Level: 2.7

Day 1: *The Early Reader's Bible* p. 363-377 (includes questions in text) **OR**
The Beginner's Bible (2005 Edition) p. 391-404 (use questions below)
Questions:
Retell the story of the good shepherd. (comprehension)
Describe what happened to the lost son. (knowledge)
Explain how God is like the good shepherd and the father in the stories. (analysis)

Day 2: *The Early Reader's Bible* p. 379-393 (includes questions in text) **OR**
The Beginner's Bible (2005 Edition) p. 405-412 (use questions below)
Questions:
What should the sick men have done differently? (evaluation)
Why did only one sick man come back to see Jesus? (analysis)
How can you tell that children are important to Jesus? (comprehension)

Day 3: *The Early Reader's Bible* p. 395-409 (includes questions in text) **OR**
The Beginner's Bible (2005 Edition) p. 413-422 (use questions below)
Question:
Tell the stories of Zacchaeus and Lazarus. (narration)

Scheduled Books for Emerging Readers
(continued)

Day 4: *The Early Reader's Bible* p. 411-425 (includes questions in text) **OR**
The Beginner's Bible (2005 Edition) p. 423-436 (use questions below)
Questions:
What can you learn about Judas from this story? (analysis)
How would you describe Jesus' ride into Jerusalem on a donkey? (knowledge)
Explain what Jesus told the disciples about the woman who gave the two gold coins. (comprehension)

Day 5: *The Early Reader's Bible* p. 427-441 (includes questions in text) **OR**
The Beginner's Bible (2005 Edition) p. 437-445 (use questions below)
Question:
Why did Jesus wash the disciples' feet? (comprehension)
What would have happened if Jesus had stopped Judas? (application)
Can you explain how we still use the wine and the bread to remember Jesus? (synthesis)

Unit 9:
Supplemental title for Unit 9 (optional): *The Salamander Room* by Anne Mazer, 1994 Dragonfly Books, ISBN 0679861874, Reading Level: 3.0
Day 1: *The Early Reader's Bible* p. 443-457 (includes questions in text) **OR**
The Beginner's Bible (2005 Edition) p. 446-458 (use questions below)
Questions:
Why did Jesus go with the soldiers? (knowledge)
After Jesus died, what happened? (comprehension)
Do you think Mary was surprised to see Jesus? Why? (evaluation)

Day 2: *The Early Reader's Bible* p. 459-473 (includes questions in text) **OR**
The Beginner's Bible (2005 Edition) p. 459-465 (use questions below)
Questions:
Why were the disciples locked in the room? (knowledge)
How did the disciples know it was Jesus that came to visit them? (comprehension)
If you were Peter, how would you have felt to see Jesus again? Why? (application)

Scheduled Books for Emerging Readers
(continued)

Day 3: *The Early Reader's Bible* p. 475-489 (includes questions in text) **OR**
The Beginner's Bible (2005 Edition) p. 466-479 (use questions below)
Questions:
What did Jesus tell His disciples before He went to heaven? (knowledge)
How did Jesus go to heaven? (comprehension)
Can you explain what happened when the disciples received the gift of the Holy Spirit? (comprehension)

Day 4: *The Early Reader's Bible* p. 491-505 (includes questions in text) **OR**
The Beginner's Bible (2005 Edition) p. 480-493 (use questions below)
Questions:
Describe the first church. (knowledge)
Why was Peter able to heal the lame man? (analysis)
What happened to Saul? (comprehension)

Day 5: *The Early Reader's Bible* p. 507-513 (includes questions in text) **OR**
The Beginner's Bible (2005 Edition) p. 494-508 (use questions below)
Questions:
Tell me about Paul's journeys. (narration)
Describe John's vision. (narration)

Unit 10:
Supplemental title for Unit 10 (optional): *Corduroy* by Don Freeman, 1976 Puffin, ISBN 0140501738, Reading Level: 3.2

Day 1: *Owl at Home* p. 5-17
Questions:
Why did Owl keep answering the door? (knowledge)
Explain what happened when Owl let Winter into the house. (comprehension)
What other way could you plan to enjoy winter? (application)

Day 2: *Owl at Home* p.18-29
Questions:
What made Owl so upset? (knowledge)
Can you explain what the bumps were? (analysis)
How did Owl solve the problem? (comprehension)

Day 3: *Owl at Home* p. 30-39
Questions:
Why did Owl think of so many sad things? (knowledge)
List some of the sad things that Owl was thinking. (analysis)
What made the tea taste salty? (synthesis)

Scheduled Books for Emerging Readers
(continued)

Day 4: *Owl at Home* p. 40-49
>   Questions:
>   *What did Owl wonder about in this story?* (knowledge)
>   *How did Owl try to fix his problem?* (comprehension)
>   *Why did Owl choose to stop running up and down?* (evaluation)

Day 5: *Owl at Home* p. 50-end
>   Questions:
>   *What happened at the beginning of the story?* (narration)
>   *Name some of the reasons Owl gave the moon to stop following him.* (knowledge)
>   *How did the story end?* (narration)
>   *Do you think the moon was really following Owl home? Explain.* (analysis)

Unit 11:
Supplemental title for Unit 11 (optional): *The Big Balloon Race* by Eleanor Coerr, 1992, Harper Collins, ISBN 006440532, Reading Level: 2.5

Day 1: *Frog and Toad All Year* p. 4-17
>   Questions:
>   *How did Frog convince Toad to come outside and sled?* (analysis)
>   *What happened when Toad found out that he was alone on the sled?* (knowledge)
>   *Think of a time that you felt alone and scared. What did you do?* (application)

Day 2: *Frog and Toad All Year* p. 18-29
>   Questions:
>   *What did Frog's father really mean when he said, "Spring is just around the corner"?* (synthesis)
>   *Describe some things Frog saw as he searched for spring.* (knowledge)
>   *Name some signs that tell you spring has come.* (application)

Day 3: *Frog and Toad All Year* p. 30-41
>   Questions:
>   *Why did Toad get ice cream for Frog?* (comprehension)
>   *What problems did Toad have as he was carrying the ice cream back to Frog?* (knowledge)
>   *Explain why Frog and Toad ate their next ice cream cones in the shade.* (evaluation)

Scheduled Books for Emerging Readers
(continued)

Day 4: *Frog and Toad All Year* p. 42-53
    Questions:
    How did Frog and Toad help each other? (comprehension)
    What happened after Frog and Toad raked the leaves? (knowledge)
    Did Frog or Toad know that their leaf pile had blown all over the lawn again? Why not? (analysis)

Day 5: *Frog and Toad All Year* p. 54-end
    Questions:
    Tell me about Toad. (narration)
    Tell me about Frog. (narration)
    How are they different from one another? (comprehension)

Unit 12:
Supplemental title for Unit 12 (optional): *Whales: The Gentle Giants* by Joyce Milton, 1989 Random House Books, ISBN 0394898095, Reading Level: 2.5

Day 1: *Frog and Toad Are Friends* p. 4-15
    Questions:
    How did Frog try to get Toad to come outside? (comprehension)
    Why had Toad been sleeping so long? (analysis)
    What did Frog do to show Toad it was spring? (knowledge)

Day 2: *Frog and Toad Are Friends* p. 16-27
    Questions:
    List some of the ways that Toad tried to think of a story to tell Frog. (comprehension)
    Can you explain what made Toad feel sick, so he had to go to bed? (synthesis)
    Retell the story that Frog told Toad. (comprehension)

Day 3: *Frog and Toad Are Friends* p. 28-39
    Questions:
    How did Frog help Toad? (comprehension)
    Describe some of the different buttons that Frog and Toad found. (knowledge)
    Did you like the way the story ended? Why, or why not? (evaluation)

Day 4: *Frog and Toad Are Friends* p. 40-52
    Questions:
    Why didn't Toad want Frog to look at him? (comprehension)
    Who were some of the animals that came to see Toad's bathing suit? (knowledge)
    What lesson did you learn from the story? (application)

Scheduled Books for Emerging Readers
(continued)

Day 5: *Frog and Toad Are Friends* p. 53-end
    Question:
    Tell me about Frog and Toad and the letter. (narration)

Unit 13:
Supplemental title for Unit 13 (optional): *Keep the Lights Burning Abbie* by Peter Roop, 1987 Lerner Publishing Group, ISBN 0876144547, Reading Level: 2.2
Day 1: *Wagon Wheels* p. 7-17
    Questions:
    What made the Muldie family come to Kansas? (knowledge)
    Describe a dugout. (comprehension)
    Why did Daddy choose to build a dugout instead of a wood house? (evaluation)

Day 2: *Wagon Wheels* p.18-29
    Questions:
    When winter came, what happened in Nicodemus? (comprehension)
    What did the Osage Indians do? (knowledge)
    How do you think the Indians knew that the settlers were cold and hungry? (analysis)

Day 3: *Wagon Wheels* p. 30-43
    Questions:
    When it was spring, what did Daddy do? (knowledge)
    How did the Muldie boys take care of themselves? (comprehension)
    What worries might the boys have? (evaluation)

Day 4: *Wagon Wheels* p. 44-51
    Questions:
    How long did it take to get a letter from Daddy? (knowledge)
    What did the letter from Daddy say to the boys? (comprehension)
    Can you explain why Daddy didn't come and get the boys himself? (synthesis)

Day 5: *Wagon Wheels* p. 52-end
    Question:
    Tell about the boys' trip to meet their father. (narration)

Unit 14:
Supplemental title for Unit 14 (optional): *A Chair for my Mother* by Vera B. Williams, 1984 Harper Trophy reprint edition, ISBN 0688040748, Reading Level: 2.5

Scheduled Books for Emerging Readers
(continued)

Day 1: *Amelia Bedelia* p. 6-15
    Questions:
    How long has Amelia Bedelia worked for the Rogers? (knowledge)
    What does Amelia Bedelia think about the Rogers? (comprehension)
    If you wanted to surprise your mom or dad, what kind thing would you do for them? (application)

Day 2: *Amelia Bedelia* p. 16-27
    Questions:
    Name some silly things that Amelia Bedelia did. (knowledge)
    Why did Amelia Bedelia do those things? (analysis)
    What do you think Mrs. Rogers really wanted Amelia Bedelia to do? (evaluation)

Day 3: *Amelia Bedelia* p. 28-37
    Questions:
    What reason did Amelia Bedelia give for hanging the lights outside? (knowledge)
    Describe what Amelia Bedelia did with the rice. (comprehension)
    Explain what Mrs. Rogers really meant. (evaluation)

Day 4: *Amelia Bedelia* p. 38-49
    Questions:
    What did Amelia Bedelia do to the steak? (knowledge)
    Can you explain why Amelia Bedelia put clothes on the chicken? (synthesis)
    How do you know Mr. and Mrs. Rogers are upset? (analysis)

Day 5: *Amelia Bedelia* p. 50-end
    Question:
    Describe some of the surprises that Mr. and Mrs. Rogers found when they came home. (narration)

Unit 15:
Supplemental title for Unit 15 (optional): *The Bravest Dog Ever: The True Story of Balto,* by Natalie Standiford, 1989 Random House Books, ISBN 0394896955
    Reading Level: 2.5
Day 1: *Buffalo Bill and the Pony Express* p. 5-17
    Questions:
    Explain what you've learned so far about Buffalo Bill. (comprehension)
    Name the rules that Mr. Majors gave Buffalo Bill. (knowledge)
    Why do you think Bill wanted to be a pony express rider? (analysis)

Scheduled Books for Emerging Readers
(continued)

Day 2: *Buffalo Bill and the Pony Express* p. 18-31
    Questions:
    What happened on Bill's ride? (comprehension)
    Why did Bill fall asleep at the table? (analysis)
    How would you explain Bill's letter to his ma? (evaluation)

Day 3: *Buffalo Bill and the Pony Express* p. 32-43
    Questions:
    Describe the problems that Bill ran into on this ride. (comprehension)
    How did Bill get away from the wolves? (knowledge)
    What did Bill leave out of his letters to his ma? (evaluation)

Day 4: *Buffalo Bill and the Pony Express* p. 44-53
    Questions:
    Explain the problems with Bill carrying the money to Three Crossings. (comprehension)
    What made Chief-Rain-in-the-Face upset? (knowledge)
    Can you guess why Bill is making a straw man? (synthesis)

Day 5: *Buffalo Bill and the Pony Express* p. 54-64
    Questions:
    Describe Bill's plan to get the money to Three Crossings. (narration)
    What was so funny about Bill's last letter to his ma? (evaluation)

Unit 16:
Supplemental title for Unit 16 (optional): *The Josefina Story Quilt* by Eleanor Coerr, 1989 Harper Trophy, ISBN 0064441296, Reading Level: 2.7

Day 1: *Prairie School* p. 4-7
    Questions:
    Can you list some of Noah's jobs on the farm? (knowledge)
    Explain why Ma and Pa want Noah to have "schooling". (comprehension)
    Why do you think Noah is upset? (analysis)

Day 2: *Prairie School* p. 8-11
    Questions:
    What happened to Aunt Dora? (knowledge)
    How is Noah acting about his "schooling"? (comprehension)
    Why did Aunt Dora choose to come to school Noah? (evaluation)

Scheduled Books for Emerging Readers
(continued)

Day 3: *Prairie School* p. 12-19
    Questions:
    What excuses did Noah come up with to miss school? (comprehension)
    Why was Aunt Dora so upset on Saturday? (analysis)
    If you were Aunt Dora, what would you do? (synthesis)

Day 4: *Prairie School* p. 20-25
    Questions:
    How did Aunt Dora get Noah to pay attention? (comprehension)
    Why did Noah think Aunt Dora was so smart? (analysis)
    What are some new things that you have learned from reading books? (synthesis)

Day 5: *Prairie School* p. 26-29
    Question:
    What did Aunt Dora tell Noah about the stars and about reading? (narration)

Unit 17:
Supplemental title for Unit 17 (optional): *The Long Way Westward* by Joan Sandin, 1992 Harper Trophy, ISBN 0064441989, Reading Level: 2.7

Day 1: *Prairie School* p. 30-34
    Questions:
    How can you tell that it was hard work for Noah to learn his letters? (comprehension)
    What is something that you have had to work hard to learn? (application)
    Why were Noah's mother and father so excited that Noah knew his letters? (evaluation)

Day 2: *Prairie School* p. 35-42
    Questions:
    How had Noah's life changed? (comprehension)
    What did Mother and Father say about Noah's reading? (knowledge)
    Why didn't Mother or Father read to the family after dinner? (analysis)

Day 3: *Prairie School* p. 43-end
    Questions:
    When Aunt Dora was leaving, how was Noah different from when she first came? (analysis)
    Tell me about Aunt Dora's letter. (comprehension)
    What did Noah's letter mean? (synthesis)

Scheduled Books for Emerging Readers
(continued)

Day 4: *First Flight* p. 4-11
   Questions:
   Retell the story Tom told Will and Orv about the fish. (comprehension)
   Explain why Will and Orv had come to Kitty Hawk. (knowledge)
   Why didn't Ned or Laura believe Tom? (analysis)

Day 5: *First Flight* p. 12-21
   Questions:
   Describe what happened when Tom flew in the flying machine. (narration)
   Then, what did Will and Orv do? (narration)

Unit 18:
Supplemental title for Unit 18 (optional): *The Story of Ferdinand* by Munro Leaf, 1977
   Picture Puffins, ISBN 0140502343, Reading Level: 2.9
Day 1: *First Flight* p. 22-27
   Questions:
   When Will and Orv came back, what happened? (comprehension)
   Why didn't Pa want Tom to ride in the machine? (knowledge)
   How can you tell that Will and Orv are discouraged? (evaluation)

Day 2: *First Flight* p. 28-31
   Questions:
   Describe the new flying machine. (comprehension)
   What did Will and Orv decide to add to the machine? (knowledge)
   How will they test the engine and propellers? (synthesis)

Day 3: *First Flight* p. 32-37
   Questions:
   List some of Will and Orv's problems. (knowledge)
   Why were the rescue workers at Will and Orv's camp? (comprehension)
   What made Will and Orv test the machine on such a stormy day? (evaluation)

Day 4: *First Flight* p. 38-end
   Questions:
   Describe Orv's flight. (knowledge)
   Why did everyone cheer? (analysis)
   What lesson can you learn from Will and Orv? (application)

Day 5: *Christian Liberty Nature Reader: Book One* p. 1-middle of 3
   Question:
   Tell me about what the mother mud wasp does. (narration)

Scheduled Books for Emerging Readers
(continued)

Unit 19:
<u>Supplemental title for Unit 19</u> (optional): *The Little House* by Virginia Lee Burton, 1978 Houghton Mifflin, ISBN 039525938X, Reading Level: 2.8

<u>Day 1</u>: *Christian Liberty Nature Reader: Book One* p. 3-5
<u>Questions</u>:
Explain how the baby mud wasp grows and changes. (comprehension)
How does the paper wasp build her nest? (knowledge)
Have you ever seen a paper wasp's or mud wasp's nest? (application)

<u>Day 2</u>: *Christian Liberty Nature Reader: Book One* p. 6-8
<u>Questions</u>:
Compare the mud wasp and the paper wasp. (evaluation)
What are some of the jobs in the colony? (comprehension)
When the weather grows cold, what do the paper wasps do? (knowledge)

<u>Day 3</u>: *Christian Liberty Nature Reader: Book One* p. 9-11
<u>Questions</u>:
How is a digger wasp different from other wasps? (analysis)
Name some ways that the digger wasp is like the mud wasp. (knowledge)
What can you tell me about spiders? (comprehension)

<u>Day 4</u>: *Christian Liberty Nature Reader: Book One* p. 12-part of 15
<u>Questions</u>:
Suppose you see a spider outside, what should you do? (synthesis)
How did the spider fool the mud wasp? (comprehension)
What part do spiders have in God's plan? (knowledge)

<u>Day 5</u>: *Christian Liberty Nature Reader: Book One* p. 15-middle of 19
<u>Question</u>:
Describe the two new types of spiders that you learned about today. (narration)

Unit 20:
<u>Supplemental title for Unit 20</u> (optional): *Doctor De Soto* by William Steig, 1990 Farrar, Straus and Giroux Reissue edition, ISBN 0374418101, Reading Level: 2.9

<u>Day 1</u>: *Christian Liberty Nature Reader: Book One* p. 19-part of 22
<u>Questions</u>:
Explain what you learned about the mother spider with the egg sac. (comprehension)
How does the spider make a bridge over the water? (knowledge)
Have you seen any of the spiders that we have read about? If so, which ones? (application)

Scheduled Books for Emerging Readers
(continued)

Day 2: *Christian Liberty Nature Reader: Book One* p. 22-middle of 26
   Questions:
   How can a spider live under water? (comprehension)
   What does a trap door spider do to make her home? (knowledge)
   Which of the spiders did you find most interesting? Why? (evaluation)

Day 3: *Christian Liberty Nature Reader: Book One* p. 26-30
   Questions:
   Name some of the animal sounds that you can hear on a summer night. (application)
   Why do the white butterflies land on cabbage leaves? (knowledge)
   Can you explain how an egg becomes a butterfly? (analysis)

Day 4: *Christian Liberty Nature Reader: Book One* p. 31-part of 35
   Questions:
   What are the 3 types of bees, and what do they do? (knowledge)
   Tell me some interesting things that you learned about the queen bee. (comprehension)
   Can you guess what would happen if the old queen bee didn't leave the hive when the new queens were hatching? (synthesis)

Day 5: *Christian Liberty Nature Reader: Book One* p. 35-38
   Question:
   Tell me what you learned about cicadas. (narration)

Unit 21:
Supplemental title for Unit 21 (optional): *The Drinking Gourd: A Story of the Underground Railroad* by F.N. Monjo, 1993 Harper Collins, ISBN 0064440427
   Reading Level: 2.5

Day 1: *Christian Liberty Nature Reader: Book One* p. 39- top of 43
   Questions:
   How are the male and female basket moths different? (knowledge)
   What is special about the caddisworm? (comprehension)
   Based on what you know, how would you explain metamorphosis? (evaluation)

Day 2: *Christian Liberty Nature Reader: Book One* p. 43-part of 46
   Questions:
   Where do mosquitos lay their eggs? (knowledge)
   Explain the changes that a mosquito goes through. (comprehension)
   Why don't you want mosquitos in your yard? (analysis)

Scheduled Books for Emerging Readers
(continued)

Day 3: *Christian Liberty Nature Reader: Book One* p. 46-middle of 49
    Questions:
    What are some special body parts on a housefly? (knowledge)
    How can a housefly make us sick? (synthesis)
    List 3 things that you learned about the ichneumon fly. (comprehension)

Day 4: *Christian Liberty Nature Reader: Book One* p. 49-middle of 52
    Questions:
    Describe the bald eagle. (comprehension)
    Where does the leaf-cutter bee lay her eggs? (knowledge)
    Do you think that the leaf-cutter bee stays with its babies? Why, or why not? (analysis)

Day 5: *Christian Liberty Nature Reader: Book One* p. 52-part of 55
    Questions:
    What did you learn about the cuckoo bee? (narration)
    Discuss what you read about the butterfly. (narration)

Unit 22:
Supplemental title for Unit 22 (optional): *The Little Red Lighthouse and the Great Gray Bridge* by Hildegarde H. Swift, 2002 Harcourt Books, ISBN 0152045732
    Reading Level: 2.9

Day 1: *Christian Liberty Nature Reader: Book One* p. 55-part of 58
    Questions:
    Where did the baby gallfly get his house (or gall)? (knowledge)
    What does the gallfly do with his house? (comprehension)
    Look at the pictures on p. 56 and 58. How big do you think a gall might be? (application)

Day 2: *Christian Liberty Nature Reader: Book One* p. 58-part of 62
    Questions:
    What special body parts did God give the grasshopper? (analysis)
    Explain how a grasshopper "molts". (comprehension)
    Where have all the little creatures gone in the winter? (knowledge)

Day 3: *Christian Liberty Nature Reader: Book One* p. 62-top of 67
    Questions:
    When spring comes, what happens to God's creation? (comprehension)
    What is a prairie? (knowledge)
    Suppose you could visit the prairie, what might you see? (synthesis)

Scheduled Books for Emerging Readers
(continued)

Day 4: *Christian Liberty Nature Reader: Book One* p. 67-top of 70
   Questions:
   List some ways that prairie animals protect themselves from prairie hunters. (knowledge)
   Why are prairie hunters needed on the prairie? (comprehension)
   What do you think of the coyote's trick? (evaluation)

Day 5: *Christian Liberty Nature Reader: Book One* p. 70-73
   Question:
   Tell about the special gifts that God gave the owl, the squirrel, and the beaver. (narration)

Unit 23:

Supplemental title for Unit 23 (optional): *Blaze and the Lost Quarry* by C.W. Anderson, 1994 Aladdin Reprint edition, ISBN 068971775X, Reading Level: 3.4

Day 1: *Christian Liberty Nature Reader: Book One* p. 74-half of 77
   Questions:
   Describe a beaver's house. (comprehension)
   Why do beavers build a dam? (knowledge)
   What unique body parts did God give the beaver? (analysis)

Day 2: *Christian Liberty Nature Reader: Book One* p. 77-79
   Questions:
   Name some of the things that are different about the hen and the duck. (comprehension)
   Have you ever see a hen or a duck? What did you notice? (application)
   What can you learn from the pages that you read today? (synthesis)

Day 3: *Christian Liberty Nature Reader: Book One* p. 80-83
   Questions:
   How does a fish's coat keep the water out? (knowledge)
   Why can birds fly when many other animals cannot? (evaluation)
   What did you learn about an oyster? (comprehension)

Day 4: *Christian Liberty Nature Reader: Book One* p. 84-part of 87
   Questions:
   In what ways does a bear's coat protect him? (knowledge)
   How does a cuttlefish get away from a big fish? (comprehension)
   Why do you think God gave each animal a way to protect itself? (analysis)

Scheduled Books for Emerging Readers
(continued)

Day 5: *Christian Liberty Nature Reader: Book One* p. 87-89
    Question:
    Tell me about the changes that a moth goes through. (narration)

Unit 24:
Supplemental title for Unit 24 (optional): *The Mitten* by Jan Brett, 1989 Putnam
    Juvenile, ISBN 039921920X, Reading Level: 3.0
Day 1: *Christian Liberty Nature Reader: Book One* p. 90-half of 93
    Questions:
    Why does a kingbird seem tough and brave? (comprehension)
    How does a robin protect his mate? (knowledge)
    Have you ever seen a robin? How could you tell if it was a male or a female?
    (application)

Day 2: *Christian Liberty Nature Reader: Book One* p. 93-part of 99
    Questions:
    What does an ant do when it finds food? (knowledge)
    Explain some strange new things that you learned about ants.
    (comprehension)
    Why are aphids so important to honey ants? (analysis)

Day 3: *Christian Liberty Nature Reader: Book One* p. 99-104
    Questions:
    Describe a flea. (comprehension)
    How is a mayfly different from other flies? (analysis)
    *What would happen if the beetles gave up rolling the ball to a safe place and
    left it?* (synthesis)

Day 4: *Christian Liberty Nature Reader: Book One* p. 105-part of 108
    Questions:
    Look at the picture on p. 106. Explain the carpenter bee's house.
    (comprehension)
    Why do you think God made the walking stick the way that He did?
    (knowledge)
    *What can you learn about God from looking at the animals and insects that He
    created?* (evaluation)

Day 5: *Christian Liberty Nature Reader: Book One* p. 108-111
    Question:
    Explain what you learned about the ladybug. (narration)

Scheduled Books for Emerging Readers
(continued)

Unit 25:
Supplemental title for Unit 25 (optional): *Bread and Jam for Frances* by Russell Hoban, 1993 Harper Trophy Reprint edition, ISBN 0064430960, Reading Level: 2.8

Day 1: *Christian Liberty Nature Reader: Book One* p. 112-116
  Questions:
  What trick does the mother quail use to protect her nest? (knowledge)
  Act out the way the inchworm walks. (comprehension)
  Have you ever seen a firefly? Explain. (application)

Day 2: *Christian Liberty Nature Reader: Book One* p. 117-top of 120
  Questions:
  What would happen if the bees didn't carry pollen from one clover to another? (knowledge)
  How are earthworms helpful to the soil? (comprehension)
  Why do you see so many earthworms after it rains? (synthesis)

Day 3: *Christian Liberty Nature Reader: Book One* p. 120-123
  Questions:
  List some interesting things about hummingbirds. (knowledge)
  Describe the changes that happen to a tomato worm. (comprehension)
  How might people confuse the hawkmoth with a hummingbird? (analysis)

Day 4: *Christian Liberty Nature Reader: Book One* p. 124-half of 128
  Questions:
  What makes the snail move so slowly? (knowledge)
  How do dragonflies help people? (comprehension)
  Why is the water a good place for the dragonfly nymph to be born? (evaluation)

Day 5: *Christian Liberty Nature Reader: Book One* p. 128-top of 133
  Questions:
  Explain what you've learned about how God's creatures care for themselves. (narration)
  How are human babies different from all other babies? (analysis)

Unit 26:
Supplemental title for Unit 26 (optional): *Miss Rumphius* by Barbara Cooney, 1985 Puffin Books, ISBN 0140505393, Reading Level: 2.8

Scheduled Books for Emerging Readers
(continued)

Day 1: *Christian Liberty Nature Reader: Book One* p. 133-top of 138
    Questions:
    What makes man special? (evaluation)
    How is man different from the animals? (analysis)
    List some inventions that God has given man the wisdom to make. (knowledge)

Day 2: *Christian Liberty Nature Reader: Book One* p. 138-141
    Questions:
    Explain how we are like the tumblebug. (comprehension)
    What lesson can we learn from the butterfly? (application)
    What does man need to do to be saved? (knowledge)

Day 3: *Christian Liberty Nature Reader: Book One* p. 142-146
    Questions:
    Why do some poems say, "Author Unknown", at the bottom? (synthesis)
    What is a hymn? (comprehension)
    Which of the poems that you read today was your favorite? Let's read it again together. (application)

Day 4: *Tornado* p. 1-5
    Questions:
    What is a twister? (knowledge)
    Why was Mother worried? (comprehension)
    How do you think the dog came to be called "Tornado"? (analysis)

Day 5: *Tornado* p. 6-12
    Question:
    Describe what the tornado did. (narration)

Unit 27:
Supplemental title for Unit 27 (optional): *Buttons for General Washington* by Peter and Connie Roop, 1987 Carolrhoda Books Reprint edition, ISBN 0876144768, Reading Level: 3.2

Day 1: *Tornado* p. 13-20
    Questions:
    Why did Tornado keep poking Pete's leg? (knowledge)
    What did Pete do to figure out the card trick that Tornado knew? (comprehension)
    How did Daddy feel about the card trick? (evaluation)

Scheduled Books for Emerging Readers
(continued)

Day 2: *Tornado* p. 21-27
    Questions:
    When did Pete find out that Tornado had the turtle? (comprehension)
    How did the children try to get Tornado to give back the turtle? (knowledge)
    Why did Tornado run wildly around the yard after he gave back the turtle? (analysis)

Day 3: *Tornado* p. 28-34
    Questions:
    Where did the cat get its name? (knowledge)
    Describe the problem between the cat and the dog. (comprehension)
    How else could Tornado have solved the problem? (application)

Day 4: *Tornado* p. 35-41
    Questions:
    Who was Buddy? (knowledge)
    Why did daddy give Tornado to the other family? (comprehension)
    Explain why daddy called his son "Petey" at the end of today's chapter. (synthesis)

Day 5: *Tornado* p. 42-end
    Question:
    Describe what happened after Tornado was gone. (narration)

Unit 28:
Supplemental title for Unit 28 (optional): *A Horse Named Seabiscuit* by Cathy East Dubowski and Mark Dubowski, 2003 Grosset & Dunlap, ISBN 0448433427, Reading Level: 3.1

Day 1: *Animal Adventures* p. 1-6
    Questions:
    Why was Pa gone? (knowledge)
    What happened to Ma and Laura when they went outside to do the chores? (comprehension)
    Was it important that Laura obeyed Ma? Why? (evaluation)

Day 2: *Animal Adventures* p. 7-11
    Questions:
    Can you guess why Ma stayed up and rocked Carrie even though Carrie was already asleep? (synthesis)
    What did Pa do to try to scare the bear? (comprehension)
    Did Laura and Mary make fun of Pa for hitting the tree stump? Why? (analysis)

Scheduled Books for Emerging Readers
(continued)

Day 3: *Animal Adventures* p. 12-16
    Questions:
    How did Pa describe the black panther? (knowledge)
    Tell the story of the black panther. (comprehension)
    Why did Grandpa jump off and leave the horse behind? (analysis)

Day 4: *Animal Adventures* p. 17-22
    Questions:
    Describe Pa's deer lick. (knowledge)
    What did Pa see at the deer lick? (comprehension)
    Have you ever sat and watched one of God's creatures in nature? Explain. (application)

Day 5: *Animal Adventures* p. 23-27
    Question:
    Retell Pa's story about the wolves. (narration)

Unit 29:
Supplemental title for Unit 29 (optional): *Kate Shelley and the Midnight Express* by Margaret K. Wetterer, 1991 Carolrhoda Books, ISBN 0876145411, Reading Level: 3.3

Day 1: *Animal Adventures* p. 28-33
    Questions:
    Why did Pa hurry home so fast? (knowledge)
    What did Laura see when she woke up? (comprehension)
    How did Pa plan to keep his family safe? (analysis)

Day 2: *Animal Adventures* p. 34-37
    Questions:
    What did Pa and the cowboys discuss? (comprehension)
    Why did the cowboys wear handkerchiefs around their necks? (knowledge)
    Have you ever seen dust blowing? What does it feel like? (application)

Day 3: *Animal Adventures* p. 38-42
    Questions:
    Tell about the surprise that Pa brought home. (comprehension)
    What did the cow do that made Pa so upset? (knowledge)
    Why did they give the milk to Baby Carrie? (synthesis)

Scheduled Books for Emerging Readers
(continued)

Day 4: *Animal Adventures* p. 43-47
> Questions:
> Name the warning that Pa gave the girls in this chapter. (knowledge)
> How did Laura get into trouble? (comprehension)
> Should Laura tell Pa what happened? Explain. (evaluation)

Day 5: *Animal Adventures* p. 48-52
> Question:
> Describe what happened to Laura in this chapter. (narration)

Unit 30:
Supplemental title for Unit 30 (optional): *Roxaboxen* by Alice McLerran, 2004 Harper Trophy, ISBN 0060526335, Reading Level: 3.4

Day 1: *Animal Adventures* p. 53-57
> Questions:
> Who did Laura and her family go to visit in this chapter? (knowledge)
> Where did Lena and Laura get to take the buggy? (comprehension)
> What do you think will happen to Lena and Laura? (synthesis)

Day 2: *Animal Adventures* p. 58-61
> Questions:
> Why did Laura want to drive? (knowledge)
> What happened on the way home? (comprehension)
> Explain what could have happened if Laura had dropped the reins? (evaluation)
> Explain what Laura and Carrie did in this chapter. (comprehension)

Day 3: *Animal Adventures* p. 62-65
> Questions:
> What did Laura see at the top of the bank? (knowledge)
> Have you ever seen a wolf? Try to describe it. (application)

Day 4: *Animal Adventures* p. 66-end
> Questions:
> What did Laura do when she saw the wolf? (comprehension)
> Tell why Laura didn't want Pa to catch the wolf. (knowledge)
> Why do you think the wolf didn't chase the girls? (analysis)

Scheduled Books for Emerging Readers
(continued)

Day 5: *The Bears on Hemlock Mountain* Chapter 1
> Questions:
> *What did you learn about Jonathan?* (narration)
> *How do you know what season it is in the story?* (analysis)

Unit 31:
Supplemental title for Unit 31 (optional): *Mike Mulligan and His Steam Shovel* by
> Virginia Lee Burton, 1977 Houghton Mifflin, ISBN 0395259398,
> Reading Level: 3.4

Day 1: *The Bears on Hemlock Mountain* Chapter 2
> Questions:
> *Why did Jonathan like Uncle James best?* (comprehension)
> *List some of the things that Jonathan and Uncle James saw and heard.* (knowledge)
> *Do you think that Jonathan will get to see a bear? Explain.* (synthesis)

Day 2: *The Bears on Hemlock Mountain* Chapter 3
> Questions:
> *Why did Mother send Jonathan to get the big iron pot?* (comprehension)
> *What excuses did Jonathan make when his mother sent him to get the pot?* (knowledge)
> *Can you guess what will happen to Jonathan?* (analysis)

Day 3: *The Bears on Hemlock Mountain* Chapter 4
> Questions:
> *What were Jonathan and his mother reciting over and over.* (knowledge)
> *How did Jonathan get the little animals to come out on Hemlock Mountain?* (comprehension)
> *Why did Jonathan feel better when all the little creatures came out?* (evaluation)

Day 4: *The Bears on Hemlock Mountain* Chapter 5
> Questions:
> *What makes Jonathan hurry down the mountain?* (knowledge)
> *Why does Jonathan seem worried that it sounds like spring?* (analysis)
> *Tell me about Jonathan's trip down the mountain.* (comprehension)

Day 5: *The Bears on Hemlock Mountain* Chapter 6
> Question:
> *Explain the problems in this chapter.* (narration)

Scheduled Books for Emerging Readers
(continued)

Unit 32:
Supplemental title for Unit 32 (optional): *The White Stallion* by Elizabeth Shub, 1995 Yearling, ISBN 0440412927, Reading Level: 3.2

Day 1: *The Bears on Hemlock Mountain* Chapter 7
Questions:
When Jonathan woke up, what happened? (comprehension)
Have you ever forgotten something? What was it? (application)
What does Jonathan's aunt say to the cat after Jonathan leaves? (knowledge)

Day 2: *The Bears on Hemlock Mountain* Chapter 8
Questions:
Describe Jonathan's walk up Hemlock Mountain now. (comprehension)
What does Jonathan do when he sees the bears? (knowledge)
Do you think that Jonathan did the right thing? Explain. (evaluation)

Day 3: *The Bears on Hemlock Mountain* Chapter 9
Questions:
Explain what the bears did. (comprehension)
How was Jonathan saved? (knowledge)
What might have happened if Jonathan's father hadn't come? (synthesis)

Day 4: *The Bears on Hemlock Mountain* Chapter 10
Question:
What did everyone do after they found Jonathan? (narration)

Day 5: *The Courage of Sarah Noble* p. 1-5
Question:
Tell me about Sarah Noble. (narration)

Unit 33:
Supplemental title for Unit 33 (optional): *Buddy the First Seeing Eye Dog* by Eva Moore, 1996 Scholastic Inc, ISBN 0590265857, Reading Level: 3.8

Day 1: *The Courage of Sarah Noble* p. 6-12
Questions:
How was this family different from Sarah's own family? (evaluation)
What does "keep up your courage" mean? (comprehension)
Why did Sarah really want her cloak near her? (synthesis)

Scheduled Books for Emerging Readers
(continued)

Day 2: *The Courage of Sarah Noble* p. 13-18
> Questions:
> Describe what the countryside looks like by Sarah's new home. (comprehension)
> What does Father tell Sarah about Mistress Robinson? (knowledge)
> If you were Sarah, what would be some of your worries? (application)

Day 3: *The Courage of Sarah Noble* p. 19-22
> Questions:
> Where did Father and Sarah spend the night? (knowledge)
> How was Sarah keeping up her courage? (comprehension)
> What do you do to keep up your courage when you are scared? (application)

Day 4: *The Courage of Sarah Noble* p. 23-28
> Questions:
> What did Sarah do when the Indian children came? (knowledge)
> Name some surprising things that Sarah noticed about the Indian children. (knowledge)
> Why did Sarah change her mind about the Indians? (analysis)

Day 5: *The Courage of Sarah Noble* p. 29-32
> Question:
> Explain what has been happening to Sarah and Father. (narration)

Unit 34:
Supplemental title for Unit 34 (optional): *Barry: The Bravest Saint Bernard* by Lynn Hall, 1992 Random House, ISBN 0679830545, Reading Level: 3.8

Day 1: *The Courage of Sarah Noble* p. 33-38
> Questions:
> Why was Sarah going to stay with Tall John? (comprehension)
> List some of Sarah's worries. (knowledge)
> How do you know that Father is worried too? (analysis)

Day 2: *The Courage of Sarah Noble* p. 39-41
> Questions:
> Why was the first night the strangest for Sarah? (comprehension)
> What did Sarah do to get ready for bed? (knowledge)
> How did Sarah keep up her courage? (evaluation)

Scheduled Books for Emerging Readers
(continued)

Day 3: *The Courage of Sarah Noble* p. 42-46
    Questions:
    What did the Indians do to keep watch for danger? (knowledge)
    How did Sarah feel about putting on her old clothes? Why? (comprehension)
    Why was Tall John sad when Sarah had to leave? (synthesis)

Day 4: *The Courage of Sarah Noble* p. 47-50
    Questions:
    Describe what Sarah saw when she got home. (comprehension)
    What does Sarah say about Arabella? (knowledge)
    Name a special object that you love. Why is it special to you? (application)

Day 5: *The Courage of Sarah Noble* p. 51-end
    Question:
    How has Sarah changed? (narration)

Additional Beginning Chapter Books

Note: When you finish the scheduled books for emerging readers, here are some additional book ideas to help ease your child's transition into chapter books.

Any books by Thornton Burgess, reprinted by Dover Publications
Aesop's Fables by Ann McGovern, ISBN 0590438808
Capyboppy by Bill Peet, ISBN 0613100263
The Chalk Box Kid by Clyde Robert Bulla, ISBN 0394891023
Dolphin Adventure: A True Story by Wayne Grover, ISBN 0380732521
Dolphin Treasure by Wayne Grover, ISBN 038073253X
Five True Dog Stories by Margaret Davidson, ISBN 0590424017
Gold Rush Winter by Claire Rudolf Murphy, ISBN 0307264130
Hannah by Gloria Whelan, ISBN 067982698X
The Light at Tern Rock by Julia L. Sauer, ISBN 0140368574
The Littles by John Peterson, ISBN 059042253
Liza, Bill and Jed Mysteries by Peggy Parish (Titles include *Pirate Island Adventure*
    ISBN 0440473942, *Clues in the Woods* ISBN 044041461X, *The Mystery of*
    Hermit Dan ISBN 0440435013)
The Matchlock Gun by Walter D. Edmonds, ISBN 0698116801
Meet George Washington by Joan Heilbroner, ISBN 0375803971
Meet Benjamin Franklin by Maggi Scarf, ISBN 0375815244
The Minstrel in the Tower by Gloria Skurzynski, ISBN 0394895983
Molly's Pilgrim by Barbara Cohen, ISBN 0688162800
Pioneer Cat by William H. Hooks, ISBN 039482038X

Additional Beginning Chapter Books
(continued)

Pioneer Trilogy by Gloria Whelan (includes *Next Spring an Oriole* ISBN 0394891252,
    Night of the Full Moon ISBN 0679872760, *Shadow of the Wolf*
    ISBN 0679881085)
Sarah Plain and Tall by Patricia MacLachlan, ISBN 0064402053
Shoeshine Girl by Clyde Robert Bulla, ISBN 0064402282
The Velveteen Rabbit by Margery Williams, ISBN 0380002558
White Bird by Clyde Robert Bulla, ISBN 0679806628

Bibliography: Suggested Storytime Titles

Note: This list of titles is <u>not necessary</u> to complete the program. It is an optional list to help you choose literature for each genre to read-aloud. These specific titles are not needed, but each book was very carefully chosen as an excellent read-aloud selection for this listening level. Descriptions are taken from the book or card catalog listing.

For ease of use, Heart of Dakota Publishing sells three different packages of the listed read-aloud selections. Each package contains nine read-aloud titles, one for each type of literature listed below. View packages on the website www.heartofdakota.com or call (605) 428-4068 for more information. Please feel free to use your own book selections or your library in order to economize.

Biography: (Unit 1-Unit 4)
Benjamin Franklin by Ingri and Edgar Parin D'Aulaire, 1998 Beautiful Feet Books
    ISBN 0964380390
    All books written by the D'Aulaires feature beautiful artwork in oversized books with storylike text. Each biography contains a carefully researched narrative that provides a providential view of our nation.
Benjamin West and His Cat Grimalkin by Marguerite Henry, 2000 Bradford Press
    ISBN 0970561806
    This is a classic book by a beloved author. With his beloved black cat Grimalkin as his constant companion, the young Quaker boy Benjamin West discovers and develops his talent as an artist. The story focuses on Benjamin's childhood and early years as a painter.
Columbus by Ingri and Edgar Parin D'Aulaire, 1996 Beautiful Feet Books
    ISBN 0964380331
    See the description under *Benjamin Franklin.*
George Washington by Ingri and Edgar Parin D'Aulaire, 1996 Beautiful Feet Books
    ISBN 0964380315
    See the description under *Benjamin Franklin.*
Gladys Aylward: The Adventure of a Lifetime by Janet and Geoff Benge, 1998 YWAM
    Publishing, ISBN 157680199
    At a revival meeting, Gladys Aylward became convinced that God was leading her to China. Even though she knew no Chinese, had no contacts in China, and flunked out of China mission school, Gladys saved her money and bought a one-way ticket to China. The adventures and close escapades she had keep you glued to the pages, all the while glorifying God and all He did for the Chinese people through His humble servant.
Helen Keller by Margaret Davidon, 1989 Scholastic Paperbacks
    ISBN 0590424041
    This is a bestselling biography of Helen Keller and how, with the commitment and lifelong friendship of Anne Sullivan, she learned to talk, read, and eventually graduate from college with honors.

Bibliography: Suggested Storytime Titles
(continued)

Squanto: Friend of the Pilgrims by Clyde Robert Bulla, 1990 Scholastic
ISBN 0590440551
Squanto tells everyone he meets that he's going on the great ship across the sea. But before Squanto can return, many, many years go by - years full of adventure. When Squanto does come back, his family is gone. His village has disappeared. New people have come - the Pilgrims.

Adventure: (Unit 5-Unit 8)
King of the Wind by Marguerite Henry, 1991 Aladdin Reprint edition
ISBN 06897141866
This is the classic story of Sham and his friend, the stable boy Agba. Their adventures take them from the sands of the Sahara to the royal courts of France and, finally, to the green pastures and stately homes of England. For Sham was the renowned "Godolphin Arabian" whose blood flows through the veins of almost every superior Thoroughbred. Sham's speed - like his story - has become legendary. This is not a story for sensitive readers.

A Lion to Guard Us by Clyde Robert Bulla, 1989 Harper Trophy
ISBN 0064403335
Left on their own in seventeenth-century London, three impoverished children draw upon all their resources to stay together and make their way to the Virginia colony in search of their father. This book is based on a true story.

Sword in the Tree by Clyde Robert Bulla, 2000 Harper Trophy
ISBN 0064421325
After his father is reported dead and his wicked uncle takes over the castle, eleven-year-old Shan hides his father's precious sword and, after escaping with his mother, makes his way to King Arthur's court to seek help in winning back his inheritance.

The Twenty-One Balloons by William Pene du Bois, 1986 Puffin Reprint Edition
ISBN 0140320970
Professor Sherman intends to fly across the Pacific Ocean. Instead, he lands on Krakatoa and discovers a world of unimaginable wealth, eccentric inhabitants, and incredible balloon inventions. In this winner of the 1948 Newberry Medal, the author of this classic fantasy-adventure combines his rich imagination, scientific tastes, and artistry to tell a story that has no age limit.

Historical Fiction: (Unit 9-Unit 12)
The Cabin Faced West by Jean Fritz, 1987 Puffin Books
ISBN 0698119363
For Ann Hamilton, life out west was anything but adventurous. In fact, she had never been lonelier. She longed for the ease and comfort of the days with her friends back in Gettysburg, until a stranger rode into Hamilton Hill and changed her life forever.

Bibliography: Suggested Storytime Titles
(continued)

Little House in the Big Woods by Laura Ingalls Wilder, 1953 Harper Trophy
ISBN 0064400018
This book is a year in the life of three young girls growing up on the Wisconsin frontier, as they help their mother with the daily chores, enjoy their father's stories and singing, and share special occasions when they get together with relatives or neighbors.

Sarah Whitcher's Story by Elizabeth Yates, 1994 BJU Press
ISBN 0440444381
Describes the search for and adventures of a young girl lost in a New Hampshire forest in pioneer days. As the long days pass, the searchers grow desperate, but her father's trust in God holds firm. Based on a true incident.

Skippack School by Marguerite de Angeli, 1999 Herald Press
ISBN 0836191242
In 1750, in Pennsylvania, mischievous young Eli, has recently arrived with his Mennonite family from Germany. He tries to adjust to his new life and especially to the teaching methods of his schoolteacher, Christopher Dock.

Fantasy: (Unit 13-Unit 16)

Charlotte's Web by E.B. White, 1974 Harper Trophy
ISBN 0064400557
Wilbur, the pig, is desolate when he discovers that he is destined to be the farmer's Christmas dinner until his spider friend, Charlotte, decides to help him. This story is a beloved classic.

The Cricket in Times Square by George Selden, 1970 Yearling
ISBN 0440415632
Chester Cricket moves into a newspaper stand in New York City and befriends the owner's son, Mario. Chester also meets Harry the cat and Tucker the mouse. Meanwhile, Chester's concerts bring new business to the stand.

Kildee House by Rutherford G. Montgomery, 1993 Walker Books for Young Readers
Reprint edition, ISBN 0802773885
Jerome Kildee is a shy stonecutter who retires to a redwood forest to be alone. He finds, instead, friendship for the first time in his life. His quiet ways allow a family of raccoons and a family of skunks to invade his space, and that is when the fun begins. The man doesn't have the heart to turn the animals away, so he enlists two neighbor children from fueding families to help him care for the animals.

The Trumpet of the Swan by E.B. White, 2000 Harper Trophy
ISBN 0064408671
Louis is a trumpeter swan who is unable to make any sound. His adventures lead him to creative solutions for declaring his love for the swan, Serena. This is a funny, yet touching read-aloud.

Bibliography: Suggested Storytime Titles
(continued)

Mystery: (Unit 17-Unit 20)

Ginger Pye by Eleanor Estes, 2000 Odyssey Classics
ISBN 0152025057
Meet Ginger Pye, the smartest dog you'll ever know. Jerry Pye and his sister, Rachel, feel pretty smart themselves for buying Ginger. Ginger steals everybody's heart, until someone steals him! The disaperance of the new puppy, Ginger, and the appearance of a mysterious man in a yellow hat brings excitement into the lives ot the Pye children.

The Key to the Treasure by Peggy Parish, 1980 Yearling
ISBN 0440444381
Each summer, Lisa, Bill, and Jed visit their grandparents and hear the story of the sketches hung above the mantel. The sketches are clues to a hidden treasure, and no one has been able to figure them out for a century. There is a missing first clue, but when the children stumble upon the seond clue, they're on their way to solving the mystery.

Phoebe the Spy by Judith Berry Griffin, 1989 Scholastic
ISBN 0590424327
Someone is planning to kill George Washington and young Phoebe Fraunces is trying to save his life. Phoebe gets a job as George Washington's housekeeper, but her real job is to work as a spy. She listens and watches very carefully, and she meets her father every day to tell him what she's learned. Phoebe is determined to figure out who is after Washington before it's too late!

The Railway Children by E. Nesbit, 1994 Puffin Reissue Edition
ISBN 0140366717
When their father mysteriously disappears, three children and their mother leave London to seek a new life in the country, finding solace in the nearby railway station. First published in 1906, this beloved children's classic has charmed generations of readers.

Nonfiction: (Unit 21-Unit 24)

If You Lived 100 Years Ago by Ann Mcgovern, 1999 Scholastic
ISBN 05909600016
Readers travel back in time to explore life in New York City 100 years ago, where there's not a television or computer in sight! This illustrated guide reveals how people both rich and poor dressed, traveled, dined, and entertained.

If You Traveled West in a Covered Wagon by Ellen Levine, 1992 Scholastic
ISBN 0590451588
This book uses an interesting question-and-answer format and a multitude of facts to bring to life the Oregon Trail in the 1840's. It is written in a new, larger format with full-color illustrations.

Bibliography: Suggested Storytime Titles
(continued)

Missionary Stories with the Millers by Mildred A. Martin, 1994 Green Pastures Press,
ISBN 096276435
This is a compilation of twenty-nine true missionary stories from around the world. Almost all the stories are about missionaries who lived and worked during the 20th century. The stories include lots of excitement, miraculous escapes, and some martydoms.

Pagoo by Holling C. Holling, 1990 Houghton Mifflin
ISBN 0395539641
An intricate study of tide pool life is presented using descriptive text and beautiful pictures. The book follows the story of Pagoo, a hermit crab. This is a classic written by Holling C. Holling that you will pour over as you read.

Humor: (Unit 25-Unit 28)

The Adventures of Happy Jack by Thornton W. Burgess, 2004 Dover Publications
ISBN 0486433218
Master storyteller Thornton Burgess charms youngsters once again with tales of life in the Green Forest. This time he recounts the adventures of Happy Jack Squirrel, who starts the day cheerily enough but soon finds himself trying every trick he knows to get away from his enemy, Shadow the Weasel.

A Bear Called Paddington by Micael Bond, 2001 Houghton Mifflin
ISBN 0618150714
A very small bear found by Mr. and Mrs. Brown at Paddington Station becomes one of the family. Their home is never the same once Paddington moves in.

The House at Pooh Corner by A.A. Milne, 1992 Puffin Books
ISBN 0140361227
This classic book contains ten adventures of Pooh, Eeyore, Tigger, Piglet, Owl, and other friends of Christopher Robin. It is full of wit, wisdom, and humor.

Mr. Popper's Penguins by Richard and Florence Atwater, 1992 Little Brown
ISBN 0316058432
The unexpected delivery of a large crate containing an Antarctic penguin changes the life and fortunes of Mr. Poppper, a house painter obsessed by dreams of the polar regions. This is a humorous, lively story that is not to be taken too seriously.

Realistic Fiction: (Unit 29-Unit 32)

All-of-a-Kind Family by Sydney Taylor, 1980 Yearling
ISBN 0440400597
It's the turn of the century in New York's Lower East side and a sense of excitement abounds for five young sisters. Together they share adventures that find them searching for hidden buttons and visiting the peddlers in Papa's shop. The girls enjoy doing everything together, especially holidays and surprises.

Bibliography: Suggested Storytime Titles
(continued)

Follow My Leader by James B. Garfield, 1994 Puffin Books
ISBN 0140364854
After Jimmy is blinded in an accident with a firecracker, he has to relearn all the things he used to know. With the help of a determined therapist and a guide dog, Leader, Jimmy's given the chance to live a more normal life. But, can he forgive the boy who blinded him?

Mountain Born by Elizabeth Yates, 1994 BJU Press
ISBN 0890847061
Wolves, weather, a black lamb, a trusty dog - all are part of Peter's life on a mountain farm. His best friend is Benj, a wise old shepherd, and Benj teaches him to care for the sprightly lamb that becomes his own special pet, his cosset. As Biddy grows into her place as leader of the flock, Peter grows too.

The Year of Miss Agnes by Kirkpatrick Hill, 2002 Aladdin
ISBN 0689851243
Fred, a ten-year-old girl, describes the year Miss Agnes takes over the one-room school. Unlike the school's other teachers, none of whom have lasted, Miss Agnes encourages the children to explore art, literature, and their own potential. This is an inspirational story about Alaska, the old and new ways, a very special teacher, and the influence she has over everyone she meets.

Folk Tale: (Unit 33-34)

Aesop's Fables by Ann Mcgovern, 1963 Scholastic
ISBN 0590438808
Here's a collection of Aesop's clever fables that you'll enjoy. The book is very plainly illustrated, but the retellings are clear enough for even the youngest listeners.

The Apple and the Arrow by Conrad Buff, 2001 Houghton Mifflin
ISBN 0618128093
This book, set in 1291 in Switzerland, tells the story of Walter, the 12-year old son of legendary archer William Tell. When Switzerland enters into a revolution against its Austrian rulers, Walter finds that he is holding a secret that could destroy the life of his beloved frather. A 1952 Newberry Honor Book.

Children's Book of Virtues by William J. Bennett, 1995 Simon and Schuster
ISBN 068481353X
This is a collection of fine fables, fairy tales, folktales and poems with colorful illustrations that are presented to teach virtues, including compassion, courage, honesty, friendship, and faith.

In Grandma's Attic by Arleta Richardson, 1999 Chariot Victor Publishing
ISBN 0781432685
A collection of tales of life in the late nineteenth century, many reflecting the Christian faith of the author's family, including stories of pride in a new dress and a little girl who was thought to be lost while asleep in her own bed.

Spelling Lists

Note: The word lists found after these directions are needed for the Spelling portion of the Language Arts box in the daily plans. Choose **either** List 1 **or** List 2 for each unit. List 1 words are typical for first grade spellers. List 2 words are typical for second grade spellers. Each unit emphasizes one spelling word pattern. Eight words on each list are pattern words. The other two words on the list are target words that do not follow the spelling pattern. Target words are marked with an '*'.

Special instructions: You need 10 index cards for each unit. On Day 1 of each unit, the plans will instruct you to write the spelling words for that unit on the index cards for the students. Label each card in the upper right hand corner with the unit number. Choose a place to store the cards to use again during the review units.

Throughout the spelling lessons, stay with the students so that you can guide them as they write the words on paper or on a markerboard to immediately erase and rewrite any incorrectly spelled words. Mentally picturing the correct spelling of a word is key to learning to spell correctly. It is important that students do not see a word spelled incorrectly any longer than necessary so that the image of the incorrect word does not become fixed in their minds.

Unit 1 - Spelling Pattern: short 'a' words

List 1	List 2
at	am
and	bad
an	tan
can	hand
man	land
ran	last
ask	fast
had	glad
* has	* back
* as	* that

Spelling Lists
(continued)

Unit 2 - Spelling Pattern: short 'e' words

List 1	List 2
let	open
set	sled
yes	end
get	send
ten	best
men	help
bed	next
red	went
* the	* then
* them	* when

Unit 3 - Spelling Pattern: short 'i' words

List 1	List 2
if	swim
in	chip
it	trip
sit	fish
did	wish
hid	sick
him	pick
big	with
* is	* which
* his	* little

Unit 4 - Spelling Pattern: short 'o' words

List 1	List 2
on	box
got	lost
hot	drop
not	chop
hop	off
stop	block
top	sock
God	rock
* was	* long
* what	* once

Spelling Lists
(continued)

Unit 5 - Spelling Pattern: short 'u' words

List 1	List 2
up	club
us	jump
bus	must
cut	shut
but	much
fun	upon
run	just
rub	lunch
* of	* some
* from	* full

Unit 6 - Spelling Pattern: short vowel words ending in 'ff', 'zz', 'll', 'ss', 'gg'

List 1	List 2
off	smell
egg	pull
will	still
hill	shall
well	bless
bell	cross
tell	dress
doll	glass
* all	* small
* call	* fall

Unit 7 - Review Week

Unit 8 - Spelling Pattern: long vowel words ending in a single 'o', 'y', or 'e'

List 1	List 2
be	shy
he	try
me	why
we	cry
go	fly
no	sky
by	zero
my	July
* she	* buy
* so	* myself

Spelling Lists
(continued)

Unit 9 - Spelling Pattern: long 'a' words formed with silent final 'e'

List 1	List 2
ate	late
came	name
game	age
same	brave
lake	grape
make	trade
tape	skate
made	shake
* have	* thank
* gave	* danger

Unit 10 - Spelling Pattern: long 'i' words formed with silent final 'e'

List 1	List 2
side	live
hide	nice
ride	mine
time	shine
line	dime
mine	bike
five	wife
like	slice
* give	* write
* find	* kind

Unit 11 - Spelling Pattern: long 'o' words formed with silent final 'e'

List 1	List 2
hope	alone
rope	stone
home	bone
note	lone
vote	rode
hole	robe
rose	joke
nose	those
* some	* done
* come	* does

Spelling Lists
(continued)

Unit 12 - Spelling Pattern: words with 'u' formed with silent final 'e'

List 1	List 2
tube	cure
cube	fuse
mule	rude
huge	rule
cute	flute
use	salute
used	tune
pure	volume
* to	* because
* you	* minute

Unit 13 - Review Week

Unit 14 - Spelling Pattern: words with 'or' as in 'horn'

List 1	List 2
or	forget
for	short
fort	sport
horn	porch
born	storm
corn	north
more	fork
Lord	store
* your	* before
* work	* yourself

Unit 15 - Spelling Pattern: words with 'er' as in 'her'

List 1	List 2
her	mother
ever	other
never	letter
over	better
river	winter
after	sister
under	helper
faster	summer
* here	* together
* were	* water

Spelling Lists
(continued)

Unit 16 - Spelling Pattern: words with 'ir' as in 'girl'

List 1	List 2
girl	thirty
sir	chirp
stir	birch
dirt	girls
bird	twirl
first	thirst
third	skirt
shirt	dirty
* there	* hurt
* where	* their

Unit 17 - Spelling Pattern: words with 'ar' as in 'farm'

List 1	List 2
arm	star
farm	start
harm	part
car	jar
far	dark
hard	yard
start	garden
barn	farther
* are	* apart
* warm	* large

Unit 18 - Review Week

Unit 19 - Spelling Pattern: words with long 'a' spelled 'ay' as in 'day'

List 1	List 2
day	tray
lay	spray
may	away
pay	today
say	pray
way	bay
stay	delay
play	gray
* they	* anyway
* away	* always

Spelling Lists
(continued)

Unit 20 - Spelling Pattern: words with long 'a' spelled 'ai' as in 'sail'

List 1
rain
pain
wait
fail
tail
nail
sail
mail
* air
* chair

List 2
train
brain
gain
stain
chain
sprain
paint
snail
* drink
* think

Unit 21 - Spelling Pattern: words with long 'e' spelled 'ee' as in 'keep'

List 1
see
tree
bee
feet
seem
sleep
green
keep
* three
* been

List 2
free
meet
cheek
sheep
street
deep
need
teeth
* these
* cheese

Unit 22 - Spelling Pattern: words with long 'e' spelled 'ea' as in 'eat'

List 1
eat
heat
read
east
leap
team
near
clean
* each
* year

List 2
ear
hear
speak
mean
peach
dream
reach
clean
* please
* easy

Spelling Lists
(continued)

Unit 23 - Spelling Pattern: words with final 'y' that sounds like 'e' as in 'baby'

List 1	List 2
baby	greedy
lady	family
happy	city
party	pretty
penny	carry
funny	glory
any	cherry
puppy	story
* every	* only
* many	* very

Unit 24 - Review Week

Unit 25 - Spelling Pattern: words with long 'o' spelled 'ow' as in 'grow'

List 1	List 2
low	grow
own	show
row	tow
bowl	throw
mow	stow
slow	bow
crow	flow
blow	glow
* yellow	* most
* know	* goes

Unit 26 - Spelling Pattern: words with 'ow' as in 'cow'

List 1	List 2
cow	towel
now	flower
how	frown
down	crown
town	growl
wow	brow
owl	plow
gown	clown
* out	* around
* our	* about

Spelling Lists
(continued)

Unit 27 - Spelling Pattern: words with 'oo' as in 'moon'

List 1	List 2
moon	roof
soon	tooth
noon	spoon
too	shoot
zoo	tool
food	fool
pool	boot
room	broom
* into	* new
* do	* who

Unit 28 - Spelling Pattern: words with 'oo' as in 'book'

List 1	List 2
book	brook
took	looked
cook	stood
look	shook
foot	wool
good	hoof
wood	cookie
hood	hook
* would	* should
* could	* put

Unit 29 - Spelling Pattern: words with 'aw' as in 'saw'

List 1	List 2
saw	straw
paw	claw
jaw	hawk
law	crawl
lawn	yawn
draw	raw
fawn	thaw
dawn	pawn
* want	* walk
* song	* wash

Spelling Lists
(continued)

Unit 30 - Spelling Pattern: words with 'oi' or 'oy' as in 'boil' or 'boy'

List 1	List 2
boy	spoil
toy	coil
joy	joint
coin	point
oil	voice
boil	boys
soil	destroy
join	employ
* going	* noise
* enjoy	* choice

Unit 31 - Review Week

Unit 32 - Spelling Pattern: color words

List 1 and List 2
- blue
- black
- brown
- green
- yellow
- white
- pink
- red
- *orange
- *purple

Unit 33 - Spelling Pattern: number words

List 1 and List 2
- one
- * two
- three
- four
- five
- six
- seven
- * eight
- nine
- ten

Spelling Lists
(continued)

Unit 34 - Spelling Pattern: days of the week and seasons

List 1 and List 2
Sunday
Monday
* Tuesday
* Wednesday
Thursday
Friday
Saturday
spring
summer
autumn
winter

Extra - Spelling Pattern: contractions

List 1	List 2
isn't	let's
she's	I've
he's	can't
it's	I'll
isn't	you'll
didn't	we'll
hadn't	we're
I'm	aren't
* don't	* they'll
* wasn't	* they're

Math Alternate Schedule:
using *Singapore Primary Mathematics 2A & 2B* (U.S. Edition)
(Times Media Private Limited, 2003)

Note: If you have already covered the concepts listed in the introduction for *Singapore Primary Mathematics 1A & 1B*, follow the alternate math schedule listed below using *Singapore Primary Mathematics 2A & 2B* instead.

Unit 1:
- Day 1: *Textbook 2A* p. 6-8; *Workbook 2A* p. 7-9
- Day 2: *Textbook 2A* p. 9; *Workbook 2A* p. 10-11
- Day 3: *Textbook 2A* p. 10-11; *Workbook 2A* p. 12-14
- Day 4: *Textbook 2A* p. 12
- Day 5: *Textbook 2A* p. 13-14; *Workbook 2A* p. 15-16

Unit 2:
- Day 1: *Textbook 2A* p. 15-16; *Workbook 2A* p. 17-18
- Day 2: *Textbook 2A* p. 17-19; *Workbook 2A* p. 19-21
- Day 3: *Workbook 2A* p. 22-23
- Day 4: *Textbook 2A* p. 20; *Workbook 2A* p. 24
- Day 5: *Textbook 2A* p. 21

Unit 3:
- Day 1: *Textbook 2A* p. 22-24 (middle); *Workbook 2A* p. 25
- Day 2: *Textbook 2A* p. 24; *Workbook 2A* p. 26-27
- Day 3: *Textbook 2A* p. 25-27; *Workbook 2A* p. 28-29
- Day 4: *Textbook 2A* p. 28-29 (middle); *Workbook 2A* p. 30
- Day 5: *Workbook 2A* p. 31

Unit 4:
- Day 1: *Textbook 2A* p. 29-30; *Workbook 2A* p. 32-34
- Day 2: *Textbook 2A* p. 31-32 (middle); *Workbook 2A* p. 35-36
- Day 3: *Textbook 2A* p. 32-33; *Workbook 2A* p. 37
- Day 4: *Workbook 2A* p. 38-39
- Day 5: *Textbook 2A* Choose **either** p. 34 **or** p. 35

Unit 5:
- Day 1: *Textbook 2A* p. 36-37 (middle); *Workbook 2A* p. 40-41
- Day 2: *Textbook 2A* p. 37-38 (numbers 3-7); *Workbook 2A* p. 42-43
- Day 3: *Textbook 2A* p. 38 (numbers 8-10) - p. 39; *Workbook 2A* p. 44-45
- Day 4: *Textbook 2A* p. 39-40; *Workbook 2A* p. 46
- Day 5: *Workbook 2A* p. 47-48

Unit 6:
- Day 1: *Workbook 2A* p. 49-50
- Day 2: *Textbook 2A* Choose **either** p. 41 **or** p. 42
- Day 3: *Textbook 2A* p. 43-44; *Workbook 2A* p. 51
- Day 4: *Textbook 2A* p. 45; *Workbook 2A* p. 52-53
- Day 5: *Textbook 2A* p. 46 (top); *Workbook 2A* p. 54-55

Math Alternate Schedule: (continued)
using *Singapore Primary Mathematics 2A & 2B* (U.S. Edition)
(Times Media Private Limited, 2003)

Note: If you have already covered the concepts listed in the introduction for *Singapore Primary Mathematics 1A & 1B*, follow the alternate math schedule listed below using *Singapore Primary Mathematics 2A & 2B* instead.

Unit 7:
- Day 1: *Textbook 2A* p. 46-47 (middle); *Workbook 2A* p. 56-58
- Day 2: *Textbook 2A* p. 47 (numbers 15-16); *Workbook 2A* p. 59-60
- Day 3: *Workbook 2A* p. 61-62
- Day 4: *Textbook 2A* Choose **either** p. 48 **or** p. 49
- Day 5: *Workbook 2A* p. 63-66

Unit 8:
- Day 1: *Textbook 2A* Choose **either** p. 50 **or** p. 51
- Day 2: *Textbook 2A* p. 52-54; *Workbook 2A* p. 67
- Day 3: *Textbook 2A* p. 55-56; *Workbook 2A* p. 68-71
- Day 4: *Textbook 2A* p. 57-58; *Workbook 2A* p. 72-73
- Day 5: *Textbook 2A* p. 59-62; *Workbook 2A* p. 74

Unit 9:
- Day 1: *Workbook 2A* p. 75-78
- Day 2: *Textbook 2A* p. 63
- Day 3: *Textbook 2A* p. 64-67; *Workbook 2A* p. 79-80
- Day 4: *Textbook 2A* p. 68-69; *Workbook 2A* p. 81-82
- Day 5: *Workbook 2A* p. 83 and 85

Unit 10:
- Day 1: *Workbook 2A* p. 84 and 86
- Day 2: *Workbook 2A* p. 87-90
- Day 3: *Textbook 2A* p. 70-73
- Day 4: *Textbook 2A* Choose **either** p. 74 **or** p. 75
- Day 5: *Textbook 2A* p. 76-77; *Workbook 2A* p. 91-92

Unit 11:
- Day 1: *Textbook 2A* p. 78 (top); *Workbook 2A* p. 93-96
- Day 2: *Textbook 2A* p. 78 (bottom); *Workbook 2A* p. 97-98
- Day 3: *Textbook 2A* p. 79-82; *Workbook 2A* p. 99-102
- Day 4: *Textbook 2A* p. 83-84; *Workbook 2A* p. 103-106
- Day 5: *Textbook 2A* p. 85; *Workbook 2A* p. 107-109

Unit 12:
- Day 1: *Workbook 2A* p. 110-111
- Day 2: *Workbook 2A* p. 112-113
- Day 3: *Textbook 2A* p. 86-87
- Day 4: *Textbook 2A* p. 88-89; *Workbook 2A* p. 114-117
- Day 5: *Textbook 2A* p. 90 (top); *Workbook 2A* p. 118-119

Math Alternate Schedule: (continued)
using *Singapore Primary Mathematics 2A & 2B* (U.S. Edition)
(Times Media Private Limited, 2003)

Note: If you have already covered the concepts listed in the introduction for *Singapore Primary Mathematics 1A & 1B*, follow the alternate math schedule listed below using *Singapore Primary Mathematics 2A & 2B* instead.

Unit 13:
- Day 1: *Textbook 2A* p. 90 (bottom); *Workbook 2A* p. 120-121
- Day 2: *Textbook 2A* p. 91 (top); *Workbook 2A* p. 122
- Day 3: *Workbook 2A* p. 123-124
- Day 4: *Workbook 2A* p. 125-126
- Day 5: *Textbook 2A* p. 91-92; *Workbook 2A* p. 127-128

Unit 14:
- Day 1: *Textbook 2A* p. 93
- Day 2: *Textbook 2A* p. 94-95; *Workbook 2A* p. 129-131
- Day 3: *Workbook 2A* p. 132-133
- Day 4: *Textbook 2A* p. 96 (top); *Workbook 2A* p. 134-135
- Day 5: *Textbook 2A* p. 96 (bottom); *Workbook 2A* p. 136-137

Unit 15:
- Day 1: *Textbook 2A* p. 97 (number 5); *Workbook 2A* p. 138-139
- Day 2: *Textbook 2A* p. 97 (number 6); *Workbook 2A* p. 140-141
- Day 3: *Textbook 2A* p. 97 (number 7); *Workbook 2A* p. 142-144
- Day 4: *Workbook 2A* p. 145-147
- Day 5: *Textbook 2A* Choose **either** p. 98 **or** p. 99

Unit 16:
- Day 1: *Textbook 2A* p. 100-101; *Workbook 2A* p. 148-149
- Day 2: *Textbook 2A* p. 102-103; *Workbook 2A* p. 150-151
- Day 3: *Textbook 2A* p. 104
- Day 4: *Textbook 2A* p. 105; *Workbook 2A* p. 152-153
- Day 5: *Textbook 2A* p. 106; *Workbook 2A* p. 154-156

Unit 17:
- Day 1: *Workbook 2A* p. 157-159
- Day 2: *Workbook 2A* p. 160-162
- Day 3: *Textbook 2A* Choose **either** p. 107 **or** p. 108
- Day 4: *Workbook 2A* p. 163-165
- Day 5: *Workbook 2A* p. 166-168

Unit 18:
- Day 1: *Textbook 2A* Choose **either** p. 109-110 **or** p. 111-112
- Day 2: *Workbook 2A* p. 169-171
- Day 3: *Workbook 2A* p. 172-174
- Day 4: *Textbook 2B* p. 6-middle of 9; *Workbook 2B* p. 7-8
- Day 5: *Textbook 2B* p. 9-10; *Workbook 2B* p. 9-10

Math Alternate Schedule:
using *Singapore Primary Mathematics 2A & 2B* (U.S. Edition)
(Times Media Private Limited, 2003)

Note: If you have already covered the concepts listed in the introduction for *Singapore Primary Mathematics 1A & 1B*, follow the alternate math schedule listed below using *Singapore Primary Mathematics 2A & 2B* instead.

Unit 19:
- Day 1: *Textbook 2B* p. 11
- Day 2: *Textbook 2B* p. 12-13 (top); *Workbook 2B* p. 11
- Day 3: *Workbook 2B* p. 12
- Day 4: *Textbook 2B* p. 13 (middle); *Workbook 2B* p. 13
- Day 5: *Workbook 2B* p. 14

Unit 20:
- Day 1: *Textbook 2B* p. 13 (bottom); *Workbook 2B* p. 15
- Day 2: *Textbook 2B* p. 14 (top); *Workbook 2B* p. 16
- Day 3: *Textbook 2B* p. 14 (bottom); *Workbook 2B* p. 17
- Day 4: *Textbook 2B* p. 15-16 (top); *Workbook 2B* p. 18-19
- Day 5: *Textbook 2B* p. 16 (middle); *Workbook 2B* p. 20

Unit 21:
- Day 1: *Workbook 2B* p. 21
- Day 2: *Textbook 2B* p. 16 (bottom); *Workbook 2B* p. 22-23
- Day 3: *Textbook 2B* p. 17 (top); *Workbook 2B* p. 24
- Day 4: *Textbook 2B* p. 17 (bottom); *Workbook 2B* p. 25
- Day 5: *Textbook 2B* Choose **either** p. 18 **or** p. 19

Unit 22:
- Day 1: *Workbook 2B* p. 26-29
- Day 2: *Textbook 2B* p. 20-21; *Workbook 2B* p. 30-33
- Day 3: *Textbook 2B* p. 22-23 (top); *Workbook 2B* p. 34-35
- Day 4: *Workbook 2B* p. 36-39
- Day 5: *Textbook 2B* p. 23-24; *Workbook 2B* p. 40-42

Unit 23:
- Day 1: *Textbook 2B* p. 25
- Day 2: *Textbook 2B* p. 26-27 (top); *Workbook 2B* p. 43
- Day 3: *Textbook 2B* p. 27 (bottom); *Workbook 2B* p. 44-45
- Day 4: *Textbook 2B* p. 28; *Workbook 2B* p. 46-48
- Day 5: *Textbook 2B* p. 29

Unit 24:
- Day 1: *Textbook 2B* p. 30-31 (top); *Workbook 2B* p. 49-51
- Day 2: *Textbook 2B* p. 31 (bottom); *Workbook 2B* p. 52-54
- Day 3: *Textbook 2B* Choose **either** p. 32 **or** p. 33 **or** p. 34
- Day 4: *Textbook 2B* Choose **either** p. 35 **or** *Workbook 2B p. 55-58*
- Day 5: *Textbook 2B* p. 36-38 (number 2); *Workbook 2B* p. 59-61

Math Alternate Schedule: (continued)
using *Singapore Primary Mathematics 2A & 2B* (U.S. Edition)
(Times Media Private Limited, 2003)

Note: If you have already covered the concepts listed in the introduction for *Singapore Primary Mathematics 1A & 1B*, follow the alternate math schedule listed below using *Singapore Primary Mathematics 2A & 2B* instead.

Unit 25:
- Day 1: *Textbook 2B* p. 38 (number 3); *Workbook 2B* p. 62-63
- Day 2: *Workbook 2B* p. 64-65
- Day 3: *Textbook 2B* p. 38 (numbers 4-5) and p. 39; *Workbook 2B* p. 66-67
- Day 4: *Textbook 2B* p. 40; *Workbook 2B* p. 68-69
- Day 5: *Workbook 2B* p. 70-72

Unit 26:
- Day 1: *Textbook 2B* p. 41
- Day 2: *Textbook 2B* p. 42-43 (top); *Workbook 2B* p. 73
- Day 3: *Textbook 2B* p. 43 (bottom); *Workbook 2B* p. 74
- Day 4: *Textbook 2B* p. 44; *Workbook 2B* p. 75-76
- Day 5: *Textbook 2B* p. 45-47 (top); *Workbook 2B* p. 77

Unit 27:
- Day 1: *Textbook 2B* p. 47 (bottom); *Workbook 2B* p. 78
- Day 2: *Textbook 2B* p. 48; *Workbook 2B* p. 79-80
- Day 3: *Textbook 2B* p. 49; *Workbook 2B* p. 81-82
- Day 4: *Textbook 2B* Choose **either** p. 50 **or** p. 51
- Day 5: *Workbook 2B* p. 83-86

Unit 28:
- Day 1: *Workbook 2B* p. 87-90
- Day 2: *Textbook 2B* p. 52-53; *Workbook 2B* p. 91-92
- Day 3: *Textbook 2B* p. 54-55; *Workbook 2B* p. 93-94
- Day 4: *Textbook 2B* p. 56; *Workbook 2B* p. 95-98
- Day 5: *Textbook 2B* p. 57 (top); *Workbook 2B* p. 99-101

Unit 29:
- Day 1: *Textbook 2B* p. 57 (bottom); *Workbook 2B* p. 102-103
- Day 2: *Textbook 2B* Choose **either** p. 58 **or** p. 59
- Day 3: *Textbook 2B* p. 60-62; *Workbook 2B* p. 104-107
- Day 4: *Textbook 2B* p. 63; *Workbook 2B* p. 108-110
- Day 5: *Textbook 2B* p. 64-67 (number 4); *Workbook 2B* p. 111-114

Unit 30:
- Day 1: *Textbook 2B* p. 67 (numbers 5-6); *Workbook 2B* p. 115-116
- Day 2: *Textbook 2B* Choose **either** p. 68 **or** p. 69
- Day 3: *Workbook 2B* p. 117-120
- Day 4: *Textbook 2B* p. 70-71; *Workbook 2B* p. 121-125
- Day 5: *Textbook 2B* p. 72-75; *Workbook 2B* p. 126-128

Math Alternate Schedule: (continued)
using *Singapore Primary Mathematics 2A & 2B* (U.S. Edition)
(Times Media Private Limited, 2003)

Note: If you have already covered the concepts listed in the introduction for *Singapore Primary Mathematics 1A & 1B*, follow the alternate math schedule listed below using *Singapore Primary Mathematics 2A & 2B* instead.

Unit 31:
- Day 1: *Textbook 2B* p. 76
- Day 2: *Textbook 2B* p. 77-80; *Workbook 2B* p. 129-130
- Day 3: *Textbook 2B* p. 81
- Day 4: *Textbook 2B* p. 82-85; *Workbook 2B* p. 131-134
- Day 5: *Textbook 2B* p. 86; *Workbook 2B* p. 135-136

Unit 32:
- Day 1: *Textbook 2B* p. 87; *Workbook 2B* p.137-138
- Day 2: *Textbook 2B* Choose **either** p. 88 **or** p. 89
- Day 3: *Textbook 2B* p. 90-92; *Workbook 2B* p. 139-142
- Day 4: *Textbook 2B* p. 93-94; *Workbook 2B* p. 143-145
- Day 5: *Textbook 2B* p. 95-97; *Workbook 2B* p. 146-149

Unit 33:
- Day 1: *Textbook 2B* p. 98-99; *Workbook 2B* p. 150-151
- Day 2: *Textbook 2B* p.100-101
- Day 3: *Workbook 2B* p. 152-155
- Day 4: *Textbook 2B* p. 102-104; *Workbook 2B* p. 156-158
- Day 5: *Textbook 2B* p. 105; *Workbook 2B* p. 159-160

Unit 34:
- Day 1: *Workbook 2B* p. 161-162
- Day 2: *Textbook 2B* p. 106-108
- Day 3: *Workbook 2B* p. 163-168
- Day 4: *Workbook 2B* p. 169-172
- Day 5: *Textbook 2B* Choose **either** p. 109-112 **or** *Workbook 2B* p. 173-176

Index of Poetry and Rhymes

Unit 1: *The Storm* by Sara Coleridge (1802-1852)

Unit 2: *Father, We Thank Thee* by Ralph Waldo Emerson (1803-1882)

Unit 3: *Uphill* by Christina Georgina Rossetti (1830-1894)

Unit 4: *Daybreak* by Henry Wadsworth Longfellow (1807-1882)

Unit 5: *Song for a Little House* by Christopher Morley (1890-1957)

Unit 6: *The Months* by Sara Coleridge (1802-1852)

Unit 7: *Mother's Jewels* by Eugene Field (1850-1895)

Unit 8: *Where Lies the Land?* by Arthur Hugh Clough (1819-1861)

Unit 9: *Maker of Heaven and Earth* by Cecil Frances Alexander (1818-1895)

Unit 10: *What Are Heavy?* by Christina Georgina Rossetti (1830-1894)

Unit 11: *Don't Give Up* by Phoebe Cary (1824-1871)

Unit 12: *The Prayer Perfect* by James Whitcomb Riley (1849-1916)

Unit 13: *We Plough the Fields, and Scatter* by Matthias Claudius (1740-1815)

Unit 14: *The Arrow and the Song* by Henry Wadsworth Longfellow (1807-1882)

Unit 15: *The Cow* by Robert Louis Stevenson (1850-1894)

Unit 16: *God, Who Made the Earth* by Sarah Betts Rhodes (1829-1904)

Unit 17: *Evening* by Thomas Miller (1807-1874)

Unit 18: *Jesus Bids Us Shine* by Susan Warner (1819-1885)

Unit 19: *Monday's Child* by Anonymous

Unit 20: *Against Idleness and Mischief* by Isaac Watts (1674-1748)

Unit 21: *A June Day* by Sara Teasdale (1884-1933)

Index of Poetry and Rhymes
(continued)

Unit 22: *Little Things* by Julia Fletcher Carney (1824-1908)

Unit 23: *Northwest Passage: In Port* by Robert Louis Stevenson (1850-1894)

Unit 24: *The Star-Spangled Banner* by Francis Scott Key (1779-1843)

Unit 25: *A Child's Prayer* by Margaret Betham-Edwards (1836-1919)

Unit 26: *The Flag Goes By* by Henry H. Bennett (1863-1924)

Unit 27: *Pippa's Song* by Robert Browning (1812-1889)

Unit 28: *Farewell to the Farm* by Robert Louis Stevenson (1850-1894)

Unit 29: *The Planting of the Apple-Tree* by William Cullen Bryant (1794-1878)

Unit 30: *Written in March* by William Wordsworth (1770-1850)

Unit 31: *Weather* by Anonymous

Unit 32: *A Child's Prayer* by Siegfried Sassoon (1886-1967)

Unit 33: *Four Seasons* by Anonymous

Unit 34: *Try Again* by William Hickson (1803-1870)

Poetry and Rhymes

The Storm

Unit 1 - All Days

See lightning is flashing,
    The forest is crashing,
The rain will come dashing,
    A flood will be rising anon.

The heavens are scowling,
    The thunder is growling,
The loud winds are howling,
    The storm has come suddenly on!

But now the sky clears,
    The bright sun appears,
Now nobody fears,
    But soon every cloud will be gone.

Sara Coleridge

Poetry and Rhymes

Father, We Thank Thee

Unit 2 - All Days

For flowers that bloom about our feet,

For tender grass, so fresh, so sweet,

For song of bird, and hum of bee,

For all things fair we hear or see,

Father in heaven, we thank Thee.

For blue stream and blue of sky,

For pleasant shade of branches high,

For fragrant air and cooling breeze,

For beauty of the blooming trees,

Father in heaven, we thank Thee.

For this new morning with its light,

For rest and shelter of the night,

For health and food, for love and friends,

For everything thy goodness sends,

Father in heaven, we thank Thee.

Ralph Waldo Emerson

Poetry and Rhymes

Uphill

Unit 3 - All Days

Does the road wind uphill all the way?
>Yes, to the very end.

Will the day's journey take the whole long day?
>From morn to night, my friend.

But is there for the night a resting-place?
>A roof for when the slow, dark hours begin.

May not the darkness hide it from my face?
>You cannot miss that inn.

Shall I meet other wayfarers for the night?
>Those who have gone before?

Then must I knock, or call when just in sight?
>They will not keep you waiting at that door.

Shall I find comfort, travel-sore and weak?
>Of labor you shall find the sum.

Will there be beds for me and all who seek?
>Yea, beds for all who come.

Christina Georgina Rossetti

Poetry and Rhymes

Daybreak

Unit 4 - All Days

A wind came up out of the sea,
And said, "O mists, make room for me."

It hailed the ships and cried, "Sail on,
Ye mariners, the night is gone."

And hurried landward far away,
Crying, "Awake! It is the day."

It said unto the forest, "Shout!
Hang all your leafy banners out!"

It touched the wood-bird's folded wing,
And said, "O bird, awake and sing."

And over the farms, "O chanticleer,
Your clarion blow; the day is near."

It whispered to the fields of corn,
"Bow down, and hail the coming morn."

It shouted through the belfry-tower,
"Awake, O bell! Proclaim the hour."

It crossed the churchyard with a sigh,
And said, "Not yet! In quiet lie."

Henry Wadsworth Longfellow

Poetry and Rhymes

Song for a Little House

Unit 5 - All Days

I'm glad our house is a little house,
Not too tall nor too wide.
I'm glad the hovering butterflies
Feel free to come inside.

Our little house is a friendly house.
It is not shy or vain.
It gossips with the talking trees,
And makes friends with the rain.

And quick leaves cast a shimmer of green
Against our whited walls.
And in the phlox, the dutious bees
Are paying duty calls.

Christopher Morley

Poetry and Rhymes

The Months

Unit 6 - All Days

January brings the snow,
Makes our feet and fingers glow.

February brings the rain,
Thaws the frozen lake again.

March brings breezes, loud and shrill,
Stirs the dancing daffodil.

April brings the primrose sweet,
Scatters daisies at our feet.

May brings flocks of pretty lambs,
Skipping by their fleecy dams.

June brings tulips, lilies, roses,
Fills the childrens hands with posies.

Hot July brings cooling showers,
Apricots and gillyflowers.

August brings the sheaves of corn,
Then the harvest home is borne.

Warm September brings the fruit;
Sportsmen then begin to shoot.

Fresh October brings the pheasant;
Then to gather nuts is pleasant.

Dull November brings the blast;
Then the leaves are whirling fast.

Chill December brings the sleet,
Blazing fire, and Christmas treat.

Sara Coleridge

Poetry and Rhymes

Mother's Jewels

Unit 7 - All Days

Aunt Eleanor wears such diamonds!
    Shiny and gay and grand,
Some on her neck and some in her hair,
    And some on her pretty hand.

One day I asked my mama
    Why she never wore them too?
She laughed and said, as she kissed my eyes,
    "My jewels are here, bright blue.

They laugh and dance and beam and smile,
    So lovely all the day,
And never like Aunt Eleanor's go
    In a velvet box to stay.

Hers are prisoned in bands of gold,
    But mine are free as air!
Set in a bonny, dimpled face,
    And shadowed with shining hair!"

Eugene Field

Poetry and Rhymes

Where Lies the Land?

Unit 8 - All Days

Where lies the land to which the ship would go?

Far, far ahead, is all her seamen know.

And where the land she travels from? Away,

Far, far behind, is all that they can say.

On sunny noons upon the deck's smooth face,

Linked arm in arm, how pleasant here to pace;

Or, over the stern reclining, watch below

The foaming wake far widening as we go.

On stormy nights when wild north-westers rave,

How proud a thing to fight with wind and wave!

The dripping sailor on the reeling mast

Exults to bear, and scorns to wish it past.

Where lies the land to which the ship would go?

Far, far ahead, is all her seamen know.

And where the land she travels from? Away,

Far, far behind, is all that they can say.

Arthur Hugh Clough

Poetry and Rhymes

Maker of Heaven and Earth

Unit 9 - All Days

All things bright and beautiful,
    All creatures great and small,
All things wise and wonderful,
    The Lord God made them all.

Each little flower that opens,
    Each little bird that sings,
He made their glowing colors,
    He made their tiny wings.

The rich man in his castle,
    The poor man at the gate,
God made them, high or lowly,
    And ordered their estate.

The purple-headed mountain,
    The river running by,
The sunset and the morning,
    That brightens up the sky.

The cold wind in the winter,
    The pleasant summer sun,
The ripe fruits in the garden,
    He made them every one.

The tall trees in the greenwood,
    The meadows where we play,
The rushes by the water,
    We gather every day;

He gave us eyes to see them,
    And lips that we might tell,
How great is God Almighty,
    Who has made all things well.

Cecil Frances Alexander

Poetry and Rhymes

What Are Heavy?

Unit 10 - All Days

What are heavy? sea-sand and sorrow:

What are brief? today and tomorrow:

What are frail? Spring blossoms and youth:

What are deep? the ocean and truth.

Christina Georgina Rossetti

Poetry and Rhymes

Don't Give Up

Unit 11 - All Days

If you've tried and have not won,
    Never stop for crying;
All that's great and good is done
    Just by patient trying.

Though young birds, in flying, fall,
    Still their wings grow stronger;
And the next time they can keep
    Up a little longer.

Though the sturdy oak has known
    Many a blast, that bowed her,
She has risen again, and grown
    Loftier and prouder.

If by easy work you beat,
    Who the more will prize you?
Gaining victory from defeat,
    That's the test that tries you!

Phoebe Cary

Poetry and Rhymes

The Prayer Perfect

Unit 12 - All Days

Dear Lord! Kind Lord!
Gracious Lord! I pray
Thou wilt look on all I love,
Tenderly today!
Weed their hearts of weariness;
Scatter every care
Down a wake of angel-wings
Winnowing the air.

Bring unto the sorrowing
All release from pain;
Let the lips of laughter
Overflow again;
And with all the needy
O divide, I pray,
This vast treasure of content
That is mine today!

James Whitcomb Riley

Poetry and Rhymes

We Plough the Fields, and Scatter

Unit 13 - All Days

We plough the fields, and scatter
The good seed on the land,
But it is fed and watered
By God's almighty hand.
He sends the snow in winter,
The warmth to swell the grain,
The breezes and the sunshine,
and soft refreshing rain.
    All good gifts around us
    Are sent from heaven above;
    Then thank the Lord, O thank the Lord,
    For all his love.

He only is the maker
Of all things near and far,
He paints the wayside flower
He lights the evening star.
The winds and waves obey Him,
By Him the birds are fed,
Much more to us, his children,
He gives our daily bread.

We thank Thee then, O Father,
For all things bright and good,
The seed-time and the harvest,
Our life, our health, our food.
Accept the gifts we offer,
For all Thy love imparts,
And, what thou most desirest,
Our humble, thankful hearts.

    Matthias Claudius
    translated J.M Campbell

Poetry and Rhymes

The Arrow and the Song

Unit 14 - All Days

I shot an arrow into the air,
It fell to earth, I knew not where;
For, so swiftly it flew, the sight
Could not follow it in its flight.

I breathed a song into the air,
It fell to earth, I knew not where;
For who has sight so keen and strong,
That it can follow the flight of song?

Long, long afterward, in an oak
I found the arrow, still unbroke;
And the song, from beginning to end,
I found again in the heart of a friend.
Henry Wadsworth Longfellow

Poetry and Rhymes

The Cow

Unit 15 - All Days

The friendly cow all red and white,
    I shall love with all my heart;
She gives me cream with all her might,
    To eat with apple-tart.

She wanders lowing here and there,
    And yet she cannot stray,
All in the pleasant open air,
    The pleasant light of day.

And blown by all the winds that pass
    And wet with all the showers,
She walks among the meadow grass,
    And eats the meadow flowers.

Robert Louis Stevenson

Poetry and Rhymes

God, Who Made the Earth

Unit 16 - All Days

God, who made the earth,
The air, the sky, the sea,
Who gave the light its birth,
Careth for me.

God, who made the grass,
The flower, the fruit, the tree,
The day and night to pass,
Careth for me.

God, who made the sun,
The moon, the stars, is He,
Who, when life's clouds come on,
Careth for me.

God, who made all things,
On earth, in air, in sea,
Who, if I lean on Him,
Careth for me.

When in heaven's bright land,
I all His loved ones see,
I'll sing with that blessed band,
"God cared for me."

Sarah Betts Rhodes

Poetry and Rhymes

Evening

Unit 17 - All Days

The day is past, the sun is set,
    And the white stars are in the sky;
While the long grass with dew is wet,
    And through the air the bats now fly.

The lambs have now lain down to sleep,
    The birds have long since sought their nests;
The air is still; and dark, and deep,
    On the hillside the old wood rests.

Yet of the dark I have no fear,
    But feel as safe as when it's light;
For I know God is with me there,
    And He will guard me through the night.

For God is by me when I pray,
    And when I close mine eyes in sleep;
I know that He will with me stay,
    And will all night watch by me keep.

For He who rules the stars and sea,
    Who makes the grass and trees to grow;
Will look on a poor child like me,
    When on my knees I to Him bow.

He holds all things in His right hand,
    The rich, the poor, the great, the small;
When we sleep, or sit, or stand,
    Is with us, for He loves us all.

Thomas Miller

Poetry and Rhymes

Jesus Bids Us Shine

Unit 18 - All Days

Jesus bids us shine
With a pure, clear light,
Like a little candle
Burning in the night.
In this world of darkness
So we must shine-
You in your small corner,
And I in mine.

Jesus bids us shine,
First of all for Him;
Well He sees and knows it,
If our light grows dim.
He looks down from Heaven
To see us shine-
You in your small corner,
And I in mine.

Jesus bids us shine,
Then, for all around;
Many kinds of darkness
In the world abound,
Sin and want and sorrow;
So we must shine-
You in your small corner,
And I in mine.

Susan Warner

Poetry and Rhymes

Monday's Child

Unit 19 - All Days

Monday's child is fair of face,
Tuesday's child is full of grace,
Wednesday's child is full of woe,
Thursday's child has far to go,
Friday's child is loving and giving,
Saturday's child works hard for a living,
But the child that's born on the Sabbath day
Is blithe and bonny and good and gay.

Anonymous

Poetry and Rhymes

Against Idleness and Mischief

Unit 20 - All Days

How doth the little busy bee
Improve each shining hour,
And gather honey all the day
From every opening flower!

How skillfully she builds her cell!
How neat she spreads the wax!
And labors hard to store it well
With the sweet food she makes.

In works of labor and of skill,
I would be busy too;
For Satan finds some mischief still
For idle hands to do.

In books, or work, or healthful play,
Let my first years be passed,
That I may give for every day
Some good account at last.

Isaac Watts

Poetry and Rhymes

A June Day

Unit 21 - All Days

I heard a red-winged black-bird singing

Down where the river sleeps in the reeds;

That was morning, and at noontime

A hummingbird flashed on the jewel-weeds;

Clouds blew up, and in the evening

A yellow sunset struck through the rain;

Then blue night, and the day was ended

That never will come again.

Sara Teasdale

Poetry and Rhymes

Little Things

Unit 22 - All Days

Little drops of water,
Little grains of sand,
Make the mighty ocean
And the pleasant land.

So the little moments,
Humble though they be,
Make the mighty ages
Of eternity.

So the little errors,
Lead the soul away,
From the paths of virtue
Far in sin to stray.

Little deeds of kindness,
Little words of love,
Help to make earth happy
Like the heaven above.

Julia Fletcher Carney

Poetry and Rhymes

Northwest Passage: In Port

Unit 23 - All Days

Last, to the chamber where I lie

My fearful footsteps patter nigh,

And come from out the cold and gloom

Into my warm and cheerful room.

There, safe arrived, we turn about

To keep the coming shadows out,

and close the happy door at last

On all the perils that we past.

Then, when mamma goes by to bed,

She shall come in with tip-toe tread,

And see me lying warm and fast

And in the Land of Nod at last.

Robert Louis Stevenson

Poetry and Rhymes

The Star-Spangled Banner

Unit 24 - All Days

O say can you see,
    by the dawn's early light,
What so proudly we hailed
    at the twilight's last gleaming,
Whose broad stripes and bright stars
    through the perilous fight,
O'er the ramparts we watched
    were so gallantly streaming?
And the rocket's red glare,
    the bomb bursting in air,
Gave proof through the night
    that our flag was still there.
O say, does that star-spangled
    banner yet wave
O'er the land of the free,
    and the home of the brave!

Francis Scott Key

Poetry and Rhymes

A Child's Prayer

Unit 25 - All Days

God, make my life a little light
Within the world to glow;
A little flame that burneth bright
Wherever I may go.

God, make my life a little flower
That giveth joy to all,
Content to bloom in native bower,
Although the place be small.

God, make my life a little song
That comforteth the sad,
That helpeth others to be strong
And makes the singer glad.

God, make my life a little staff
Whereon the weak may rest,
And so what health and strength I have
May serve my neighbors best.

God, make my life a little hymn
Of tenderness and praise;
Of faith, that never waxeth dim,
In all his wonderous ways.

Margaret Betham-Edwards

Poetry and Rhymes

The Flag Goes By

Unit 26 - All Days

        Hats off!
Along the street there comes
A blare of bugles, a ruffle of drums,
A flash of color beneath the sky:
        Hats off!
The flag is passing by!

Blue and crimson and white it shines,
Over the steel-tipped, ordered lines.
        Hats off!
The colors before us fly;
But more than the flag is passing by.

Sea fights and land fights, grim and great,
fought to make and save the State:
Weary marches and sinking ships;
Cheers of victory on dying lips;

Days of plenty and years of peace;
March of the strong land's swift increase;
Equal justice, right, and law,
Stately honor and reverend awe:

Sign of a nation, great and strong
To ward her people from foreign wrong;
Pride and glory and honor - all
Live in the colors to stand or fall.

        Hats off!
Along the street there comes
A blare of bugles, a ruffle of drums,
And loyal hearts are beating high:
        Hats off!
The flag is passing by!

        Henry H. Bennett

Poetry and Rhymes

Pippa's Song

Unit 27 - All Days

The year's at the spring,

And day's at the morn;

Morning's at seven;

The hill-side's dew-pearled;

The lark's on the wing;

The snail's on the thorn;

God's in His heaven--

All's right with the world!

Robert Browning

Poetry and Rhymes

Farewell to the Farm

Unit 28 - All Days

The coach is at the door at last;
The eager children, mounting fast
And kissing hands, in chorus sing:
Good-bye, good-bye, to everything!

To house and garden, field and lawn,
The meadow-gates we swang upon,
To pump and stable, tree and swing,
Good-bye, good-bye, to everything!

And fare you well for evermore,
O ladder at the hayloft door,
O hayloft where the cobwebs cling,
Good-bye, good-bye, to everything!

Crack goes the whip, and off we go;
The trees and houses smaller grow;
Last, round the woody turn we swing:
Good-bye, good-bye, to everything!

Robert Louis Stevenson

Poetry and Rhymes

*The Planting of the Apple-Tree
(Verse 2)*

Unit 29 - All Days

What plant we in this apple-tree?

Buds which the breath of summer days

Shall lengthen into leafy sprays;

Boughs where the thrush, with crimson breast,

Shall haunt, and sing, and hide her nest;

We plant, upon the sunny lea,

A shadow for the noontide hour,

A shelter from the summer shower,

When we plant the apple-tree.

William Cullen Bryant

Poetry and Rhymes

Written in March

The cock is crowing,

The stream is flowing,

The small birds twitter,

The lake doth glitter,

The green field sleeps in the sun;

The oldest and youngest

Are at work with the strongest;

The cattle are grazing,

Their heads never raising;

There are forty feeding like one!

Like an army defeated

The snow hath retreated,

And now doth fare ill

On the top of the bare hill;

The ploughboy is whooping--anon--anon:

There's joy in the mountains;

There's life in the fountains;

Small clouds are sailing,

Blue sky prevailing;

The rain is over and gone!

William Wordsworth

Poetry and Rhymes

Weather

Unit 31 - All Days

Whether the weather be fine

Or whether the weather be not,

Whether the weather be cold

Or whether the weather be hot,

We'll weather the weather

Whatever the weather,

Whether we like it or not.

Anonymous

Poetry and Rhymes

A Child's Prayer

Unit 32 - All Days

For Morn, my dome of blue,
For Meadows, green and gay,
And Birds who love the twilight of the leaves,
Let Jesus keep me joyful when I pray.

For the big Bees that hum
And hide in the bells of flowers;
For the winding roads that come
To Evening's holy door,
May Jesus bring me grateful to his arms,
And guard my innocence for evermore.

Siegfried Sassoon

Poetry and Rhymes

Four Seasons

Unit 33 - All Days

Spring is showery, flowery, bowery.

Summer: hoppy, choppy, poppy.

Autumn: wheezy, sneezy, freezy.

Winter: slippy, drippy, nippy.

Anonymous

Poetry and Rhymes

Try Again

Unit 34 - All Days

Tis a lesson you should heed,
Try again;
If at first you don't succeed,
Try again;
Then your courage should appear,
For if you will persevere,
You will conquer, never fear,
Try again.

Once or twice though you may fail,
Try again;
If you would at last prevail,
Try again;
If we strive, 'tis no disgrace
Though we did not win the race;
What should we do in that case?
Try again;

If you find your task is hard,
Try again;
Time will bring you your reward,
Try again;
All that other folk can do,
Why with patience, may not you?
Only keep this rule in view,
Try again.

William Hickson

Other books by this author:

Little Hands to Heaven

A Preschool Program for Ages 2-5

*Follows the Bible chronologically from creation through Apostle Paul's missionary journeys

*Coordinates daily activities with stories from the Bible, so there is no literature to gather

*Includes simple daily plans with quick activities that require little or no preparation

*Can be done in one 30-minute session or throughout the day in 5 minute blocks of time

*Is a complete preschool program that includes letter recognition, letter formation, letter sounds and motions, early math skills, Bible activities, devotional topics, art projects, dramatic play, active exploration, fingerplays, and music

*Offers a choice of resources so you have the option of selecting what best suits your needs

*Written to use with multiple ages at the same time

Available from Heart of Dakota Publishing
(605) 428-4068
Visit our website: www.heartofdakota.com

Other books by this author:

Little Hearts for His Glory

An Early Learning Program for Ages 5-7

*May be used as a follow-up to *Little Hands to Heaven*

*Is a complete early learning program

*Includes a full year of easy-to-follow plans

*Emphasizes quick and easy activities that require little or no preparation

*Follows history chronologically from creation through present day

*Coordinates daily activities with stories from the Bible and from history

*Offers a choice of resources so you have the option of selecting what best suits your needs

**Available from Heart of Dakota Publishing
(605) 428-4068
Visit our website: www.heartofdakota.com**